In no region of the world have changes in religion and ethnic identity had a greater impact on political life than in the three countries that are the subject of this volume. The book examines the changing relationship of the state, religion, and ethnicity in three contiguous, non-Arab, Muslim countries in Southwest Asia. Each country has experienced a major political upheaval in the last two decades: the 1979 revolution in Iran, the Soviet invasion of Afghanistan, and the partition of Pakistan.

In Iran the Pahlavi regime sought for more than half a century to build its foundations and claim to legitimacy mainly upon a pre-Islamic Persian heritage. That endeavor collapsed in a religiously inspired popular revolution. In Afghanistan a Soviet-dominated Afghan state replaced a weak secular, tribal-based regime and has been promoting a Marxist political ideology as a means of creating greater loyalty to the state. In Pakistan one ethnic group, the Bengalis, successfully tore the Pakistani state in two.

(Continued on back flap)

The STATE, RELIGION, and ETHNIC POLITICS

Contemporary Issues in the Middle East

Sponsored by the
JOINT COMMITTEE ON THE NEAR AND MIDDLE EAST *and the*
COMMITTEE ON SOUTH ASIA OF THE AMERICAN COUNCIL OF
LEARNED SOCIETIES *and the* SOCIAL SCIENCE RESEARCH COUNCIL.

The STATE, RELIGION, and ETHNIC POLITICS

Afghanistan, Iran, and Pakistan

Edited by
ALI BANUAZIZI
Boston College

and
MYRON WEINER
Massachusetts Institute of Technology

SYRACUSE UNIVERSITY PRESS 1986

Library of Congress Cataloging-in-Publication Data

The State, religion, and ethnic politics.

(Contemporary issues in the Middle East)
"Sponsored by the Joint Committee on the Near and Middle East and the Committee on South Asia of the American Council of Learned Societies and the Social Science Research Council."
Includes bibliographies and index.
1. Iran—Politics and government—1979- —Congresses.   2. Afghanistan—Politics and government—1973- —Congresses.   3. Pakistan—Politics and government—1971- —Congresses.   4. Islam and state—Iran—Congresses.   5. Islam and state—Afghanistan—Congresses.   6. Islam and state—Pakistan—Congresses.
7. Iran—Ethnic relations—Congresses.   8. Afghanistan—Ethnic relations—Congresses.
9. Pakistan—Ethnic relations—Congresses.   I. Banuazizi, Ali.   II. Weiner, Myron.
III. Joint Committee on the Near and Middle East.   IV. Joint Committee on South Asia.
V. Series.
DS63.1.S73   1986   950   86-6048
ISBN 0-8156-2385-2 (alk. paper)

The paper used in this publication meets the minimum requirements of American National Standard for Information Sciences—Permanence of Paper for Printed Library Materials, ANSI Z39.48-1984. ∞™

Manufactured in the United States of America

CONTENTS

FIGURES

TABLES

PREFACE

THIS VOLUME had its origin in a conference on "Islam, Ethnicity and the State in Afghanistan, Iran, and Pakistan," which was sponsored by the Joint Committee on the Near and the Middle East and the Committee on South Asia of the American Council of Learned Societies and the Social Science Research Council, and held in November 1982, in Tuxedo, New York. The Planning Committee for the Conference included Robert Canfield, Ainslee Embree, Amal Rassam, and John Richards, as well as the editors of the present volume.

The idea of comparing Afghanistan, Iran and Pakistan—three contiguous, non-Arab, Muslim countries in Southwest Asia—seemed appealing from the start. All three have experienced significant political changes over the past decade with lasting ramifications not only for each of them individually, but for the region as a whole. The nature, causes, and patterns of these changes have been, of course, quite different in each society. However, important cultural and other similarities among these three states afford a unique opportunity for examining a number of key questions which fall under the major conceptual foci of the present volume—the themes of state, religion, and ethnicity. Different academic disciplines have explored these themes from their own particular vantage points: political scientists have focused on the problems of state building and processes of legitimation; anthropologists on the study of tribal, ethnolinguistic, and minority groups; and Islamists (joined in the more recent years by scholars of all other persuasions) on the study of the role of Islam in politics and society. However, given the highly intricate, variable, and historically unique interrelationship among Islam, ethnicity, and politics in these societies, a comparative analysis of these themes by scholars from the relevant disciplines seemed highly desirable. The present volume, we hope, serves as a step toward fulfilling this objective.

In addition to the contributors to this volume, others who participated in the original conference were Bashiruddin Ahmad, Akbar S. Ahmed, Lois Beck, Girilal Jain, and Amal Rassam. Their contributions to the conference, while not reflected directly here, were most valuable and much appreciated. Two of the chapters in the volume (those by Patricia Higgins and John Esposito) were commissioned for the present volume after the conference.

We are pleased to acknowledge the continuing advice and support of the sponsoring ACLS-SSRC committees, the Joint Committee on the Near and the Middle East, and the Committee on South Asia, as well as their respective staff, Nikiforos Diamandouros and David Szanton.

And finally, we would like to record our debt to Jessie Janjigian, whose critical and discerning judgment as our editorial consultant bettered this book at every stage, and to Ramesh Farzanfar for her fastidious work on the index.

January, 1986   ALI BANUAZIZI
                                                          MYRON WEINER

CONTRIBUTORS

SHAHROUGH AKHAVI is Professor, Department of Government and International Studies, University of South Carolina. He is the Editor of the SUNY Series in Middle Eastern Studies, State University of New York Press, and the Book Review Editor of *Iranian Studies*. He has written articles on Egyptian and Iranian politics and is the author of *Religion and Politics in Contemporary Iran: Clergy-State Relations in the Pahlavi Period*.

ALI BANUAZIZI is Professor of Social Psychology and Modern Iranian History at Boston College. He served as the Editor of *Iranian Studies* from 1968 to 1982, and is currently on the Editorial Board of the *International Journal of Middle East Studies*. His publications include "Iranian 'National Character': A Critique of Some Western Perspectives," in *Psychological Dimensions of Near Eastern Studies* (edited by L. C. Brown and N. Itzkowitz); "Iran: The Making of a Regional Power," in *The Middle East: Oil, Conflict & Hope* (edited by A. L. Udovitch).

LEONARD BINDER is Professor of Political Science at the University of California, Los Angeles. His books include *In a Moment of Enthusiasm: Political Power and the Second Stratum in Egypt; Iran: Political Development in a Changing Society;* and *Religion and Politics in Pakistan*.

ROBERT L. CANFIELD is Professor and Chair, Department of Anthropology, Washington University in St. Louis. His recent publications include "Western States in the Afghanistan War" in *Central Asian Survey,* "Soviet Gambit in Central Asia" in *Journal of South Asian and Middle Eastern Studies:* and "Islamic Coalitions in Bamiyan: A Profile in Translating Afghan Political Culture" in *Revolutions and Rebellions in Afghanistan: Anthropological Approaches* (edited by M. Nazif Shahrani and Robert L. Canfield).

STEPHEN P. COHEN is Professor of Political Science at the University of Illinois and heads the Regional Security Project of the university's Program in Arms

Control, Disarmament and International Security. He is the author of *The Pakistan Army* and several other books on South Asian security problems. He served as a member of the Policy Planning Staff of the Department of State from 1985 to 1987. His chapter for this volume was written before he joined the State Department and does not represent the views or policies of the U.S. government.

JOHN L. ESPOSITO is Professor of Religious Studies at the College of the Holy Cross. Among his published works are *Women in Muslim Family Law* and *Islam and Politics*. He has also edited *Islam and Development, Voices of Resurgent Islam* and *Islam in Transition: Muslim Perspectives*.

SELIG S. HARRISON, a Senior Associate of the Carnegie Endowment for International Peace, has written extensively on ethnic problems in South Asia, including *In Afghanistan's Shadow: Baluch Nationalism and Soviet Temptations* and *India: The Most Dangerous Decades*. He has served as Senior Fellow in Charge of Asian Studies at the Brookings Institution and as South Asia Bureau Chief of the *Washington Post*.

PATRICIA J. HIGGINS is Associate Professor of Anthropology at the State University of New York, College at Plattsburgh. Her recent publications include "Anthropologists and Issues of Public Concern: The Iran Crisis" in *Human Organization* and "Women in the Islamic Republic of Iran: Legal, Social, and Ideological Changes" in *Signs*.

NIKKI R. KEDDIE is Professor of History at the University of California, Los Angeles. She is the past President of the Middle East Studies Association of North America and the author of numerous articles and books on Iran and the Middle East, including *Roots of Revolution: an Interpretive History of Modern Iran*, editor of *Religion and Politics in Iran: Shi'ism from Quietism to Revolution*, and coeditor, with Juan R. I. Cole, of *Shi'ism and Social Protest*.

EDEN NABY is Faculty Associate at the Center for Middle Eastern Studies and Lecturer at the Extension School of Harvard University. She has written on the problem of ethnic minorities in Iran, Afghanistan, the Soviet Union and the People's Republic of China. Currently she is writing a book on Islam and the Afghan Resistance.

RICHARD S. NEWELL is Professor of History and Asian Studies at the University of Northern Iowa. With Nancy Newell, he is the author of *The Struggle for Afghanistan*.

M. NAZIF SHAHRANI is Assistant Professor of Anthropology at the University of California, Los Angeles. He is the author of *The Kirghiz and Wakhi of Afghanistan: Adaptation to Closed Frontiers* and coeditor (with Robert L. Canfield) of and contributor to *Revolutions and Rebellions in Afghanistan: Anthropological Perspectives.*

ALI REZA SHEIKHOLESLAMI is the coauthor, with Rostam Kavoussi, of *Political Economy of Saudi Arabia* and the author of a forthcoming study, *The Central Structure of Authority in Qajar Iran, 1871-1896.*

MYRON WEINER is Ford International Professor of Political Science at the Massachusetts Institute of Technology. He served as chairman of the Joint Committee on South Asia of the Social Science Research Council and the American Council of Learned Societies from 1980 to 1984. His studies of ethnicity in South Asia include *India's Preferential Policies: Migrants, the Middle Classes and Ethnic Equality* (with Mary F. Katzenstein) and *Sons of the Soil: Migration and Ethnic Conflict in India.*

The STATE, RELIGION,
and ETHNIC POLITICS

INTRODUCTION

Ali Banuazizi and Myron Weiner

I

In no region of the world have changes in religion and ethnic identity had a greater impact on political life than in the three countries that are the subject of this book.

In Iran, the Pahlavi state, which for over half a century had sought to build its foundations and claim to legitimacy mainly upon a pre-Islamic Persian heritage, and to strengthen that heritage in relation to the country's myriad linguistic and tribal minorities, collapsed in the face of a mass-based, religiously inspired, and popular revolution. In contrast to its predecessor, the new theocratic state founded by the Islamic clerics is seeking to build its foundations upon an Islamic identity and to eliminate, neutralize, or weaken those who do not closely follow its fundamentalist line or those who choose to adhere to secular or non-Islamic identities.

In neighboring Afghanistan, a Soviet-dominated Afghan state replaced a secular, but weak, tribal-based regime and is promoting a Marxist political ideology as a means of creating greater loyalty to the state. Opposition to the state comes primarily from the tribes and ethnic groups, as well as the urban middle classes, for whom an Islamic identity has served as a rallying point capable of unifying otherwise antagonistic ethnic communities and other groupings.

In Pakistan, one ethnic group, the Bengalis, successfully tore the Pakistani state in two. And now, some decade-and-a-half after the secession of 55 percent of the country's population and a sizable segment of its land, the ruling Punjabi military elite still views the country's non-Punjabi ethnic minorities as a potential threat to the

1

ι, it is

as an

ιnolin-

ιe uses

ιve had

on. The

of both

ι, and ·in

s the de-

ιnary, op-

obscured

ιns of eth-

d, further-

attach the

ibes, to the

ιnities—are

times, such

purposes of

ethnic iden-

ιrity and the

legitimacy oι the ...

It is this complex interplay ιcι.... and religious
and ethnic identifications that is the central problem of the present
volume. In the case of each of the three countries, the following
chapters examine the role of Islam as a political force, both historically and in its present and more militant form, in relation to the
state, on the one hand, and the region's major ethnic groups on the
other.

II

We use the term "ethnic" to refer to the way individuals and groups
characterize themselves on the basis of their language, race, place of
origin, shared culture, values, and history. Ethnicity is generally but
not always a matter of birth. Central to the notion of ethnicity is a
conception of a common descent, often of a mythic character. In this
volume we have distinguished between religious identity and certain
other forms of collective identity for which we have used the term

"ethnic." But even this version of the term requires further differentiation, for ethnic can mean traditional clan, tribal, and subtribal identities, as well as the historically more recent forms of ethnolinguistic identities. In the case of many Middle Eastern societies, the latter have usually resulted from the erosion of the traditional forms of tribal authority through the voluntary or forced settlement of tribes in urban settings. Thus, for example, whereas the urbanized Baluch and Pashtun tribesmen may no longer feel attached to their particular tribes, they may still feel strongly about a Baluch or Pashtun identity. Moreover, while traditional tribes may be content to strike a bargain with the central authority to preserve their political autonomy, the large ethnolinguistic groups continue to assert their nationhood and often even press for independent statehood. Finally, it should be emphasized that the presence of an ethnic identity does not in itself imply that the ethnic group is politically articulate and assertive. Here as elsewhere in the world a central problem for political analysis is to determine the conditions under which ethnic groups become politically active.

Historically, in all three countries, the erosion or breakup of the traditional forms of tribal authority led to the creation of new forms of ethnic identity. The process is sufficiently well along in Iran so that tribal identities have been replaced almost entirely by ethnolinguistic ones, particularly among the country's largest minorities, the Azerbaijanis and the Kurds. In Afghanistan, the process is more advanced among some communities (e.g., Hazaras and Tajiks) than among others (e.g., Pashtuns and Baluchis). And in Pakistan, tribes remain significant among the Pashtun and Baluchi communities, but are of little or no importance among the peasantized and urbanized Sindhis and Punjabis.

Broadly speaking, there are at least three reasons for the continuing significance of ethnicity in the region covered by these three countries. The first is that all three societies are multiethnic. In Iran, the politically dominant Persians form an estimated 55 percent of the total population of 44.5 million (1985 estimate). The country's largest linguistic minority is the Azeri(Turkish)-speaking Azerbaijanis, who comprise about a quarter of the population. Next in numerical strength are the Kurds, who make up about one-twelfth of the population. The other major ethnic groups are the Qashqa'is, Boir Ahmadis, Turkomans, Afshars, Bakhtiaris, Baluchis, Arabs, and Lurs. Shi'ite Islam is the professed religion of close to 90 percent of the population; the Sunni minority includes the Baluch, the Turkomans, the vast majority of the Kurds and segments of the Arab population. Non-Muslims, comprising less than 2 percent of the total population, include the Baha'is, Zoroastrians, Jews, and Assyrian and Armenian Christians.

In multilingual Afghanistan, the arithmetic of the ethnic balance between Pashtuns and non-Pashtuns has been a continuing subject of controversy. Although the Pashtuns claim to constitute a majority of the country's 18 million (1985 estimate, including the Afghan refugees in Pakistan and Iran), this is at best a precarious margin, if it exists, and the Pashtuns themselves are divided into numerous tribes. They have been the politically dominant group since Ahmad Shah Durrani built a tribal confederacy in the eighteenth century. Efforts by the Pashtuns, especially by the Durrani Pashtuns, to centralize authority and to assert their control over other tribes and ethnolinguistic groups have continued through most of the twentieth century. The Dari (Persian or Farsi)-speaking Tajiks are the second largest linguistic group, estimated at approximately one-fifth of the population; the Tajiks, too, are divided into a variety of ethnic communities. The Shi'ite Hazaras, an estimated one million, are the second-largest Dari-speaking group, while the Uzbeks, who almost number about a million, are the largest Turkic-speaking group in Afghanistan. Other linguistic groups include the Turkomans, the Baluch, the Aimaq, the Brahui, and the Nuristani.

In Pakistan, the Punjabis, constituting some 55 percent of the total population of 95 million (1985 estimate), are the politically dominant group within the bureaucracy and the military. Muhajirs, mainly Urdu-speaking refugees originating from India, though only a small percentage of the population, exercise considerable influence, and their language, Urdu, is the country's official language. Sindhis, Baluchis, and Pashtuns are the major minority groups.

A second feature of the ethnic mosaic of these countries is that many of the ethnic groups are transborder peoples. The borders of all three countries divide major ethnic groups (see Figure 1). In the case of Pakistan, each of its major ethnic groups is a transborder people. Punjabis and Sindhis live in both India and Pakistan, but religious cleavages coincide with the national boundaries. A majority of the Baluchis live in Pakistan, but substantial minorities live in Iran and in southern Afghanistan. The Pashtuns are a majority in Pakistan's North-West Frontier Province, but a majority of the Pashtun-speakers live in neighboring Afghanistan.

In addition to the Pashtuns, the other linguistic groups in Afghanistan are also divided by international borders. Its northern-

FIGURE I.1   MAJOR ETHNIC GROUPS of IRAN, PAKISTAN, and AFGHANISTAN

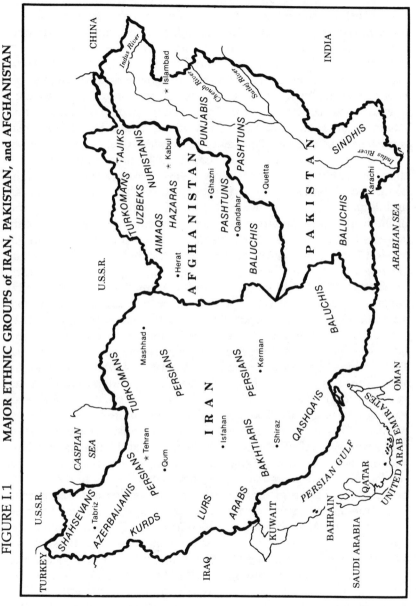

most peoples—the Tajiks, Uzbeks, and Turkomans—also live on the Soviet side of the border. And the Baluch population is divided among Afghanistan, Iran, and Pakistan. The Hazaras are the only major ethnic group in Afghanistan that is not internationally partitioned.

The Azerbaijani and Turkoman populations are divided between Iran and the Soviet Union; the Kurds among Iran, Iraq, Turkey, and the USSR; and the Baluch among Iran, Pakistan, and Afghanistan. Finally, the region's Arab population is shared among Iran, Iraq, and the littoral states of the Persian Gulf.

The borders of the three countries are sufficiently porous so that population movements among their transborder peoples are not blocked by international boundaries. The borders dividing Pakistan and Afghanistan are relatively open and have been so since the time of the British rule. So too are, though to a lesser degree, the Iranian-Afghan and Iranian-Pakistani borders. The civil conflict within Afghanistan has significantly accelerated population movements: there are now an estimated three million Afghan refugees in Pakistan and an additional one million or more in Iran. Only the northern borders separating Iran and Afghanistan from the Soviet Union and Pakistan's borders with China are closed to any population movements.

Each of the countries is at odds with at least one of its neighbors over its borders. Successive Afghan regimes have rejected the Durand Line separating Afghanistan from Pakistan and insisted that the Pashtun population of Pakistan be given the right to choose between autonomy within Pakistan, an independent Pashtunistan or reversion to Afghanistan. As Selig Harrison points out in his contribution to this volume, the Pashtuns of Afghanistan have looked to the unification of all Pashtuns as a means of establishing secure Pashtun dominance in Afghanistan. However, he emphasizes that the Pashtuns of Pakistan are ambivalent with respect to their future because they have a greater sense of power sharing in Pakistan than either the Baluch or the Sindhis. Moreover, he notes, they have been divided by the Afghan conflict, which has opened the way for greater Islamic fundamentalist influence among the Pashtuns than among the other two communities. Nonetheless, writes Harrison, sections of all the minorities, including the Pashtuns, continue to clamor for greater power sharing, autonomy for the provinces, and above all, for the acceptance of the notion that Pakistan is a multiethnic state, positions that are rejected by the present government.

The Baluch in Pakistan waged civil war against the Pakistani government from 1973 to 1977 in pursuit of their demands for autonomy or, failing that, independence, a movement which received some support from the Baluchis living in Afghanistan and Iran, but which was opposed by both the Pakistani and Iranian governments. The Kurds, as is well known, have fought for autonomy within Iraq and, in recent years, within Iran. When the Iraqis tried to lay claim to the loyalty of the Arab population of southwest Iran in the early days of their current conflict with the Islamic Republican regime in Iran, however, they had no apparent success. Hence, the porousness of the borders and the irredentist and secessionist claims made by various ethnic groups and governments contribute to the persistence of ethnic group identity throughout the region and undermine their loyalty to each of the states.

A third and in some respects the most critical factor in the continued importance of ethnicity is the relative weakness and the limited capacity of each of the states, a problem to which we shall turn next.

III

A central concern of successive rulers in all three countries has not only been the enhancement of their own personal power but extending the authority of the state itself. In all three countries religious, tribal, and ethnolinguistic leaders have had an uneasy and at times hostile relationship with central authority and have been regarded by those in authority as impediments to state building.

The term "state" itself is an elusive one, for it is so associated with modern European conceptions that in some respects it is not appropriate to apply the term to the institutions of these countries. The state implies a sovereign authority, a sovereignty based upon both consent and coercion. The state is associated with a particular bounded territory over which it exercises a monopoly of coercive authority. Legitimacy implies myths and symbols which provide a kind of ideological rationalization and justification for this monopoly of coercive authority. In modern Europe the expansion of the state was linked to the expansion of the monarchies at the expense of other authorities, notably the church and feudal magnates. Initially the authority of the modern European state rested on the notion of the sacredness of the office of the king; subsequently, the notion of the sovereign state rested on conceptions of legal rights on the part of citizens in relation to authority, on sovereignty as an inalienable right of the people, and, above all, on the capacity of the state to command resources.

In the case of Iran and Afghanistan, the monarchs, and in the case of Pakistan the military rulers, aspired to create modern states with an exclusive monopoly of coercive authority and control over the entire territory over which they had international judicial authority and to gain some form of popular legitimacy. But none of the states in question could be said to have been successful in these respects. For one thing, none of the three states have had legitimacy in the eyes of all the major ethnic groups and social classes in their respective societies. Furthermore, in their effort to strengthen central authority and the hegemonic position of the dominant ethnic group, state officials have often pursued antagonistic and discriminatory policies toward ethnic minorities. In return, the authority of the state has been repeatedly challenged by one or more ethnic groups in all three countries.

Weakest of all has been the Afghan state. The various tribes and regional communities of Afghanistan have operated relatively independently of the authority of a central state whose writ has often extended outside of Kabul only to the most accessible territories and the weakest of minority groups. The capacity of the Afghan state bureaucracy to extract resources, to deliver benefits, and to enforce law and order has been limited. When the authority of the state over the tribes has increased, it has been largely with the aid of an external power—the British in the nineteenth and early part of the twentieth centuries, and the Soviets over the past three decades.

In his contribution to this volume Richard Newell points to three major obstacles to state building in Afghanistan: (1) the country's geopolitical setting at the crossroads of three of Asia's most enduring civilizations (the Indian, the Chinese, and the Irano-Islamic) and its rugged landscape and harsh and arid climate; (2) its segmentary social structure, resulting from localized patterns of origin and migration, and leading to distrust, rivalry, and conflict among the various social and ethnic groups; and (3) the ambivalent political role of Islam as a basis for national unity. As Newell points out, in spite of the near universality of Islam (with a Sunni preponderance of about 80 percent), attempts to coopt Islamic leaders and to enlist the teachings of Islam in the service of the state have largely failed because of the segmented nature of Afghan society. With each community tending to identify Islam with its own particularistic usages, attempts to impose an official version of Islam have been viewed locally as interference or even heresy. At the same time, the secular features of state building (e.g., modern public education, some public health measures, public employment of women, and commercial banking) have invited opposition on the grounds that they threaten or violate Islamic precepts. Thus, Newell argues, rather than serving as a unifying factor in consolidating the authority of the state, religion has been at times a source of internal resistance against the state. Nonetheless, Newell believes, considerable progress toward the creation of a national state was achieved prior to the Marxist seizure of power in 1978.

It was Pashtun "nationalism" rather than Islam that served as the basis for the centralization of political power in Afghanistan. Nazif Shahrani's historical analysis of the development of the Afghan state and the role within it of the Pashtuns points to the impact of Moghul rule on the emergence of a strong Pashtun consciousness and to the importance of kinship ties among the Pashtuns as the basis for forming alliances. It was not, however, until the 1930s that the monarchical regime sought to replace Persian with Pashtu, first in the schools, then as the official language of the government. Pashtu language, culture, and values, not Islam, he notes, became the cornerstone of Afghan nationalism. Furthermore, as Eden Naby suggests in her chapter, the state sought to undermine religious groups by extending its authority in the educational and judicial spheres and over *waqfs* (endowments supporting religious authorities). However, many of King Amanullah's (1919–29) social reform programs were undermined by Islamic groups who used religiously inspired resistance to his reforms as the rallying point for all those who were opposed to the centralized authority of the state.

Meanwhile, the country's more remote regions were, in turn, hardly touched by the central government, as Robert Canfield notes in his analysis of the social-structural underpinings of Afghan political authority. Although the central government attempted to expand its revenue base by appointing provincial governors who in turn were to collect taxes from local rulers, provincial tax revenues were not always passed on to the national treasury. Canfield describes the variety of ways—through smuggling, bribery of officials and periodic rebellions—in which the rural populace, including the Pashtuns, skillfully resisted the central authority.

The limited expansion of state authority was accompanied by a weakening of the traditional institutions, many of which were controlled by the clergy. Furthermore, the government's policy of providing the clergy with regular stipends incorporated many of them, at least partially, into the state bureaucracy. In the 1950s, the social base of Muhammad Daoud's government, Shahrani notes, was primarily the rural aristocratic elites, especially among the Pashtuns. With this relatively narrow social base and with limited resources, it became increasingly dependent upon foreign financial support. By the 1960s, the government was under attack by the left for failing to adopt a more radical reform program and by the Muslim youth movement for having eroded the position of Islam. The republican Daoud regime, says Shahrani, chose to suppress the Islamic movement, while the Marxist parties were given relatively free rein.

The Pakistani state, as a successor to a comparatively strong British colonial administration, has had considerably more authority, although even its authority has been limited in the tribal areas of the country. Portions of the northwest, the Pashtun area adjacent to the Afghan border, were what the British described as "unadministered" areas, an arrangement continued by the Pakistani government. But what is "unadministered" by the central government is often administered by local tribal chiefs. Similarly, for many years the Baluch sardars (tribal chiefs) continued to exercise authority independent of the central government.

Attempts by the post-independence Pakistani governments to establish their authority were resisted by two distinct groups. The strongest resistance came from the Bengalis who, while forming a majority, lacked any real authority, especially after a Punjabi-dominated military assumed power in the late fifties. In the western regions of the country, resistance came from among the three major linguistic minorities, the Pashtuns, Baluchis, and Sindhis. Meanwhile, the Punjabis and Muhajirs, through their role in the bureaucracy and the military (but not in parties and representative institutions where they were a minority) dominated the state.

Selig Harrison's chapter traces the growth of Baluch, Sindhi, and Pashtun ethnic identities, the demand within these groups for greater autonomy, and the political and constitutional response of the Punjabis and Muhajirs. While there has been a weakening of tribal ties and a strengthening of Baluch and Pashtun identities, neither community has been able to acquire the kind of political cohesion achieved by Bengalis in the 1960s. Nonetheless, fictive kinship ties and a sense of attachment to a territorial homeland have been persistent characteristics of all three ethnic groups.

Opposition to the state has also come from the clergy and their supporters. Indeed, a large part of the clerical establishment in pre-partition India opposed the creation of Pakistan; they regarded its advocates as a secularized, Westernized elite concerned not with creating an Islamic state but with creating a state in which Muslims were in the majority. To a considerable extent, these perceptions were accurate. The early leaders were indeed modernized, secularized and Westernized individuals who believed in the separation of church and state. They reacted with alarm, therefore, at the subsequent demand by orthodox elements that Pakistan be made an Islamic state, that non-Muslims be excluded from positions of power, and that Islamic heterodox groups be declared non-Islamic. A particularly traumatic event for the new state in the early 1950s was a popular and violent demand by fundamentalists that the Ahmadiyah (an Islamic splinter sect that rejects the fundamental Muslim belief that Muhammad was the last of the prophets) be declared non-Muslim and denied positions in the government. The Punjabis and the Muhajirs thus felt threatened by two quite disparate groups, the Islamic fundamentalists and the non-Punjabi, non–Urdu-speaking linguistic communities.

While post-independence Pakistan was less dependent upon external resources than Afghanistan, it too relied substantially upon external assistance. American economic and military aid was important in the 1950s through the mid-sixties. U.S. military assistance diminished thereafter, but the Chinese, and to a lesser extent the French, became Pakistan's major military suppliers. With the Soviet invasion of Afghanistan, U.S. military aid was resumed, and, today, U.S. economic aid, support from international agencies (notably the International Monetary Fund and the World Bank), and assistance from Saudi Arabia constitute a significant and growing share of the central government's revenues.

In contrast to both Afghanistan and Pakistan, the Iranian state has been comparatively strong in its capacity to deliver benefits and enforce law and order without recourse to external support. As Shahrough Akhavi writes, Reza Shah (1925–41), confronted with a near collapse of state authority, domination by foreign powers, and economic and financial chaos in the aftermath of World War I, took a series of decisive measures to centralize state power through the establishment of a modern army, an aggressive industrialization program, and a major expansion of the country's civilian bureaucracy. The ideological orientation of his regime was an intense, secularist Persian nationalism which stressed Iran's ties to its pre-Islamic past. A central concern of Reza Shah, who was the first Persian to establish political control following centuries of rule by Turkish-speaking Safavid, Afshar and Qajar dynasties, was to break the power of the various tribes that had long ignored or threatened the authority of the central government and to assimilate the non– Persian-speaking linguistic communities into the Persian culture and language. Indeed, it is often argued that the strengthening of the central authority vis-à-vis the country's powerful tribal groups was the primary contribution of Reza Shah to state building in contemporary Iran.

While the Pahlavi monarchs had considerable success in dealing with the tribes and with the linguistic minorities, they had far less success in dealing with the country's religious hierarchy. The clerics were officially deprived of many of their traditional functions and privileges, particularly in such areas as education and law, though they continued to enjoy the support of the popular classes and the more traditional segments of the society. Thus, in addition to their spiritual leadership of the faithful, the *ulama* (Islamic clergy; literally "learned men") ran a number of religious seminaries, operated the country's vast network of mosques, religious shrines and charitable endowments, and performed a variety of ceremonial, juridical and social-welfare functions. The payment of religious "taxes" directly to the ulama by members of the more religious and traditional strata of the society helped augment the independence and autonomy of the clerical establishment as a whole. Finally, the fact that some high-ranking ulama resided in the holy Shi'ite centers in Iraq gave the religious hierarchy some degree of immunity and independence from the often arbitrary power of the monarch in Tehran.

A key element in the expansion of the Iranian state in the present century has been its increasing resource base, the consequence primarily of the discovery and production of oil. But oil as the main source of state revenue has been a mixed blessing: while the sale of oil has provided the central government with financial resources to expand its coercive arm and to deliver public services, it has also relieved the government from having to depend on its population for extracting revenues. As a rule, states which do not need to depend for revenues upon their populations—whether, as in the case of Iran, because they earn rents from the sale of natural resources, or, as in the cases of Afghanistan and Pakistan, because they obtain assistance from outside—are less likely than regimes that tax their citizens to be able to effectively penetrate local power structures. Consequently, they are less dependent upon the active support of a wide social base of their population.

IV

In all three countries, the state is once again in a centralizing phase. The Islamic Republic of Iran, the People's Democratic Republic of Afghanistan, and the present military regime in Pakistan are all committed to the creation of strong states, though each has of course a different conception from its predecessor of what constitutes a "strong" state and how best to achieve it. But what was said earlier about their predecessors still remains true today: none of the present regimes in these states has legitimacy in the eyes of all its various minority groups and major social strata.

In Pakistan, the Punjabi-Muhajir dominance continues to be rejected by the ethnic minorities, military rule is rejected by the country's political parties, and the claim by the military to Islamic legitimacy is rejected by a substantial segment of the middle class. In Afghanistan, the flight of millions and the persistent struggle of the insurgents against the regime are sufficient testimony to the lack of legitimacy by the Communist government. And in Iran, in spite of the enormous charismatic appeal of Ayatollah Ruhollah Khomeini and the popular and zealous support for the Islamic Revolution that brought him to power, the clerically dominated regime has had to resort to political repression and terror in order to neutralize its challengers and impose its authority over the country's ethnic groups and others who have opposed its monopolistic control over all political, economic, social and cultural institutions.

Moreover, in all three countries once again the periphery resists the attempts by the center to extend its authority, although the current forces in the periphery differ significantly from the ones that had opposed the states earlier. In contemporary Iran, opposition is strongest from the Kurdish minority, Islamic-leftist, and intensely anticlerical Mojahedin-e Khalq and members of the modern middle classes. The Mojahedin, various other leftist groups, and, to some extent, segments of the middle class had played a critical role in bringing about the downfall of the Pahlavi regime, but they were gradually pushed off the political arena as the Islamic clerics began to tighten their grip on all organs of power after the triumph of the Revolution. In Afghanistan, opposition to the Marxist regime comes primarily from among ethnic communities, urban middle classes, and Islamic elements in the form of a major and sustained armed resistance. And in Pakistan, while religious opposition has become somewhat attenuated, ethnic opposition to central authority persists. Although the latter may be less violent than it has been in the past, it has sufficient power to restrain the center from intervention in some areas of the country. And even today, the linkage between an ethnic regional movement and an external power is what most concerns the ruling authorities in Pakistan. For example, an alliance between the Baluch or Pashtun minorities and the Afghans and their Soviet allies is, in the minds of the military leadership, the one coalition that could undermine their rule and the very existence of Pakistan itself. For this reason, foreign policy is understood as an integral feature of the internal security of the Pakistani state. In none of these countries, it should be noted, is the opposition monolithic; indeed, differences among those who oppose the state are often as great as the differences between the state and the opposition.

One other feature of state authority is characteristic of all three countries: the comparative strength of the military and the comparative weakness of other political institutions. The army has been a central institution of state formation in all three countries. It was so during the reign of the two Pahlavi shahs (1925–79), who modernized the Iranian army and used it principally to strengthen the state's control over society, to provide teeth, as it were, for the bureaucratic institutions. The army has not disappeared as a centralizing force in Iran, but for the most part its authority has been replaced by the *Pasdaran* (Islamic Revolutionary Guards) and other paramilitary organizations which were established during and shortly after the 1978–79 Revolution.

In Pakistan, the military proved ultimately ineffectual in holding the state intact in 1971 against the combined threats of a secessionist movement and the Indian army. However, as Stephen Cohen points out, the military continues to perceive itself as the only force for keeping the country intact. In the absence of representative institutions or of a system of political decentralization to facilitate power sharing among the ethnic groups, there have been some pressures to make the military more representative ethnically, but with little success. Instead, the military under President Zia ul-Haq has turned to Islamic ideology as an instrument for identifying itself with popular sentiment; ties between Pakistan and regimes in the Middle East have been used by the military to emphasize their Islamic affiliation, and in turn to create an increasingly centralized state. It remains to be seen whether the recent ending of martial law, the lifting of restrictions on political participation, and elections to the national assembly will weaken the military's control of the state. The result may well be a period of increasing conflict between the military and the political parties and among the political parties themselves.

The military has proven to be an even less effective unifying force in Afghanistan than in the other two countries. Financial support from outside, especially from the Soviet Union, substantially enhanced its size and firepower. Sovietized sections of the military, working with (and infiltrated by) Afghanistan's Communist Party, were able to overthrow President Daoud in April 1978, but the government was subsequently unable to defeat its many armed opponents in the countryside. The Soviet invasion in December 1979 has not, as the Soviets had evidently hoped, bolstered the Afghan military. Indeed, it is reported that the military has actually dwindled in size as a result of desertions and has thus far been an unreliable instrument of control by the government.

The Babrak Karmal regime moved away from the state-building strategy of the Hafizullah Amin regime, with its emphasis upon the destruction of the clergy, the landed elites, and tribal leaders, and toward a policy intended to isolate the Pashtuns who are regarded as the backbone of the resistance movement. A Nationalities Ministry within the government thus seeks support from the Uzbeks, Tajiks, and Turkomans by teaching their languages in the schools and by giving their languages official status. If the new language policy is successful, the non-Persian minorities will no longer speak Dari, the lingua franca of Afghanistan, and the minorities will have closer linguistic ties to their ethnic brothers in the Soviet Union. The Soviets evidently view a nationalities policy as a way of weakening Islamic-based opposition to the state and of establishing political ties between the various ethnic groups in Afghanistan and their ethnic kinsmen in neighboring Iran and Pakistan.

The search for cadres to serve in the People's Democratic Party of Afghanistan (PDPA), in the Afghan army, in the secret police (KHAD), and in the state bureaucracy is the centerpiece of Soviet/Afghan state-building efforts. (In May 1986 the Soviets chose Dr. Najibullah, the head of KHAD, to succeed Babrak Karmal as the head of government.) Several thousand Afghans have been sent to the Soviet Union and to Eastern Europe for training while in Afghanistan itself the government has organized a Soviet-style Young Pioneers in the schools to provide ideological training for future cadres.

In all three countries, the question of whether the state in its present form will be able to integrate diverse ethnic and religious groups into a single political system, to gain legitimacy in the eyes of the population, and to establish effective control over the country's juridical territory still remains a central problem. In characterizing the three states, we believe that it would be as much an oversimplification to assert that they represent the hegemonic interests of a single ethnic group—the Pashtuns, the Persians, or the Punjabis—as it would be to assert that they reflect the interests of a single social class within each of these societies. Rather, we would argue that these states, though certainly not representative of all the major ethnic minorities and classes in their respective societies, have by now acquired considerable autonomy, and that in each instance a particular institution—the Communist Party in the case of Afghanistan (or, more precisely, the Soviet state operating through the PDPA), the clerical establishment in Iran, and the military in Pakistan—exercises power primarily to promote its own interests.

V

Does this emphasis on institutions neglect the crucial role of Islamic, nationalist, and Marxist ideologies for purposes of political centralization or countermobilization in these countries? And, aside from their instrumental functions—serving the interests of the ruling elites and dominant classes in some contexts and of those challenging the status quo in others—are such ideologies deeply felt, meaningful, and moving forces whose appear can cut across the various segments of such ethnically heterogeneous societies? The analyses and evidence presented by the contributors to this volume, we believe, cast doubt on the view that any of the aforementioned ideologies has provided the regimes in power with a firm enough basis for achieving popular legitimacy and political integration. This fact is underscored by the continuing reliance of the governments in all three countries on coercion for the maintenance of their authority. On the other hand, these same ideologies, and particularly "resurgent Islam," seem to have been more effective as instruments for mobilizing political opposition to the states in the form of parties, guerrilla organizations, or mass protest movements.

The considerably different and variable roles that Islamic ideologies have played in the recent history of Afghanistan, Iran, and Pakistan should be taken as strong evidence against a monolithic

view of Islam as either inherently oppositional or fundamentally ac-
commodationist and supportive of the status quo. That Islam as political ideology has been used to legitimize both conservative or
radical regimes, as well as a variety of reactionary or revolutionary
movements in Muslim societies, may be seen, furthermore, in its
many diverse interpretations by the ruling elites or their challengers
in such countries as Saudi Arabia, Libya, Morocco, Egypt, and Indo-
nesia.

The triumph of the Iranian Revolution and the subsequent
historically unprecedented rise of the ulama to the position of direct
rule have provided a new impetus for analyzing the political character of Islam. In part as a result of the ensuing scholarly debate, an
earlier, more or less dominant, view of Shi'ite clerics believing all
temporal rulers to be illegitimate, maintaining their independence
from the state and siding with the populace against tyranny, corruption, injustice, and impiety—a view which seemed to fairly portray
the leading role of the ulama in the protest movements that led to the
Constitutional Revolution of 1905–11 in Iran—has given way to a
greater appreciation of the highly variable relationship of religious
leaders to the state from one historical period to another, if not within
the same period. As Nikki Keddie points out in her commentary on
the chapters dealing with Iran, questions concerning the relationship
between religion and state cannot be addressed satisfactorily by examining only the written doctrinal materials. Of at least equal significance to an understanding of the ramifications of the issue at the
mass-political level, Keddie argues, is the prevalence of the notion of
illegitimacy of temporal rule in the orally expressed views, popular
beliefs, and cultural symbols among the people and the ability of the
clerics and their allies to modify and apply such doctrines in such a
way as to meet populist demands.

Looking at the problem from a somewhat different, social-
structural perspective, Ali Reza Sheikholeslami attempts to explain
the changing stance of the Shi'ite clerics toward the Iranian state in
terms of significant changes in the Iranian class structure and in the
social origins of the ulama themselves. What is essential to the understanding of the Iranian Revolution and the role of the ulama in it,
Sheikholeslami argues, are the changes in the social fabric of the
Iranian society, especially in the last two decades of the Pahlavi rule,
which led to the emergence of a new, radical Shi'ism, successfully
utilizing traditional religious symbols as instruments of mobilization
and social control in the context of a new class-structured society.

In postrevolutionary Iran, the regime has sought to shift the fundamental basis of unity between the state and society from a secular nationalist ideology to that of an Islamic ideology which covers every sphere of political, economic, social, and cultural life of the nation. Islam is seen as an overarching ideological link between the state and the people, on the one hand, and as a primary bond uniting all segments of the populace on the other. This emphasis on the role of Islam as the focal symbol of national unity has ramifications for the relationship between the state and the various minority groups. For example, as Patricia Higgins points out, while the Azeri-speaking Shi'ite Azerbaijanis could, at least potentially, be better integrated within the symbolic and the actual power structure of the state, the non-Shi'ite minorities have been relegated to a more marginal status in the economic, political and cultural spheres than they held previously. Moreover, as under the Pahlavis, the Sunni Kurds remain the largest and the most significant marginal group challenging the authority of the central government in contemporary Iran.

In the case of Pakistan, as John Esposito writes, successive governing elites have sought to harness Islam as an instrument for strengthening the state and legitimizing their power. The attempts of the secular, socialist Zulfiqar Ali Bhutto to woo Islamic support failed, but the efforts of the martial-law government of President Zia ul-Haq, Esposito suggests, have been somewhat more successful. New Islamic institutions have been put into place, and Islamic social and economic policies have been adopted. The government has won the support of some Islamic fundamentalists without threatening the military, the bureaucratic, the business, and the landholding communities. But President Zia's interpretation of Islam, he concludes, has also created new schisms between Sunni and Shi'ite communities and has not healed the cleavages among the country's ethnic groups.

In a similar vein, Leonard Binder points out that the Punjabi-dominated Pakistan government has denied the legitimacy of politicized ethnicity while insisting upon the legitimacy of politicized Islam, viewing the former as a subversive force and the latter as an instrument of integration and legitimation. But Islam as political ideology, Binder points out, also serves specific socioeconomic goals, for in the Pakistan context, politicized Islam is a conservative ideology with respect to agrarian policies, property rights, and social issues. On the question of popular political participation, the religious elements and the military and bureaucratic elites share a conservative political orientation. Thus, while Islam proved to be a powerful ideological weapon for undermining political authority in Iran, in Pakistan it is used not only by the government, but by the ulama and the Jama'at-i Islami critics of the military to, in Binder's words, maintain and enhance social control.

Perhaps one reason then for the resurgence of religion is that nationalism as the basis for a civil society has proven to be a weak force in all three countries. The Pahlavi dynasty sought to create a Iranian nationalism, but given the circumstances under which the second Pahlavi monarch was reinstalled on the throne—by the overthrow of the popular, nationalistic government of Premier Mohammad Mosaddegh through a CIA-sponsored coup in 1953—he was never able to gain credibility as a nationalist in the eyes of most of his countrymen. In Pakistan, the post-independence ruling groups, the Muhajirs and Punjabis, appealed to a newly created Pakistani nationalism ("Five Thousand Years of Pakistan," heralded the founding fathers, claiming an identity dating to the ancient Indus valley civilization), an appeal that fell upon the deaf ears of the non-Punjabi ethnic groups and religious fundamentalists. And in Afghanistan, nationalism is being expressed mainly as a negative force in the form of a widely based opposition to the Soviet presence. But even here, as Eden Naby suggests in her chapter, religion and ethnicity have thus far proven to be more powerful forces than Afghan nationalism in uniting the various insurgent elements resisting the Soviet occupation.

Nor has war proven to be a force for nationalism in the region to the extent that it has been elsewhere in the world. In Iran, whatever nationalistic sentiments are aroused by the present conflict with neighboring Iraq are partly attenuated by the intense propaganda efforts of a regime that prefers to mobilize its young men for battle under the call of *jihad* (holy war) and martyrdom rather than a secular nationalist ideology. Similarly, neither Pakistan's various struggles against India nor Afghanistan's conflicts with Pakistan have proven to be a significant force for nationalist cohesion. In short, forces that have been regarded elsewhere as bolstering nationalism—e.g., the growth of a national market, the spread of transportation and communication, and the existence of an external adversary—have only had limited success in bringing about genuine societal cohesion in these states, suggesting that other forms of social identity continue to maintain a powerful hold on the political consciousness of their peoples.

Building institutions that cut across diverse religious and ethnic divisions continues to be difficult in all three societies. In Iran, despite the fact that the vast majority of the population professes a belief in Shi'ism, efforts by the postrevolutionary regime to "Islamize" such institutions as the judiciary, banking, education, labor unions, and the like have had a divisive rather than a unifying impact on the society as a whole. Not only have these policies not helped bridge the longstanding ethnic rifts (particularly between the Kurds and the government), but they have further marginalized the country's religious minorities and created new bases of opposition. The policies have been opposed in particular by the urban middle classes who view them to be as much a reflection of the clerics' desire to extend their power of control into every facet of people's lives as a fundamentalist commitment on the part of the ulama to fashion a truly Islamic community governed by strict Islamic laws and teachings. In Afghanistan, given the circumstances under which the present Marxist regime assumed power, Marxist ideology has certainly not served as a banner to unify the highly fragmented Afghan society. Islam and a quest for independence, as indicated earlier, have been the only effective grounds for whatever unity exists today among the various segments of the population. And finally in Pakistan, where the major social divisions remain ethnic, none of the country's political institutions, including both the military and political parties, have as yet been successful in bridging these differences.

The chapters herein address the fundamental questions of how society, polity, and the state are linked in societies that have a history of ethnic fragmentation and where religion has alternately been used as an instrument for solidifying and undermining state authority. These chapters point to the reasons for the lack of a civil society in all three countries and the resulting failure to create a political process that can provide the basis for stable, legitimate state authority.

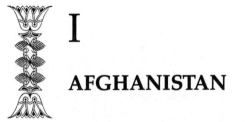

I

AFGHANISTAN

1

STATE BUILDING and SOCIAL FRAGMENTATION in AFGHANISTAN
A Historical Perspective

M. NAZIF SHAHRANI

THE BROAD OBJECTIVE OF THIS CHAPTER is to systematically examine the relationships between state-building efforts, Islam, and ethnicity within the field of changing political, economic, and historical realities in Afghanistan. Such an attempt (however brief and schematic due to space limitations) is formidable, particularly in the case of Afghanistan, since none of these issues has been well investigated, even separately.[1] Thus, the explanations offered here can be only tentative and suggestive.

Canfield, Naby, and Newell detail a wide range of significant facts herein regarding Afghanistan's physical, environmental, and ecological conditions, geopolitical and strategic position, sociocultural and structural pluralism, the segmentary nature of the social order, increasing power and control of central government over the reluctant peoples of the rural peripheries, as well as the definite, but somewhat ambiguous, role of Islam in the country's political processes, past and present. A common theme in the three chapters, also found in other writings on Afghanistan, particularly those following the current political conflict in the country, is the existence of persistent tensions, conflicts, and ongoing adversarious relations between the center and the periphery, i.e., Afghan governments ("state") and the tribal and ethnic groups, especially in the rural areas. The principal focus of this chapter, therefore, will be a critical examination of this particular complex issue. This focus rests on the belief that the articulation of relationships between Islam, ethnicity, and state in Afghani-

23

stan may be best explained, or explicable, through the systematic exploration of the nature and causes of the alleged tensions between the government and society.

The failure of Afghan governments to achieve their goal of building a strong, centralized, and unified nation-state is generally justified and explained, by government officials and researchers alike, in terms of the country's geophysical problems, ethnolinguistic and religious-sectarian differences, and tribal organization extant in the nation. From this perspective, the problems of state building are safely externalized by blaming the alleged intrinsic and inherent conflictual and fragmentary character of the Afghan society. More specifically, social and cultural heterogeneity and pluralism are equated with social and political disagreement, fragmentation, and opposition to centralized rule, independent of the policies and practices of the state-building agents. While the geophysical characteristics of Afghanistan and the sociocultural and social structural heterogeneity of Afghan society have played some part in affecting the processes of state building in the country, it is argued here that it has been the particular policies and practices of the central governments in Afghanistan toward the various peoples of Afghanistan that have transformed existing sociocultural pluralism into articulated forms of social structural fragmentation and opposition to centralized powers along ethnic, religious sectarian, regional, and tribal parameters. These policies and practices have thereby produced a cumulatively negative impact on state-building efforts. It is with the above thesis in mind that the nature and causes of the tensions between the Afghan state and society will be explored.

Ethnicity and kinship, which are expressed linguistically through the same terms, *qawm* (people, tribe, community), *wulus* (nation, tribe, relatives), and *tyfah* (clan, tribe, group), represent the same or similar ideological frameworks in Afghanistan. Together with Islam they provide the most fundamental bases for individuals and collective identities and loyalties, and they are the most persistent and pervasive potential bases for the organization of social formations, for the mobilization of social action, and for the regulation of social interaction among individuals and between social groups.

As generalized social organizational principles, Islam, ethnicity, and kinship have been equally available to individuals and collectivities in the society at large, as well as to those who have controlled the central government powers. They could be applied and manipulated not only to further common or similar collective national goals, but also to pursue separate, often divergent, and sometimes conflicting and contradictory aims by individuals, groups, and institutions. Other sources of tension in the social processes emanate from the fact that ethnic, kinship, and religious ideologies, like other social organizational principles, are also filled with internal ambiguities, contradictions, limitations, and conflicts. Therefore, the use of these principles by individuals, organized pluralities, and governments for instrumental purposes has often manifested many unforeseen consequences. However, social organizational principles, whether based on ethnicity, kinship, religion, or any other sources of social identity, are not in themselves causal in the actual organization of social relations. Rather, individuals, organized social pluralities, and governments apply such principles according to the specific political, economic, and historical contexts in which they find themselves. It is within the context of the operations of real economic and political forces, both internal and external to the particular society, that the value of particular ethnic, kinship or religious identities, loyalties, and ideologies, and their efficacy in organizing social relations, as well as their relation with the state, can be studied. It is also within the changing historical contexts of the political economy of both the state and society that the nature of relations between the ongoing formation and reformation of ethnic, tribal, and religious-sectarian groupings in the country, and the formation and transformation of the government power structures at the center, can be examined and understood.

For reasons of clarity and easier recognition of continuities and changes, this discussion will be presented in a chronological scheme in which socioeconomic and political developments in Afghanistan are divided into five major phases:

1. The rise of frontier feudalism (1500–1747)
2. The rise of the Durrani empire (1747–1800)
3. The disintegration of the Durrani empire (1800–80)
4. The creation and consolidation of a "buffer state" (1880–1955)
5. Toward the creation of a "nation-state" (1955–79)

The emergence of Afghanistan as a separate political entity in the mid-eighteenth century is almost coterminous with the rise of Pashtun tribal power on the national scene. In fact, the sociology of Pashtun dominance over the other ethnic communities in the country forms the very substance of political developments and state building in Afghanistan. Yet, the fact of Pashtun dominance is often taken for granted rather than as a subject for inquiry. Traditionally their political dominance has been generally explained by reference to certain assumed inherent Pashtun qualities, such as their warlike behavior, their love of freedom and individuality, their "lawlessness," "fanaticism," and "pride." It is also often added that Pashtun society is characterized by a high level of internal and external conflict and by weak internal authority patterns.[2] In such explanations Pashtun society and polity are often presented in monolithic terms which most recent anthropological studies of the Pashtun in Afghanistan contradict.[3] Even if found to be sociologically true, the personality traits attributed to Pashtun individuals and the authority pattern said to be characteristic of the society do not explain the historical rise of the Pashtun to political preeminence in the mid-eighteenth century.

A more reasonable explanation of the rise of the Pashtun to power must be sought in the sociopolitical conditions that prevailed in the region prior to their rise to political dominance in the mid-eighteenth century. It is, therefore, a brief examination of the situation before the founding of independent Pashtun politics in Afghanistan that we will address first.

The RISE of FRONTIER FEUDALISM, 1500–1747

Following the disintegration of the Timurid (Koragani) dynasty of Herat in 1506, the territories constituting Afghanistan became the object of the political ambitions of three newly emergent empires in the region. The Shaybanid Uzbeks fought with the Moghuls for possession of Badakhshan and the northern areas, and with the Safavid Persians for control of Herat, while the Safavids and Moghuls fought several wars over Qandahar. The Safavids, ardent Shi'ites, and the Uzbeks, determined Sunnis, were strongly opposed to each other. This opposition was motivated, at least in part, by "racial" or ethnic differences, but their wars were justified on religious-sectarian grounds.[4] The Safavids and Moghuls also engaged in similar destructive wars with one another. As a result, Shi'a and Sunni sectarian affiliations became extremely politicized.[5] The cities of Herat and Qandahar were ravaged by the Uzbek-Safavid and Moghul-Safavid wars respectively, as they changed hands from one rival power to another. Divided Afghanistan became the remote, isolated, and embattled frontier areas of the three empires, resulting in a significant economic, social, and cultural decline. Urban centers and merchant classes suffered severely. Major *madrasahs* (advanced schools for Islamic learning) and *ulama* (Islamic clergy, literally, "learned men") lost their endowments, and scores of indigenous scholars, artists, and poets turned to the Moghul Indian courts and to Bukhara and Samarkand.[6] The isolation and economic and cultural decline was further aggravated by the discovery of a maritime route between Europe, India, and the Far East, which resulted in a substantial decrease in the volume of international overland trade through Afghanistan.[7]

On the local and regional level the consequences of this prolonged experience of subjugation and territorial division were the manifestation of distinct social and cultural orientations, important demographic movements, and the articulation of new ethnic and tribal power relations. The Shaybanid rule in northern Afghanistan resulted in the establishment of Uzbeks as the dominant political force in the area, leading to the subjugation, and often displacement, of some indigenous Tajiks and Hazaras, especially the Shi'as, in the fertile valleys.

The central highlands, where the ancestors of the modern Hazaras had been established since the early decades of the thirteenth century, were conquered by the armies of the Safavid King, Shah Abbas I (1588–1629), who may have been responsible for the conversion of the Hazaras to Shi'ism.[8] This event undoubtedly set the stage for almost continuous raids and wars between the Hazaras and their Sunni neighbors until the end of the nineteenth century.

The most critical development of the period of foreign imperial rule, and one which had significant consequences for the future of Afghan political processes, was the imperial policies toward the Pashtun tribes and the resultant development of Pashtun tribalism. The Moghuls controlled Pashtun-inhabited areas to the south and east of the Hindu Kush, while the Safavids were in control of the western regions. The impact of the policies of the two contending empires over their respective Pashtun subjects was by no means identical. For example, the Moghul policies proved particularly advantageous to the sedentary agriculturalist Pashtun living in the fertile valleys and plains to the east of the Sulayman range. For this segment of the population, the so-called *qalang* (taxpayer) Pashtun, their dominant position within a caste-like hierarchical arrangement, in which the indigenous non-Pashtun peoples assumed a subservient role, was confirmed and maintained. On the other hand, Pashtun tribes who lived in the ecologically and economically marginal, but much more defendable, mountain areas, the so-called *nang* (honor-bound) Pashtun, did not fair well under Moghul rule. It was among the hill Pashtun that a number of popular opposition movements against the Moghul rule occurred.[9]

Moghul policies toward the Pashtun and the Pashtun anti-Moghul agitations played a very important role in the development of Pashtun tribal structure and articulation of a strong sense of Pashtun consciousness, which became increasingly manifest through the emergent Pashtu poetic and literary tradition during the sixteenth and seventeenth centuries. The differences between the so-called nang Pashtuns, living in ecologically marginal mountain areas, and the qalang Pashtuns, living in well-watered, fertile agricultural plains, also became more marked.

Safavid control of western Afghanistan differed from that in other areas in a number of important ways, the most significant being the Safavids' attempt to impose Shi'ism upon the local population and the persecution and killing of Sunni ulama. Consequently, they met with more widespread popular resistance than did the Moghuls. Although, like the Moghuls, they had an elaborate feudal administrative system, their control of the western region was contingent primarily upon their strong military presence; they maintained twenty thousand Persian soldiers in both Herat and Qandahar.[10] To ensure their rule, the Safavids recruited local fighting men into the Persian armies, then stationed them in Persia, banished individuals, transplanted entire kinship groups in distant areas, and relied on a policy of divide and rule, creating conflicts and competition between local leaders, both religious and secular. The most notable example of such manipulations involved the long-standing tribal feuds between the Abdali and Ghilzai Pashtun, one in which the parties were willing participants, and which had profound consequences for the Safavids, for the development of Pashtun tribalism, and for the future history of Afghanistan.[11]

The two centuries of indirect imperial rule produced significant changes in the kin-ordered social, economic, and political structure of the Pashtun, ultimately catapulting them into a position of political dominance in the region. Among the Pashtun, as well as other ethnic communities in the region, kinship had been an important force in mobilizing social labor for economic and social production on the household level. Under Safavid and Moghul imperial rule, the internal dynamics of the Pashtun kin-ordered, socioeconomic, and political structure were further developed by using kinship and ethnic groups as administrative units of indirect rule. Perhaps the most significant influence of indirect foreign imperial rule was the rise of aristocratic clans of Popalzai among the Abdali tribes, and Hotaki[12] and Tokhi clans among the Ghilzai, with the development of further internal rankings within the two major tribes and their respective subdivisions.[13] Such rankings created opposition among various segments of the tribes and their leaders which sometimes broke out into open conflict and shifts in alliances. While groups rose and fell depending on their demographic strength, equally important was the ability (or lack thereof) of their leaders in managing people, resources, and effective alliances, especially with the imperial powers, their success or failure in military campaigns in support of or against the empires, and the judicious distribution of resources, whether war booty, subsidies, or land grants. The critical factors involved in the rise of the Pashtun to political ascendency were also the sedentarization of large numbers of nomads, particularly of the Abdali tribes, the establishment of wealthy and aristocratic elements in urban areas, and their developing interest in commerce, and the participation of Pashtun tribesman in the imperial armies in Persia and India, which contributed significantly to the kin-ordered subsistence economy of the tribesmen through booty or remittances.

Therefore, the successful attempt to establish an independent political entity in Qandahar (1709) by Haji Mirways Hotaki (a prominent merchant and appointed mayor of Qandahar), the Safavid court's officially confirmed *ra'is* (paramount chief) of the Ghilzai tribes, and his sons' subsequent control of the Safavid empire during the early decades of the eighteenth century, however brief, were important outcomes of Pashtun tribal developments in relation to the Moghul and Safavid empires' imperial policies and practices during the sixteenth and seventeenth centuries. The rise of the Hotakis to power also signaled the rising political fortunes of the Pashtun and laid the foundations for the establishment of a lasting Pashtun political entity following the short reign of the Sunni Persian ruler, Nadir Afshar, who had effected the reunification of all three regions of Afghanistan under his control by 1739.

The RISE of the DURRANI EMPIRE, 1747–1800

The sudden and violent death of Nadir Shah Afshar provided the opportunity for Ahmad Khan Abdali, his most trusted Pashtun commander, to create an independent government in Qandahar in 1747 and to subsequently launch a successful campaign to establish the Durrani empire. In this venture Ahmad Khan Abdali had the support and active collaboration of a number of Ghilzai and Uzbek officers who were his comrades in the Persian army. The process through which Ahmad Khan Abdali was selected by tribal, ethnic, and religious leaders as the King of Afghanistan was both a reflection of the kinship and ethnic-based nature of the articulation of the existing power structure and its reaffirmation and legitimation by precedent in the new independent country and polity.[14]

On assuming the leadership of the new government in Qandahar, Ahmad Shah, with the help of his small military force and a substantial amount of revenues captured in transit from Kabul and Peshawar to the court of Persia (which he regarded as gifts from God—'Atayayi hazrati yazdan), set out to organize his court and government. Not surprisingly, in this effort he followed the model he knew best—Persia. In Elphinstone's words, "The forms of his court, the great officers of state, the arrangement of the army, and the pretensions of the crown, were exactly the same as those of Naudir Shauh [sic]."[15] In accordance with the practice of Muslim rulers, he issued coins for circulation in his own name,[16] and in the Friday prayers his name was mentioned in the khutbah (sermon) as the sovereign.

Ahmad Shah Abdali, who assumed the title of Durrani for himself and his tribe, adopted an imperial policy of indirect rule. In the absence of any reliable alternative bases of support, he tried to strengthen his position among his own kinsmen and tribesmen. The ownership of all the lands held by the Durrani were confirmed in return for the provision of a fixed number of troops on call. Special privileges were also awarded to his own Sadozai clan.[17] He tried to obtain the allegiance of other Pashtun tribes, with the exception of the Ghilzai whom he vanquished militarily, by appealing to their spirit of nationalism, claiming that he had delivered them from foreign domination. He did not attack the rebellious groups out of a sense of unwillingness "to bring any calamity upon his countrymen."[18] Major non-Pashtun tribal-ethnic communities submitted peacefully to indirect rule through their own local leaders.[19]

Ahmad Shah's most effective strategy for consolidating his power within the country was his foreign wars of conquest. He had no desire for Western conquest against the Persians and Uzbeks, except in the defense of Khurasan and Turkestan, south of the Oxus, and he directed his conquests toward the east and south to India. He did not exact heavy taxes from his western territories; such exactions were, after all, associated with foreign rulers and the agents of foreign empires in the past. He employed the men from the west in his many successful military campaigns in India, which brought him increased reputation and loot with which to maintain an army and keep the continued allegiance of the khans through favors and rewards. Many local chiefs from all parts of the country joined him with their forces in the campaigns in the hope of plunder and then willingly submitted to his authority after serving under his command in the battlefield.

In addition to the obvious attraction of booty from his wars of conquest in India, Ahmad Shah Durrani's Islamic zeal may have also played an important role.[20] He was, by all available accounts, a pious Muslim, a Sufi disciple of the saint of Chamkani, and a man with deep respect for the ulama and holy men, both as a matter of personal inclination and of public policy.[21]

By the time of his death in June 1773, Ahmad Shah had created a great empire stretching from Khurasan to Kashmir and Punjab, and from the Oxus to the Indian Ocean. He had secured the allegiance of these areas either through treaties, sometimes involving exchange of women in marriage, or by actual possession. Ahmad Shah, also in the manner of other emperors, built his own capital city in a new location, Qandahar, but failed to create an independent urban economy. The kin-ordered mode of production persisted, especially in his western territories, complemented by the tributary mode of the partimonial empire. His Durrani empire was more of a confederation of many Pashtun and non-Pashtun tribes and khanates than a centralized kingdom.[22] This achievement was a testament to his personal charisma and leadership abilities, but also clear evidence of what Wolf calls:

> one of the Achilles' heels of the kinship mode, [and] one of its diagnostic points of stress. For as a chief or other leader draws a following through judicious management of alliances and redistributive action, he reaches a limit that can only be surpassed by breaking through the bounds of the kinship order . . . To break through the limitations of the kin order, a chief must gain independent access to reliable and renewable resources of his own.[23]

The particular strategy used so effectively by Ahmad Shah to break through the limitations of kin order was the fruits of war, but that proved to be transient. The problem of finding or developing reliable and renewable resources has persisted to this day as the central problem of the political economy of the state for all the aspiring leaders of the Afghan governments.

The successor to Ahmad Shah's throne, his son and heir-designate, Timur Shah (1773–93), was immediately confronted by all the instability of a kin-based system of political patrimonialism he had inherited. Timur Shah was challenged for the throne by one of his brothers and faced strong opposition from among his own Durrani tribesmen. Revolts by other Pashtun khans near his capital in Qandahar, as well as in the distant provinces of Punjab, Sind, and Kashmir, underlined the unreliability of tax-tribute revenues from these areas upon which the central political authority was so totally dependent.

Due to internal threats to his power Timur Shah did not indulge in wars of conquest, focusing his attention upon the defense of territories and tax and tributes he had inherited. He was only partially successful and as his grip on the distant revenue-producing provinces of the east weakened toward the end of his reign, his government lost both reputation and influence. In the face of declining revenues from the Indian provinces he also began to increase taxes on the non-Pashtun populations, which resulted in more revolts and a further weakening of central authority. Timur Shah's measures to ensure his power by relying on non-Pashtun troops and courtiers led to growing resentment among some Pashtun tribal leaders and many attempts at revolts. The conditions for strengthening central authority, however, grew worse on the death of Timur Shah, since he left twenty-three sons from his ten wives of diverse tribal and ethnic origins, without designating a successor.[24]

Despite the feverish efforts of his successor, Zaman Shah (1793–1802), to secure the continuation of the tax tributes from the eastern provinces and to improve centralization of power, the results were far from satisfactory. In the escalating conflicts and competitions among Timur Shah's sons for the Afghan throne, under conditions of increasingly closed resources (both money and allies), the long-existing alliance between the two powerful Sadozai and Barakzai clans of the Durrani tribes was shattered by the execution in 1800 of Sardar Payinda Khan, the leader of the Barakzai, at the hands of Zaman Shah.

The DISINTEGRATION of the DURRANI EMPIRE, 1800–80

The murder of Sardar Payinda Khan Barakzai, who left twenty-one sons, most of them eager to seek revenge on Zaman Shah, provided an excellent opportunity for the king's contending brothers. There ensured a bloody fratricidal squabble among the Sadozai princes, which resulted in the fall of their dynasty in 1818 and the transfer of power to the Barakzai sardars (tribal chiefs), i.e., the sons of Sardar Payinda Khan Barakzai. Competition among the Barakzai sardars for paramount authority in turn launched a destructive and debilitating internal war (1818–34) in the country. A semblance of unity returned to the country only in the face of foreign threats and the ensuing Anglo-Afghan wars (1839–42 and 1878–80).

The kin-based political disorders did not disrupt the kinship order within the society; rather, it strengthened it. This is principally due to the fact that kinship "oppositions as they are normally played out are particulate, the conjunction of a particular elder with a particular junior of a particular lineage at a particular time and place, and not the general opposition of elder and junior as classes. In everyday life the kin-ordered mode contains its oppositions by particularizing tensions and conflicts."[25] Thus the bloody internal wars were fought by many on various sides not for or against any ideological or institutional cause or causes, but rather for or against specific individuals out of personal loyalties (categorical and/or acquired) and a sense of personal obligation. Yet, the importance of this period of particularistic political conflicts, and its consequences for the future dynamics of Afghan political culture, cannot be underestimated.

One of the earliest and most significant legacies of the conflicts surrounding succession to the Afghan throne was politicization of Islam in the form of Shi'a-Sunni conflicts in the internal national politics. Although Sunni antagonism toward the Shi'a Persians has existed for a very long time, particularly among the Pashtun and Sunni non-Pashtun in western regions of the country, the prominence of Qizilbash and Bayat Shi'a troops and officers in the Durrani court, beginning with Ahmad Shah and growing in numbers and political importance during the reign of his sons and grandsons, was of growing concern to some Pashtun chiefs. Finally, a minor incident between a Qizilbash officer and a Sunni man in Kabul in 1804 provided the opportunity for an opponent of the reigning monarch, Shah Mahmud, to exploit the situation. A devastating riot broke out in Kabul between the Sunni and Shi'a communities, leading to the mobilization of the peoples of Kohistan and Logar on the Sunni side, and some 10,000 Hazaras from Hazarajat on the side of the Shi'as. Thus, Shah Mahmud's first reign ended as a result of this unprecedented Shi'a-Sunni conflict in Kabul.[26]

This event also marked the beginning of the active use of Islam and the employment of ulama and *ruhanis* (religious dignitaries, spiritual leaders, Sufis) by contenders for, and occupants of, the Kabul throne in the decades to follow. Thus, this development inaugurated a new role for Islam and religious leaders in the political culture of Afghanistan at the national level. Until then, relations between central governments and the religious establishment had been, for the most part, nonpolitical. Although individual ulama had been appointed to serve in the royal court, or the government courts, the religious establishment generally had enjoyed some economic support in the form of *tiyul* (land assignments) from the state. The ulama and mullahs were in charge of informal Islamic education, interpretation of the Shari'a (the sacred Law of Islam), and the administration of local justice, and more importantly, they acted as guardians of public morality and as a voice against the excesses of government officials, and even the royal court. Though enjoying only moral, not political, power in the country, religious leaders (both ulama and ruhanis) were active in mediating local conflicts.[27] By the 1820s and 1830s their active role in national politics expanded, not only in the service of Afghan leaders vying for political ascendancy, but also in the service of foreign powers seeking to influence domestic political processes for their own ends.

The second significant legacy of the particularistic conflicts and civil wars during the early decades of the nineteenth century was the loss of political control over the major revenue-producing provinces of Punjab, Kashmir, and Sind to the rising power of the Sikhs and the local chiefs. Baluchistan was permanently lost to local independent khans. Afghan Turkestan, Badakhshan, and Hazarajat also fell to the many independent local chieftains and remained outside the influence of Kabul governments, except for brief periods, until well into the last decade of the nineteenth century. Under these conditions, prolonged and immensely destructive intratribal (within Uzbek, Hazara, Taimani, Aimaq, Jamshidi tribes) and interethnic (between Hazara, Uzbek, Tajik, Jamshidi, etc.) wars ensued, particularly between Shi'a and Sunni groups. The object of most of the wars was *chapawul*, plunder of one another's territory for slaves, portable goods, and, occasionally, exaction of tribute. The eastern, southern, and western parts of the country were divided among the sons of Sardar Payinda Khan Barakzai, who were constantly at war with one another. Under these plural power centers and power holders, old feuds were rekindled and intensified among subunits of Durrani tribes, as well as those between Durrani and Ghilzai Pashtun, as the various warlords pursued new possibilities for furthering their personal ambitions. Because of the insecurity, regional and international trade declined, the towns and countryside were pillaged and plundered by contending armies, and heavy taxes were imposed on merchants, artisans, and non-Pashtun ethnic groups, forcing the emigration of Armenian, Hindu, and Jewish merchants and artisans from Afghanistan.[28]

At this time, when the Durrani empire was in a state of total disarray, the rise of the Qajar dynasty in Persia and a confederation of Sikh powers in northern India began to pose a serious threat to the survival of an Afghan political entity. The Persians had already claimed most of Khurasan and were repeatedly attacking Herat. The Sikhs had taken most of the Durrani empire's eastern provinces and were fighting for control of Peshawar and its environs. By the 1820s and 1830s the Western colonial powers, principally the Russians and the British, were aiding and encouraging such attacks against the Afghans. Even in the face of this growing threat, the warring Barakzai brothers were unable to come together. At last, the limitations of kin-based particularistic political conflicts had to be overcome by the universalizing power of an Islamic ritual of *jihad* (holy war) in the face of overwhelming foreign threats.

An Indian Muslim and Sufi named Sayyid Ahmad Brelwi, who had been active in the jihad against the British in northern India, had come to Afghanistan in 1827 to warn of the Sikh menace and to encourage the Barakzai sardars and the Afghans to take up a jihad against the Sikhs. But it was not until 1834, during a direct attack on Peshawar by the Sikhs, that a Barakzai sardar, Dost Muhammad, who had held Kabul since 1826, was willing to face the Sikhs in the name of Islam. Upon the declaration of his intentions, the Kabul ulama conferred upon him the title of *Amir al-Mu'minin* (Commander of the Faithful) and leader of the jihad against the Sikhs. This act formally marked the foundation of the Barakzai dynasty by making Dost Muhammad the Amir (not king) of Afghanistan (1834–38 and 1842–63). Upon his declaration in 1835 of a jihad against the Sikhs, Amir Dost Muhammad received considerable financial and military support from all segments of the population, thus establishing the potency of the concept of jihad as a means of defending the country and consolidating the power of his dynasty against external threats.[29]

The prolonged period of particularistic internal political conflicts surrounding the succession, the struggle against the Sikhs, and two major wars of invasion by the British, had profound and long-lasting effects upon future economic, social, and political developments in Afghanistan. The most obvious consequence of these events was the permanent loss of territories and, thus, loss of crucial revenues for the government. The country's declining urban economy and population, particularly in Kabul, Jalalabad, Qandahar, and Herat, were also seriously affected. Consequently, because of the extremely

> weakened position of the urban sectors, the nationalist, anti-British struggle was led primarily by the Afghan tribes and religious establishment, and became a religious war as well as a nationalist one. Islam became a potent national force, a unifying force that overrode, to a great extent, ethnic, racial, and linguistic division, a force used by Afghan rulers to mobilize popular opinion and enlist the support of the masses in their struggle against the Sikhs and against British imperialism.[30]

Not surprisingly, the position of religious leaders and ulama was strengthened, as was the continuing significance of tribal and feudal relations, for the defense of the country and continuation of the Barakzai dynasty. The wars and occupation of the country by British troops, the banishment of some of the ruling elite to British India, as well as official government visits to the subcontinent resulted in a familiarity with Western technology, institutions, and values. In the limited modernization of the army, weaponry, and government-sponsored industry, the Afghan monarchy found the means to strengthen its own power over the tribal and religious leadership and to create a politically and economically united country. Yet, lacking in financial resources, necessary technology, and sufficient weapons and ammunition to achieve centralization of power, the Barakzai dynasty became increasingly dependent on British financial and military assistance. The British played a substantial part in the succession of Amir Dost Muhammad (1842–63) and Amir Sher Ali (1868–79) to the throne. The provision of money and modern arms to both rulers played an important role in their attempt to politically reunite the country. As the British and Russian "Great Game" in Central Asia intensified during the 1870s, the very survival of the monarchy and the country became subject to British goals and intentions in the region.

The CREATION and CONSOLIDATION of a "BUFFER STATE," 1880–1955

At the end of the Second Anglo-Afghan War (1878–80) Britain decided against the direct control and incorporation of Afghanistan into her British-Indian empire. Instead, Britain retained control of the country's foreign relations and helped Sardar Abdur Rahman, a grandson of Amir Dost Muhammad, to become the Amir of Afghanistan, thereby creating a buffer state between tsarist Russia to the north and British India to the south. Amir Abdur Rahman was the product of, and participant in, the political chaos that had reigned in the country during the previous decades. He had also witnessed Russian colonial rule in Turkestan during his self-imposed exile in Samarkand (1868–80) and was well acquainted with British policies in Afghanistan.[31] Thus, keenly aware of the intentions of both colonial powers in the "Great Game," he was determined to safeguard his own rule, and the political integrity of the territorially much reduced country, from external threats. To do so, however, he had first to cope with the internal problems of reuniting the country and establishing a strong centralized government. The conditions he inherited posed a tremendous challenge. In Amir Abdur Rahman's own words to his biographer, at the beginning of his reign in 1880,

> every priest, mullah and chief of every tribe and village considered himself an independent King, and for about 200 years past the freedom and independence of many of these priests were never broken by their sovereigns. The Mirs of Turkistan, the Mirs of Hazarah, the Chiefs of Ghilzai were all stronger than their Amirs, and so long as they were the rulers, the King could not do justice in the country. The tyranny and cruelty of these men were unbearable. One of their jokes was to cut off the heads of men and women and put them on red-hot sheets of iron to see them jump about![32]

Amir Abdur Rahman viewed this situation as the product of a policy of indirect rule by his predecessors, and he aimed to establish direct rule by the central government throughout the country. Unlike his predecessors, he did not believe that the power of the King or Amir derived from the support of the people or tribal khans. He was convinced that his power as a monarch emanated from Allah. He claimed that the purpose of Allah in honoring him with "His vice-regency" was "to relieve Afghanistan from foreign aggression and internal disturbances."[33] His sole purpose for claiming an Islamic basis for the monarchy was to establish the fact that those who opposed the King's authority in the efforts to build a strong, Muslim nation were committing anti-Islamic acts, and as such they deserved the harshest punishment. He thereby elevated political conflicts from their traditional particularistic and kinship dominated form to a universalistic and moral level. He saw his task as Amir as that of a nation

builder. He believed that "a nation could be built . . . by the concerted efforts of a king as an architect, the army as masons, and the
people [common men] as workmen. The 'middlemen' [tribal elders,
local khans, and the ulama and the Durrani sardars] then had to be
reduced or destroyed."[34] To justify the destruction of the "middlemen" who opposed him or posed a threat, he accused them of cooperating with the anti-Islamic colonialist powers and of oppressing the
common man.

Despite the Amir's antiforeign rhetoric and sentiments, he
was able to negotiate and accept significant material assistance from
British India in the form of cash grants, annual cash subsidies, quan-
tities of modern arms and ammunition, and the technology to produce arms locally in order to build a relatively powerful and
self-sufficient regular army.[35] He then used the army to reunify the
country and consolidate his authority throughout the country.

Through the use of military force, savage reprisals, tyranny,
marriage alliances, subsidies, intrigues, religious injunctions, and a
policy of divide and rule, the Amir was able to weaken, and effectively contain, the powers of local, regional, tribal, and religious leaders who either opposed him or posed a threat to his rule. The Amir's
internal policy favored the Sunni over the Shi'a and the Pashtun over
the non-Pashtun, and among Pashtun he relied on his own clan, the
Muhammadzai and the Safis of Tagaw. Only after his authority over
the entire country was made secure during the middle of the 1890s,
and when the Russian and British threats were on the rise, did the
Amir begin to promote the idea of national unity, emphasizing common religion, common land, and systems of interethnic marriages as
the bases for such unity. He established a *jashn-i mutafiqqiyya-i milli*
(National Festival of Unity day) in 1896, and ordered its annual observance. But, even in his call for such unity, Pashtun preeminence
was preserved.[36]

He deprived the religious dignitaries of their economic independence by nationalizing the *waqf* (endowments supporting religious authorities), taking charge of religious schools and
establishments, and instituting annual salaries for those mullahs who
agreed to preach the kind of Islam the Amir wanted to propagate.
Central to the doctrine were "giving of *Zakat* (taxes), taking part in
Jehad, service at the borders of the Islamic state, and *obedience to the
ruler*" (emphasis added).[37] As head of an *Islamic state*, the Amir
claimed to be the sole interpreter of religious doctrine and asserted
that jihad or *ghazaawat* (holy war) "could not be fought except under
the orders and instructions of the ruler of the country."[38] He further

claimed "whether just or despotic, the king must be obeyed, provided his command does not violate the Shari'a."[39] Courts were set up throughout the country and in order to curb the local influence of the ulama and religious dignitaries, settlement of disputes outside the courts was forbidden. Books of sermons, pamphlets, guidelines for preaching, and religious rules of conduct were published and widely distributed by the state for the first time. Many of the same books are still in use in the *masajid-i jami* (Friday mosques) in Afghanistan. The most important achievement of Amir Abdur Rahman's religious policies, which had a lasting effect upon the rural population in Afghanistan, was the establishment of the role of central government as the guardian of Islam and Muslim territory and as the single most important factor of its legitimacy.

By the time of Amir Abdur Rahman's death in 1901 he had, for the first time, created an Afghanistan that had recognized international boundaries, was politically unified, and governed directly by a centralized authority, within the framework of fairly well-defined and universally applied administrative and judiciary rules and regulations. Thus, during the last two decades of the nineteenth century, a clear transition was made from the period of indirect rule based on feudal ties, which had been instituted by the rulers of the Durrani empire in the mid-eighteenth century, to the establishment of a centralized government based on superior military force.[40]

Amir Abdur Rahman's political and administrative achievements were not, however, accompanied "by fundamental socioeconomic reforms affecting the structure of the rural economy of Afghanistan."[41] He did not encourage modern education or improve the communication infrastructure, and because of his extreme fear of colonialist intervention, he adopted a policy of cultural isolationism, avoiding extensive foreign contact, trade, and communication.[42] His reform efforts suffered from lack of resources, capital, and skilled personnel. Most of the meager revenues collected by means of heavy taxation were spent on the upkeep of his standing army (some 50,000–60,000 strong) and the expenses of the royal court. While the peasantry, who had suffered for so long from lack of security, benefited from the centralization of authority, and many landless farmers benefited from the government's sale of lands confiscated from local large landholders who had fallen from favor, these policies of the Amir were not in any way designed specifically to alter the conditions of the rural villagers. Rather, as an indirect consequence of his main policy of centralizing authority and increasing government revenues, he perpetuated the previous processes which hindered the development of a stable, landed aristocracy in Afghanistan. As a result, the majority of the Afghan peasantry continued, into the twentieth century, their kin-ordered, subsistence-oriented household economy of mixed herding and farming, with a large degree of self-sufficiency within the regional economic schemes. The ranks of sedentary village populations were swelled to some extent because of Amir Abdur Rahman's policies of sedentarizing the nomads. While his plans aimed at the settlement of Pashtun nomads, few Pashtuns settled, though most of them benefited from the opening of new grazing grounds in Hazarajat and Turkestan and continued their profitable pastoral nomadic economy with greater vigor. The people who were most affected by Amir Abdur Rahman's sedentarization and resettlement policies were the non-Pashtun nomadic and sedentary *maldar* (herders), the great majority of whom, impoverished after losing their productive land to the state or to the Pashtuns, lost their herds, and turned to marginal sedentary agriculture.[43] As a further consequence of the weakening of tribal and larger local power structures, the village rather than the traditional clan or other tribal segment became the principal administrative unit for most purposes. As a defense mechanism in response to increasingly oppressive and exploitative government officials, the rural villagers also began to evolve their own diffused parallel power structures for handling local conflicts and thereby avoided contact with government officials as much as possible.

Amir Abdur Rahman had a clear understanding of the historical problems of succession to the throne in Afghanistan, and he took unprecedented measures to ensure a smooth transition of power after his own demise.[44] He intentionally avoided naming a successor, but had trained and groomed his eldest son, Habibullah, who was the first monarch to accede to the throne without violence. Amir Habibullah (1901–19) basically followed the policies of his father. Assured by the strength of his military forces, which maintained peace and order throughout the country during his reign, Amir Habibullah relaxed some of the harsher and more despotic aspects of his father's rule. He allowed local chieftains detained in Kabul to return to their homes and tried to improve relations with local leaders by asking for their cooperation with provincial administration in resolving local problems, rather than confronting them with force. Habibullah also proclaimed an amnesty and invited Afghan families his father had sent into exile to return home. Most of them did so and were given important government jobs, and all adult members of his own Muhammadzai clan were offered government allowances as a privileged class.

During the early years of his reign, Amir Habibullah tried to underscore his own personal piety by some symbolic gestures.[45] Emphasis on the divine source of the Amir's power and his principal duty as guardian of the Islamic country of Afghanistan against foreign threats, which had begun during his father's reign, remained strong. Traditionalist ulama reinforced these notions during the Amir's coronation ceremonies and through new and elaborate court rituals. He was given the title of *Siraj al-Millat-i wad Din* (The Light of the Nation and of the Faith) by a group of conservative ulama for his services to Islam.[46] In the early years of his reign Amir Habibullah was also a strong supporter of education. In 1903 he laid the foundation for the modern educational system in Afghanistan by opening Habibiyah School, followed by a number of other schools.[47] Because of the relatively peaceful situation within the country, urban conditions began to improve and urban populations grew. However, the success and scope of modernization programs were restricted to Kabul and were hampered by limited government resources, estimated at about eighty million Kabul rupees a year.[48]

After the signing of the Anglo-Afghan treaty of 1905 and the Amir's official visit to British India in 1907, Habibullah apparently felt secure on his throne and left much of the administrative tasks to his brother and eldest son. He became preoccupied with organizing his opulent court on the Western model and indulged more in sports, hunting, and other leisure activities, becoming less and less concerned in the affairs of state. Large sums of money were spent by the court and members of the royal family, and to cover the costs a variety of new taxes were introduced and collected. Tax collection had become the major task of government and provided an ideal pretext for corruption, bribery, extortion, and fraud. Some six hundred Hazara households attempted to flee to Iran, and poverty, hunger, and loss of peasant land in many parts of the country ensued. Major popular armed uprisings in protest against the local officials, who were frequently Muhammadzai sardars, occurred only in the well-armed frontier area of Paktya (1912–13) and in Qandahar (1912). Although both uprisings were resolved without major military confrontations, the particular officials involved were not punished, but simply either transferred by the court to other areas, or to a more lucrative posting.[49]

Following the Qandahar incident, the problem of official cor-

ruption was addressed in *Siraj al-Akhbar Afghaniyah* (The Lamp of the
News of Afghanistan) by Mahmud Beg Tarzi in an article entitled
"Aman wa Asayush" (Peace and Security), which in part said:

> Public morality has become poisoned, and this lack of morality
> among the people has produced such an undesirable effect that we
> have totally forgotten the Commandments of God, His Prophet, the
> Qur'an and our duty to the country, our national honor, our tribal/
> ethnic respect and dignity, the rights of *'ibadullah* (God's slaves, i.e.,
> Muslims), and our conscience and faith. All to satisfy our lascivious
> and treacherous *nafs* or worldly passions. The King selects and ap-
> points governors and officials to his provinces: if you enquire
> whether or not a candidate [is] of noble birth, he is! a white beard,
> he is! a man who says his prayers, he is! a pious person, he is! an
> *'alim* [scholar], he is! a wise person, he is! Who would not come
> forth and testify to his goodness?! . . . When he is appointed, he is
> so indigent and unfortunate that he has to borrow money to hire
> horses and help, and with thousands of difficulties and heartaches
> reaches his place of provincial appointment. The moment he
> reaches there, he becomes a man-devouring snake, an *azhdaha*, if
> you will! a shark, if you will! a demonic beast, if you will! . . . He
> becomes the owner of stables full of horses! flocks and flocks of
> small animals! rows and rows of camels!—bundles and bundles of
> cash! houses full of boxes of goods! The wonder of it all is, if one
> asks him "What are all these?" he says, "They are my *peshkash and
> tartuq*." The meaning of these word you cannot find in any dictio-
> nary, save the honorable govenor's own dictionary of knowledge
> and sciences! . . . If this confirmed malady, this despicable lack of
> ethics, was limited to only a few [it would have been as well to
> forget it, as] what ever it was, it was. But regretfully any indigent
> clerk who is appointed to a provincial government office, in a short
> while becomes the owner of houses, properties, lands, this, that
> and more! . . . Some governors have given gifts of hundreds of
> thousands of rupees to individuals and to the royal court. Where are
> they coming from? How do we know where from? . . . All from the
> embezzlement of the public treasury, and all from the blood of citi-
> zens.[50]

The chronic and systematic abuse and exploitation of the rural and
peripheral populations at the hands of government officials, which
was the direct consequence of the centralization of power, continued
unabated during Amir Habibullah's rule, as well as that of his successors.

Amir Habibullah's power was challenged, not for the injustices to the majority of rural populations, but for its autocratic nature and for his devotion to the pursuit of a policy of friendship with the British during World War I, at the expense of Afghanistan's external independence. The challenge did not come from the tribes and rural masses, but from among the very small, nascent urban intelligentsia, which included members of his own family and courtiers. This opposition to Habibullah, unlike opposition in the past, was not a simple dynastic struggle. Instead, it was guided by particular political ideological inclinations with aims to alter or modify the existing power structure. These political leanings were closely linked to the ideals of constitutionalism, nationalism, and reformism, and of Islamic modernism. All of these ideologies, while new to the political culture of Afghanistan, were prevalent in the Muslim world and in Asia at that time. The principal sources of these ideas in Afghanistan were two policy developments early in Habibullah's rule. First, the return to the country of the educated sons of exiled Afghan families from British India and the Ottoman empire. Among them were the children of two leading Muhammadzai families, the Musahiban family of the Yahya Khel clan (1901), and those of Mahmud Beg Tarzi (1903 and 1905). Both of these families established marriage ties with Habibullah's family and played significant roles in Afghan politics for decades to come.[51] Second, the opening of the Habibiyah School and the opportunity for modern education for the children of the Kabul aristocracy and the court page boys, the *ghulam bachagan khasi Amir* (Amir's special slave boys), recruited from among the sons of rural nobility.[52]

With the introduction of these ideas, new and qualitatively different bases for the organization and consociation of individuals for political action at the national level emerged. As a result, among the intelligentsia and courtiers several small groups, some secret and others public, some supporting, others opposing the rule of Amir Habibullah, were formed. Among strong opponents of the regime was a group called Jami'at-i Siraiyi Milli (Secret Society of Nationalists) which called for a democratic and constitutional government. A number of *mawlawi*s (religious scholars) and mullahs, were active members of the movement. Their radical plans were revealed to the court in 1909, the movement was suppressed and the Amir's interest in promoting modern education was considerably diminished.[53]

Another group, which attracted many nationalist, reformist, and Islamic modernist elements from among the Kabul intelligentsia, was headed by Mahmud Beg Tarzi and his associates, the "Young Afghans." Mahmud Tarzi, who had spent seven months in Istanbul with Sayyid Jamal al-Din al-Afghani, was well acquainted with his and other Islamic modernist writings, as well as Western literature through Turkish translations. The sociopolitical thinking of Tarzi and his associates was also profoundly affected by the major political events of the first two decades of the twentieth century: the anticolonialist movements of Asia; Pan-Islamic movements; constitutional movements in Persia and the Ottoman empire; the Russo-Japanese war; the Anglo-Russian convention of 1907; World War I; and the Russian Revolution. Upon his return to Kabul from Damascus, Tarzi became the principal advocate of Afghan independence from Great Britain, the major architect of Islamic modernist reform, and articulator of Afghan nationalism on territorial and general historical and cultural bases, rather than its common particularistic and ethnic referents. He believed that under the prevailing conditions of extreme illiteracy, economic backwardness, and the ignorance and opposition of the traditionalist religious establishments, reform and modernization was only possible from above, implemented by the central government. Thus, he used the pages of *Siraj al-Akhbar* (1911–19) as the main vehicle for "the political and social education of the Afghan ruling class."[54] In his attempt to educate the ruling elite and the traditionalist ulama, Tarzi presented the views of himself and his associates, the Young Afghans, in a series of rational and ethical arguments that justified the interdependence of Islam, national independence, the monarchy, a strong centralized political power, and formulation and implementation of social and economic reforms and modernization. To him, however, the success of any kind of national reform and modernization policy required the full independence of the country as a prerequisite.[55]

Amir Habibullah welcomed the support of the *Siraj al-Akhbar*, particularly its efforts to justify the legitimacy of the monarchy through Islamic modernist ideologies and its support for the centralization of authority. However, the extreme nationalistic Pan-Islamic and pro-Turkish views expressed in the *Siraj al-Akhbar*, particularly during World War I, which called for an armed struggle against the British, angered the Amir. He had declared Afghanistan neutral during the war and while he was under tremendous pressures from the Ottoman and German powers to support their cause, he remained loyal to Britain, which he regarded as a friend and guardian.[56] This particular policy brought existing political tensions within the court into sharper focus. His brother, Nasrullah Khan, and his traditionalist faction were strongly anti-British and favored a war of independence. Inayatullah, his eldest son, and his "court liberals" were strongly pro-Turkish and, as such, favored Pan-Islamic and anti-British policies. Amanullah, one of the Amir's younger sons, was a supporter of the modernist-nationalist faction of his father-in-law, Mahmud Tarzi, the editor and publisher of *Siraj al-Akhbar*.[57] The Amir's pro-British diplomacy during the war resulted in the formation of a coalition of traditionalists, court liberals, and Islamic modernist forces due to the appeal of the Pan-Islamic sentiments they shared. All three factions, therefore, stood in opposition to the monarch. The Amir's policies prevailed and *Siraj al-Akhbar* was ordered to cease publication. On 21 February 1919, shortly after the end of the war, Amir Habibullah was assassinated in what appears to have been a joint conspiracy of all parties. A brief contest for the throne followed between his brother, Nasrullah Khan, who had the backing of the traditionalist ulama and tribal forces, and his son, Amanullah, who belonged to the modernist-nationalist faction. Amanullah, who was the governor of Kabul at the time of his father's assassination, made his claim to the Afghan throne good with the help of a promised pay raise to the Afghan army and declared himself King, *not* Amir, of Afghanistan.[58]

King Amanullah (1919–29) thus succeeded to the Afghan throne without any disturbances. In his first address to the people he expressed gratitude to the "honorable nation of Afghanistan" for "putting the crown of the Kingdom" on his head. He promised total national independence for the country, and proclaimed that internally all citizens would be granted complete freedom and safety from "all forms of oppression and transgression and will be subject only to the obedience of the law." He also declared that "all forms of forced labor and corvee is forbidden." Amanullah promised that he would rule through consultation *(shura)* and urged the nation to be alert in guarding their *din* (faith), *dawlat* (state), and *millat* (nation), and to remain awake to, and aware of, the threats to the security of their *watan* (country).[59] His declaration of independence from Britain meant the loss of the traditional promise of political and military support against outside aggression, principally Russia, and, more significantly, the loss of annual British subsidies and access to arms, which had been an important source of internal security since 1880. Amanullah also declared his uncle, Nasrullah Khan, the head of the traditionalist ulama and tribal faction, responsible for the assassination of his father, and sentenced him to life imprisonment. The handling of this situation by Amanullah resulted in significant acts of disaffection among traditionalist religious and tribal leaders, such as not reading the khutbah in the king's name in Qandahar on 25 April 1919. Amanullah immediately regained the support of the tradition-alist ulama and tribal leaders, as well as that of the army, by declaring a jihad against Britain in pursuit of his goal of achieving Afghan national independence. The independence of the country was granted after the Third Anglo-Afghan War (1919), and Amanullah became known as *ghazi* (victor) and a national hero.[60]

In 1919 Amanullah established friendly relations with Soviet leaders, who hailed Amanullah as the head of "the only independent Muslim State in the World" and urged him to lead other Muslim peoples on the road to freedom and independence.[61] Between 1919 and 1922 Amanullah continued to pursue the Pan-Islamic cause and supported both the anti-British Khilafat and Hijrat movements in India and the anti-Bolshevik Basmachi resistance movements among the Muslims of Central Asia. He also established strong ties with Persia and Turkey and gained much popularity as the champion of Islamic causes, both at home and abroad.

By 1921 his Pan-Islamic policies had alienated both Britain and the Soviets. The Soviets, who had earlier promised large cash and arms assistance, withheld some of their help, and under finan-cial and political pressure from both sides, especially after the Rus-sian takeover of Bukhara and Khiva in 1920, King Amanullah began a policy of rapprochement with both powers. The independent Af-ghanistan's status as a buffer state was thus reaffirmed when Amanullah signed a treaty of friendship with the Soviets in 1921 and allowed the establishment of a British legation in Kabul in 1922.[62] His interest in Pan-Islamic, anti-colonialist, and anti-Bolshevik move-ments was significantly curtailed or stopped altogether. Amanullah's change of policy, after several years of a strong anti-British stance, particularly angered the frontier Pashtuns, the traditionalist ulama, and some nationalist intelligentsia. His withdrawal of support for the Basmachi resistance caused distrust and disillusionment in Kohistan and northern Afghanistan.[63] The presence of Muslim Central Asian refugees in Afghanistan and their accounts of the Soviet atrocities against Bukhara, Samarkand, Khiva, and all of Muslim Central Asia, together with Amanullah's apparent policy of friendship toward the Soviets, resulted in the lasting alienation of the population of Kohis-tan and northern Afghanistan.[64]

Following the war of independence, Amanullah launched a plethora of Western-inspired administrative, legal, social, economic, and political reforms. These programs aimed to achieve further centralization of power and a strengthening of direct rule, and the radical transformation of Afghan society. Amanullah's reforms, if successful, would have achieved both his objectives—true centralization of authority and the radical transformation of Afghan society and politics. Instead, they failed miserably and resulted in the total collapse of central authority, as well as that of his own rule in 1929. Amanullah's failures left important legacies for the Afghan political processes and became a celebrated topic of investigation.[65]

Prior to 1924, many of Amanullah's social political and economic reforms drew enthusiastic support from a wide spectrum of the country's population. The promulgation of the first Constitution of Afghanistan in 1923 and several other laws that curtailed or eliminated the privileges of the Muhammadzai sardars, the feudal interests of some Pashtun khans, the ulama, and especially the judges of the Shari'a courts undoubtedly resulted in grudges and disagreements. But, for the first time the constitution and some of these laws legally acknowledged the fact that citizens had rights in relations to the government, and that they had equal rights without discrimination. The Hindus were allowed to shed their officially imposed distinctive garments, and the Shi'a population could hold their religious rituals in public. These policies earned Amanullah the support of the Hazaras throughout his reign. During the early part of his reign an ardent attempt was made to create a sense of nationality and nationhood in Afghanistan that would transcend ethnicity and other claims of distinctiveness. However, these reforms and modernization programs were put forth without long-range planning or any regard for the variability of national resources, both financial and human, with which to implement them. Although any regard through tax reform and the elimination of tax farmers and other middlemen, national revenues were more than doubled during the early years (from 80 million to more than 180 million Kabuli rupees), the number and scope of projects undertaken far exceeded the revenues.[66]

Apart from the financial constraints on the implementation of Amanullah's reform programs, there was the critical problem of political ideological differences between him and his prime minister, Sardar Abdul Quddus Khan, and some members of his cabinet. The prime minister and his supporters seriously questioned King Amanullah's drive toward constitutionalism and social reform, and they were actively engaged in propaganda against the King's programs among prominent ulama and ruhanis in Kabul.[67] Differences of political ideology among high government officials and the lack of harsh measures against government opponents resulted in political infighting within the government administration, thus implying government weakness, which encouraged corruption, bribery, graft, and oppression by government officials in rural areas. The central government became less responsive to local and regional complaints against the tyranny of provincial officials, who were in league with local oppressive khans, thus providing greater opportunities for the propaganda of Amanullah's enemies.

The central focus of the anti-Amanullah campaign became his reform and modernization policies.[68] In 1923 the first formal reaction came in the form of a petition from two mullahs from Paktya (which ultimately led to the so-called Khost rebellion). The Paktya mullahs exploited the immediate local grievances among the Mangal and Zadran tribes, who were particularly disenchanted with the oppressive rule of the governor of Paktya and other provincial officials, in addition to their earlier disappointment with the government's pro-British policies concerning the frontier Pashtuns. This local administrative conflict was thus turned into a jihad against Amanullah's regime and reforms. The conflict lasted almost a year and antigovernment agitation spread among the Ghilzai and the Khugiani tribes in the eastern frontier areas and in Kohistan. At the end, only in response to the possibility of British interference was the government able to mobilize extensive support in northern Afghanistan, in Kohistan, and from among the Hazaras to confront the rebel forces. Some segments of the Paktya population also began to side with the government. The rebels were defeated, and government control reestablished in the area. However, the immediate and long-term costs of this rebellion to the government, and ultimately to Afghan society, were tremendous. Economically, the rebellion cost the government the equivalent of one to two years' state revenues. Socially, the incident caused Amanullah to further distrust the traditionalist religious establishment and, in particular, resulted in the alienation of a prominent ruhani family, the Hazrats of Shor Bazar, whom Amanullah had earlier respected and consulted regularly in public matters. Politically, Amanullah rescinded some important articles of reform from the Criminal Code, the Constitution, and other administrative laws and regulations.[69]

After the end of the rebellion King Amanullah did not take any strong measures to curb the abuses of government officials or strengthen the armed forces. Instead, claims Mir Ghulam Muhammad Ghubar[70] (who was a politically active member of the Young Afghans party at the time), the King was totally isolated from the public by some members of his court, and the problems of effective governance of the country, as well as public security, steadily deteriorated. To meet the added costs of the war and the King's ambitious, but erratic, modernization programs, taxes were raised and new taxes imposed. This provided a lucrative opportunity for government officials, and corruption and oppression continued unabated.

It was under these conditions that King Amanullah left the country for a seven-month grand tour (December 1927 to June 1928) of British India, Egypt, most of the Western European countries, the Soviet Union, Turkey, and Iran.[71] During the King's absence the government ordered that all tax arrears from previous years were to be collected immediately. The task of collecting arrears was first begun in the non-Pashtun regions between Kohdaman, Bamyan, and Tagaw, just to the north of Kabul, and in Herat. The guidelines for the officials were strict and treatment for those who could not comply extremely harsh.[72] Enforcing this policy in the areas of Kohistan and Shamali, where population density was high and people were generally poor, compared with the relatively more affluent people of Herat, caused much suffering and anger. The people in these areas anxiously awaited the return of their reformer king from his travels so that he could relieve them from these oppressive conditions. They were bitterly disappointed, however, for on his return, instead of attempting to relieve the burdens of taxation, he launched his final series of reforms. Many of these reforms were superficial imitations of those of the Europeans, Kemal Ataturk of Turkey, and Reza Shah of Iran, both of whom were known for their anti-Islamic and secularist policies. Some of King Amanullah's proposals, however, contained important sociopolitical reforms and modernization programs, while others clearly played into the hands of his enemies. In the end, all of them fell victim to the events that followed.[73]

In November of 1928 an ordinary incident between a group of Pashtun nomads and Pashtun villagers in Shinwar, which was not properly handled by local officials, quickly developed into a full-fledged war of rebellion against the central government.[74] It was then that Habibullah, Bacha-i Saqaw (the "water carrier's son"), a native of the village of Kalakan, the district center of Kohdaman, staged his attacks against Kabul, under the banner of a jihad against an "infidel king," Amanullah.[75]

After his capture of Kabul, Habibullah took the title of Amir (not King) and was also endowed with the religious title of *Khadim-i Din-i Rasulullah* (the servant of the faith of the Prophet). It is important to note that while Amir Habibullah II, the only Tajik ruler of Afghanistan in recent memory, received support from the predominantly non-Pashtun Turkestan and Herat during his reign, he also received support from some Pashtun groups, including the Ghilzai tribes. On the other hand, his support among the non-Pashtun was by no means unanimous: the Hazaras, for example, remained totally loyal to Amanullah and opposed Habibullah's rule. It is tempting to explain his success and wide-ranging support among non-Pashtun in terms of "Tajik resentment of Pashtun dominance,"[76] but the objective experiences of the populations in Kohistan, Herat, and Turkestan, particularly those relating to the Basmachi movement, Amanullah's policy of friendship toward the Soviets, a large influx of Central Asian refugees following Soviet attempts at collectivization during the latter part of the 1920s, and, finally, the Soviet invasions of northern Afghanistan in 1925 and 1929 (the last invasion clearly intended to return Amanullah to the Afghan throne) deserve due consideration.[77] Ultimately Amir Habibullah's success was less a function of his personal qualities or programs than a clear testament to the growing personal unpopularity of Amanullah, partly due to the effective propaganda of his internal and external enemies, but also because of some of his own policy failures, especially some of his cosmetic Western "reforms," poor management of his administration, and, more significantly, his abandonment of the Islamic cause, notably in Soviet Central Asia.

Amir Habibullah's short reign failed because of many of the same administrative maladies that he and his peasant followers so despised—corruption, oppression, and arbitrary rule by government officials in rural areas.[78] His inability to consolidate his power throughout the country, especially in the frontier tribal zone, together with lack of recognition by foreign powers, deteriorating urban economic conditions, and depletion of all state revenues made the collapse of his regime inevitable. Opposition to Amir Habibullah was led by an experienced Muhammadzai general and seasoned politician, Muhammad Nadir Khan, who, together with his four brothers and the help of Pashtun tribes from Paktya, the Wazir tribes across the frontier, and the family of Hazrat of Shor Bazar in Kabul, managed to overthrow the Bacha-i Saqaw regime and establish the Musahiban dynasty in Afghanistan (1929–78).[79]

On 17 October 1929, shortly after the defeat of Amir Habibullah II and the capture of Kabul, General Muhammad Nadir Khan was proclaimed King (not Amir) of Afghanistan, by a *jirgah* (assembly) of Pashtun tribal leaders and religious dignitaries who had helped to bring about his military success. During his brief rule (1929–33) as the founder of the Musahiban dynasty, Nadir Shah introduced policies that had a fundamental impact upon the future course of Afghanistan's political, social, and economic developments. His policies were significantly influenced by a number of factors: Nadir Shah's own moderate modernist-reformist and nationalist orientation; legacies of Amanullah's failures; the consequences of the Civil War; and outside political realities, particularly the neighboring colonialist superpowers.

During his campaign against Amir Habibullah, Nadir Shah attempted to rely on Islam as a major justification for his cause. This proved difficult since Habibullah was championing Islamic orthodoxy in the manner of the extreme egalitarianism of the Kharijites, dating back to the period of the rightly guided caliphs of Islam. Thus, Nadir Khan concentrated his campaign against Habibullah on personal grounds, vilifying him as a robber, plunderer, and bandit of lowly ethnic Tajik background, who had usurped the throne from the Pashtuns.[80] It was the ethnic factor and the promise of loot from Kabul and Kohistan that ultimately galvanized the Pashtun tribes from the southern frontier regions to rally round Nadir Shah. This politicization of Pashtun and non-Pashtun relations, strongly biased toward the Pashtun, became a major element of Musahiban politics throughout their rule.

Although Nadir Shah won the throne with the help of the Pashtun tribal *lashkar* (army), the consolidation of his power depended largely on financial and military assistance from Britain, Germany, and France in the form of loans and gifts, which enabled him to organize an effective army.[81] He, however, attributed his success to "the exclusive help of the Almighty God" and "the sacrifices of the people of Afghanistan."[82] In order to legitimize his dynastic rule and institutionalize his concessions to the Pashtun tribes and the traditionalist religious establishment, he relied on one of the most important legacies of Amanullah's period—constitutionalism. By calling a Loyah Jirgah (Grand Assembly) of the traditional local leadership from all parts of the country, a new constitution, which differed significantly in symbolic as well as substantive terms from that of King Amanullah's, was promulgated on 31 October 1931.[83]

In the constitution Nadir Shah's right to rule and the claim of the Musahiban family to the Afghan throne was justified on the basis of his role "in obtaining the independence and deliverance of the land of Afghanistan, and the uprooting of oppression and despotism."[84] But, in article 6, the obligations of the King were also clearly spelled out in the following oath that future kings of Afghanistan were to take in the chamber of the Majlis-i Shura (National Consultative Assembly) in the presence of its members:

> I swear by Almighty God and the sacred Quran, knowing that God the Glorious is omnipresent and omniscient, to rule according to the *Shariat* of Muhammad (peace be upon him!) and the fundamental rules of the country (and to strive) for the protection of the glorious religion of Islam, the independence of Afghanistan and the rights of the nation, and for the defense, progress and prosperity of the country. So help me God through the blessings of the sacred spiritual force of the blessed saints (the approval of God be upon them!).[85]

From this oath it is clear that the most important concern of the monarchy was to appease the traditionalist ulama and ruhani elements by emphasizing the Shari'a and the blessed saints. To achieve the support of these forces, Nadir Shah established a Jami'at ul-Ulama (Society of Islamic Scholars), ordered the first-ever printing of the Qur'an in the country, removed all restrictions imposed by Amanullah on the role of mullahs and mawlawis in education, institutionalized the primacy of the Sunni Hanafi school of Shari'a orthodoxy over Shi'a, institutionalized inequality of men and women, curtailed the rights of non-Muslims in the country, closed girls' schools, and reimposed veiling. Nadir also appointed members of the influential Hazrat of Shor Bazar family, which had secured the support of the Ghilzai tribes for him, to cabinet and other high government posts.[86] He also rescinded the secularist legal measures instituted by Amanullah by bringing both civil and criminal cases within the domain of the Shari'a. Thus, as in Amir Abdur Rahman's period, some 106 *mahkama-i ibtida'iyah* (lower courts), 19 *mahkama-i murafi'a* (courts of appeal), and a *mahkama-i tamiz* (supreme court) served as the most important vehicles for the centralization and penetration of central authority, even in the frontier Pashtun tribal areas.[87]

The power and influence of Pashtun tribal groups, especially those from the southern frontier regions, were ensured through exemption from military conscription and taxation. Many rural aristocrats were also elected to, or selected for, the two houses of parliament. Their participation in what turned out to be a rubber-stamp parliament served two purposes. It gave the local khans the satisfaction of sharing government power, but it also helped the centralization of the government by keeping the local leaders in Kabul for more than seven months of each year under the watchful eye of the police. The government also tried to recruit the sons of these local leaders into schools to ensure more long-term support by the rural aristocracy.

By these constitutional and legislative means, through total control of the cabinet, the organization of police, gendarmerie, and the army, the Musahiban family began to encapsulate local tribal and ethnic power structures. By formalizing and fusing tribal, religious, and dynastic interests, the Musahiban attempted to create a clear conception of the monarch as the personification of the *dawlat* (state) and the *hukumat* (government). As such, political power became concentrated within the Musahiban oligarchic circle and the traditional local political and religious elite which ran both the army and the bureaucracy. However, the consolidation of Musahiban power was not free of challenge. There was active opposition from among the pro-Amanullah political elite, the intelligensia who opposed the Musahiban policy of slow reforms and modernization programs, and disillusioned nationalists who objected to Nadir Shah's policy of friendship with the British in the face of their forward policy toward the frontier Pashtun. Also there were incidents of armed resistance against Nadir Shah in Kohdaman, northern Afghanistan, and disturbances in the southern frontier regions. Many of these incidents were linked, correctly or not, to the pro-Amanullah forces led by the powerful Yusufzai Pashtun family of the Charkhis, and one of them, Ghulam Nabi Charkhi, was summarily executed in October 1932 upon the order of Nadir Shah. By 1933 the political squabbles had developed into a full-fledged feud between the Musahiban and the Charkhi families, leading to several assassinations, including Nadir Shah's own, on 8 November 1933.[88]

These events had a radical impact on the domestic and foreign policies of the Musahiban rulers. Domestically, it caused the liquidation, imprisonment, suppression, or cooption of a large number of members of the Young Afghans political movement, who were calling for more rapid modernization and reform and a more truly constitutional government. The Musahiban family also used Pashtun tribal forces to brutally suppress the Kohdaman rebellion, which further aggravated the hate and disaffection between Pashtun and non-Pashtun groups in both the region and the country as a whole. Although with the consolidation of Musahiban power, the physical insecurity that the people had suffered during the civil war eased, a new and more subtle sense of uncertainty, suspicion, and insecurity, especially among the non-Pashtun ethnic groups, settled in.[89] To further safeguard their hold on the domestic scene, the Musahibans signed treaties of friendship and nonaggression with the Soviet Union and Great Britain and adopted what has been termed a policy of "benevolent neutrality" toward both superpowers. This involved nonencouragement of the frontier Pashtun tribes against Britain, forcing anti-Soviet Basmachi resistance fighters across the border into Soviet hands, and the transfer of Central Asian refugees from Afghan Turkestan to the southern provinces, thereby curbing their anti-Soviet activities. Their leaders were encouraged to emigrate to Turkey and Saudi Arabia.[90]

Zahir Shah, the only son of Nadir Shah, succeeded him, but the real power remained in the hands of his uncles, Hashim Khan (1933–46) and Shah Mahmud Khan (1946–53), as prime ministers of the country. They followed policies similar to those laid down by Nadir Shah. The main focus of Musahiban policies during the 1930s, 1940s, and early 1950s was based on the philosophy of "limited guided modernization," aimed principally at decreasing the government's economic dependence on the rural population for direct land and livestock taxation. Education was promoted in order to convince the traditionalists of the compatibility of Islam with gradual reform and modernization, to develop a national ideology, and to secure long-term loyal support for the monarchy.

In order to decrease government dependence on the rural population, the Musahiban dynasty began to create new sources of income. It established the first commercial bank in the country, the Bank-i Milli (National Bank) in 1932 and began to issue paper money in 1935. Bank-i Milli was a private venture headed by a Herati capitalist entrepreneur, Abdul Majid Zabuli, who was able to raise capital from other rich merchants. The bank was extended substantial monopoly rights and guarantees by the government and was soon able to launch "a score of commercial and industrial enterprises founded as joint stock companies and known as *shirkats.*"[91] One of Bank-i Milli's most significant development projects was the establishment of the Spinzar (White Gold in Pashtu) Cotton Company in Kunduz. This development involved the relocation into Qataghan area of tens of thousands of Pashtun from the south and east, changing the ethnic makeup of the region, and resulting in the loss of more lands by the non-Pashtun (Uzbek and Tajik) inhabitants.[92] The laissez-faire economic policy of the government resulted in unprecedented commercial and industrial growth during the 1930s and brought about a radical change in the political economy of the Afghan state: The major source of government revenues shifted from direct taxation, which had made up two-thirds of the national revenue during Amanullah's rule, to indirect taxes and custom duties, with less than one-third of the revenues coming from land and livestock taxes.[93] The success of private enterprises, especially those headed by non-Pashtun entrepreneurs, led the government to restrict the activities of the Bank-i Milli and to inaugurate an etatist policy of economic development.

The government's initial policy of encouraging private capitalism to launch very profitable commercial ventures, which relied almost exclusively on the export of agricultural products to foreign markets, was extremely successful for the entrepreneurs and generated a large proportion of the government's revenues. However, the events of World War II proved the unreliability of such sources of capital accumulation and revenue enhancement for the government and the country. During the war the markets for primarily nonessential agricultural produce disappeared. Neither the state nor the capitalists had invested in long-term domestic productive industries, and the government in particular had consciously avoided awarding foreign concessions or soliciting large foreign loans for the development projects, adopting instead an industrial policy of "pay-as-you-go."[94] The government's determination to build a strong army and police, which claimed one half of the entire national budget, also made any meaningful agricultural or industrial development impossible. Yet the encroachment of a capitalist economy in the form of large amounts of manufactured consumer goods began to severely affect home industries and handicrafts. The economic problems of the war era caused high inflation, shortages of food, increased poverty among the rural and urban populations, and loss of much peasant land. The deterioration of economic conditions during World War II was viewed by the proponents of a more rapid industrialization and modernization, the modernist-nationalist intelligentsia, as clear evidence of the failure of the Musahiban policy of limited-guided modernization. Therefore, they opposed the policies as against national interests and began agitating against the government during the postwar years, which resulted in the resignation of Hashim Khan as the prime minister in 1946.[95]

The post-World War II political developments in Afghanistan were also directly linked to the educational policies of the Musahiban dynasty, which in turn had significant implications for their policies toward Islam, their efforts toward the development of a national ideology, and ethnic policies. For the Musahiban rulers, education was the principal means to combat what they regarded as the legacy of

Amanullah's approach to reform. In an interview in 1937 Hashim Khan aired this concern when he said, "We are devoting a sum to public education equal to half our war budget. . . . We must transform the thoughts of Afghans before we can build an ultra-western capital, as Amanullah tried to do. He saw only the outward forms of modernization."[96] In 1936 the Musahiban policy for a national ideology became clear when they made Pashtu the official language of the country and launched a program to teach Pashtu to all government officials. Hashim Khan told a reporter in a 1937 interview that "from next year it [Pashtu] is to become the language of our officials, doing away with Persian. Our legends and our poems will then be understood by *everyone*. We shall draw from them a pride in our culture of the past which will unite us" (emphasis added).[97] Thus, Pashtu, which was ranked equally with Dari (Afghan Persian) by Amanullah, gained supremacy during the Musahiban period. The Pashtu Tulana (Pashtu Academy) was established to engage in research in, and the propagation of, the "Afghan" national ideology. The cornerstone of nationalism was based on the promotion of the Pashtu language and Pashtun culture and values, which remained a major preoccupation of the government's educational system. It was only in the Constitution of 1964 that Dari was accorded coequal status as an official language of the country.

In order to broaden the appeal of this national ideology to achieve national unity, important considerations were given to the common history, common religion, and the common Aryan origins of the majority of the Afghan population, principally the Pashtun, Tajiks, Nuristanis, and other minority Indo-Iranian speaking groups.[98] Emphasis on Aryan origins and the Pashtu language and culture was also to justify the unity of the Pashtun across the Durand Line within the emergent notion of Afghan nationalism. This proved to be a crucial issue for the political processes in Afghanistan following the partition of India in 1947.[99]

In this formation of Afghan national ideology, Islam was invoked at every opportunity by the Musahiban leaders and regarded as an important basis for national unity and a critical force for preserving national independence. During the early decades Islamic subjects constituted a substantial part of the modern school curriculum. The purpose of this emphasis on Islam was, for the most part, to appease traditionalist sensitivities, but at the same time it was hoped that secular education would weaken the traditionalist forces. The Musahiban rulers had an ambivalent view of the role of Islam in Afghan national politics. This view was well articulated by Zahir

Shah (1933–73) who told Donald Wilber that "the strength of Muslim faith in Afghanistan did not necessarily guarantee stability and national unity," since religious force and fervor could be "suborned to unworthy purposes."[100] Because of this strong ambivalence toward Islam, and wary of strong reaction from the traditionalist elements toward Western ideologies, the educational system had no political ideological orientation, other than Pashtun-based nationalism.

Despite the expressed goals of achieving national unity and training more loyal and patriotic citizens, the system only functioned to produce, for the most part, semiliterate bureaucrats to fill the expanding government administrative apparatus. Through its control of religious schools the government anticipated that the graduates of these schools would resist "antireligious" threats, but the school curriculum in no way indicated what the sources or nature of these threats might be or how to respond to them. Religious leaders who supported government policies confidently expressed the view that "religion guides every phase of our life and we all—young and old, learned and illiterate—have a love for and a need for Islam. Our religious leaders are confident that Islam answers all the inner demands of man so that no 'isms' can find a place in Afghan hearts."[101] The fact that religion has been so well entrenched in Afghan society is in no way the function of the policies of any particular Afghan government. Nor could it safeguard the society against the penetration of Western political ideologies. The Musahiban educational policy and practices increasingly and progressively failed, whether intentionally or not, to prepare educated Afghans to effectively meet the challenge.[102]

The Musahiban policies were successful, however, in creating an alliance between the royal court and the rural aristocracy, in preserving their common interests, and in maintaining relative domestic peace and order. This stable alliance was shaken only briefly, in the face of deteriorating social and economic conditions, by the emergence of the Wish Zalmiyan (Awakened Youth) movement (1947–51). The Wish Zalmiyan campaigned against official corruption, bribery, and rampant injustice and proposed major social and economic reforms, including land redistribution for the poor peasants and liberalization of politics. They were successful in electing a number of reform-minded deputies during the parliamentary elections of 1949 to the Shura-i Milli (National Council), but after brief experimentation the movement was ruthlessly suppressed.[103]

Several other significant developments occurred during the decade following World War II, all of which had important consequences for the future dynamics of political processes in Afghanistan. These developments included the inauguration of the Helmand Valley project, contracted by the Morrison-Knudsen Company of the United States (1946); the rise of the Pashtunistan issue in the wake of the partition of British India; the Safi Pashtun revolt (1947–49); and the rising tensions between the government and the Bank-i Milli group of private capitalists. The Helmand Valley project was a precedent-setting development program for at least three reasons: its large-scale, "white elephant" characteristics, its justification based on political (i.e., development in a Pashtun region essentially to benefit the Pashtun) rather than on rational, economic bases, and its heavy reliance on foreign loans and capital investment.[104] This pattern and policy of economic development continued into the 1970s with disastrous consequences.[105] Beginning in 1949 the Pashtunistan issue resulted in a series of border closures by the Pakistan government which prevented the movement of Afghan trade goods through Pakistan and had a considerable negative impact on the economy. It also resulted in the expenditure of large sums of national revenues to subsidize in various ways the Pashtun tribes living in the southern and eastern frontier areas.[106] The Safi revolt in Nangahar province brought Sardar Muhammad Daoud, the general who brutally suppressed the rebellion, to national attention. It also brought about the forced relocation of thousands of Safi Pashtun to penal colonies throughout northern Afghanistan, once again aggravating Pashtun and non-Pashtun relations in Afghan Turkestan.[107] The conflict between the government and the Bank-i Milli group was also ethnic in origin. The Bank-i Milli group, which had proven so successful as private industrial-mercantile entrepreneurs, did not include any significant Pashtun or dynastic interests among them; thus Abdul Majid Zabuli, the group's leader, was forced out of the Cabinet in 1950. Extensive limitations and restrictions were placed on the activities of the group after 1953, when Sardar Muhammad Daoud became the prime minister, and new, stringent etatist economic policies inspired by those of Turkey and Egypt were put into effect.[108]

TOWARDS the CREATION of a "NATION-STATE," 1955–79

The decade of Daoud rule as prime minister (1953–63) proved to be a crucial period for the development of the Afghan state and its relations with both Islam and ethnic communities in the country. The constraints of the country's "buffer state" status removed after the departure of Great Britain from the Indian subcontinent, Daoud inaugurated an active policy on the Pashtunistan issue causing strain in relations with Pakistan. His focus served two important purposes. First, it provided the context for promoting Pashtun nationalism as Afghan nationalism by making the Pashtunistan issue a national issue. Second, it provided the pretext for the government to create a strong and modernized military power base. The cold war situation in the 1950s, in turn, made it possible for Daoud's regime to receive substantial foreign aid from both the Soviets and the Western bloc countries. Thus, with the first major Soviet loan of $100 million for long-term development projects and a $25 million arms sale in 1955–56, the Afghan government entered an entirely new phase in its history. For the first time the government was able to build, and rely upon, a secure military base of power against any kind of internal challenge and also to become economically independent of its citizens, urban or rural. The government also found itself in the enviable position of providing social services to the populace on a scale that was hitherto impossible.

Secure in his military power, Daoud launched his program of national integration and national development through a series of five-year economic plans. The economic objectives of these development programs were not realized, but an extensive communication infrastructure was built and education was made available to large numbers of rural youth in most parts of the country. The bureaucracy was enlarged to accommodate the graduates of new schools and to implement government programs. The emancipation of women was declared in 1959, and education for girls expanded. Traditionalist reaction to these reforms, principally in Qandahar, was brutally suppressed by the new, mechanized armed forces. The army cadet school, for the first time, opened admission to non-Pashtun youth and the sons of nonaristocratic rural Pashtun. Secularism and less emphasis on Islamic education, particularly in large urban schools, became the norm. The penetration of the capitalist market economy grew in rural areas, which profited a few but added to the poverty of many. For the most part, development projects benefited a few, densely populated Pashtun areas and some corrupt government officials, but their contribution to the national economy was negligible, despite government promises and expectations to the contrary. Conditions reached crisis point when Daoud's Pashtunistan policies led to the closure of the borders by Pakistan (1961–63). This situation finally resulted in Daoud's resignation, followed by a decade of experimentation in "democracy" based on the new liberal constitution of 1964.[109]

The decade of King Zahir's rule from 1963 to 1973 witnessed the entry of a new force into the political processes of the country—the increasing numbers of educated Afghan youth. During this period attempts were made to strike a more balanced ethnic policy toward non-Pashtun groups. However, the thaw in the cold war and a substantial decline in foreign aid once again proved the unreliability of the most recent bases of the Afghan government's political economy. Discontent increased with the decline in foreign aid, the saturation of the wastefully overextended bureaucracy, the unemployment of new graduates from schools, and lack of mobility of those in the lower ranks of the bureaucracy.[110]

In the absence of any concerted effort to promote a particular national political ideology or ideologies in the Afghan educational system, and increasing lack of attention to the promotion of Islam as a basis of government legitimacy, a prophetic diagnosis made in 1952 by Donald Wilber began to come true. He said that "two forces may threaten the present political life and social structure of the country: democracy, with all its appendages, and communism."[111] Indeed, following the 1964 liberal constitution and the passage of press laws, a variety of political movements, with diverse Western-inspired ideologies, emerged. Among them were several Communist groups, including the Khalq party, which began to publish papers and actively engage in antigovernment agitation. Although no systematic attempt was made in the Afghan educational system to teach Western political ideologies, the availability of foreign scholarships, the expansion of mass media, and the availability of books and propaganda from foreign cultural missions in Kabul made the penetration of a wide range of such ideologies possible. The emergence of Khalq and other Communist parties and groups was not opposed by the government. Instead, the movement that emerged to oppose the Communist parties was a Muslim Youth movement inspired by the Egyptian Muslim Brotherhood and organized by several professors of the Faculty of Shara'iyat (Islamic Studies) at Kabul University, who had studied on scholarships at al-Azhar University in Cairo during the 1950s and 1960s. Thus began the politicization of Kabul University and the high schools in Kabul and the provinces, and a bloody struggle between the Islamic movements and the Communists ensued. While the government did not support the Communists, at least not publicly, it began to brutally suppress the Muslim Youth movement, killing and imprisoning many of its leaders.

In addition to these factional struggles amongst themselves, the educated youth in Afghanistan also opposed the government for various political and ideological reasons. Thus, the traditional political idioms of tribe, ethnicity, region, and sect were not replaced but augmented by new political ideological sympathies and loyalties. A common theme in the attacks, although expressed in different terms, was the oppression and corruption of the government officials who "openly and ruthlessly squeezed the poor peasants, often in collaboration with village and community elders (*maliks, khans, arbab, mirs, aqsaqals*)."[112] Although not all government officials or local leaders were oppressive and corrupt, most people in rural Afghanistan, whether poor or rich, peasant or nomad, considered government officials far more oppressive than the local large landowners. In fact, the rural population clearly distinguished between oppressive local khans who were in league with corrupt officials and those who helped protect their collective interests against official abuse. Indeed, since the beginning of etatist economic policies in the mid-1950s, the end of government dependence upon direct taxes and tributes, and the establishment of a secure military base of power, the generally tenuous relations between the government and the rural populations became even more so, despite the expansion of administrative and institutional apparatus during this period. Rural populations had successfully created their own parallel power structures at the village level to resolve local disputes with the aid of their own respected local leaders, thereby avoiding extensive and costly relations with the government whenever possible.[113] Consequently, during the 1960s and 1970s the nature of political conflict was no longer that of periphery versus the center, or tribe versus the state. Instead, there were new bases for political conflicts, most concerned with the questions of the legitimacy of the government, and articulated by the newly educated youth of Afghanistan. These conflicts were manifested on two levels: the ideological, which was either expressed in terms of a Marxist class struggle or in terms of Islamic social, economic, and political justice; and the generational-class differences which were manifested in a broader conflict between the traditional, aristocratic, and well-entrenched elite and the newly emergent intelligentsia, most from the rural and urban middle and lower classes. An added complication to the oppositional politics directed against the government in the 1960s and 1970s was the ongoing political and ideological conflicts between the Marxist and Islamic elements who opposed the Musahiban rule.[114]

By the late 1960s and early 1970s, ideological and

generational-class struggles pervaded all levels of Afghan government institutions, including the military, the schools, and even the Cabinet. The attack on the Musahiban regime came from all sides. During the 1965 and 1969 parliamentary elections the attack on the Musahiban regime was directed by all opposition groups against "the 'state' (dawlat), 'bureaucrats,' and 'reactionaries' more than they attacked the 'feudals,' 'khans,' 'arbab,' and 'capitalists'."[115] Governments changed quickly and political discontent mounted as economic conditions continued to deteriorate in the face of shrinking foreign aid and the dismal failure of large-scale development projects. In 1972 a last-ditch effort was made by Zahir Shah to turn the situation around when he invited a relatively young and energetic prime minister, Muhammad Musa Shafiq, to form a government. Shafiq, trained as an Islamic scholar, had also been well exposed to Western liberal thinking, but in the absence of any consistent political ideology or fundamental programs for social and economic change, he was not able to mobilize much support for his government. Thus, on 17 July 1973, aided by the Parcham faction of the Communist party, which had recruited a small number of low-ranking military officers, Sardar Muhammad Daoud staged a military coup and overthrew his cousin, Zahir Shah, proclaiming Afghanistan a republic.

In his initial radio address Daoud called the republican system more "consistent with the true spirit of Islam" and promised to introduce " 'basic reforms' aimed at the actualization of 'a real democracy to serve the majority of the people' as opposed to the 'pseudo-democracy' of the 'corrupt system', that was based on 'personal and class interests, intrigues and demagogy'."[116] Daoud's coup met with no resistance from the armed forces or the public. In fact, most people, except for the Muslim Youth group and other Islamic-minded individuals, initially welcomed the change, particularly since Daoud also attacked the policies and practices of the previous regimes. For example, during his Independence Day radio address shortly after the July 1973 coup, he described the social conditions in the country in this way:

> In the last decade the standard of living in Afghanistan has continually declined, and the cost of living risen. . . . While prices have gone up, the salaries of low ranking officials, government servants, and wage earners have remained at an eat-not-to-starve level. Poverty and unemployment in the society, misfortune and homelessness among the people has increased. Sickness has spread more than ever. . . . Lack of security and disregard for the implementa-

tion of laws became the rule. Autocracy, oppression and the arbitrariness of despots and influential people, and the cruelty of high ranking officials intensified. Immorality in state institutions reached a disgraceful level. Stealing from the public treasury, from the national wealth, from the people's pockets became a habit. Graft, bribery, hoarding, smuggling, fraud, and usury intensified from day to day. As a result, the living conditions of the majority of the people, which were already constrained, became even more restricted.[117]

These conditions were, thus, used by Daoud to justify his coup, and the solutions he promised to remedy these evils in the society provided him initially at least with a degree of legitimacy.

During his five years of rule as the President of the "Royal Republic" no positive social, economic, or political changes were seen, although a new constitution, a land reform law, and other legislation were introduced to strengthen his personal power. In order to further this effort he eliminated some influential nationalist politicians and ruthlessly attacked the Muslim Youth organization, especially after their brief armed attacks against the government during the summer of 1975. He quickly alienated his coconspirators, the Parcham group of Communists, but left them and their other pro-Soviet counterparts, the Khalq party, unharmed. During these years, as in past decades, no attempt was made to alter or improve the conditions of the rural populations. Segments of some pastoral nomadic groups and a few rich landowners and mixed herders in the villages benefited from the further penetration of the capitalist market economy, but many more rural peoples became impoverished and rural-urban migration increased. The government once again began to reaffirm the state capitalist approach to economic development through large-scale industries, but the changed political circumstances made the financing of such enterprises almost impossible.[118] Although Daoud spoke of national unity and the elimination of ethnic inequities, he in fact abolished the few rights that non-Pashtun and non-Dari speakers had been granted by the 1964 Constitution and subsequent parliamentary legislation. These included recognition of minority languages as national languages and weekly radio broadcast time for a few of the languages.

Daoud tried to reaffirm the traditional Musahiban ties of patronage with the rural aristocratic elite, and although he remained basically indifferent to the masses of rural peasantry, just as his predecessor had been, there was no threat of rural opposition to him. His supporters and opponents came from among the *munawarin*, the "enlightened youth." He had attacked his enemies ruthlessly and considerably weakened them, but had not been able to destroy them. Ultimately, his former allies, the Communists, whom he had not been able to, or did not want to, attack (perhaps for fear of upsetting the Soviets) caused the downfall of his regime on 27 April 1978. The real force behind the coup was the same group of military officers who had helped him return to power five years earlier.

The Khalq-Parcham Marxist coup was a bloody one, but their overthrow of the Musahiban dynasty brought some support and initial claim to legitimacy for them. However, their Communist ideology, their close links with, and total reliance upon, the Soviets, and their harsh and oppressive measures against their presumed enemies soon resulted in rising discontent. The assumption of government power by the Communists not only revived their running conflict with the Muslim Youth organization and Islamic-minded individuals, but elevated it to a popular nationwide armed struggle. The direct military intervention of the Soviet Union changed the character of the conflict from an internal war to an Islamic jihad against the Khalq-Parcham Communists and the Soviets for national independence and for the creation of an Islamic government. Thus, the structural articulation of the current political conflict reflects both significant changes and continuities in the evolution of relationships between state, ethnicity, and Islam in Afghanistan over the last two centuries.[119]

In conclusion, on the eve of the Khalq-Parcham Marxist takeover of political power in April 1978, Afghanistan displayed all the main characteristics of a state: recognized national territory; a claim to sovereignty by a ruling body over that territory, and paramount control over the peoples occupying it; and a claim of "legitimacy," i.e., some justification for the existence of the state, the particular social order and hierarchies, and the means of maintaining them.[120] However, as subsequent events have demonstrated, the particular structural articulation achieved by the Afghan state was not viable. It is suggested here that the failure of Afghan governments to build a viable state structure may be due, in large part, to two major factors: First, the Afghan government's inability to find or create adequate, reliable, and renewable sources of state revenue. Second, the specific policies and practices of the various Afghan governments toward Islam and toward ethnic and tribal groups within the context of changes and continuities in the political economy of both Afghan society and the state during the last two to three hundred years. More specifically, it is argued that the virtual collapse of the Afghan state apparatus in 1979 under the Khalq-Parcham Marxist party was not the function of any inherent aversion to central authority on the part of the people of Afghanistan because of such factors as their tribal organization, ethnic diversity, or extreme individualism. In fact, the formation and perpetuation of tribal structures and conflictual ethnic relations have been direct products of their relations with the central government. The real difficulty with the development of state structure in Afghanistan has been the government's inability or unwillingness to try to establish an organic relationship with its citizens based on just and equitable treatment of them. A mechanical relationship between the state and its citizens based on the expanding, corrupt bureaucracy was nothing more than a castle built on sand. When challenged, the collapse of the Afghan state was inevitable.

NOTES

The work on this chapter was begun under a Haynes Summer Research Fellowship (1984) awarded by the Haynes Foundation through Pitzer College. It was completed during my tenure as an Andrew W. Mellon Fellow (1984–85) at the Stanford Humanities Center, Stanford University. I gratefully acknowledge the generous support of both institutions.

1. A systematic study of religious institutions, beliefs, and practices in Afghanistan is the least developed, as it is apparent from Naby's chapter in this volume. A few exceptions are Wilber on the general structure and position of Islam, Dupree and Ghani on Islam and politics, and Canfield on Islam and social organization. See Donald N. Wilber, "The Structure and Position of Islam in Afghanistan," *Middle East Journal*, 6:1 (Winter 1952), pp. 41–48; Louis Dupree, "Islam in Politics: Afghanistan," *Muslim World*, 56:4 (October 1966), pp. 269–76; Louis Dupree, "The Political Uses of Religion: Afghanistan," in *Churches and States*, ed. K. H. Silvert (New York: American Universities Field Staff, 1977); Ashraf Ghani, "Islam and State-Building in a Tribal Society: Afghanistan 1880–1901," *Modern Asian Studies*, 12:2 (1978), pp. 269–84; Ashraf Ghani, "Disputes in a Court of *Sharia*, Kunar Valley, Afghanistan, 1885–1890," *International Journal of Middle East Studies*, 15:3 (August 1983), pp. 353–67; Robert Leroy Canfield, *Faction and Conversion in a Plural Society: Religious Alignments in the Hindu Kush*, Anthropological Papers No. 50 (Ann Arbor: Museum of Anthropology, University of Michigan, 1973); Robert L. Canfield, "Suffering as a Religious Imperative in Afghanistan" [Paper presented at the Ninth International Congress of Anthropological and Ethnological Sciences, Chicago, August-September 1973]; Robert L. Canfield, "Religious Myth as Ethnic Boundary," in Jon W. Anderson and Richard F. Strand, eds., *Ethnic Processes and Intergroup Relations in Contemporary Afghanistan*, Occasional Paper No. 15 (New York: Afghanistan Council of the Asia Society, 1978), pp. 35–41; Robert L. Canfield, "What They Do When the Lights Are Out: Myth and Social Order in Afghanistan" (Paper presented at the Conference on Symbols and Social Differentiation, Social Science Research Council and American Council of Learned Societies, Joint Committee on the Near and Middle East, 25–28 May 1978); and Robert L. Canfield,

"Islamic Coalitions in Bamyan: A Problem in Translating Afghan Political Culture," in *Revolutions and Rebellions in Afghanistan: Anthropological Perspectives*, ed. M. Nazif Shahrani and Robert L. Canfield [Berkeley: Institute of International Studies, University of California, Berkeley, 1984].) What passes for the study of the state in Afghanistan, with a few exceptions (e.g., Kakar, Gregorian), are no more than descriptions of dynastic successions, reports of internal disturbances, and development of government institutions. See Hasan Kawun Kakar, *Government and Society in Afghanistan: The Reign of Amir 'Abd al-Rahman Khan* (Austin: University of Texas Press, 1979); and Vartan Gregorian, *The Emergence of Modern Afghanistan: Politics of Reform and Modernization, 1880–1946* (Stanford, Calif.: Stanford University Press, 1969). The study of ethnicity, as may be apparent from Canfield's bibliography (in this volume), has improved considerably during the last two decades, but much work still needs to be done.

2. For example, see Leon B. Poullada, *The Pushtun Role in the Afghan Political System*, Occasional Paper No. 1 (New York: Afghanistan Council of the Asia Society, 1970), pp. 19–34.

3. See Richard Tapper, ed., *The Conflict of Tribe and State in Iran and Afghanistan* (New York: St. Martin's Press, 1983), especially the chapters on Afghanistan.

4. See René Grousset, *The Empire of the Steppes: A History of Central Asia*, trans. Naomi Walford (New Brunswick, N.J.: Rutgers University Press, 1970), pp. 482–83; R. M. Savory, "Safavid Persia," in *The Cambridge History of Islam*, vol. 1, ed. P. M. Holt, Ann K. S. Lambton, and Bernard Lewis (Cambridge: Cambridge University Press, 1970), pp. 399–400; and B. Spuler, "Central Asia from the Sixteenth Century to the Russian Conquests," in Holt, Lambton, and Lewis, eds., *The Cambridge History of Islam*, vol. 1, pp. 468–94.

5. See Gregorian, *The Emergence of Modern Afghanistan*, p. 21.

6. See Mir Ghulam M. Ghubar, *Afghanistan dar Masiir-i Tarikh* (Afghanistan's Path Through History) (in Persian) (Kabul: Government Press, 1967), pp. 303–4; also see W. K. Fraser-Tytler, *Afghanistan: A Study of Political Developments in Central and Southern Asia*, 2nd ed. (London: Oxford University Press, 1953), pp. 35–40.

7. See Gregorian, *The Emergence of Modern Afghanistan*, pp. 19–24, and Ghubar, *Afghanistan dar Masiir-i Tarikh*, pp. 281–307.

8. See M. Hasan Kakar, *The Pacification of the Hazaras of Afghanistan*, Occasional Paper No. 4 (New York: Afghanistan Council of the Asia Society, 1973), p. 2.

9. See Ghubar, *Afghanistan dar Masiir-i Tarikh*, pp. 313–14; Martiras Aslanov, "The Popular Movement 'Roshani' and Its Reflection in the Afghan Literature of the 16th-17th Centuries," in "Social Sciences Today" Editorial Board, *Afghanistan: Past and Present*, Oriental Studies in the U.S.S.R., No. 3 (Moscow: U.S.S.R. Academy of Sciences, 1981), p. 36; J. Leyden, "On the Rosheniah Sect and its Founder Bayezid Ansari," *Asiatic Researches* or *Transactions of the Society Instituted in Bengal*, 11 (1812), pp. 363–428; Andre Singer, *Lords of the Khyber: The Story of The Northwest Frontier* (London: Faber & Faber, 1984), pp. 26–35; and Gregorian, *The Emergence of Modern Afghanistan*, pp. 43 and 421, fn. 49; also see Mountstuart Elphinstone, *An Account of the Kingdom of Caubul*, 2 vols. (1815; London: Oxford University Press, 1972), vol. 1, pp. 274–76.

10. See Ghubar, *Afghanistan dar Masiir-i Tarikh*, p. 305.

11. See Gregorian, *The Emergence of Modern Afghanistan*, p. 44.

12. The Hotak branch of the Ghilzai faction inhabited areas contiguous to the Abdalis near Kadahar. The Hotaks by comparison to other Ghilzai further to the north were more sedentary and urban oriented. As the *Khan-Khel* (chiefly clan) of the

Ghilzai they provided the paramount chiefs of the entire tribe (see Igor Reisner, "Specific Features of the Development of Feudalism Among the Afghans," in *Afghanistan: Past and Present*, p. 56).

13. See Ghubar, *Afghanistan dar Masiir-i Tarikh*, p. 301; Elphinstone, *An Account of the Kingdom of Caubul*, vol. 2, pp. 84–173.

14. See Ghubar, *Afghanistan dar Masiir-i Tarikh*, pp. 354–55; and also see Charles M. MacGregor, ed., *Central Asia*, Part II: *A Contribution Towards the Better Knowledge of the Topography, Ethnology, Resources and History of Afghanistan* (Calcutta: Office of the Superintendent of Government Printing, 1871), p. 142; and Elphinstone, *An Account of the Kingdom of Caubul*, vol. 2, pp. 281–82.

It is important to point out that despite the statements by many historians that Ahmad Shah Abdali was a youthful khan of a relatively weak Sadozai clan of the Abdali tribes, he was by no means an ordinary nomadic Pashtun tribal chief. His grandfather had been a paramount chief of the Abdali tribes, officially confirmed by the Safavid court, and his father, for a time, was an independent ruler of Herat. As commander of the elite Afghan troops of Nadir Shah Afshar's court, he had personally accompanied the Persian king on his triumphant military campaigns against the Moghuls in Dehli (1739) and to the capital of the Uzbek rulers of Transoxiana, in Bukhara (1740).

15. Elphinstone, *An Account of the Kingdom of Caubul*, vol. 2, p. 281; also see R. Tapper, ed., *The Conflict of Tribe and State in Iran and Afghanistan*, p. 13.

16. Ahmad Shah also set a precedent by inscribing the following Persian poetic verse with a strong religious sentiment on the coins issued by him:

Hukum Shud az Qadiri Bechun ba Ahmad Padshah
Sikka zan bar sim-u zar az pushti mahi ta ba mah

(Commandment came from the peerless Almighty to Ahmad the King
Strike coins of silver and gold from the back of fish to the moon.)

From Ghubar, *Afghanistan dar Masiir-i Tarikh*, p. 360; *Siraj al-Tawarikh* [The Light of History, a history of Afghanistan compiled by Fayz Muhammad Katib, a scribe in the court of Amir Habibullah (1901–1919) on the order of the Amir], vols. 1 and 2 combined [Kabul: Matba'a-i Hurufi, 1912 (1331 A.H.)], p. 10.

The importance of this declaration on the coins, the most public symbol of government authority, carrying a message of religious legitimacy of the ruler, has not been assessed to date. But the fact that all of his descendants and the later Barakzai amirs followed the practice testifies to the power of the precedent he set.

17. See Elphinstone, *An Account of the Kingdom of Caubul*, vol. 2, p. 283.

18. Ibid.

19. See MacGregor, ed., *Central Asia*, Part II, p. 142; Elphinstone, *An Account of the Kingdom of Caubul*, vol. 2, p. 249.

20. Among his known symbolic and politically motivated Islamic acts are: the transfer of *Khirqa-i Mubarak* (the Prophet's Holy Cloak) from Badakhshan to his capital, Qandahar *(Siraj al-Tawarikh*, pp. 27–30); the construction of a mosque and establishment of a charitable foundation in Mecca to serve the needs of the Afghan pilgrims (Elphinstone, *An Account of the Kingdom of Caubul*, vol. 1, p. 280); and his positive response to a call for jihad against the Maratha and Jat threat to Delhi, by Shah Wali-Ullah, the great eighteenth-century Muslim leader of India (1761), who

praised him as a compassionate Muslim ruler. See Aziz Ahmad, *Studies in Islamic Culture in the Indian Environment* (London: Oxford University Press, 1964), pp. 208–9; Ahmad Asghar Bilgrami, *Afghanistan and British India 1793–1907: A Study in Foreign Relations* (New Delhi: Sterling Publishers, 1972), pp. 4–10; and Munshi 'Ata Muhammad Shikarpuri, *Taza Nawayi Ma'arik*, with corrections and commentary by Abdul Hay Habibi Afghani (Karachi: Sindhi Adaby Board, 1959), pp. 776–77, 787–89.

Ahmad Shah is also praised for his modesty and commitment to social justice. His sense of devotion to Islam is best expressed in the following verse by him:

> I capture every province with the aid of God:
> It is with his help that I go everywhere without failure.
> Yet I, Ahmad, consider the world worthless and unimportant.
> I shall leave the world behind and go to the next, armed only with my faith.
>
> Quoted in Singer, *Lords of the Khyber,* p. 39.

21. Elphinstone, *An Account of the Kingdom of Caubul,* vol. 1, p. 289, and vol. 2, p. 299.

22. For an excellent discussion of the distinction between an empire and centralized state from legal and political perspectives, see Rob Hager, "State, Tribe and Empire in Afghan Inter-Polity Relations," in R. Tapper, ed., *The Conflict of Tribe and State in Iran and Afghanistan,* pp. 83–118.

23. Eric R. Wolf, *Europe and the People Without History* (Berkeley: University of California Press, 1982), p. 94.

24. See Ghubar, *Afghanistan dar Masiir-i Tarikh,* pp. 372–79; also see *Siraj al-Tawarikh,* pp. 36–45, and Elphinstone, *An Account of the History of Caubul,* vol. 2, p. 302.

25. Wolf, *Europe and the People Without History,* p. 95.

26. See Elphinstone, *An Account of the History of Caubul,* vol. 2, pp. 335–37; Ghubar, *Afghanistan dar Masiir-i Tarikh,* p. 393; *Siraj al-Tawarikh,* pp. 66–67; and Shikarpuri, *Taza Nawayi Ma'arik,* pp. 802–3.

27. Elphinstone, *An Account of the History of Caubul,* vol. 1, pp. 280–89, and vol. 2, pp. 258, 260.

28. See Gregorian, *The Emergence of Modern Afghanistan,* pp. 52–60.

29. See John William Kaye, *History of the War in Afghanistan* (London: Richard E. Bentley, 1851–57), vol. 1, pp. 129–30; *Siraj al-Tawarikh,* pp. 127–28; and Ghubar, *Afghanistan dar Masiir-i Tarikh,* pp. 517–18.

30. Gregorian, *The Emergence of Modern Afghanistan,* p. 126.

31. See Mir Munshi Sultan Mahomed Khan, *The Life of Abdur Rahman, Amir of Afghanistan,* 2 vols. (London: John Murray, 1900), vol. 1, pp. 131–84.

32. Ibid., vol. 1, p. 217.

33. Ibid., vol. 2, p. 80.

34. Kakar, *Government and Society in Afghanistan,* p. 8.

35. Gregorian, *The Emergence of Modern Afghanistan,* pp. 130–32; see Kakar, *Government and Society in Afghanistan,* pp. 93–114.

36. See Kakar, *Government and Society in Afghanistan,* pp. 10–11.

37. Ghani, "Islam and State-Building in a Tribal Society," p. 278.

38. Gregorian, *The Emergence of Modern Afghanistan,* p. 135.

39. Ghani, "Islam and State-Building in a Tribal Society," p. 282.

40. See Hager, "State, Tribe and Empire in Afghan Inter-Polity Relations"; Sir George MacMunn, *Afghanistan from Darius to Amanullah* (1919; Quetta, Pakistan: Gosha-e-Adab, 1977), pp. 243–47.

41. Gregorian, *The Emergence of Modern Afghanistan*, p. 160.

42. See ibid., pp. 124–28.

43. See Kakar, *Government and Society in Afghanistan*, pp. 113–45; also see Nancy Tapper, "Abd al-Rahman's North-West Frontier: The Pashtun Colonisation of Afghan Turkistan," in R. Tapper, ed., *The Conflict of Tribe and State in Iran and Afghanistan*, pp. 233–61; and Klaus Ferdinand, "Nomad Expansion and Commerce in Central Afghanistan," *Folk*, 4 (1962), pp. 123–59.

44. See Khan, *The Life of Abdur Rahman*, vol. 2, pp. 1–13.

45. For example, he divorced his fifth wife to conform with the Shari'a; ordered that women's veils be of darker colors and simpler design; and forbade women to visit shrines or appear in city streets without male escorts. Professional women singers and dancers were prohibited and were moved from their traditional residential district of Kharabat. New clothing restrictions were imposed on Hindus, and their conversion to Islam was encouraged. The Amir also opened a school in each of the eleven major cities and towns at government expense for the memorization of the Qur'an *(Dar ul-Hifaz)* and offered public feasts during the month of Ramadan (fasting) for Kabul residents. The sale of male and female slaves was forbidden (although slavery was not abolished), some prisoners kept in dungeons were released, and the practice of harsh and cruel punishments forbidden. In reality, however, these practices were maintained, even by the Amir himself. See Ghubar, *Afghanistan dar Masiir-i Tarikh*, pp. 699–702.

46. See Gregorian, *The Emergence of Modern Afghanistan*, pp. 182–83, and Ghubar, *Afghanistan dar Masiir-i Tarikh*, p. 700.

47. The Habibiyah School (grades 1–10) followed a modern curriculum with much emphasis on Islamic education, and it was staffed by Turkish, Indian Muslim, and Afghan teachers. A school for training military officers *(maktabi harbiyah)* was also founded in 1909. A teachers' training school and a religious educational school for the children of newly converted Nuristanis were also inaugurated during this period. See Ghubar, *Afghanistan dar Masiir-i Tarikh*, pp. 702–4; Payenda Muhammad Zahir and S. M. Yusof Elmi, *De Afghanistan de Ma'arif Tarikh* (History of Education in Afghanistan) (in Persian and Pashtu) (Kabul: Ministry of Education Press, 1960), pp. 28–31.

48. See Gregorian, *The Emergence of Modern Afghanistan*, pp. 181–205, and Ghubar, *Afghanistan dar Masiir-i Tarikh*, pp. 704–6.

49. Ghubar, *Afghanistan dar Masiir-i Tarikh*, pp. 706–16.

50. A. G. Rawan Farhadi, comp., *Maqalati Mahmud Tarzi dar Siraj al-Akhbar, 1290-97* (Mahmud Tarzi 1867-1933) (pamphlets, editorials, and major articles from *Siraj al-Akhbar, 1911-18)* (in Persian) (Kabul: Baihaqi Publishers, 1977), pp. 516–17; for some important commentary on the issues, see also Ghubar, *Afghanistan dar Masiir-i Tarikh*, pp. 714–16.

51. See Sir Percy Sykes, *A History of Afghanistan*, 2 vols. (London: Macmillan, 1940), vol. 2, p. 266n.

52. See M. Nazif Shahrani, "Causes and Context of Responses to the Saur Revolution in Badakhshan," in Shahrani and Canfield, eds., *Revolutions and Rebellions*

in Afghanistan: Anthropological Perspectives, p. 147; and Kakar, *Government and Society in Afghanistan*, pp. 15–20.

In addition, two other factors also helped hasten the spread of ideals of nationalism, reform, constitutionalism, and Islamic modernism in Afghanistan during Habibullah's reign: The presence of a number of anti-British Muslim nationalists (from the Pan-Islamic and later Hijrat movements) and leftist revolutionaries from India, who were granted asylum in Kabul; and the arrival and activities of German and Ottoman Turkish agents in Kabul during World War II. See Sadhan Mukherjee, *Afghanistan: From Trajedy to Triumph* (New Delhi: Sterling Publishers, 1984), pp. 40–41.

53. Ghubar, *Afghanistan dar Masiir-i Tarikh*, pp. 716–27; also cf. Gregorian, *The Emergence of Modern Afghanistan*, pp. 163–80.

54. Gregorian, *The Emergence of Modern Afghanistan*, p. 164; also see Farhadi, *Maqalati Mahmud Tarzi dar Siraj al-Akhbar*, pp.2–31, 442–58.

55. See Farhadi, *Maqalati Mahmud Tarzi dar Siraj al-Akhbar*, pp. 117–434; and M. Nazif Shahrani, "Introduction: Marxist 'Revolution' and Islamic Resistance in Afghanistan," in Shahrani and Canfield, eds., *Revolutions and Rebellions in Afghanistan: Anthropological Perspectives*, p. 31.

56. See MacMunn *Afghanistan from Darius to Amanullah*, pp. 253–56.

57. See Gregorian, *The Emergence of Modern Afghanistan*, p. 220; Sykes, *A History of Afghanistan*, vol. 2, p. 246.

58. See Ghubar, *Afghanistan dar Masiir-i Tarikh*, pp. 740–52.

59. See Ghubar, *Afghanistan dar Masiir-i Tarikh*, p. 752; also cf. Sykes, *A History of Afghanistan*, vol. 2, p. 264.

60. See Sykes, *A History of Afghanistan*, vol. 2, pp. 264–82, and Sir Percy Sykes, "Afghanistan: The Present Position," *Journal of the Royal Central Asian Society*, 27:2 (April 1940), pp. 149–54.

61. See Thomas T. Hammond, *Red Flag Over Afghanistan: The Communist Coup, the Soviet Invasion, and the Consequences* (Boulder, Colo.: Westview Press, 1984), p. 10; also see Mukherjee, *Afghanistan: From Tragedy to Triumph*, pp. 45–72.

62. See texts in Ludwig W. Adamec, *Afghanistan, 1900–1923: A Diplomatic History* (Berkeley: University of California Press, 1967), pp. 183–91.

63. The people and ulama of both of these predominantly Tajik and Turkic areas had been mobilized against the Soviets by a mawlawi, Abdul Hay of Panjsher Valley, and had fought under the command of Anwar Pasha. Habibullah (Bacha-i Saqan, the "water carrier's son"), who later drove Amanullah out of the country, had also taken part in the campaign against the Bolsheviks with Mawlawi Abdul Hay. See Khalilullah Khalili, 'Ayari az Khurasan: Amir Habibullah, Khadim-i Din-i Rasul Allah (A "Robin Hood" from Khurasan: Amir Habibullah, the Servant of the Faith of the Prophet) (in Persian) (Peshawar: Jamiat-i Islami Afghanistan, 1980), pp. 73–75, 93–101.

64. See Khalili, *'Ayari az Khurasan*, pp. 73–75, 91–101; Hammond, *Red Flag Over Afghanistan*, pp. 10–12, also cf. Ghubar, *Afghanistan dar Masiir-i Tarikh*, pp. 785–89, Leon B. Poullada, *Reform and Rebellion in Afghanistan 1919–1929: King Amanullah's Failure to Modernize a Tribal Society* (Ithaca, N.Y.: Cornell University Press, 1973), pp. 172–195; Gregorian, *The Emergence of Modern Afghanistan*, pp. 231–39.

65. See, for example, Poullada, *Reform and Rebellion in Afghanistan*; Rhea Talley Stewart, *Fire in Afghanistan, 1914–1929: Faith, Hope and the British Empire* (Garden City, N.Y.: Doubleday, 1973); Ludwig W. Adamec, *Afghanistan's Foreign Affairs to the*

Mid-Twentieth Century: Relations with the USSR, Germany, and Britain (Tucson: University of Arizona Press, 1974), pp. 42–147.

66. See Ghubar, *Afghanistan dar Masiir-i Tarikh*, pp. 789–99; cf. Gregorian, *The Emergence of Modern Afghanistan*, pp. 239–54; Adamec, *Afghanistan's Foreign Affairs to the Mid-Twentieth Century*, pp. 77–112; for a text of the constitution see Poullada, *Reform and Rebellion in Afghanistan*, pp. 277–91.

67. See Ghubar, *Afghanistan dar Masiir-i Tarikh*, pp. 801–806.

68. See ibid., pp. 799–801; Khalili, *'Ayari az Khurasan*, pp. 88–90; cf. Poullada, *Reform and Rebellion in Afghanistan*.

69. See Ghubar, *Afghanistan dar Masiir-i Tarikh*, pp. 806–11; also see Gregorian, *The Emergence of Modern Afghanistan*, pp. 254–56; Poullada, *Reform and Rebellion in Afghanistan*, pp. 122–25, 277–91.

70. Ghubar, *Afghanistan dar Masiir-i Tarikh*, pp. 811–18.

71. See Gregorian, *The Emergence of Modern Afghanistan*, pp. 256–58; Fraser-Tytler, *Afghanistan: A Study of Political Developments in Central and Southern Asia*, pp. 207–10; Sykes, *A History of Afghanistan*, vol. 2, pp. 302–309.

72. See Khalili, *'Ayari az Khurasan*, p. 97.

73. See M. Mobin Shorish, "The Impact of the Kemalist 'Revolution' on Afghanistan," *Journal of South Asian and Middle Eastern Studies*, 7:3 (Spring 1984), pp. 34–45; and for details of Amanullah's reform policies see Poullada, *Reform and Rebellion in Afghanistan*, pp. 66–110; Adamec, *Afghanistan's Foreign Affairs to the Mid-Twentieth Century*, pp. 113–47.

74. See Ghubar, *Afghanistan dar Masiir-i Tarikh*, pp. 818–20.

75. According to Ustad Khalilullah Khalili (1980), a contemporary of Habibullah, his most recent biographer, and also once an official in his government and later poet at the Musahiban court, Habibullah was a sensitive and pious man with martial skills. He had taken part in anti-Bolshevik wars in Bukhara and had received a note of recognition from Anwar Pasha for his bravery on the battlefield. On his return from Bukhara, Habibullah joined the Afghan army and, on the basis of the note from Anwar Pasha, the Turkish officers in charge of the *qit'a-i namuna* (the model battalion) recruited him into their ranks. During the Paktya rebellion of 1924 he took part in the war as a member of his battalion and proved himself a capable soldier. At the end of the rebellion in early 1925 he returned to Kabul and was again serving in the model military unit. On his way home during a religious holiday, Habibullah came across two notorious bandits in Kohdaman. They stopped him but he was able to kill them both. This made him eligible for a large government cash prize as a reward, but when he reported the incident to the *hakim* (district officer) in Kalakan, the hakim had him imprisoned as a thief and bandit in order to collect the reward for himself. After spending some months in prison, Habibullah was able to escape with the help of some of his village friends, and after his escape he engaged in agitations against corrupt officials and in some Robin Hood-like activities in the Kohdaman area that increased his popularity. It was this illiterate Tajik peasant who ultimately mobilized the suffering peasants and launched the successful rebellion which drove Amanullah out of Afghanistan and made it possible for Habibullah to rule the country for an eventful nine months. See Khalili, *'Ayari az Khurasan*, pp. 102–55; Adamec, *Afghanistan's Foreign Affairs to the Mid-Twentieth Century*, p. 164; Ghubar, *Afghanistan dar Masiir-i Tarikh*, pp. 172–84; also see Shahrani, "Introduction: Marxist 'Revolution' and Islamic Resistance

in Afghanistan," in Shahrani and Canfield, eds., *Revolutions and Rebellions in Afghanistan: Anthropological Perspectives*, pp. 32–33; Gregorian, *The Emergence of Modern Afghanistan*, pp. 263–80; Sykes, "Afghanistan: The Present Position," pp. 155–57. For a radically different account of the life of Habibullah, one which is closer to the official Musahiban version, see the alleged autobiography of Amir Habibullah, Amir Habibullah, *My Life: From Brigand to King, Autobiography of Amir Habibullah* (London: Sampson Low, Marscon & Co., nd.).

76. Poullada, *Reform and Rebellion in Afghanistan*, p. 28n.

77. See Mawlawi Muhammad Idris, "Taqriz" (Commendation) (in Persian), in Khalili, *'Ayari az Khurasan*, pp. 170–76; Hammond, *Red Flag Over Afghanistan*, pp. 12–18; Anthony Arnold, *Afghanistan: The Soviet Invasion in Perspective* (Stanford, Calif.: Hoover Institution Press, 1981), pp. 5–7; also cf. Mukherjee, *Afghanistan: From Tragedy to Triumph*, pp. 38–72.

78. See Khalili, *'Ayari az Khurasan*, pp. 156–64.

79. See Sykes, *A History of Afghanistan*, vol. 2, pp. 312–21; Adamec, *Afghanistan's Foreign Affairs to the Mid-Twentieth Century*, pp. 148–72.

80. See Adamec, *Afghanistan's Foreign Affairs to the Mid-Twentieth Century*, pp. 177–78.

81. See Gregorian, *The Emergence of Modern Afghanistan*, p. 297, 321.

82. Ibid., p. 322.

83. For the text see Ramesh C. Ghosh, *Constitutional Documents of the Major Islamic States* (Lahore: Muhammad Ashraf, 1947), pp. 126–43; also see Gregorian, *The Emergence of Modern Afghanistan*, pp. 300–307.

84. Ghosh, *Constitutional Documents of the Major Islamic States*, p. 127.

85. See ibid., p. 128.

86. See Gregorian, *The Emergence of Modern Afghanistan*, pp. 293–96, 298–300, 305–307; Sykes, *A History of Afghanistan*, vol. 2, pp. 324–25.

87. See Gregorian, *The Emergence of Modern Afghanistan*, p. 299; for later expansions of the court system see Wilber, "The Structure and Position of Islam in Afghanistan," pp. 42–43.

88. See Adamec, *Afghanistan's Foreign Affairs to the Mid-Twentieth Century*, pp.191–99; Gregorian, *The Emergence of Modern Afghanistan*, pp. 338–40; Sykes, *A History of Afghanistan*, vol. 2, pp. 327–28.

89. See Ghubar, *Afghanistan dar Masiir-i Tarikh*, pp. 834–37; Khalili, *'Ayari az Khurasan*, pp. 168–69.

90. See Sykes, *A History of Afghanistan*, vol. 2, p. 323; Gregorian, *The Emergence of Modern Afghanistan*, pp. 330–32; Adamec, *Afghanistan's Foreign Affairs to the Mid-Twentieth Century*, pp. 202–12.

91. Peter G. Franck, "Problems of Economic Development in Afghanistan. Part II: Planning and Finance," *Middle East Journal*, 3:4 (October 1949), p. 431; Peter G. Franck, "Economic Progress in an Encircled Land," *Middle East Journal*, 10:1 (Winter 1956), p. 47.

92. See Thomas J. Barfield, "The Impact of Pashtun Immigration on Nomadic Pastoralism in Northeastern Afghanistan," in Anderson and Strand, eds., *Ethnic Processes and Intergroup Relations in Contemporary Afghanistan*, pp. 26–34; Thomas J. Barfield, *The Central Asian Arabs of Afghanistan: Pastoral Nomadism in Transition* (Austin: University of Texas Press, 1981), pp. 29–32; and Thomas J. Barfield, "Weak Links on a

Rusty Chain: Structural Weaknesses in Afghanistan's Provincial Government Administration," in Shahrani and Canfield, eds., *Revolutions and Rebellions in Afghanistan: Anthropological Perspectives*, p. 177.

93. See Maxwell J. Fry, *The Afghan Economy: Money, Finance and the Critical Constraints to Economic Development* (Leiden: E. J. Brill, 1974), pp. 155-56; Gregorian, *The Emergence of Modern Afghanistan*, p. 317.

94. See Gregorian, *The Emergence of Modern Afghanistan*, p. 363.

95. See R. T. Akhramovich, *Outline History of Afghanistan After the Second World War* (Moscow: "NAUKA" Publishing House, 1966), pp. 11-21, 45-67; Peter G. Franck, "Problems of Economic Development in Afghanistan. Part I: The Impact of World Conditions," *Middle East Journal*, 3:3 (July 1949), pp. 293-314; Peter G. Franck, "Problems of Economic Development in Afghanistan. Part II: Planning and Finance," *Middle East Journal*, 3:4 (October 1949), pp. 421-40; Gregorian, *The Emergence of Modern Afghanistan*, pp. 318-20.

96. Ella Maillart, "Afghanistan's Rebirth: An Interview with H. R. H. Hashim Khan in 1937," *Journal of the Royal Central Asian Society*, 27:2 (April 1940), p. 224.

97. Ibid., p. 227. Emphasis added.

98. See Mohammed Ali, *The Afghans* (Lahore: Punjab Educational Press, 1965), pp. 3-16; also see Gregorian, *The Emergence of Modern Afghanistan*, pp. 345-48.

99. See A. Rahman Pazhwak, *Pakhtunistan: A New State in Central Asia* (London: Royal Afghan Embassy, 1960), pp. 7-8; Afghanistan Information Bureau, London, *Pakhtunistan: The Khyber Pass the Focus of the New State of Pakhtunistan* (London: Key Press Ltd., n.d.).

100. Wilber, "The Structure and Position of Islam in Afghanistan," p. 47.

101. Ibid., p. 46.

102. See Gregorian, *The Emergence of Modern Afghanistan*, p. 395; M. G. Weinbaum, "Legal Elites in Afghan Society," *International Journal of Middle Eastern Studies*, 12 (1980), pp. 39-57.

103. See Akhramovich, *Outline History of Afghanistan After the Second World War*, pp. 45-67; Gregorian, *The Emergence of Modern Afghanistan*, p. 392; Louis Dupree, *Afghanistan* (Princeton, N.J.: Princeton University Press, 1973), pp. 494-98; Shahrani, "Introduction: Marxist 'Revolution' and Islamic Resistance in Afghanistan," in Shahrani and Canfield, eds., *Revolutions and Rebellions in Afghanistan: Anthropological Perspectives*, pp. 35-36.

104. See Dupree, *Afghanistan*, pp. 482-85; Richard B. Scott, *Tribal and Ethnic Groups in Helmand Valley*, Occasional Paper No. 21 (New York: Afghanistan Council of the Asia Society, 1980); Franck, "Problems of Economic Development in Afghanistan. Parts I and II"; Franck, "Economic Progress in an Encircled Land," p. 56.

105. See Mir Ahmad Zekrya, "Planning and Development in Afghanistan: A Case of Maximum Foreign Aid and Minimum Growth" (Ph.D. dissertation, Johns Hopkins University, 1976).

106. Dupree, *Afghanistan*, pp. 485-94; Pazhwak, *Pakhtunistan: A New State in Central Asia*.

107. Dupree, *Afghanistan*, p. 537; Barfield, "The Impact of Pashtun Immigration on Nomadic Pastoralism in Northeastern Afghanistan"; Barfield, *The Central Asian Arabs of Afghanistan*, p. 31.

108. See Franck, "Economic Progress in an Encircled Land," pp. 48#50.

109. For a text of the constitution see "Constitution of Afghanistan, with commentary by Donald N. Wilber," Middle East Journal, 19:2 (Spring 1965), pp. 125–29; see also Dupree, Afghanistan, pp. 499–558.

110. Shahrani, "Introduction: Marxist 'Revolution' and Islamic Resistance in Afghanistan," in Shahrani and Canfield, eds., Revolutions and Rebellions in Afghanistan: Anthropological Perspectives, pp. 36–37.

111. Wilber, "The Structure and Position of Islam in Afghanistan," p. 48.

112. Hasan Kakar, "The Fall of the Afghan Monarchy in 1973," International Journal of Middle East Studies, 9:2 (May 1978), p. 205.

113. See Shahrani, "Introduction: Marxist 'Revolution' and Islamic Resistance in Afghanistan," in Shahrani and Canfield, eds., Revolutions and Rebellions in Afghanistan: Anthropological Perspectives, pp. 34–35, 50–52; Shahrani, "Causes and Context of Responses to the Saur Revolution in Badakhshan," in Shahrani and Canfield, eds., Revolutions and Rebellions in Afghanistan: Anthropological Perspectives, p. 149; M. Nazif Shahrani, The Kirghiz and Wakhi of Afghanistan: Adaptation to Closed Frontiers (Seattle: University of Washington Press, 1979), pp. 208–12; Richard F. Strand, "The Evolution of Anti-Communist Resistance in Eastern Nuristan," in Shahrani and Canfield, eds., Revolutions and Rebellions in Afghanistan: Anthropological Perspectives, pp. 82–86; R. Lincoln Keiser, "The Rebellion in Darr-i Nur," in Shahrani and Canfield, eds., Revolutions and Rebellions in Afghanistan: Anthropological Perspectives, pp. 127–33; Barfield, "Weak Links on a Rusty Chain: Structural Weaknesses in Afghanistan's Provincial Government Administration," in Shahrani and Canfield, eds., Revolutions and Rebellions in Afghanistan: Anthropological Perspectives, pp. 174–75; and Kakar, "The Fall of the Afghan Monarchy in 1973."

114. See Shahrani, "Introduction: Marxist 'Revolution' and Islamic Resistance in Afghanistan," in Shahrani and Canfield, eds., Revolutions and Rebellions in Afghanistan: Anthropological Perspectives, pp. 37–41; Shahrani, "Causes and Context of Responses to the Saur Revolution in Badakhshan," in Shahrani and Canfield, eds., Revolutions and Rebellions in Afghanistan: Anthropological Perspectives, pp. 139–69.

115. Kakar, "The Fall of the Afghan Monarchy in 1973," p. 206.

116. Quoted in ibid., p. 214.

117. Muhammad Daoud, Khitab ba Mardumi Afghanistan: Bayaniya-i Radyu-i (An Address to the People of Afghanistan on Radio) (in Persian), Supplement to Volume 6 of the journal Merman (Women) (Kabul: Government Press, 1973), pp. 6–7.

118. See Mukherjee, Afghanistan: From Tragedy to Triumph, pp. 88–91.

119. See Shahrani, "Introduction: Marxist 'Revolution' and Islamic Resistance in Afghanistan," pp. 41–54, and other chapters in Shahrani and Canfield, eds., Revolutions and Rebellions in Afghanistan: Anthropological Perspectives; also see R. Tapper, ed., The Conflict of Tribe and State in Iran and Afghanistan.

120. See Morton H. Fried, "State. I: The Institution," in International Encyclopedia of the Social Sciences, vol. 15, ed. David L. Sills (New York: Macmillan Company & The Free Press, 1968), p. 143–47.

2

ETHNIC, REGIONAL, and SECTARIAN ALIGNMENTS in AFGHANISTAN

ROBERT L. CANFIELD

THE PROBLEM

A NY ATTEMPT TO EXPLAIN how the various peoples of Afghanistan align themselves must give close attention to what they are like in their rural settings, for, as it happens, the rural peoples—ethnically diverse and politically divided as they are—have more political influence than some observers have recognized.[1] One reputed authority of the region has said that "politics [in Afghanistan] had been confined mainly to Kabul," confined, in fact, "mainly to the royal family, to an urban elite . . . to a very select group of people."[2] Quite the contrary, the rural populations of this nation have repeatedly exerted a decisive influence on public affairs. These groups—tribal, ethnic, sectarian, and regional in their loyalties—have quarreled among themselves and with the government, particularly when administrative vigor was either too harsh or too lax, so as repeatedly to distract the government with fresh provincial brushfires. A few times—actually only rarely, but the social implications were momentous—large numbers of the provincial peoples collectively, as much by fortuitous coincidence as by coordination, have risen up against the government.[3] But their importance to national affairs goes beyond their periodic squabbles and localized restiveness. They are, in fact, numerically quite preponderant. Before the current civil war, in which, as is well known, thousands have been killed and millions dislocated, the rural populations accounted for 87 percent of the nation.[4] Of their number about a fifth were pastoral nomads and the rest were mainly sedentary agriculturalists. So by virtue of sheer numerical strength the ru-

75

ral peoples have exerted a powerful distinctive influence on public affairs for the nation as a whole. That influence may have been somewhat intensified by the decline of the cities in the eighteenth and nineteenth centuries, the result of a general decline in economic and cultural interchange throughout Central Asia.[5] The Second Anglo-Afghan War culminated the process, leaving the cities—especially Kabul, but also Qandahar and Herat—in ruins. Yaqub Khan, who succeeded Sher Ali Khan as ruler of the nation in 1879, complained that "the troops, the city [Kabul] and surrounding country have thrown off their yoke of allegiance [to the government]. The workshops and magazines are totally gutted. . . . In fact, my kingdom is ruined."[6] Because the peoples of the provincial areas had been spared much of this calamity, it was on them that the government, struggling to lift itself out of the ashes, had to rely for stability and strength. Eventually, of course, the government regained its footing and the national economy recovered a degree of health. But the rural populations, restive and factious as they were, continued to act as a distinctive influence on national affairs.

Thus, in order to assess how, within the context of this book, the ethnic minorities articulate with the Afghan government, we have to rephrase the question so as to place the focus on the significant units of sociopolitical action. Contrary to what might be supposed, the actual operating units of sociopolitical coalition among these populations are rarely genuinely "ethnic" in composition. The collectivities of people who act together for social or political purposes are better identifiable by some other term, such as "subtribe," "regional group," or "Islamic coalition." Even if these terms lack specificity, and so must be explained as to their actual content in Afghanistan, they in any event diverge far from what is implied by the term "ethnic." There are, to be sure, "ethnic types" in Afghanistan, in the sense of bodies of people who share common linguistic and cultural heritages and are regarded by most people as being distinctive in some sense. In fact, there are perhaps two dozen such ethnolinguistic types, depending on how one counts. But the main ones—that is, the largest and most influential ones—never act as a single social unit and are, on the contrary, riven with internal factions. Except in the cases of the smallest ethnolinguistic types, such as the Qirghiz, in which the boundaries of the type coincide with some other social unit, the real units of cooperation are normally based on other grounds of loyalty than common ethnic identity. The categories of ethnic ascription are not in fact the categories of sociopolitical action.[7]

Accordingly, this chapter will raise and attempt to answer[8] the following set of questions:

1. What are, in fact, the characteristic units of social and cultural significance (including the units of ethnic ascription)?
2. What conditions control the alignment and composition of the viable sociopolitical units among the rural populations?
3. What impact has Afghan government policy and practice had on these populations over the years and how have they responded?

This discussion will suggest in the concluding section some of the reasons why these peoples have responded as they have to the recent Marxist and Soviet regimes.

IMPORTANT SOCIAL AND ASCRIPTIVE UNITS IN RURAL AFGHANISTAN

The main ethnolinguistic types in Afghanistan are listed in Table 2.1. Their locations are indicated on Figure 2.1. As already stated, the actual units of sociopolitical action—except in the cases of the very small ethnolinguistic types—are not coterminous with ethnolinguistic boundaries. These social units will here be called "coalitions," but seem to be what Whiteford and Adams[9] have called "operating units." I describe the actual units of sociopolitical cooperation—coalitions—as three types: those that commonly exist among "tribalized" societies, those that exist among "peasantized" societies, and those that unite people from different ethnolinguistic types.

One type of coalition exists within the "tribalized" ethnolinguistic types. The term "tribalized" here suggests segmentary systems based on agnatic relationships; they are nested systems of obligation based upon degree of relationship through male ancestors. The more closely related people are, the stronger their obligations to cooperate, help, avenge, and so forth. The less closely related they are, the less their obligation. The widest lines of connection are seldom activated; some have not been active for generations. This is the system of alignments extant among the Pashtuns, Turkomans, Baluch, Qirghiz, and some others. A similar structure exists among the Nuristani peoples, except that their lineages, unlike those in the other "tribal" societies, are ranked.

TABLE 2.1 MAJOR ETHNOLINGUISTIC GROUPS in AFGHANISTAN*

Group	Language	Religion	Population Estimates‡	Location
Pashtun (Afghan)	Pashtu	Sunni (a few Imami Shi'ites) Islam	6,500,000	All over; concentrated in South and Southwest
Tajik (eastern and northern)	Dari (Persian)	Sunni (Ismai'li in NE) Islam	3,500,000	North, northeastern
Farsiwan†	Dari†	Imami Shi'ite Islam	600,000	Western
Hazara	Dari	Imami (a few Isma'ilis, Sunnis) Islam	1,000,000	Hazarajat, Northwest (Qala-i Nao)
Uzbek	Uzbek (Turkic)	Sunni Islam	1,000,000	North
Aimaq tribes	Dari (some Turkic words)	Sunni Islam	800,000	West Central
Brahui	Brahui (Dravidian)	Sunni Islam	200,000	Southwest
Turkoman	Turkic dialects	Sunni Islam	125,000	North, Northwest
Baluch	Baluchi	Sunni Islam	100,000	South, Southwest
Nuristani	"Katiri" languages (Indo-European)	Sunni Islam	100,000	Northeast
Pamiris	Indo-Iranian dialects	Sunni and Isma'ili Islam	"several thousand"*	Northeast
Kohistani	Dardic dialects	Sunni Islam	n.a.*	Northeast
Gujar	Indo-European dialects, Pashtu	Sunni Islam	n.a.*	Northeast
Qirghiz	Turkic	Sunni Islam	n.a.*	Northeast Pamir (now Turkey); gypsy-like, itinerant
Jat	Indo-European, Pashtu	Sunni Islam	"several thousand"*§	
"Arab"	Dari	Sunni Islam	n.a.*	North; Sayyid Arabs widely dispersed
Mongol	Dari (with some Mongol words)	Sunni Islam	"several thousand"*	West Central

*Adapted from Dupree, *Afghanistan*, pp. 58–64.

†These populations are sometimes called "Tajiks," but, being Imami Shi'ite and distinctly Mediterranean in appearance, they are clearly different from the northeastern Tajiks, who are either Sunni or Isma'ili and bear traces of Mongoloid ancestry. Dupree reports (in a personal communication) that part of the confusion results from the tendency for Farsiwans to identify themselves as "Tajik" when in other parts of the country, especially in Kabul, probably because "Tajik" is a rather generalized, nonspecific ethnic category. However, compare the somewhat different usage of Richard Tap-per, "Ethnicity and Class: Dimensions of Intergroup Conflict in North-Central Afghanistan," in *Revolutions and Rebellions in Afghanistan: Anthropological Approaches*, ed. M. Nazif Shahrani and Robert L. Canfield, pp. 230–46 (Berkeley, Calif.: Institute of International Studies, 1984).

‡Figures on total population are only estimates. They range from 15 million to 18 million.

§Shahrani now says the number is less than 1,000. They fled and are now in Turkey.

FIGURE 2.1   MAJOR ETHNOLINGUISTIC TYPES in AFGHANISTAN

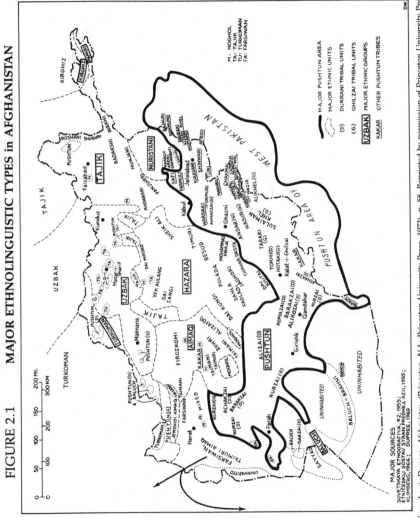

From Louis Dupree, *Afghanistan*, (Princeton, N.J.: Princeton University Press, 1973), p. 58. Reprinted by permission of Princeton University Press.

The actual size of the social unit suggested by the word "tribe" varies significantly among the largest tribalized group. The Pashtuns as a whole have, as already stated, rarely acted together. They are divided into two main branches, the Durrani and Ghilzai, and the various sub-branches of these have likewise seldom united for political action. It is the subbranches of these—or some subdivision within them—that are the viable sociopolitical units entailed in the concept of tribe. Because the Pashtuns are segmentary, sometimes broken into smaller localized agnatic groups, and sometimes drawn together on a larger scale, depending on issues and circumstances, the "tribe" that is extant at a given time can be a larger or smaller unit, a higher or lower level of agnatic coalition. Circumstances in different areas can favor the persistence of larger units than in others. Kakar, for example, notes that the Durrani tribes are larger than those of the Ghilzai.[10] Using the term "tribe" for what I have just called a "subbranch," he says, "the Ghilzai elders . . . exercized only limited authority over the nearest sections of their tribe. The Ghilzai tribe, as a whole, was broken up into small independent groups ['tribe' as used here]. But in a state of emergency, such as war, this was altered. Among the Sulaiman Khel [for example] *chel washtees* (fighting forces?), commanded by an able person who was given wide power . . . were organized. During the campaign each clan ['tribe'] of the Ghilzais elected leaders, presumably in the above manner."[11]

A different type of coalition exists among "peasantized" ethnolinguistic types and includes the Tajiks, Farsiwans, Hazaras, Pamiris, and perhaps also the Uzbeks. The term "peasantized" is used here to suggest that the higher-level agnatic associations that unite the subunits of "tribes" are no longer significant; the viable units of sociopolitical affiliation are smaller. They include, as they do among tribes, patrilineal extended families, localized agnatic groups, and regional or neighborhood groupings whose members recognize affiliation through agnates.

The important sociopolitical alignment beyond the agnatic community and neighborhood are patron-client networks. These may be highly agnatic in composition, one of the agnates being the preeminent person of wealth and influence, and his close kinsmen serving as loyal colleagues and supporters. But there may be other kinds of loyal "friends" in the network as well: the patron's affines, affines of his neighbors, and the like. The strength and wealth of such a person may change or vary partly in respect to the fortunes of other prominent patrons, for there are other prominent men who with their relatives and friends form other nuclei of social and political activity. Sometimes the prominent person becomes a malik, or *arbab*, an official government representative of some of the people in his area. Sometimes he and his friends may support another person to be the malik, often a close relative or loyal associate. Patron-client networks appear to vary greatly in size; such networks appear to be larger among the Uzbeks than the Hazaras.[12] Specific patron-client networks may also vary a great deal over time; a patron's fortunes rise and fall, depending on how he handles his affairs since social influence can very much be a matter of impression management.

The third type of coalition includes people from different ethnolinguistic types that unite under religious authorities. But they are religious authorities of a certain type. They are learned in Islam, like mullahs, but in addition they are reputed to have special access to God and His blessing. This reputation may derive, depending on the emphases of the sect, mainly from their descent from Muhammad (and his son-in-law Ali) or from one of the caliphs or another ancient person that is sacred to some Muslim groups, or it may derive from an extreme piety that has enabled them putatively to be infused with the character of God, or it may derive from their control of spiritual powers, such as the jinns. Such people are known variously as pirs or shaykhs or *ruhanis*, among the Sunnis and are the focal persons of the Sufi orders; among the Shi'ites they are the paramount Sayyids; they are called "saints" in Western literature.[13] Believed to be *walis*, "friends" of God, their favor, because of their unusual access to the blessing of God, which brings prosperity and healing in this life and the next, is highly valued. The great "saints" are sought for advice, favor, and blessing by people from far and wide. This makes them nodes of informal "friendship" networks. Some of these "saints" would never use their social position for political, or at least materialistic, ends. But under certain circumstances some of them have induced, or allowed, their followers to act collectively on some public issue. In such a case, the saint may avoid becoming personally involved, but nevertheless assign one or several of his prominent "friends" to take the lead in the matter. When the members of a "saint's" personal network of friends act in concert to bring something about in a public arena, they may be called a "saint coalition."

There is yet a wider network than this that can become activated as a coalition. This occurs when the saints presiding over different coalitions decide for some special purpose to work together in common cause. This may be called an "Islamic coalition." Coalitions of this type have rarely arisen, and when they have, they have been short-lived. Always, of course, they have arisen in special and extreme circumstances. But they are nonetheless potential, for it is common for Islamic authorities to maintain contacts with other authorities in their own sect. If they have been in association for a long time, their "friends" may intermarry with members of their family. This tends to integrate the "friends" more firmly into a network of associations having not only religious or sectarian loyalties but also affinal and agnatic ones. Because "saints" of different Islamic sects do not recognize each other, the outer limits of such Islamic coalitions are the sect.

Such are the units of active cooperation among the rural populations of Afghanistan. Let us now examine the conditions that affect their emergence as political units.

CONDITIONS AFFECTING the SOCIOPOLITICAL ALIGNMENTS of the RURAL POPULATIONS

As should be evident, some of the sociopolitical groupings mentioned or described above are perpetually operational; extended families are an example. Others are operational only on specific occasions for specific tasks, such as tribal movements. Some are rarely operational; they only take shape under extreme circumstances and perhaps only because of the Herculean efforts of some key individuals; Islamic coalitions are presumably of this sort.[14] It should also be evident that ephemeral social units can be especially important in the relations of the rural populations to the Afghan government, for by virtue of their size they can exert a significant influence on public affairs. The next three sections seek to explain the conditions under which ephemeral coalitions take form.[15] Three kinds of determinative circumstances will be described, the material conditions, the relevant cultural heritages of these peoples, and the policies and practices of the Afghan government.

Important Material Conditions

The material[16] conditions to be emphasized here are associated with the geophysical conditions of this region. These significantly affect—in the sense of setting a limiting context for—the sociopolitical alignments of Afghanistan's rural populations. They are

(1) the terrain, which, because of its dramatic features, drastically affects spatial relations among these peoples; (2) the climate and ecology, which influence the production systems of these peoples; and (3) the location of the country as a whole, which establishes its geopolitical context.

Few regions of the world are topographically more various and abrupt than Afghanistan. Descending from northeast to southwest through the heart of the country, the Hindu Kush mountain range, which is the westernmost spur of the Himalayas, lifts dozens of peaks higher than any in Europe or the continental United States, the highest to above 25,000 feet. Nestled between the crests and folds of this range, sometimes bounded by abrupt cliffs, are alluvial plains of varying shapes and sizes. Because most of them are well watered by the runoff from melting snow and ice, they are suitable for settled human habitation.

Existence on these sharply bounded plains often entails a measure of isolation. Many of these plains are "islands," bounded, perhaps on several sides by forbidding cliffs and steep ascents, sometimes open to neighboring plains only along the stream banks above and below. As a result, the natural lines of contact, such as they are, between communities on these plains follow the lines of drainage (Figure 2.2). Along these lines of contact, the "islands" vary in their accessibility. Normally the higher ones are the most isolated; they are usually also, of course, smaller. But downstream they get progressively larger and, as the folds that bound them broaden and flatten, the lowest ones become easily accessible from several directions. But even many of the downstream "islands" are rather isolated because they are situated in arid places, for surrounding the Hindu Kush range from which lines of drainage flow are wide, expansive deserts.

The major highway in this region (Figure 2.3) skirts wherever possible the central mountain massif. Only at one place—at Salang, the pass above Panjsher to the south and Andarab to the north—does it approach the Hindu Kush. From this paved highway extend four paved roads that link Afghanistan to its neighboring nations, one going east to Peshawar, Pakistan; one south to Chamand, Pakistan; one west to Iran; and one (and now possibly two) north to the Soviet Union.

The great circle highway connects, of course, the population centers of the country: Kabul, Ghazni, Qandahar, Herat, Mazari-Sharif. These cities are relatively well integrated into a national system of commerce and communication. But the other populations of the country—those situated far off any roads, paved or unpaved, and

FIGURE 2.2   RIVERS and DRAINAGE in AFGHANISTAN

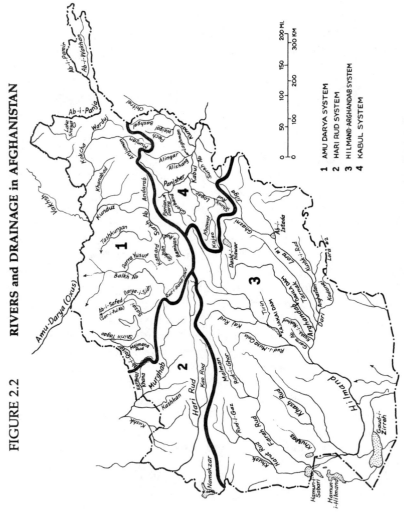

1 AMU DARYA SYSTEM
2 HARI RUD SYSTEM
3 HILMAND-ARGHANDAB SYSTEM
4 KABUL SYSTEM

From Dupree, *Afghanistan*, p. 32. Reprinted by permission of Princeton University Press.

FIGURE 2.3   HIGHWAYS and ROADS in AFGHANISTAN

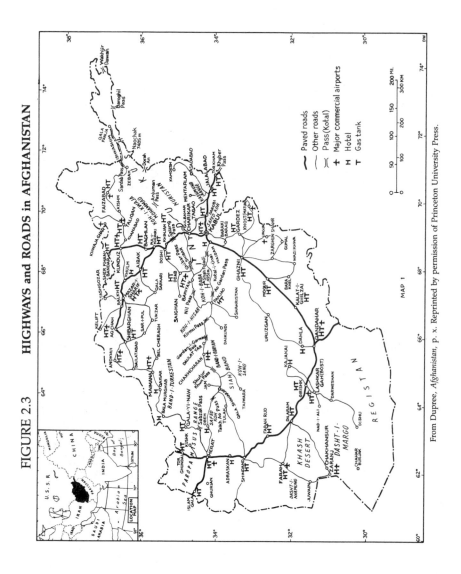

MAP 1

From Dupree, *Afghanistan*, p. x. Reprinted by permission of Princeton University Press.

those dwelling on the further "islands"—are more isolated. As a result of the terrain, most of the rural populations are relatively inaccessible and poorly integrated into the nation as a whole. Their loyalties and interests remain local (see Figure 2.4).

Climate and ecology in turn are geophysical features that directly influence rural production systems and sociopolitical alignments. Two major wind currents pass across this terrain. The monsoon winds that blow in summer from east to west are thoroughly dried by the time they arrive, having already dumped their moisture on Indochina and India. Alpine winds flowing from west to east still have enough moisture to blanket the mountains with heavy snow in winter. It is the runoff from winter snow that feeds most of the people in Afghanistan. Surface water is abundant in spring and summer, which is ideal for the irrigation grain farming practiced by most of the sedentary rural population. The variation in altitudes provides the context for the other major production system in rural Afghanistan, pastoral nomadism, by which the flocks of migratory peoples subsist on the luxuriant grasses of the highlands in summer and those of the lowland plains in winter.

As is well known, these two systems of subsistence, irrigation grain farming and nomadic pastoralism, affect the ways people cooperate and organize. Irrigation requires cooperation among the people who use the natural surface water flows. They must arrange, first, to build the canal that brings the water to their fields; then they must arrange to clean it—an important task in many parts of Afghanistan where the swift mountain runoff may fill canals with debris— and they must arrange to use the water according to some schedule. The nomadic system of the pastoralists similarly requires cooperation, especially during the migration when the pastoralists come into closest contact with the settled populations, and when there is the greatest chance of conflict over the straying flocks onto the lands of the agriculturalists.[17]

One other significant geophysical feature is the location of Afghanistan in respect to the resources and population centers elsewhere. This region of Central Asia, of which Afghanistan is a part, is bounded on the northeast by the Himalayas and on the northwest by the Caspian Sea and Kara Kum desert, and constitutes the historic corridor of diffusion, trade, and conquest connecting the great population centers of South Asia, China, the Middle East, and Europe. Diverse linguistic, cultural, political, and religious heritages have met and mingled here, and their impact on the sociopolitical alignments

FIGURE 2.4   The LARGER "ISLANDS" of CULTIVATION

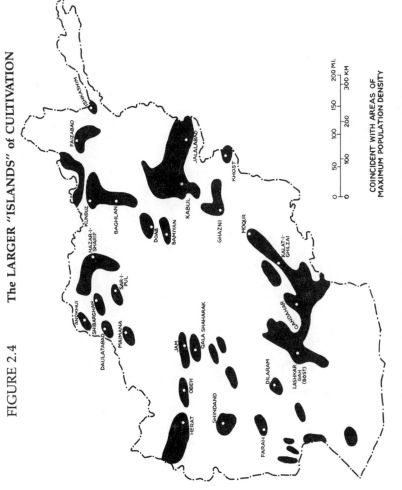

COINCIDENT WITH AREAS OF
MAXIMUM POPULATION DENSITY

From Dupree, *Afghanistan*, p. 46. Reprinted by permission of Princeton University Press.

of the peoples living in this region will be explained in the next section.

Traditions

The word "tradition" is used intentionally here, that is, as the statements, beliefs, legends, customs, understandings, terms, and categories of experience and social relationship that are handed down from one generation to another. Tradition, used alone, can never explain a people's behavior, since behavior is always situational, contextual, circumstantial. But there are frames of meaning, biases, and entrenched understandings that people have received from their past, which are already intact when they are confronted with exigencies, and these affect how people understand their problems, how they perceive what is of immediate or of prior importance, and thus how they will be prone to act. However unpopular the notion of "tradition" as a social force may be in some circles,[18] it is a necessary concept for the analysis here since it is precisely the prejudices, assumptions, established perspectives, and so forth, that these rural populations *bring to* their experience that make them distinctive; these affect how they organize their affairs and solve their problems in ways different from other peoples. This is especially necessary if we want to take note not only of how they are aligned but also of the particular moral understandings which shape their particular alignments.

This is not to say that tradition is a static, unbendable force, constraining creative thought and innovative behavior. Rather, tradition changes—is revised, lost, revived, corrupted—as people use it to interpret and respond to the problems they face.[19] But if tradition is tractable, it is not infinitely plastic. It does not conform neatly to every human exigency as it appears.[20] It exerts a weight of its own by being, in Sahlins's words, a system "in place" at any given moment, setting the context of new and emerging problems, limiting the range of acceptable responses to them. Tradition is therefore an important determining condition of a people's existence, distinct from other determinants. In the case of the problem before us, it is, along with the material conditions already described, the second of three conditions that govern the sociopolitical alignments of Afghanistan's rural peoples. We shall explain the tradition controlling these alignments as a set of heritages and will describe each—ethnic diversity, Islam, and xenophobia—in terms of the important antecedents that give each its distinctive influence in social affairs today.

The diverse ethnolinguistic heritage results from a busy history of invasion and immigration in the area. The Indo-Aryan peoples who in ancient times occupied the region now called Afghanistan were invaded, mostly from the north, by more kinds of people than anyone will ever count—peoples whose identities, if they are known at all, are only vaguely familiar to most of us: Scythians, Massagetae, Sakas, Dards, Huns, and Ephthalites. In the more recent past Arabs, Turks, Mongols, and Persians invaded the region. These many and diverse kinds of people passed through, hid in, or were trapped in this territory. And they left behind the melange of phenotypic features, tongues, and customs now extant in modern Afghanistan.

They bequeathed to the present at least one feature of social alignment that is shared, I believe, by all the Afghanistan peoples: the rule of patrilineal descent. They also bequeathed to the present a history of interethnic hostility. The various occupants of this territory have competed with each other for desirable goods—land, water, flocks, women, and silver—and have captured and enslaved or sold each other for too many generations for their differences to be easily forgotten. Their irritations may be said to run deep in the sense that each group "remembers"—in the form of stories, sayings, and monuments—the offenses done against them by their enemies. This is the basis of the interethnic separations that exist today. Even if the large ethnic types cannot get together, neither can any portion of them easily unite with other ethnic types who were once their enemies.

The heritage of Islam originated with Islamic invaders, mostly Arabs, who reached into the area less than a century after the death of Muhammad. By the third Islamic century (our tenth) prominent rulers were striking coins in the name of God and his Prophet.[21] The influence of Islam, as it did almost everywhere it stayed, shaped the whole world view of the peoples of the area. Islam brought to the rulers the notion that they were answerable to God for guarding the faith. It brought an extensive and growing literature which covered many subjects, but especially it brought a system of jurisprudence, which the peoples of this region not only imbibed but also expanded and in significant ways reshaped. It brought new concepts of authority enshrined in words for new kinds of specialists—terms like *mazhab, faqih, gazi, mufti, muhtasib, mullah, mawlawi,* and *mawlana,* for specialists in law and learning; terms like *imam* and *rowzakhan* for ritual leaders; terms like *fakir, shaykh,* and *sayyid* for sacred persons. How thoroughly Islamic notions have permeated Afghan society is shown by pointing out that (with the exception of the word *pir*) the most common terms of self-ascription—*watan,* "one's homeland," *qawn,* "one's clan or kinship group," *mazhab* (or *madhhab*), "one's sect group"—are Arabic words.

Islam also brought a new kind of issue over which people took up arms against each other: religious sect. This kind of antagonism—between Sunnis and Shi'ites—had already existed among Muslims before it came into this area. But here it became intensified by many political struggles that went on for generations. One of the most important took place in the sixteenth and seventeenth centuries, between the Safavids, who were Shi'ites, and the Turko-Mongols, who were Sunnis. Their struggles were not merely interethnic conflicts, for the Safavis, it will be remembered, had self-consciously promoted Shi'ism in order to win the support of the oppressed Shi'ite populations of Khorasan. Dogmatic differences were thus deliberately wedded to power and territorial interest. It could have no other effect than to politicize sectarian categories. The Sunni-Shi'ite opposition was further intensified during the reign of Abdur Rahman (1880–1901). Amir Abdur Rahman fought four wars to subjugate the dissenting peoples of the region that had recently been ceded to him by the British and Russians. In each war he sought the support of the religious authorities, and in each he sought to identify the opposition with heresy. In the third war, against the Hazaras, who were Shi'ites, he won the support of essentially all the Sunni authorities; the Hazaras, on their side, had gained the support of all the Shi'ite authorities, and one served as their leader. The intersectarian tensions of that war are well preserved in the memory of the Hazaras, who lost, and they are evident today in the discriminating practices of the Sunnis against the Hazaras.[22]

Islam brought yet one more cultural feature of importance to Afghanistan life: Sufism. Indeed the peoples of Khorasan—which at one time concluded Afghanistan and a portion of Central Asia as well as eastern Iran—made some of the most significant contributions to the development of early Sufism. Some of the greatest of Sufi thinkers came from this region. Hujwiri, for example, who wrote the first great treatise on Sufism in the Persian language, was born in Ghazni, and died, after many travels throughout Khorasan, in Lahore. Moreover, many of the Sufi orders, especially in the earliest period of

Sufism, developed in this region, for example, the Naqshbandis and Chishtis.[23]

Sufism introduced many notions to Islam, but one that may be mentioned here, because it has had a significant influence on Afghanistan society, is the belief in walis, "friends" (i.e., of God). Hujwiri in the eleventh century, drawing from the teaching of another Khorasani, al-Tirmidhi (whose work is lost), made the classic statement of this notion in Persian:

> God has saints (awliyaa) whom He has specifically distinguished by His friendship (wulaayat) and whom He has chosen to be governors of His Kingdom and has marked out to manifest His action and has peculiarly favored with diverse kinds of miracles (karaamat) and has purged of natural corruption . . . so through the blessing of their advent the rain falls from heaven, and through the purity of their lives the plants spring up from the earth, and through their spiritual influence the Moslems gain victories over unbelievers. . . . They have power to loose and to bind and are the officers of the Divine Court.[24]

Throughout Islamic history, since this belief became widely disseminated, there has been difficulty and disagreement over who might be the true walis—Hujwiri believed that some of them did not even know they were walis—but that such sacred persons exist, or may exist, is not doubted by most of the rural populations of Afghanistan. This popular belief is an important basis for the influence of the "saints."

The heritage of xenophobia took form mainly in the nineteenth century as a reaction to the persistent interventions and invasions of the region by the British, who sought a defensible northern frontier for its empire in India, and by the Russians, who were rapidly expanding into Central Asia. In a period of eighty years the Afghanistan peoples fought three wars with the British and several skirmishes with the Russians. Despite many internecine tensions among themselves, the menacing presence of the nonMuslim ("Christian") British and Russians generated a strong anti-European (and anti-Christian) xenophobia among these peoples throughout the last century. This xenophobia was defined in Islamic terms. All the conflicts with the outside powers were seen as clashes between Muslim believers and infidel outsiders. Appeals of the government for popular support made in these terms drew large numbers of warriors from varying tribal backgrounds, and the Afghanistan peoples became known for their fanatical Muslim zeal.[25]

The geophysical setting and the various heritages of the rural peoples of Afghanistan have been two influences affecting their sociopolitical alignments. There is yet another, namely, the impingements of the Afghan government, and it is to these and the responses to them that we turn in the following section.

Policies and Actions of the Afghan Government

The government of Afghanistan took shape toward the end of the previous century under the influence of Amir Abdur Rahman of Kabul, and the institutions which he established were in some ways still in place in the 1970s. I will describe the policies and practices of the government as they existed initially, the general trends that developed afterwards, and their effects.

By the turn of this century effective provincial administration had been imposed and provincial governorships were strong enough to exert a significant force upon the affairs of the rural populations. The main assignments of the governors were to keep order, collect taxes, and conscript young men for the military. The maintenance of order was a major concern because opposition to the government was common in the provinces. To the Amir this "necessitated breaking down the feudal and tribal system and substituting one grand community under one law and one rule."[26] This entailed strengthening his control of the provinces by means of the standing army he was forming. He made military contingents available to the provincial governors so that they could improve the government's control of recalcitrant populations and replace troublesome leaders. He also instituted policies that would strengthen government control at the expense of "the feudal and tribal system." He drew provincial and subprovincial boundaries through tribal territories so as to make different segments of a tribe answerable to different provincial governments. He enlarged his bureaucracy so that it could take over some of the functions of the local leaders, the maliks or arbabs, some of whom had been extremely powerful. Disaffected elements of a malik's following became more able to break away and arrange to have their own representatives to the government. As a result, the number of maliks increased and the sizes of their followings, and hence their influence, declined.

Besides being responsible for maintaining order, the other main tasks of the provincial governors were to collect taxes and conscript men for the army. Given extensive powers, sometimes they were abusive, demanding excessive fees and keeping large amounts for themselves. In some of the more distant provinces the governors began to collect taxes as "rent," turning their provinces into virtual fiefdoms. Dupree says "the right to collect taxes sometimes became confused . . . with bona fide ownership of land. Land was sold and resold by government officials without any regard to the traditional joint ownership of village lands by the clan or lineage."[27] The effect, in any case, was to disenfranchise some people, to abuse traditionally sanctioned rights to land, and to fragment the social units associated with it. The conscription of men for the army, if it abused established customs, had the effect of mixing the ethnic groups, but on different echelons, since the officers were nearly always Pashtuns. The mixing of the ethnic groups in the military sometimes worsened the interethnic tensions, especially so among the smaller and weaker ethnic groups. It did have the salutary effect, however, of broadening the outlook of the troops from the provinces and fostering a national cosnciousness. As will be explained below, conscription was required of only some groups, certain Pashtun groups being exempted, and thus the impact of the military experience varied considerably.

Since that time the central government has increased its direct control over provincial affairs. The number of provincial governments increased from four at the turn of the century to twenty-eight in 1970. More boundaries cut across old coalition territories, and more governors deal with smaller numbers of people, thereby leaving maliks with fewer numbers of people to represent. Moreover, the staffs of the provincial governments have increased, and they have been involved in many more activities.[28]

Other policies and practices of the government were directed toward control of the religious authorities. The Afghan rulers had already in the nineteenth century been paying stipends to mullahs who expressed loyalty and helped encourage the warriors to fight. But under Abdur Rahman efforts were made to bring the Islamic learned establishment under more direct control. Some of the Muslim authorities to whom the people had informally turned for counsel and adjudication were given positions as judges in the provincial governments. They were required to pass government-controlled examinations in Islamic jurisprudence and their judgments were made subject to review by secular officials. *Madrasahs* (advanced schools for

Islamic learning) were established. Mosques in the major cities were built or improved and refurbished by government grants, and their mullahs supported by stipends. *Waqfs* (endowments which supported religious authorities) were taken over by the state.

Thus were the authorities of Islamic learning brought under the control of the central government. There were some Islamic authorities who were less easily controlled, however. These were the shaykhs or pirs, those who claimed to be, or were reputed to be, walis, the sacred persons through whom special grace putatively passed to the common people. Their social influence was exerted mainly through the Sufi orders that formed around them. The Sufi orders had long been troublesome to the Afghan rulers as in many other Islamic nations, and before the turn of the century they had been banned. Many pirs, like the mullahs—which most of them also claimed to be—were provided pensions. The pirs and their clients were thus brought under a degree of control. But the belief in sacred authorities who have direct and special access to God could not be outlawed, and the informal ties of dependence which the rural peoples formed with the pirs have persisted. Small groups of people under the tutelage of a Sufi authority still meet to practice the Sufi rituals of worship. Informal networks of religious affiliation have thus persisted. In fact, many of the rulers and prominent leaders of the country—and especially the women of their families—have retained informal ties with pirs.

The degree to which these informal "friendship" networks have been under the control of the government has therefore been unclear. Officially the pirs and the Sufi orders have no legitimacy and no capability of exerting any significant influence on public affairs. But unofficially they continue to be important in informal ways, and especially so to the common people, for nonpolitical reasons. These networks remain socially viable. That they could, under special conditions, become the basis of powerful political coalitions has made them potentially significant, for at the time when they have coalesced they were capable of exerting much pressure on public affairs.

Another policy of the government that significantly affected the sociopolitical alignments of the rural populations involved ethnic favorites and discrimination. The government treated the various ethnic groups differently. The Pashtun tribes were given, on the whole, favorable treatment. Some of them were absolved from conscription to the military and from taxation. Some were paid stipends. Some of the nomadic Pashtuns were awarded special grazing rights in the

Hindu Kush. These privileges were given as rewards for loyalty and assistance to the government in its military campaigns.

Troublesome populations, on the other hand, received no such favors. The Hazaras, who rebelled and fought an extended war against the Afghan government, were stripped of their control over the Hindu Kush pastures and the pastures were given to the Pashtun pastoralists. This had a devastating impact on the Hazara's society and economy. These pastures had been held in common by the various regional Hazara groups and so had provided important bases for large "tribal" affiliations to be maintained. With the loss of their summer pastures the units of practical Hazara affiliation declined. Also, Hazara leaders were killed or deported, and their lands were confiscated. These activities of the Afghan government, carried on as a deliberate policy, sometimes exacerbated by other outrages effected by the Pashtun pastoralists, emasculated the Hazaras. Today they are peasants owning relatively small tracts of land and, as of the 1970s, gradually declining economically. Large numbers were migrating seasonally to find work and many were permanently situated in the cities seeking to survive as day laborers.

The Nuristanis fared better. After they were subjugated and forcibly converted to Islam, and some of their young men were carried off to be servants of elite Kabul families, they were left relatively alone. That they had become Sunnis when they converted to Islam may also have contributed to their being treated better than the Hazaras, who were Shi'ites. The inaccessibility of Nuristan and the personal ties with their young men in the capital—some of whom eventually advanced to prominent positions in the military—combined to give the Nuristanis a comparatively comfortable relationship with the central government.

Other rural populations for a long time remained relatively unaffected by the Afghan government. These were the groups situated in more inaccessible regions of the country, groups like the Baluch, Qirghiz, and Mountain Tajiks. Having been relatively unaffected by government controls, they tended to retain wide segmentary and kinship-based social units.

This differential treatment of the ethnic types in the country of course created wide differences in their political and economic fortunes. As a whole, the Pashtuns have prospered and the Nuristanis have done well. On the other hand, the Hazaras lost ground, becoming Afghanistan's underprivileged ethnic minority.[29]

But at the same time, as the government has become stronger

and more effective, it has tended toward impartiality. The favored status of the Pashtuns has been eroding for some time. The government has trod ever deeper into local Pashtun affairs, just as it has into those of other groups. As everywhere, the government has built roads and set up telephone lines in rural Pashtun territory. As everywhere also, it has brought in more officials to inquire into local Pashtun affairs. Moreover, the government's dependence upon the Pashtun tribes' support declined as it acquired more advanced weapons for its military. The purchase in 1955 of heavy arms from the Soviet Union enabled the government to possess, for the first time, more firepower than all the Pashtun tribes combined. In another realm, the development of a national educational system further eroded the Pashtun advantage, for eventually the government began allowing bright non-Pashtun students to study at advanced levels, and eventually to study abroad. As a result, Uzbeks and Tajiks as well as Pashtuns have reached responsible positions in the Afghanistan bureaucracy.

The development of an infrastructure by the government to protect and facilitate these policies had a major impact on the rural populations by affecting economic opportunities and patronage links. As already mentioned, existing roads were improved, especially those connecting the provincial seats with Kabul, thereby opening the way for a better transport and trade system. A few entrepreneurs organized and promoted industries—cotton and karakul, for example—which eventually flourished and of course increased the number and value of products sold for cash. The marketing of goods within the country—not to mention to the outside—has radically expanded.

These developments have fostered a kind of class differentiation among the rural populations. Agriculturalists who were favorably located on or near a main road have begun to raise crops that bring a high cash value in the cities. Some of the more well-to-do families have ventured into trucking and transshipping. Seasonal labor in the cities has been more feasible for the poor. On the whole, the rural families that have by such means been able to tie into the cash economy have done well. Those that have not done so have tended to decline.[30] Of course, with the growth of the importance of cash, there have also been more opportunities for cultural brokering. Because the services provided by the government have for the common people been difficult to obtain without the recommendations of well-placed "friends," the broadening of government influence that accompanied the development of the national infrastructure fostered the importance of well-placed patrons.

As the Afghanistan government became more powerful and efficient the range of feasible responses by the rural populations became narrower. There was less local autonomy, less room for the formation of coalitions, less room for leaders to maneuver. The obvious response of the rural populations to the pressures of the Afghan government, then, has had mainly to be compliant. But some of the peoples have complied as little as possible, in fact, avoided compliance, in three ways that may be mentioned: by smuggling, by other forms of evasion including bribery, and by rebellion.

What is now called smuggling was normal among the Pashtun nomads of eastern Afghanistan for many generations. As the nomads migrated between lowland pastures in India and Pakistan and the highland pastures in central Afghanistan, they carried besides their personal effects, some goods for trade or barter. They have long bought and sold and bartered and traded with the settled populations of Afghanistan, Pakistan, and India. The animal products of the highlands—wool, ghee, *qurut* (dried yogurt)—were exchanged in the lowlands for the products of the subcontinents—tea, cloth, and other manufactured goods. When national governments began carving up the landscape, the British, with reluctant acquiescence from the Afghan rulers, drew a national boundary between the usual summer and winter territories of the Pashtun nomads. Initially, the boundary made no difference, as neither the British nor Afghans had the wherewithal to enforce it. But shipping of goods across this boundary has continued, even though both governments are now trying to control it, basically because the region in Pakistan across the border is still essentially under tribal control. Members of the tribes in Afghanistan have kinsmen in the urban centers of both countries who can help them market their goods, and they have relatives and allies on the other side of the border who can help them continue to avoid the officials.

As the government has felt it necessary to intrude more directly into local affairs, the local populations, unable to resist by force, frequently resist by evasion. They underreport their livestock holdings, underreport the size and productivity of their land, and until fairly recently fail in many instances to report the births of sons so as to avoid sending them to the army. Moreover, they prefer to settle their disputes without involving the government. There are in many communities strong pressures to withhold information on sensitive matters from outsiders, but especially government officials.

Another way the local populations try to control government intrusion into their affairs is by bribing the officials. A subject of great sensitivity among Afghan officials, bribery is openly and at length talked about among the rural peoples. Two conditions seem to foster the payment of bribes. One is the desire, sometimes the demand, of the officials for them. Most officials are underpaid, and, in fact, it has been said that the government assumes that local officials will receive some supplementary income. I found no evidence, however, that the higher-paid officials such as governors and judges accepted bribes. But some of the lower-echelon officials, clerks, *alaqadars* (subdistrict administrators), and hakims sometimes accepted bribes. Even so, many of them claimed that they did not want the bribes, but were being forced to accept them by the insistence of the people. This is the second condition that fosters the payment of bribes, for the rural peoples often doubt that their case will get adequate attention, or their claims receive a fair hearing, unless some sort of special gratuity is given. Even though they resent the necessity, as they see it, of paying a bribe, once they are obliged to deal with the government they want to pay it in order to make the most of the situation.

The bribery system has helped the local maliks to prosper. As the bribe is paid through them, and the client who pays the money has no direct access to the officials except through him, the malik is able to keep a portion of the amount paid; in fact, it is normally understood that he will keep some of it. It was often said of the "good" maliks that they do not take much of the money paid to the government—that is, as taxes or bribes.

The payment of bribes is therefore both a way of relating to the government and a way of evading it. Because the price of bribes is so great, people make every effort to avoid letting the government know about a case. It was better, many people in Bamyan told me, to resolve a case internally. Once it becomes "official" it becomes far more costly—even though in principle such government services are supposed to be free. Anyway, they say, no matter how much one pays, one cannot be sure of not being outbid by one's opponent. Such is their sense of alienation from the government.

Rebellion has been, of course, a rare response to the influence of the government. But in fact a number of rebellions have been reported. Most of them have been brief and abortive, but, as is well known, not all of them.

The typical units of rebellion have of course been the rather large coalitions—smaller groupings easily recognize the impossibility of success. The type of coalition that is most often mentioned in the historical literature is the "tribe." That term, as already explained, says little about how large the coalition may be. Another kind of rebellious group sometimes discussed is the "bandit" group. Bandits seem to arise among less tribalized peoples, such as Tajiks and Hazaras. Still another kind of rebel coalition is the saint coalition or Islamic coalition. This sort of coalition is almost never mentioned in the literature. But that such groupings have formed is frequently suggested by the fact that they are led by religious authorities, almost always referred to as "mullahs' in the literature. The key instigators in the successful rebellion against Amanullah in 1929—in which several tribes and several ethnic types were involved—were the Mujadidi brothers and a prominent "mullah" from Panjsher, all of whom appear to have been regarded as "saints" by the rural populations.[31]

CONCLUSION

The viable units of sociopolitical activity among the rural populations of Afghanistan have not, on the whole, been ethnolinguistic types. Rather, they have been other kinds of sociopolitical units. Those have taken form in respect to three types of influences, the geophysical conditions of the region, the historic traditions of obligations and understanding existing among these populations, and the impingements of government. Despite the government's impingements, however, some of the rural populations do find ways to evade or resist the government.

There is no need to elaborate further. But it may be useful to make, in conclusion, an analytical point: In identifying the structures that were "in place" among the rural popualtions of Afghanistan in the late 1970s—when the rural populations so generally and vigorously rose up against the "reforms" of the Marxist government—it is wise to consider not only the sociopolitical structures that were viable and active and thus "visible" at that time, but also those that were implicit in the biases and orientations of these people, the structures that were "potential" in Afghanistan rural society. Perhaps one failing of Soviet strategists, when they decided to invade Afghanistan, was the failure, as had earlier rulers, to consider the scope and strength of the implicit and potential coalitions of the rural populations. We social scientists who sympathize with the resistance activities of the Afghans may congratulate ourselves for having kept the importance of these coalitions from any Soviets whom might have consulted our work.

NOTES

1. One's obligations seem to grow in respect to one's knowledge. I have received a number of grants and fellowships that have in one way or other enhanced this research: from the Social Science Research Council, the University of Michigan Center for Middle Eastern and North African Studies, the National Endowment for the Humanities, Washington University, and the School of American Research. Gratitude is expressed to all these organizations. In the preparation of this chapter I have benefited from the comments of Jon Anderson on another paper on a similar topic. I also am grateful to A'i Banuazizi, Lois Beck, Louis Dupree, and Nazif Shahrani for comments on the chapter. Also, as there have been delays in publication, much has changed in Afghanistan and the article should be read as a statement of the situation in *circa* 1980. Some recent works on the topic are: M. Nazif Shahrani and Robert L. Canfield (editors), *Revolution and Rebellions in Afghanistan: Anthropological Perspectives* (1984, Berkeley: Institute of International Studies); Robert L. Canfield "Islamic Sources of the Resistance," *Orbis* 29 (1985), pp. 57–71; the proceedings of the Conference on "Le Fait Ethnique en Iran et en Afghanistan" at the Centre National de la Recherche Scientifique edited by Jean-Pierre Digard (in press); and above all the writings of Olivier Roy, most important of which is his *L'Afghanistan: Islam et Modernité Politique* (Paris: Editions du Seuil, 1985).

2. Jim Paul, "The *Khalq* Failed to Comprehend the Contradictions of the Rural Sector: Interview with Feroz Ahmed." *Middle East Research and Information Project* (hereafter *MERIP) Reports* (No. 89), 10:6 (July-August 1980), pp. 13, 14.

3. Mountstuart Elphinstone, *An Account of the Kingdom of Caubul and Its Dependencies in Persia, Tartary and India, Comprising a View of the Afghaun Nation and a History of the Dooraunee Monarchy,* 3rd ed. (1815; London: Richard Bentley, 1839) vol. 1, p. 281; Leon B. Poullada, *Reform and Rebellion in Afghanistan 1919–1929: King Amanullah's Failure to Modernize a Tribal Society* (Ithaca, N.Y.: Cornell University Press, 1973); Rhea Talley Stewart, *Fire in Afghanistan: Faith, Hope and the British Empire,* (Garden City, N.Y.: Doubleday, 1973).

4. See *Keesing's Contemporary Archives,* 26 (11 January 1980), pp. 30031–32. See also the final reports, based upon an incomplete census project in the 1970s, of the Afghan Demographic Studies Program in the Ministry of Planning.

5. Vartan Gregorian, *The Emergence of Modern Afghanistan, 1919–1929: King Amanullah's Failure to Modernize a Tribal Society* (Stanford, Calif.: Stanford University Press, 1969), pp. 69–73.

6. Quoted in ibid., p. 126.

7. For fuller arguments on ethnic processes see Frederik Barth, ed., *Ethnic Groups and Boundaries: The Social Organization of Culture Difference* (Boston: Little, Brown, 1969); and Abner Cohen, *Custom and Politics in Urban Africa: A Study of Hausa Migrants in Yoruba Towns* (Berkeley: University of California Press, 1969).

8. This analysis must be regarded as preliminary, approximate, and suggestive. Almost anything that might be said about Afghanistan is probably in some sense wrong, as this region contains one of the most disparate populations of the world. My best field experience has been with Hazaras, although I have had some contact with Pashtun nomads, and extensive contact with urban, middleclass Afghans. All the statements concerning matters beyond this range of knowledge should be considered schematic and suggestive.

The best published attempt to survey the structure of rural Afghanistan as a whole is Dupree's *Afghanistan* with which this analysis differs somewhat at a few points. See Louis Dupree, *Afghanistan* (Princeton, N.J.: Princeton University Press, 1973). To augment the schematic analysis in this chapter see also the publications cited in Dupree, *Afghanistan,* and in M. Jamil Hanifi, *Bibliography of Afghanistan* (New Haven, Conn.: Human Relations Area Files, 1982). Because Kakar's 1979 study is a social history of the reign of Amir Abdur Rahman, it tends to be ignored as an ethnographic source. It is, in my opinion, a rich store of ethnographic information. See Hasan Kawun Kakar, *Government and Society in Afghanistan: The Reign of Amir 'Abd al-Rahman Khan* (Austin: University of Texas Press, 1979).

9. Scott Whiteford and Richard N. Adams. "Migration, Ethnicity and Adaptation: Bolivian Migrant Workers in Northwest Argentina," in Brian M. Du Toit and Helen I. Safa, eds., *Migration and Urbanization: Models and Adaptive Strategies* (The Hague: Mouton, 1975). See also Richard N. Adams, *Crucifixion by Power* (Austin: University of Texas Press, 1970).

10. Hasan Kakar, *Afghanistan: A Study in Internal Political Development, 1880–1896* (Lahore: Educational Press, 1971), p. 132.

11. Ibid.

12. Cf. G. Whitney Azoy, *Buz Kashi: Game and Power in Afghanistan* (Philadelphia: University of Pennsylvania Press, 1982); and Robert Leroy Canfield, *Faction and Conversion in a Plural Society: Religious Alignments in the Hindu Kush,* Anthropological Papers No. 50 (Ann Arbor: Museum of Anthropology, University of Michigan, 1973). Professor M. Nazif Shahrani noted in a personal communication that Azoy's description of patron-client networks in northern Afghanistan is less typical of the Uzbeks than the Pashtuns.

13. The Mujadidi and Gailani families mentioned by Naby in this volume are prominent leaders in the Sufi orders, the Mujadidi's in the Naqshbandiyya order, the Gailanis in the Qadiriyya order. The great saints of the Shi'ites are Sayyids. Even though the Shi'ites have no formal Sufi orders, they have imbibed many of the same concepts of sainthood as the Sunni Sufis, but associated with concepts of the Islam and by derivation with the Imam's representatives; these are normally the Sayyids, sacred descent from Ali (and the Prophet) being especially venerated among Shi'ites.

(See Roy, *L'Afghanistan*.) There is a vast literature on the subject. See, for example, Fazlur Rahman, *Islam*, 2nd ed. (Chicago: University of Chicago Press, 1979), pp. 174 ff.

14. Robert L. Canfield, "Islamic Coalitions in Bamyan: A Problem in Translating Afghan Political Culture," in *Revolutions and Rebellions in Afghanistan: Anthropological Perspectives*, ed. M. Nazif Shahrani and Robert L. Canfield (Berkeley, Calif.: Institute of International Studies, 1984), pp. 21129.

15. Underlying this presentation is the notion that societies may take different "structural poses" depending on different conditions. (See Fred Gearing, "The Structural Poses of 18th Century Cherokee Villages," *American Anthropologist*, 60 [1958], pp. 1148–57.) Our discussion includes both ecological and sociopolitical matters as impingements or controlling conditions that affect their "poses," but it also includes something that Gearing took for granted, the traditions or heritages that affect the way the impinging influences are perceived and defined.

16. I assume "material conditions" to include (1) those that are "natural," that is, that are inherent in or closely allied to the geophysical features of the region; and (2) those that are technological. Technology, some would argue, for example, Sahlins, is actually part of the cultural tradition, which I discuss in the section on tradition. See Marshall Sahlins, *Culture and Practical Reason* (Chicago: University of Chicago Press, 1976). But the technology to which I refer has a closer link to the land and the requirements of human subsistence than the types of traditional culture I describe. It is necessary to deal with the aspects of human culture that are closely allied to biological needs and the material resources for satisfying them, and it is necessary to deal with the aspects of human culture that express and serve the moral and spiritual need of humans to be placed in fields of significance. Kroeber's distinction between material culture and moral culture, and Redfield's between technology and world view, continue to be necessary and utile. See Alfred L. Kroeber, *Anthropology* (New York: Harcourt, Brace, 1948); and Robert Redfield, *The Primitive World and Its Transformations* (Ithaca, N.Y.: Cornell University Press, 1953).

17. Frederik Barth, "Nomadism in the Mountain and Plateau Areas of Southwest Asia," *Problems of the Arid Zone* (Paris: UNESCO, 1960), pp. 341–55.

18. See Marvin Harris, *Cultural Materialism* (New York: Random House, 1980); and Eric A. Ross, ed., *Beyond the Myths of Culture: Essays in Cultural Materialism* (New York: Academic Press, 1980).

19. See Emile Durkheim, *The Evolution of Educational Thought*, trans. Peter Collins (London: Routledge and Kegan Paul, 1977).

20. See Sahlins, *Culture and Practical Reason*; and Edward Shils, *Tradition* (Chicago: University of Chicago Press, 1981).

21. See Jere L. Bachrach, "Andarab and the Banijurids," *Afghanistan Journal*, 3:4 (1976), pp. 147–50.

22. Dupree has an interesting discussion of the discriminatory pressure placed on the Qizilbashes, who were Shi'ite. See Louis Dupree, "Further Notes on Taqiyya: Afghanistan," *Journal of the American Oriental Society*, 99:4 (1979), pp. 68–82; see also Louis Dupree, *Saint Cults in Afghanistan*, American University Field Staff Reports, South Asia Series, vol. 20, no. 1 (1976).

23. See Marshall G. S. Hodgeson, *Venture of Islam* (Chicago: University of Chicago Press, 1974), vol. 2.

24. Ali B. Uthman Hujwiri, *The Kafsh al-Mahjub: The Oldest Persian Treatise on Sufism,* trans. R. A. Nicholson (London: Luzac, 1910 [c. 1050]), pp. 212–14.

25. Arnold Fletcher, *Afghanistan: Highway of Conquest* (Ithaca, N.Y.: Cornell University Press, 1965).

26. Quoted in Dupree, *Afghanistan,* p. 419.

27. Ibid., p. 420.

28. Robert L. Canfield, *Hazara Integration into the Afghan Nation: Some Changing Relations Between Hazaras and Afghan Officials,* Occasional Paper No. 3 (New York: Afghanistan Council of the Asia Society, 1971).

29. Klaus Ferdinand, "Preliminary Notes on Hazara Culture," *Historiskfilosofiske Meddelelser Udgivet af Det Kongelige Danske Videnskabernes Selskab,* Bind 37, nr. 5. (Copenhagen: Ejnar Munksgaard, 1959); Klaus Ferdinand, "Nomadic Expansion and Commerce in Central Afghanistan: A Sketch of Some Modern Trends," *Folk* 4 (1962), pp. 123–59; Canfield, *Hazara Integration into the Afghan Nation;* Robert L. Canfield, "Suffering as a Religious Imperative in Afghanistan," in Thomas R. Williams, ed., *Psychological Anthropology* (The Hague: Mouton, 1976), pp. 465–86.

30. Canfield, "Suffering." Thomas J. Barfield, *The Central Asian Arabs of Afghanistan: Pastoral Nomadism in Transition* (Austin: University of Texas Press, 1981), provides an excellent example of the impact of the sudden availability of cash markets on pastoralists in Qataghan.

31. See Stewart, *Fire in Afghanistan;* and Poullada, *Reform and Rebellion in Afghanistan* and Canfield, "Islamic Coalitions in Baurian."

3

The PROSPECTS for STATE BUILDING in AFGHANISTAN

RICHARD S. NEWELL

AMONG THE MANY VICTIMS of the Marxist usurpation of 1978 and the Soviet invasion of 1979 has been the Afghan state. Since mid-1979 the government based in Kabul has been incapable of functioning as a credible and legitimate source of political authority within Afghan society. Instead, the apparatus of the state has been overwhelmed by the anarchy and violence ignited by virtually universal resistance to Soviet occupation forces and their client regime, the Democratic Republic of Afghanistan.

Amidst the turmoil, the writ of all the political protagonists in Afghanistan is severely limited. It runs hardly at all for the government led by Babrak Karmal, which has not been able to unite its warring Parcham and Khalq factions and is reduced to posing as an administrative and political facade for its Soviet sponsors. The authority of the occupation forces extends further, but only to the cities and provincial capitals which account for little more than 10 percent of the population. Effective governance also eludes the grasp of the resistance despite its popular support. Lacking the weapons and military organization to dislodge the heavily armed Soviet forces, the resistance is further hampered by parochial and ideological fragmentation which prevents it from asserting a unified claim to national political authority. Accordingly, there is no complex of institutions currently operating in Afghanistan that can meet the minimal criteria for the broadest definition of a state.

In order to assess the breakdown and the prospects for the Afghan polity, we must attempt to define the state in an inclusive way that is applicable to a wide variety of cultural and political circumstances. To paraphrase Richard Cohen,

> the state is a political authority, organized hierarchically, capable of overcoming internal factionalism and succession disputes in order to perpetuate itself for at least several generations. It has the administrative capacity to impose a monopoly of coercive sanctions upon the society it governs (which its practitioners may elect not to exercise completely). Its functions require a persistent, professional bureaucracy designed to supercede, coopt or absorb such preexisting authority structures as were rooted in the primordial elements of the society in question. The state's greater capacity to control and mobilize human resources enables it to initiate new levels of activity, e.g., new or expanded modes of production, extensive long-distance trade, complex logistical connections. Frequently, it energetically modifies its ecological setting and economy, most notably through irrigation or changes in cultivation and land tenure, through new technologies of mineral extraction and processing, or through imposition of new relationships between major participants in the economy such as farmers and herders, capital and labor, etc. The state is controlled by an elite which either created it to protect or extend its previously established interests or which seized authority from other contenders in the process of creating a governing apparatus.

In addition to these features, it is essential to add the dimension of ideology which furnishes religious sanction or identity to the state, and in recent times generates secular nationalism as the basis for its popular support. Ideology legitimates state claims to authority by mixing bodies of received knowledge and myth regarding the origin, history, and cultural traits which set the state and its society apart from rivals.

The state is not synonymous with society since the latter can be organized for political purposes through other institutions—kin or peer groups, charismatic leaders, sacral or cultic arrangements—all of which lack the structural and functional capacities of states. Moreover, society possesses intrinsically nonpolitical dimensions—esthetic, sensual, intellectual, technical—which overlap politics (and which the totalitarian state attempts to appropriate and control), but which exhibit distinctive institutional, motivational, and behavioral patterns.

Nor does the state necessarily require the modern, industrial capabilities of mass production and distribution, rapid transportation and instant communication, pervasive indoctrination or coercive technology in order to function viably for extended periods over large populations and land masses. Such different polities as the Roman, Mauryan, and several Chinese and Persian empires attest to this, as do the early modern monarchies of Western Europe. The modern state, however, is set apart from its precursors by the intensity of its impact on society as made possible by innovations in organization, ideology, and technology. The modern state is also associated with the formulation of a national identity, so much so that the twentieth-century concept of "state" is virtually synonymous with "nation-state."

The latter usage creates difficulties when the concept is applied to polities which have developed outside of the context of Western culture, the concept of nation being exclusively European in origin. Attempts to apply the hybrid concept "nation-state" universally are further complicated by its association with the phenomenon of nationalism generated by the American and French revolutions. Thus, isolation from such developments before the twentieth century meant that no polity outside of the West fitted the definition of a nation-state—with the possible exception of Japan. Non-Western polities have come to be doubly suspect in contemporary social science analysis of the nature of the state. Their national character is open to question since it must inescapably be the result of a recent adaptation of exotic ideas and institutions. Moreover, whether applied by Western or non-Western social scientists, the tools for examining the state have been derived from the experience and perspectives of Western culture. The most venerable and visible of the Western nations, France, Great Britain, and the United States, serve as the models against which political systems that have emerged in the past century are compared. Evaluation of the character of such polities is burdened, therefore, with inherited or adopted ethnocentrism.

The possibility of confusion when the concept of the state is applied to societies such as Afghanistan's is particularly acute because of the massive impact of foreign influences that have been thrust upon them within little more than the past generation. The pressures of assimilation of alien skills, ideas, institutions, products, and funding have led to responses that suggest labeling their political systems as derivative, not integral, states. Examination of polities like Afghanistan's, therefore, calls for both a careful monitoring of cross-cultural assumptions and a sensitivity to the international pressures that have affected Afghan state building. Exaggeration of the significance of such exogenous factors must also be avoided. The recent collapse of political authority in Afghanistan dramatizes the persistence of endogenous features that have and presumably will continue to shape its polity regardless of the outcome of the current struggle. Three such factors warrant special comment: Afghanistan's physical legacy, its segmentary social institutions, and its Islamic heritage.

The IMPACT of LAND, SOCIETY, and ISLAM

Afghanistan's geopolitical setting and topography have set distinctive parameters for state building. It occupies a transitional region where the Iranian Plateau, the Central Asian steppes, and the northwestern corner of the Himalayan range intersect. Location has subjected it to a combination of influences from three of Asia's most enduring civilizations: the Indian, the Chinese, and the Irano-Islamic. It has also been continuously exposed to the marauding and occasional settlement of the most restless of inner Asia's nomadic peoples from the Indo-Aryans, Huns, and Turks, to their latter-day Uzbek and Turkoman counterparts. The political vacuum which opened between the collapsing Safavid and Moghal empires permitted the seeds of an indigenous Afghan polity to sprout in the mid-eighteenth century. Yet a new imperial rivalry, between the British and the Russians, shaped the actual boundaries of Afghanistan in the decades before the First World War. Exterior forces have thus played a large role in determining the demography and regional patterns of power within which Afghanistan's politics have developed.

The boundaries created by these imperial rivalries hold almost no value for either defending or defining an Afghan state. Only the Amu Darya River in the north can be considered a natural border. On nearly all sides Afghanistan's boundaries bisect major communities, leaving their population either hostage to the politics of neighboring governments or subject to irredentist impulses among Afghans themselves. Thus, the frontiers which cross plains, deserts, and mountainous regions are not amenable to the development of internal control or the creation of a political identity. Only the Hazaras, among Afghanistan's major communities, are not internationally partitioned.

Its interior geography has been no less inimical to state building. A harsh, arid climate of seasonal extremes and a rugged landscape have forced the scattering of most of the population into small ecological niches. Such niches demand tenacious subsistence-oriented economies and political competition underscored by scarcity and the mutual isolation of settlements. The largest peasant communities have developed within the basins of the four largest river systems, the Hari Rud, the Kunduz, the Helmand/Argandab, and the Kabul. These basins are separated from each other by difficult mountain terrain or by extensive arid plains. Most of the rest of the population is scattered in agricultural pockets squeezed within the narrow, upland valleys of the more mountainous regions. Some degree of outside contact has been maintained by the annual movements of nomads between the lower plains lying along the edges of Afghanistan and the alpine meadows in the central mountain core. These physical conditions joined with the constant pattern of invasion across the country to produce sociocultural systems organized to wrest subsistence from a stubborn environment and to protect themselves from a continual stream of dangerous intruders.

Closely linked to the broken and unyielding landscape is the intensely segmented nature of Afghan society. Circles of affiliation, mutual dependence, and loyalty extend outwards from individuals who possess a highly developed sense of self. When linkage becomes tenuous, reaching beyond the intimate degrees of kinship, exchange, or cooperation possible within close-knit village and nomadic communities, such common interests become progressively outweighed by rivalry, distrust, and prejudice. Localized patterns of origin and migration have interacted with the demographic fragmentation induced by the landscape to create a great degree of local particularism whose most obvious results are wide diversity of language, religious sectarianism, and economic isolation. The product has been an extraordinary proliferation of small agrarian enclaves, localized loyalties, and highly regionalized polities.[2]

For the great majority of the population this intensely local focus of institutions and behavior patterns is founded on sedentary, subsistence agriculture, commonly tied to complex small-scale irrigation networks. The immobility required by such economic arrangements tends to make many of the peasant settlements vulnerable to external interference and control. To some extent this threat has been mitigated by physical isolation and the limited wealth available to plunder or to tax. Throughout much of Afghanistan surpluses are too small and difficult to transport to attract exploitation. Local security is further buttressed by the development of inward-oriented attitudes and organization which stress kinship and intimate functional interdependence.

The resulting tendency toward clannishness of behavior and attitudes, often misleadingly associated with "tribalism," has been reinforced by two factors operative in most regions of Afghanistan, i.e., the interplay of mutual dependence and rivalry between herders and cultivators, and the prominence of individual self-assertion. The peasant-nomad connection has generated both rivalry and exchange. It offers wider political and economic horizons to sedentary communities while often forcing them to accept hierarchical status for the chiefs who are capable of defending their corporate interests against the nomads. Countering the tendency toward clientage has been the widespread pattern of independent land ownership which provides a foundation for an ethos of individualism. Taken together, these attitudinal and land tenure features account for the most pronounced aspects of segmentation in Afghan society. This inward-looking individualism is frequently identified with "tribalism" in explanations of Afghan institutions, social codes, and personality patterns. In fact, tribal affiliation applied in the literal sense of affiliations beyond the immediate linkages of kinship has little salience for nearly all of the non-Pashtun communities and for many sedentary and town-dwelling Pashtuns themselves.[3] The tribal misnomer, notwithstanding, the segmentary features that permeate the society—patriarchal, patrilinear organization of households and intensely localized arrangements for property control, labor division, dispute settlement, security maintenance, and marriage arrangements—do present difficult barriers against the successful imposition of centralized state authority.

Perhaps the most attractive advantage offered by a unifying state authority in a segmented society is the suppression of the violent rivalries endemic between essentially autonomous communities living in permanent scarcity. This pacification comes at the cost of extraction of goods, as taxes or tribute, and labor, as corvee or military conscription, and the imposition of sanctions that violate or interfere with locally derived mechanisms for maintaining security and justice. Given the primordial basis for segmentation in Afghan society, local responses to state authority can range from reluctant acceptance through elaborate avoidance devices to outright violent resistance. Such resistance can present a severe challenge to a state whose coercive powers are limited by the difficulties of extracting resources from a fragmented society and a mostly subsistence-oriented economy.

Islam has also proved to have an ambivalent effect on state building in Afghanistan. The near universality of Islam and a great Sunni preponderance, commonly estimated at 80 percent of the population, would appear to offer strong ideological and perhaps institutional support for the establishment of a state. The importance of Islam as a rallying force throughout Afghanistan against the Marxist governments and especially against the Soviet occupation, adds further credence to this assumption. Yet employment of Islamic symbols and interpretations of doctrine against the expansion of government authority has been notable throughout the twentieth century. Resistance based on religion has occurred despite determined efforts to coopt religious leaders and to enlist Islam's teachings into service to the state. Such attempts have largely failed because the segmented nature of Afghan society makes it extremely difficult for the state to manipulate religion to its own ends. The same social diversity that fragments politics and economics has also resisted a monolithic interpretation or application of Islam. Each community tends to identify Islam with its particualrist usages which are a mixture of local belief, practice, and sense of unique identity. This often results in dogmas that clearly contradict orthodox Shari'ah (the sacred Law of Islam) doctrines regarding rights of women, inheritance, management of disputes, and criminal punishments. Consequently, attempts to impose consensual or official versions of Islam tend to be seen locally as worse than interference, even as heretical. And when the state has been successful in using Islam to strengthen itself internally, as in Abdur Rahman's *jihad* (holy war) against the Shi'a Hazaras in the 1890s, the attempt brought a mixed result. It incited a popular Sunni movement to crush an alleged heresy, while it created lingering Hazara resentment which continues to impede the molding of a common sense of Afghan nationality.

The secular features of modern state building have incited opposition on the ground that they threaten or violate Islam. Such threats are seen in the content and organization of modern education, public health measures, public employment of women, and commercial banking, especially when any of these activities can be identified with Western origins. Thus, while religion has frequently been a unifying factor in the face of foreign interference, it has often been a source of internal resistance to the growth of state authority.

Despite the obstacles presented by its landscape, society, and religion, there is much evidence that supports the conclusion that considerable progress toward the creation of a national state had been achieved prior to the Marxist seizure of power in 1978. The nature of that achievement offers a number of insights into Afghanistan's political future regardless of the outcome of the present struggle.

STATE BUILDING UNDER the AFGHAN MONARCHY

State building in Afghanistan was carried out by a series of monarchs who transformed an amorphous tribal confederacy into a quasi-centralized state by the beginning of the twentieth century. Initially, Ahmad Shah Durrani gained ascendency over rival claimants to royal status within a loose grouping of Pashtun tribes that dominated Afghanistan after it became free of Iranian and Indian control early in the eighteenth century. For more than a century monarchy meant little more than a recognized claim to leadership among equals; Pashtun tribal khans offered their (often shifting) loyalties on a personal basis and presided over their own followers with little royal interference. Dynastic struggles between royal claimants remained chronic until the early twentieth century. Competition between royal candidates was waged between clans and within households divided by rivalries between cousins, halfbrothers, and brothers. Dynastic claims to Afghanistan as a whole were disputed until Dost Muhammad brought Herat under his control in 1863. Throughout this chaotic process royal authority largely rested on individual achievement, reputation and personality, and patronage links formed through tribal, regional, and cross-ethnic connections.[4]

The beginnings of an apparatus that could maintain rudimentary revenue records, collect taxes, and support an armed central force came under Sher Ali (1868–79) and, especially, Abdur Rahman (1880–1901). The latter built a standing army that eventually was well enough organized, disciplined, and equipped to overcome all regional challenges. Even so, it was recruited primarily through Durrani tribal connections.[5] Alternatively using terror and guile and the classical tactics of central aggrandizement—the holding of hostages against good behavior, divide and rule (between Pashtuns, between the minorities and the Pashtuns, between Sunnis and Shi'as), exemplary punishments, the championing of religious orthodoxy—Abdur Rahman eliminated or silenced all rivals. Yet the basis for perpetuating royal authority remained tenuous. Its fragility was demonstrated a generation later when tribal and peasant forces overwhelmed Amanullah's government (1919–29) after it had embarked on an ambitious set of social and constitutional reforms. The lack of an adequate administrative and political foundation on which to base such changes gave opponents the opportunity to whip up popular resentments against the most radical of Amanullah's reforms into a revolt that drove him from the throne.[6]

Among other things Amanullah's political demise in 1929 called the Pashtun's dominance of Afghanistan into question. They suffered the trauma of losing political control to the short-lived Tajik monarchy of Bacha-i Saqao (Amir Habibullah II) after Pashtun ascendency had earlier appeared assured with the successes of Abdur Rahman against the Uzbeks, Turkomans, and Hazaras. The backing of several of the Pashtun tribes made possible the restoration of royal authority by the Musahiban family under Nadir Shah (1929–33) after the nine-month reign of Bacha-i Saqao. Afghan state building has since been characterized by a double standard in policy and treatment applied to Pashtuns generally in contrast to the minorities. Musahiban policy was especially influenced by the debt it owed to levies of the Jaji, Mangal, Jadran, Ahmadzai, and Waziri tribes who lived across from or adjacent to the frontier shared with British India.[7] The dynasty acknowledged this support by exempting them from taxation and military conscription and giving special recognition to the autonomy of their tribal institutions. To a lesser degree this policy diluted Musahiban authority over most of the principal Pashtun groups. Later, this ethnic favoritism was expressed in the development priorities given to Pashtun regions. All three of the most ambitious agricultural projects developed since the late 1940s are located in Pashtun areas: the Helmand Valley and Ningarhar and Paktya provinces. Hydroelectric projects are likewise clustered in eastern Afghanistan where Pashtuns live in valleys adjacent to Kabul. Development in northern and western Afghanistan came more slowly and has also been associated with a marked movement of Pashtuns to the sites of such projects.

Indulgence of the Pashtuns also had a great impact on Afghanistan's foreign relations and internal cultural policies. By far the most portentous results came from Musahiban policy on Pashtunistan. Reacting to the British refusal to offer Pashtuns living east of the Durand Line the alternative of independence in the transfer of power to Pakistan in 1947, the Kabul government refused to recognize Pakistan's claims to the territory west of the Indus River. Afghan policy was instead to insist upon the establishment of an independent state, Pashtunistan, in the ambiguously defined region. Devised at least partially as a means to retain internal Pashtun loyalty, the policy led to a series of confrontations with Pakistan climaxing in border skirmishes and the blocking of Afghan transit rights through Pakistan in 1961. Bilateral relations were poisoned by the impasse and this led directly to the decision to accept greatly expanded military and economic assistance from the Soviet Union following Moscow's declarations of support for Afghanistan's Pashtunistan policy. Ethnic politics thus came to be linked to events that greatly increased Soviet influence.

Cultural policy was similarly shaped to assure Pashtun support of the Musahiban government. Pashtu was declared the national language, although Persian (Dari) was the interethnic language spoken in nearly all of Afghanistan's communities. Strenuous efforts were made, especially in the 1950s, to require exclusive use of Pashtu in government operations. This included the mandatory study of Pashtu by the largely Persian speaking bureaucracy and the establishment of a Pashtu Academy to purify the language and stimulate the development and dissemination of its literature.

Under Nadir Shah (1929–33) and Hashim Khan (1933–46) the government combined Pashtun favoritism with a studied policy of reversing the social and educational policies, especially regarding women, that had led to religious opposition to Amanullah's rule. Such conservatism was designed to support its primary goal: the creation of the institutional, economic, and military basis for unchallengeable control over Afghanistan. The effort bore fruit in clear military superiority over all regional groups, including the Pashtuns, by the late 1950s. The Safi Pashtuns of (present-day) Laghman province were routed by the central forces under then General Muhammad Daoud in 1947. The Kabul government did not have to resort to the previous practice of recruiting levies of rival tribes in order to put down the revolt. When the more dreaded Mangal Pashtuns of Paktya province inadvertently killed a military officer in the course of an intertribal dispute in 1959, thousands of them fled headlong into Pakistan rather than face a confrontation with the armored and air units sent against them by the government.[8]

This successful exercise of central power was largely the achievement of Daoud after he had become Prime Minister under Zahir Shah (1933–73) in 1953. This became possible as a result of the air and armored equipment and extensive military training provided by the Soviet Union. Government control over the population thus came at the cost of an open-ended political relationship with a neighboring global power. There was considerable precedent for accepting military aid. Afghan rulers had received military subsidies from British India as early as the reign of Dost Muhammad (1842–63) and in the early 1920s Amanullah had accepted Soviet technical and military assistance in establishing an air force. Daoud was to find, however, that assistance on a scale that insured control of internal affairs and a modest deterrent of a usually hostile Pakistan required a degree of dependence that substantially affected Afghanistan's international posture and domestic political climate.

Soviet influence increased primarily through the presence of military advisers in Afghanistan and the training of officer candidates in the Soviet Union. Once these Afghan trainees returned to duty, their careers were tied both to their ability to carry out Soviet military technique and doctrine and by their relationship to the Russian advisers assigned to modernize the armed forces. Even if Afghan officers were not influenced by political indoctrination, their dependence on Soviet military assistance created an institutional ethos which inescapably separated the armed forces from the rest of Afghan society. The government was fashioning a tool for control which increasingly acquired the capacity and would eventually generate the inclination to seize political power itself.

Backed by this dangerous instrument, the royal government in the late 1950s embarked on programs of national integration and development which were unprecedented in their impact on the population as a whole. Large-scale foreign aid, mostly Soviet and American, made it possible to build the physical infrastructure that enabled the government to extend its contact with and deepen its impact on the great majority of the population. By the mid-1960s Afghanistan's principal economic and political regions were linked by a system of all-season roads. Regular air service and telecommunications made possible effective supervision of subprovincial agencies in all but the most isolated and least populated areas of the country. As a result, central authority steadily penetrated most segments of Afghan rural society. A simultaneous expansion of the education system quickly produced a new generation of officials which was employed to bring the towns and many villages to the threshold of a largely foreign-supported modernization process.

Wherever it became firmly established, the administrative machinery abruptly became potent in its effect upon individuals. Photo-identity cards, the *tazkiras*, introduced in the 1940s became required of all males. They provided the information base for imposing a virtually universal military and police conscription system and for improving the collection of taxes and the maintenance of order. General success in establishing the tazkira system not only markedly increased government authority over most regional communities, but also served as an index to the accompanying spread of government services. Possession entitled the holder to medical treatment, enrollment in school, eligibility for employment, and public assistance when indigent. Depending upon the region, three or four tiers of government were installed in the provinces. They were able to move beyond policing and tax collection to dispute resolution, public education, and rudimentary public works. As the role of government in the countryside became more active in the 1960s and 1970s, it became more positively oriented toward development and its capacity to identify, manipulate, mobilize, and motivate rural Afghans greatly increased.

Simultaneously, the government took advantage of modern techniques of state building. It invested heavily in stimulating public consciousness of its presence by expanding cultural and propaganda programs through Radio Afghanistan and by increasing the number and sophistication of national and provincial newspapers and magazines. A high government profile was also generated by a nearly constant stream of senior government officials and their deputies traveling to the more accessible of the provincial capitals and subcapitals. Through display of its own officials, perhaps more than developmental and cultural programs, the central government became a presence to the large majority of Afghans who had paid it little attention previously. The linkage between government and population was reinforced by the holding of generally open elections for parliament in 1965 and 1969.

Whatever its successes in introducing public relations and popular political representation, the presence of a greatly reinforced rural bureaucracy also meant the imposition of arbitrary justice, labor extortion, and conscription with little chance for local complaint or redress. In the relationship between an official and residents of local communities, this often led to quasi-systematic arrangements for corruption and bribery. The patrimonial leaders of households, lineages, and peasant communities increasingly were forced into the position of having to negotiate moderation of government demands.

As the positive functions of the tazkira imply, government presence brought services as well as demands, although the former usually came more slowly and diffidently. By the mid-1960s the central impact began to include educational innovations in the towns and some villages and a scattering of multipurpose rural development projects, most notably in the more populous, politically crucial, and economically promising regions, i.e., Jalalabad, Kunduz, Paktya, and the Helmand Valley. Acquiescence to government authority grew as it became increasingly associated with development programs.

The popular mushrooming of interest in public education (usually for males) was the most remarkable example of rural enthusiasm for government innovations. The degree of support and the demands for expansion of the school system led actually to the swamping of higher education facilities in the early 1970s and thus to the ominous political problem of a swelling number of secondary and university-level graduates with new economic and political horizons but poor or no prospects for prestige jobs.

Health facilities grew more slowly; rudimentary rural clinics did not become common until the early 1970s. At about the same time a national system of community development projects was beginning to have an impact on cultivation practices, crop yields, and access to more favorable credit. But new forms of bureaucratic arrogance crept in as well, e.g., in crop-processing programs which arbitrarily set prices on the cotton and sugar beets that farmers were forced to sell to government-run mills. Despite such interference and the obvious favoritism shown the cities—above all, Kabul—expanded central control and innovations in development stimulated new interests and activity among a large section of the rural population. Internal trade and travel grew rapidly. Legitimate commerce more effectively competed against smuggling networks. Urban migration accelerated and it became increasingly diverted from Kabul to the larger provincial capitals. Institutional linkages within education, commerce, culture, and religion began to lengthen. While most villages in the more remote valleys and corners of Afghanistan—the Hazarajat, Badakshan, Maimana and the northwest, and Sistan in the far southwest—remained cut off from the new arteries of transport, bulk movements of goods and public transportation rapidly spread between all of the cities and most of the regions.

The new institutional connections were accompanied by partially fulfilled efforts to co-opt rural and regional communities into new forms of political involvement. Despite limitations in its implementation, the popular parliamentary system created in the Constitution of 1964 provided an inducement for participation by community leaders, secular and religious. This was most clearly demonstrated in the 1969 election after the potential political importance of the lower house, the Wolesi Jirgah, had been demonstrated.[9]

Evidence that centrally based institutions, virtually all identified with government, were spreading and beginning to penetrate society throughout Afghanistan can be documented abundantly. For the first time policy makers in Kabul appeared to be in a position to shift their concern from control of the population to the development of the economy and the fashioning of a sense of a common national culture. Subsequent events have amply demonstrated, however, that the segmentary nature of Afghan society had not been fundamentally altered and the changes introduced had yet to penetrate to the point where widespread religious resentment was generated. Barriers to a definitive achievement of central control and national integration remained.

MARXIST RULE, SOVIET INVASION, and the RESURGENCE of REGIONAL RESISTANCE

Marxists were able to seize control of government as a result of the success of the quasi-conspiratorial Khalq party in winning the cooperation of military officers dissatisfied with the Daoud regime for a variety of ideological, sociological, and political reasons. Within a few days of the April 1978 coup, it was clear that the Khalq leadership under Noor Muhammad Taraki had wrested control of the revolutionary government from officers who advocated a military dictatorship.

The purge of Khalq's Marxist rivals in the Parcham party took longer. By the fall of 1978 Khalq was in a position to initiate the set of policies that was to determine its relationship with the rural population. The resulting chaos and civil warfare led once again to the loss of central control over the great majority of the population. The mixture of coercion and consensus created under the monarchy dissolved as a consequence of Khalq's obtuse and feckless application of Marxist ideology.[10] Ironically, most of the content of the reforms that inflamed all sectors of the rural population, Pashtuns and minority communities alike, had been tentatively attempted by earlier governments. Land redistribution had been begun by Daoud's republic. Universal compulsory education had been a major aim of policy during the constitutional period (1963–73), although sensitivity to custom and limited expectations caused female enrollment to lag far behind. Registration and minimum age requirements for marriage and discouragement of expensive bride prices had been attempted several times beginning with Abdur Rahman. What convulsed the population were the heavy doses of Marxist propaganda combined with abrupt, confused, and arbitrary attempts of newly posted, inexperienced officials to impose such changes. The irrelevance of Marxist class theory to the essentially segmentary character of Afghan society aside, the peasants and the nomads reacted to what they saw as interference in religious and social matters, not improvements, in the fiats declared by the new regime.

Obscured by the resulting turmoil were Soviet-inspired and directed efforts by the new government to win minority support through the promotion of cultural—especially linguistic—identity. The languages of the Uzbeks, Turkomans, Baluchis, and Nuristanis were recognized as national languages. Minorities were represented prominently in appointments to the cabinet and the revolutionary council. Government television and radio programming placed a heavy emphasis on the visual and literary facets of the northern minorities in patterns clearly derived from policies developed in Soviet Central Asia. Soviet language and culture experts were quickly installed in the ministry of education where they were able to oversee the preparation and distribution of classroom materials in the minority languages. Editions of the works of minority poets which had been denied publication by previous governments suddenly appeared.[11]

These attempts to attract minority support drew little involvement beyond the cultural programming generated by the media and the co-opting of nominal representatives of the minorities who later attended the rallies of Parcham's National Fatherland Front. The strategy of using education backfired as well since it too required making the school system a major conduit of political persuasion. To meet Marxist objectives the schools were turned over to young teachers who were enthusiasts for the revolution. Compulsory attendance was required. Such steps produced a direct confrontation with rural sensitivities regarding state intrusion into family authority over children and government dictation of the roles and status of women. Thus, the cultural/political enticements offered by Kabul were lost in the storm of resentments touched off at the local level by the attempted reforms. The minority communities were the first to rebel against Khalq policies and officials.

Fighting first began in Nuristan largely over resentment against the purging and execution of senior military and police officers from the community who had prominently benefited from political patronage under Daoud. Nuristanis attacked police outposts in the summer of 1978, leading the Khalq government to mobilize neighboring groups, most notably the Gujars, in a so-called jihad. This revolt was followed by an Uzbek/Tajik uprising in the far northeastern province of Badakshan and by a concerted revolt throughout the Hazarajat. In both regions large areas were sealed off from government control and the towns were either seized or besieged. During the winter of 1978-79, revolt spread to the Pashtuns. When warm weather returned, the Khalq regime faced an uprising that included all of Afghanistan's major ethnic and regional communities.

RETROSPECT and PROSPECT

The Marxist coup and the Soviet invasion have severed central authority from the painfully built architecture of coercion, co-option, and mutual restraint that had previously held Afghanistan together under the monarchy. The patrimonial connections that helped legitimize Kabul's rule, especially with the Pashtuns and some of the more remote minority chiefs, died with Daoud. The identification of the state with Sunni Islam that had been achieved by Abdur Rahman and revived by the early Musahibans ended in the fall of 1978 when the Khalq government literally raised the red banner of Marxism-Leninism. Parcham's claims that it is returning to state protection and support of religion are negated by its military dependence on the Soviet army and the legion of Russian advisers running the government. All of the ideological and nearly all of the paternalistic foundation on which central authority had rested has been destroyed. Between government and population only force remains. It is orchestrated by the application of modern military technology on the one side and by the elusive, small-group tactics of lightly armed guerrilla forces on the other. With few exceptions, the central regime has lost control of all but the urban population (which is deeply penetrated by the resistance and in several instances has made bloody attempts at revolt).

The Afghan resistance is rooted in the primordial social bases available in the various regional/ethnic communities. Its leadership is a blend of traditional community notables and members of the urbanized elite, civilian and military, who have returned to the countryside to oppose the central regime. As in the past, opposition is fragmented and factionalized, reflecting the social and spatial segmentation of Afghan society. These divisions limit its effectiveness, especially in gaining international support, but together with the sense of outrage at interference with Islam they virtually assure its universality. The resistance is supported by the population but cannot dislodge the government and its patron without at the very least a large infusion of suitable military equipment, the achievement of tactical coordination, and a Soviet judgment that the costs of subduing Afghanistan exceed the benefits.

Prospects for the Afghan state, therefore, remain profoundly in doubt. Its collapse in 1979 has to be seen as the result of more than Marxist incompetence and miscalculation. Earlier failures to broaden popular affiliation and participation had left the monarchy under Zahir Shah and Daoud's republic vulnerable to internal political threats. This weakness reflected the incomplete nature of the Afghan state. Personal loyalties to the monarchy had not been substantially reinforced by a state apparatus which could simultaneously assert control, expand services, and generate ideological allegiance. Control over the population depended on foreign inputs which were highly visible, most notably from the Soviet Union and the United States. Economic, educational, and institutional development were also closely identified with foreign technical and financial assistance. Almost all of the rapidly growing new class of modern educated, socially mobile Afghans had studied abroad. Their political and economic expectations were shaped by foreign models; their prospects were constrained by the inability of the political system to provide promising careers or political roles for them. In the very process of attempting to create a modern state, the government had raised the expectations of the elite needed to operate it beyond a level it could satisfy. By allowing the pace of political and social change to be determined by foreign assistance and advice, the government also ran the risk of alienating the governing elite from the bulk of the population whose chances of participating in or profiting from the expansion of the state apparatus remained marginal. State building in Afghanistan was thus constricted by the failure to root institutional and political change in the human resources and social institutions integral to its indigenous culture. Alienated both from the rural communities and from the new educated class they had created, the monarchy and later the republic increasingly faced a political vacuum.

Perhaps a different set of policies might have overcome the obstacles presented by Afghanistan's land, society, and religion. To have done so would have required a more indigenously supported process, certainly one that was less dependent on foreign ideas and resources than was undertaken by the liberals under Zahir Shah and by Daoud in an attempt at populist dictatorship. Given their failures, one can say that Afghanistan had an incipient state which succumbed to the pressures of internal demands compounded by its dependence on foreign assistance.

Recent attempts to build a Marxist state have fared even worse. The dependence of the post-1979 government on foreign military and political support has become absolute. Afghanistan's future polity is now subject to the dialectic of a war of occupation and resistance. It has already become protracted, the material superiority of the Soviets being offset by the tenacity and universality of the resistance.

Given the complexity of the global and regional factors playing on the conflict, concrete prediction of its outcome and, therefore, the prospects for a future Afghan polity is impossible. There are enough variables to make for innumerable alternative results. Even so, the realities that have already confronted the building of political systems in Afghanistan suggest that the following alternatives are the most likely:

Alternative One: Soviet forces eventually prevail by driving so much of the population off the land (into refugee status in Pakistan or Iran or to Afghan cities) that the resistance level is reduced to a point that allows control over the majority of the population and the reconstruction of the economy. This makes possible the installation of a Marxist totalitarian state on the model of those operating withint the Soviet bloc. Its authority rests on drastic demographic and economic changes that fundamentally alter the character of Afghan society. Traditional herding and subsistence agriculture are limited to the most remote and marginal communities. The polity comes to function on an economic base of extractive and processing industries and state-controlled commodity agriculture. The logistical problems facing Afghan unity are solved by ambitious construction programs. Social segmentation is overcome by large-scale relocation, especially urbanization, and massive attempts at indoctrination and education. Islam receives official recognition as the national religion, but its leadership and institutions become totally co-opted by the state as in Soviet Central Asia. There will be a state in Afghanistan; it will not be an Afghan state.

Alternative Two: The resistance forces prevail, forcing a Soviet withdrawal which is prompted by a combination of global and regional pressures on Moscow. This culminates a long process of tactical, political, and ideological amalgamation among the various resistance groups. An overriding sense of Afghan nationality emerges, born of a common struggle for physical, cultural, and religious survival. A representative, federal system of popular government consistent with the segmentary, locally autonomous character of Afghan society is accepted. Afghanistan survives as an agrarian polity with no dominant ethnic community, weakly governed at the center. (Presumably its national sovereignty would be guaranteed by international agreement.)

Alternative Three: Soviet withdrawal under similar circumstances to Alternative Two is followed by the emergence of a strong national government in Afghanistan motivated and disciplined by a commitment to a militant Islamic revival. This movement overcomes regional and sectarian opposition to the imposition of a unitary political order dedicated to carrying out a reformist interpretation of the Shari'ah. Led by a disciplined, highly organized elite that was created in the process of successfully combating the Soviet occupation, the new state embarks on a highly selective policy of economic development and social consolidation. It orients its foreign associations and trade closely to the Islamic community. Galvanized by the process of liberation, a strong, centralized Afghan state emerges which has modest and gradualist ambitions for economic and logistical integration.

Alternative Four: A partition of Afghanistan is imposed by the Soviet Union and surrounding regional governments. No Afghan state as such becomes possible.

Alternative Five: The present turmoil continues indefinitely with the Soviet forces consolidating control of the cities, administrative centers, military installations, and logistical network. Resistance groups continue to control all but the most accessible rural areas, sporadically challenging Soviet and Kabul government forces in the more populous, fertile valleys near Kabul, Herat, Qandahar, and Jalalabad. Afghanistan remains subject to a truncated garrison regime surrounded by hostile, often mutually contentious rural communities. The level and incidence of combat gradually drop to a point tolerable to both sides. Economic development, except possibly for some extractive gas and metals industries, remains stagnant because of security constraints on transportation.

In the last two alternatives Afghanistan's natural and social legacies combine with prevailing political factors to destroy the prospects for a functionally genuine Afghan state. A strong political order is imposed in the first alternative, but only under conditions that either make it a substate (of the Soviet system) or eventually a state governed by native Afghan Marxists over a society bearing little resemblance to the Afghanistan considered here.

Alternatives Two and Three offer the possibility of an independent Afghan state, but Alternative Two would be too weak to survive without an international guarantee, thus partially continuing Afghanistan's dependent status. Alternative Three presents the possibility of a centrally strong, internationally independent state. Its success would require not only great political discipline, presumably under a one-party system, but also a combination of imaginative and repressive solutions to the obstacles to national unity inherited from Afghanistan's legacy of individualism, social segmentation, and physical fragmentation.

NOTES

1. Ronald Cohen and Elman R. Service, eds., *Origins of the State: The Anthropology of Political Evolution* (Philadelphia: Institute for the Study of Human Issues, 1978), pp. 2–5. The quoted statement is a summary paraphrase of several points made in Cohen's introductory chapter.

2. See Robert L. Canfield's chapter in this volume, "Ethnic, Regional and Sectarian Alignments in Afghanistan," pp. 3–4.

3. Ibid., pp. 1–4.

4. Vartan Gregorian, *The Emergence of Modern Afghanistan: Politics of Reform and Modernization, 1880–1946* (Stanford, Calif.: Stanford University Press, 1969), pp. 49–51, 74.

5. Ibid., p. 161.

6. Leon B. Poullada, *Reform and Rebellion in Afghanistan, 1919–1929: King Amanullah's Failure to Modernize a Tribal Society* (Ithaca, N.Y.: Cornell University Press, 1973). See especially chap. 7, 9, and 12.

7. Louis Dupree, *Afghanistan* (Princeton, N.J.: Princeton University Press, 1973), p. 459.

8. Ibid., pp. 534–35.

9. Ibid., p. 652.

10. Nancy Peabody Newell and Richard S. Newell, *The Struggle for Afghanistan* (Ithaca, N.Y.: Cornell University Press, 1981), pp. 74–85.

11. Eden Naby, "The Ethnic Factor in Soviet-Afghan Relations," *Asian Survey*, 20:3 (March 1980), pp. 247–52.

4

The CHANGING ROLE of ISLAM as a UNIFYING FORCE in AFGHANISTAN

EDEN NABY

THE POSITION OF ISLAM as a component of Afghan self-identity and national identity has been radically effected by the events since April 1978. Following the ascent to political power of the Khalq/Parcham Marxist parties, and particularly subsequent to the Soviet invasion of their country in December 1979, Afghans in general and prominent leaders of the resistance in particular have come to assume, if not openly state, that the only force for uniting the broad spectrum of the Afghan people is a real or perceived threat to their Islamic way of life. This assumption provides but the first major reason why Islam has shifted from playing a relatively passive role toward an active role in integrating a diverse, multiethnic society. We may call this kind of resulting integration, tentative as it may prove to be, defensive integration. That is, fearing a loss of their traditional way of life, a life perceived to be bound together with Islam, disparate groups, some often antagonistic to each other, are waging battle against the same enemy. In some cases, the integration has advanced to a next stage. Groups and communities that had been traditionally enemies—for ethnic, religious, or economic reasons—have shown signs not only of not fighting each other, but of actually cooperating in the field. This kind of united front does not permeate all levels of Afghan society nor perhaps all segments of any one section. Nevertheless, a significant lessening of interethnic tensions is apparent.

A second, and possibly more significant, reason for the manifestation of Islam in its new integrative role within Afghan society, however, is less understood and studied. That is, the amalgam of newly educated rural elites from diverse ethnolinguistic backgrounds into a new community of like-minded persons, allied to each other mainly through aspiration for the formation of an Islamic republic in Afghanistan. This amalgam seeks to transcend previous allegiances of its members and to exhort them to struggle, not for the restoration of Afghan independence alone, but for the establishment of an Afghanistan that would forsake its former emulation of Western ("anti-Islamic") practices.

The significance of the role of the religious issue in Afghanistan since the Soviet invasion has eluded attention for several reasons. First, because the Afghan situation has degenerated into an East-West propaganda contest, and because neither Moscow nor Washington places political value on Islamic ideology or perceptions, the Afghan resistance is largely viewed in secular terms such as nationalism, international socialism, secure borders, and Persian Gulf oil. Second, most Westerners, be they seasoned scholars or journalists, are unable to divest themselves of the assumption that the separation of church and state remains the only logical and realistic political path open to modern man. Therefore, Islam as a genuine political force as opposed to a political tool is regarded with skepticism. Third, not only does the Soviet government share with the West this disbelief in the political significance of Islam, but it attempts to portray the Afghan resistance in the kind of ideological light it chooses to shed on the anti-Bolshevik movement in Central Asia during the 1920s. Calling the Afghan resistance "bandits" and even "Basmachis," the pejorative term applied to Central Asian resisters to the Red Army, the Soviet government seeks to accomplish two purposes: to convince the Afghan resistance that its opposition to Soviet power will be similarly crushed; and to remind would-be sympathizers among Soviet Central Asians that opposition to Soviet rule there would be meted the same fate it was sixty years ago.[1] Finally, less from political cynicism and more out of ignorance, the West too has mislabeled the Afghan Islamic revolutionary movement, attaching to it the uninformative and misleading term "fundamentalist," a catchall label that obfuscates that which may be new, innovative, and vital.

Thus, despite a substantial volume of recent literature on the subject in Dari (Afghan Persian) and in Pashtu, the nature of Islamic ideology among the Afghan resistance has received only cursory attention from most writers. Nor have past works on the country focused on Islamic beliefs and practices among the Afghan elites and the general population in the countryside and their effects on state formation, patterns of allegiance, and social and ethnic coherence. A few anthropological studies form the exception, but these are less concerned with theology and history of religion than with folk religious custom and the superstitions attached or associated with Islam.[2]

A further handicap results from the virtual absence of any intellectual or institutional histories of Afghanistan.[3] This is in sharp contrast to Iranian and Pakistani studies where such research forms a prominent part of the materials available on the cultural history of each country. While there may be some validity in the assumption that Afghan intellectual history exists as an appendage to that of Iran and that, on its own, Afghan cultural life has been negligible, nevertheless, since the 1920s Afghanistan has been perceived as a place of refuge for Muslims from north, south, and east. This interpretation is based on the existence of an Islamic climate in the country, especially as it is associated with the Sufi (Islamic mystical) orders. Thus, a systematic study of Islamic institutions, leaders, and thought during this century in Afghanistan remains a lacuna in our knowledge. The present contribution is intended to serve as a very preliminary effort to fill part of this gap.

In this chapter I will describe the position of Islam in Afghanistan during this century, first from the period in which full independence from Great Britain was achieved in 1919 to the occurrence of the Marxist coup in 1978, and then during the subsequent years in which the Afghan resistance has organized, aligned, realigned, and sharpened its ideological position.

ISLAMIC INSTITUTIONS and LEADERSHIP

Islam in the Afghan Context

It has been argued that because Islam has not been a force in ruling Afghanistan in the past, the religious motivation of the Afghan resistance does not translate into a long-term political role for Islamic leaders in a future Afghanistan.[4] Nevertheless, most of those who look at the character of the Afghan resistance movement are struck with the Islamic symbolism and the appearances and expressions of piety that are made.[5] To assume that all of the Afghan resistance leadership is attempting to use Islam as a substitute for an absent political or national unity, however, would be to view the matter of religion in Afghan history too simplistically. For although the role of religion has differed in Iran, Pakistan, and Afghanistan, the interaction between Islam and secular government has played and continues to play a major role in shaping Afghan history.

To begin with, one may look at Afghanistan's population. Statistics in a formal sense do not exist by confession as they do in Iran and Pakistan. In Afghanistan, however, only a negligible number of non-Muslims may be found. These include relatively poor urban Jews, most of whom emigrated to Israel by the 1960s, and some Sikhs and Hindus, scattered, again, in urban areas. These groups never wielded political influence whether by virtue of wealth, professional and intellectual attainment, or number.[6] In Iran, on the other hand, Zoroastrians, Christians, and Jews, and more recently Baha'is, break the Islamic homogeneity of the country and have played some political role either individually or collectively. In Pakistan, Christians, Sikhs, and Hindus, albeit to a lesser extent than their counterparts in Iran, have played a similar role. In this respect, Afghanistan may be more profitably compared to the rest of Central Asia where, during the pre-1917 period the only indigenous non-Muslims consisted of relatively small numbers of Bukharan Jews and Hindus who lived in towns.

Thus, when one speaks of Islam as a political force in Afghanistan, one must place it within the appropriate social context: within Afghanistan Islam has not, until the Soviet invasion, faced a formidable challenge from the outside. Colonial or missionary pressures have been negligible in comparison with neighboring countries. On those occasions when the rural or to a lesser extent, the urban popualtion, but especially the religious tribal leadership, has perceived an internal challenge to its authority, the opposition to that challenge has been clothed in Islamic garb. Witness the undoing of the reign of King Amanullah (r. 1919–29) which, although the result of a power struggle between the center and the countryside, especially of eastern Afghanistan, nonetheless took on a religious overtone. This culminated in the nine-month reign in 1929, by the Tajik Habibullah II (Bacha-i Saqao), the sole interruption of Pashtun rule of the country since its eighteenth-century origins. The opposition to

Amanullah succeeded in convincing large segments of the Pashtun and non-Pashtun population that the social reforms put into effect by the King were Western-instigated attacks on Islam. Thus, the Habibullah II period was marked by a reversal in the controversial and obviously antitraditional changes, i.e., dress codes for men and women and educational and juridical changes. Religion became a focal point for opposition that was essentially political.[7] More frequently than not, however, political struggle in modern Afghan history has revolved around power bases apart from Islam. This is not to say that they have not included religious leadership as in the above example. But the religious leadership has acted in its capacity as a political power base. Past power struggles have been waged between pastoral nomads and sedentary agriculturists vying for land in the countryside and highlighted by virtual autonomy of the rural Pashtun tribes and the continuing modus vivendi of the Hazarajat with the central government where limited direct authority was exerted by Kabul.

Another traditional arena for political struggle, tribal versus nontribal struggle for territory and power, may be illustrated by Kirghiz versus Tajiks in the Wakhan and foothills, as well as by Turkomans versus villagers of western Afghanistan. Ethnolinguistic groups also provide a constant source of friction, sometimes involving subtribes but frequently engaging two separate ethnolinguistic groups such as the Hazara and Pashtun. In many cases, these three categories overlap; for example, the Hazara case involves settled versus nomadic, tribal versus nontribal, as well as different ethnolinguistic groups.

One source of potential conflict, that between the dominant Sunni and the minority Shi'ite population, has in fact not served as the source of widespread friction. However, once a conflict has erupted, sectarianism has become a point for unified action on either side. Thus, Sunni ulama (Islamic clergy) at the request of Amir Abdur Rahman (r. 1880-1901) issued fatwas (formal legal opinions) condoning attacks on the Shi'ite Hazaras as well as on the Amir's rebellious cousin, Ishaq Khan, who, it was alleged, had sold his religious values for Russian aid.[8] In the case of Abdur Rahman, what was invoked to supplement the muscle needed to uphold central authority was traditional religion. The Shi'ites were condemned for simply being Shi'ite, while Ishaq Khan was condemned for being unIslamic in a broad sense.

The Religious Establishment and the State

During the twentieth century, tensions between the Afghan state and the religious establishment have generally resulted in the apparent victory of the state until the erosion of the power of the ruling clique offers a vacuum in which the religious elements can attempt to redress the balance of power. The history of Islamic institutions in Afghanistan, however, for the most part, reveals a decline in two important spheres: the educational and the juridical.

The cornerstone of intellectual and theological activity, prior to the eventual establishment of Western-style schools, had been the Islamic educational system. This sytem, however, had not developed as fully in Afghanistan as in neighboring countries because Afghanistan traditionally remained part of a far larger cultural sphere with ties to the subcontinent, Central Asia, and Iran. Political pressures, coupled with Afghan xenophobia, reduced channels for continued cultural contact with neighbors. With no recognized centers of learning and a lean economy, the endowed Islamic institutions never fully developed in the cultural isolation into which Afghanistan plunged during the height of the colonial struggles of the eighteenth and nineteenth centuries. Herat and Balkh, both centers of Muslim culture and learning, even as late as the fifteenth century, became provincial battlegrounds in the political struggle waged between warring Pashtun factions for control of Kabul. It was not until the relative stability of the Abdur Rahman period in the late nineteenth century that some attempt was made to revive educational institutions.[9]

With the loss of vigor of the educational establishment came a decline in religious leadership. Not only could fewer persons understand the Arabic in which the scriptures were read and the prayers recited, but the quality and availability of traditional education were affected. The *maktabs* (elementary schools for Islamic learning) that operated in the countryside, and even into the 1950s provided the major source of literacy in rural villages for Afghan boys, depended solely on the quality of the local *mullah* (religious scholar). Since the 1930s these mullahs have been partially financed by the government (and partly paid from local contributions) and over the last few decades more elementary schools have been established in villages. But even these and other steps have not helped to offset the drawbacks presented by secularization of the curriculum and the language of instruction, the quality of teachers, and the availability of teaching materials. The few *madrasahs* (advanced schools for Islamic learning) that existed in the country suffered from insufficient curriculum update and lack of contact with Islamic centers elsewhere. Moreover, their limited number meant that only the well-to-do could afford a good Qur'anic education. Few Afghans could undertake the expense of attending Indian, Bukharan, or other foreign institutions.[10]

An added casualty of the decayed educational establishment was the closing of an important avenue for exceptional members of traditionally less privileged ethnic groups to escape from existing social and economic restrictions. Bright and hardworking boys could not hope to climb the social and political ladder through strength of exceptional intellect. In contrast, in the neighboring Bukharan Khanate, a backwater of the Islamic world, numerous well-endowed madrasahs operated even during periods of relative intellectual stagnation. As poor and ethnically denigrated boys benefited from the scholarship system of the madrasahs and rose above the station into which they were born, they were able to champion the cause of their ethnic group.[11] Thus, the religious educational institutions that in other parts of the Muslim world have traditionally served to some extent to unify elements of ethnic groups, especially the budding intellectuals of society, did not operate to any appreciable degree in Afghanistan.

The weak position of clerics affected their ability to deal with two other power sources in Afghan society: the Sufi orders and the Kabul authorities. The Sufi orders, important in the religious and political life of Afghanistan for centuries, have continued to remain traditionally relatively free of formal institutions: that is, the two important orders, the Naqshbandiyya and the Qadirayya orders, rely for support upon the prominence of two important families (though not unchallenged, especially among the Naqshbandiyya) where leadership devolves along accepted Islamic lines of heredity. While these families may support and study at religious schools, their position is not dependent on scholarly recognition but on loyalty to the pir. In theory, then, these leaders evolve quite differently from the ulama in Muslim society and certainly from the Shi'ite scholastic leadership in Iran. In reality, the Mujadidi family that has long been associated with the Naqshbandiyya in Afghanistan has aspired to Islamic learning while the Gailani family that head the Qadiriyya order has not. In critical periods, the alienation of the Mujadidi family has resulted in considerable conflict between secular power and the religious establishment. The activities of the Hazrat of Shor Bazar (Mujadidi) in the overthrow of King Amanullah (1929) and his cooperation with Habibullah II and later with Nadir Shah (r. 1929–33) were pivotal, and in 1978-79, the Noor Muhammad Taraki government's arrest of key members of this family resulted in large-scale religious opposition. As the prestige of the clerics has decreased, the influence of the Sufi leaders has increased, although not proportionally due to the introduction of stronger secular institutions and a new wave of Islamic revivalists.

The eroded position of the clergy led to ultimately successful attempts by the government to gain control of key institutions such as the legal, educational, and *waqf* (endowments supporting religious authorities) systems. Although some setbacks occurred in the late 1920s, in subsequent decades the efforts of the Kabul authorities to introduce secular constitutions and secular schools gradually diminished the role of Islam on a formal level.

The Legal System, the Shari'ah, and the Pashtunwali

The four constitutions of Afghanistan (prior to 1978), called basic laws, reflect the changing role of Islam in the country. All agree on Islam as the state religion of the country: however, the insistence on the Hanafi school of Sunni jurisprudence as the school to be followed (as in the 1923 and 1931 Constitutions) has been relaxed.[12] By the time that the 1977 Constitution was presented to the Loyal Jirgah (Grand Assembly) for discussion, no mention appeared of any particular school of Sunni Islam nor even Sunnism. This development reflects, on the one hand, the decline of the role of religion in state affairs as perceived by the Kabul educated elite who drafted the constitution and, on the other, the increased jurisdiction of secular law. In addition, the dropping of this insistence on Sunni Islam paved the way for potentially easier integration of non-Sunni Muslim minorities into the slowly evolving national identity.

While, for example, non-Muslim religious minorities, specifically Hindus and Jews, have enjoyed tolerance of their beliefs and practices, they paid the *jaziyah* (poll tax for non-Muslims), were excluded from the military, and were enjoined from proselyzation and otherwise "disturbing" the Muslims, as stated in the 1923 Constitution. Payment of jaziyah and exclusion from the military were deleted in later constitutions to reflect the reduced attention to Islamic law.

As another example, Muslim sects that have been considered heretical have at times been outlawed, as during the relatively moderate period of Amanullah. According to the 1923 Constitution (Article 123), the Sabi, the Zendiq, and especially the Qadyani "were to be killed."[13] This reference to unacceptable sects has been dropped from later constitutions.

Through the introduction and gradual refinement of the legal codes, both in family and criminal law, the secular authorities also have attempted to reduce the jurisdiction of the Shari'ah (the sacred law of Islam) in various ways. At first, the rulers tried to increase their discretionary legal powers by removing from the Shari'ah those crimes that they wished to adjudicate personally. In most of these cases the crimes were of a civil nature where the Shari'ah did not prescribe the death penalty but the ruling group wished to do so.[14] In other cases, punishments prescribed by the Shari'ah, while on the books, have been retired from practice. For example, the stoning of a married adulterer or adultress no longer occurs.[15] Later taxes on polygamous marriages and the like marked the entry of secular courts into areas reserved for Islamic law.

In addition to the struggle to wrest jurisdiction from the *qazis* (religious judges), Afghan rulers also attempted to create uniformity in the legal codes by instituting national penal codes that would subject the Pashtunwali, the special rules of Pashtun tribal society, to the Shari'ah and later to secular courts. Certain basic rules of the Pashtunwali are clearly contrary to Islamic law and, moreover, endanger the establishment of a stable government. Since the 1920s Kabul has attempted to limit and control *badal* (blood feuds and clan or tribal vendettas), a primary element of Pashtunwali for which an elaborate code exists. *Riwaj* (sole male inheritance), again essential to the social structure of Pashtun tribes, though modified by Islam, has not been discarded in tribal areas without government intervention.[16] The government has justified this intervention into tribal law by drawing upon Islamic law where personal vengeance is codified and estates are inherited by females as well as males.[17]

Thus, in a sense, the secularization and codification of the legal system have offered rulers an opportunity to weaken the powers both of the religious establishment and of the tribes by fostering reliance on the ruler as the final arbiter of law. To perform this function as judge, the early amirs (rulers), including Amanullah, held periodic durbars at which time subjects would personally petition the monarch. To what extent this practice assured loyalty to the monarch is not clear. It would appear, however, to have increased reliance on him, raised his personal prestige, and damaged that of the qazis. By the 1920s, slavery, often practiced with ethnic discrimination, had been abolished. Although, in practice, access by either minorities or the poor to the monarch appears to have been limited, all Afghan Muslims were assumed equal before the law.

Accompanying the increased stature of the ruler as judge, an area largely allocated to Muslim law previously, was his rising position as an actual religious leader. Aside from having the *khutbah* (Friday sermon) mention his name, a traditional practice, the first constitution established a hereditary monarchy that bestowed on the monarch the title of Defender of the Faith. Indeed, as it became clear even to the hopeful Afghans that the Kemal Ataturk regime in Turkey would not reinstate the caliphate it had abolished, some discussion took place regarding the establishment of the caliphate in Afghanistan, with Amanullah at its head. Financial restraints, perhaps among other considerations, limited the pursuit of this idea. Its proposal, however, demonstrates the relatively high status as a Muslim that Amanullah enjoyed prior to his fatal missteps in tribal management. Afghanistan's initial generous reception of the subcontinental *muhajirin* (refugees) of the Hijrat movement (1920s) further attests to the regional importance of Afghanistan as an independent Islamic state despite the low quality of its religious establishment.

As the country moved toward secularization and erosion of the legal jurisdiction of the ulama, the need to create in the ruler a religious figurehead declined. Instead, the monarchy shifted toward becoming a military figurehead enjoined to defend the independence of the country and, only by extension, Islam. This tradition, begun at the time of Nadir Shah, an actual general, continued in the Musahiban family where several of the last monarch's generation received military training exclusively. With the creation of of Pakistan and contention over the issue of Pashtunistan, the military issue became more pronounced. Afghanistan armed itself against a fellow Muslim country and until the Islamic issue came to the fore again with the development of revivalist feelings among the newly educated rural youth in the 1960s, Kabul's concern was with the control of the Pashtun tribes rather than with disaffection by the religious establishment.

The Educational System and the Waqf

As the case of the Iranian religious political elites demonstrates, Islamic clergy depend upon the network of religious schools and upon charitable endowments to build and secure a cadre of followers, develop ideas, and disseminate them. In the absence of a viable madrasah system in Afghanistan, individuals aspiring to higher education, and those wishing religious education in particular, traditionally journeyed abroad, frequently to Russian Central Asia or British India.[18] This practice restricted the opportunity to organize a following on the home turf, to which the scholars returned, except in unusual cases or in cases where the scholar also could claim a Sufi following. When in the 1920s study at Deoband was barred, and simultaneously Soviet Central Asian madrasahs were shut, Afghans were bereft of inexpensive and easily accessible places to study. During the following decades only a few undertook the trip to the Arab world, mainly to al-Azhar in Cairo, as did Burhanuddin Rabbani, for example. Study there was complicated by the necessity to communicate, as well as study, in Arabic, rather than in Persian as had been the case in Bukhara and India. In 1944 the government began to exert its influence by establishing a school for the study of Islamic law. Six years later this facility became the Faculty of Islamic Studies, a part of Kabul University, and is held in high regard as the center for the training of young religious leaders and teachers. Interestingly, many important figures in the Afghan resistance movement have had direct or indirect ties to this Faculty.

Another useful method followed by clerics traditionally to gain and keep followers was through the disbursement of funds from charitable endowments. This avenue was shut to the Afghan clergy early in this century when Amir Habibullah (r. 1901-19) took over the waqf system. The Afghan government has continued to administer the purse since that time. The doling of these funds thus became one more method of government control over the religious establishment as mullah and mosque had to be maintained at the pleasure of the ruling clique. Even before the official takeover of the waqf institution by Habibullah, its actual control had begun to revert to the monarch. Amir Abdur Rahman withheld salaries and subsidies from the clergy of the Ghilzai confederation when it rebelled.[19] His grandson attempted to control the activities of Central Asian refugees of particular orthodoxy by refusing them subsidies or paying them very low ones.[20]

The isolation and restriction of the Afghan religious establishment, however, is quite different from the reduction of Islamic sentiment in the country and from the piety, real or superficial, that the general population expected. As the major cities, especially those closely associated with the royal family, lost contact with the major portion of the Afghan people. The traditional religious leadership, the clergy, received their training at a government institution (the Faculty of Islamic Studies), were paid by the government, and had their jurisdiction curtailed. The educational system, especially the secondary educational system, was beyond their control although the curriculum still included Islamic subjects. The Shari'ah courts operated within reduced spheres. In fact, the clergy had become part of the government bureaucracy. Its ability to mediate between the government and the people or to form bridges between the Kabul elites and the countryside had diminished.

By 1978 when the sudden Marxist coup occurred, the Kabul elites, clerical and secular, were left in disarray, imprisoned or shot. The Khalq government adopted an uncompromising attitude toward Islam and was quickly perceived as atheistically tyrannical. Leadership for the opposition, however, was slow to emerge and, when it finally did appear, it came from three chief sources: the Sufi orders, the ethnotribal leadership, and the newly educated revolutionary Islamic elements.

These three groups, often drawing on mutually antagonistic parts of the population, have attempted to strike a new path toward the amalgamation of state power and religious authority. In the process they choose to profess that Islamic egalitarianism and idealism will overcome ethnic rivalry and diversity. This proposed experiment seeks to reconstruct a new Afghanistan in which both ethnic differences and a modern state would emerge under the banner of Islam. In the following section we turn to the organizational dynamics of the Afghan religious resistance.

The AFGHAN RESISTANCE MOVEMENT

The Background of the Religious Parties

It has become common to hear the Afghan resistance described as fragmented and to interpret that fragmentation as the result of ethnic and tribal rivalry. This assumption, has become less true as the Afghan struggle has evolved. The acceptance of the fact that the Russians cannot be driven out through sheer military means, but must be forced out with a combination of methods, military and political, has sobered much of the resistance as have the heavy losses in life and property that their numbers have suffered. In Peshawar, for the first time, men who since the mid-1960s have called for change have an opportunity to put some of their ideas into practice among several millions of their countrymen. At the same time, the hardship of exile in Pakistan has thinned the ranks of some of the resistance groups, particularly those in which results were expected quickly and whose members had been accustomed to a relatively easy urban lifestyle. For these reasons, idealism and rhetoric have begun to give way to pragmatism.

Under pressure from the military resistance units in the field and from external funding sources, in 1985 the major political parties formed a unified structure with a three-month rotating leadership from among the leaders of the political parties. While this structure allows for increased cooperation and reduced intra-party suspicion, nevertheless the ideological differences continue. The six main Afghan resistance parties in Pakistan formed into two ideologically opposed camps in 1981 that reflected the basic conflicting ideology of the resistance. Below the surface of a unified resistance lies the ideological pattern that continues to affect political thought and possible future state formation under war free conditions. The pattern grows out of the recent history of confrontation between traditional conservative forces in uneasy alliance with a small group of urban intellectuals that seek a return to the pre-1978 conditions, and the newly emerging revolutionary Islamic groups that insist on making a fresh start toward construction of an Islamic state.[21] The following brief description highlights the essential philosophical differences of the two opposing groups.

The first camp, formalized in 1981 as the Islamic Alliance of the Mujahidin of Afghanistan, has gradually distanced itself from Islam as the primary driving force for resistance and has concentrated instead on appeals to Afghan nationalism. The Islamic Alliance follows the guidance of Sayyid Ahmad Gailani. Gailani, an urbane Kabul businessman, although lacking in personal charisma, is held in great reverence by large sections of Pashtun tribes because of his position as a Sufi pir and head of the Qadiriyya order in Afghanistan. His family's intermarriage with the ruling Kabul elites, his personal wealth, and generally Western orientation have earned him a reputation that attracts former bureaucrats to his side, makes him more acceptable to the West, especially to the United States, and, in the opinion of some, renders him a better candidate to compromise with the Soviet government on the restoration of an independent Afghanistan. Gailani and his coalition have become active in attempts to recruit the former king, Zahir Shah (r. 1933–73) into an active role in either leading the resistance or offering himself as a compromise figurehead leader in the event of a political settlement with the Soviet government. Gailani apparently views the former monarch as capable of attracting segments of the peasantry within the country, the refugees, and moderate Islamic countries to his Islamic Alliance camp. This hope is based on the assumption that many of the parties involved in the struggle for Afghanistan would regard a return to the pre- 1973 monarchist period, in foreign and domestic policy, as desirable. This assumption may not be valid and we shall explore the reasons why as we examine the second and opposing camp and the background and present position of the Afghan Islamic resistance.

The second camp, the Islamic Unity of Afghanistan Mujahidin, formed during the spring of 1981 also, is composed of revolutionary Islamic parties, opponents of the status quo ante position of the Islamic Alliance, and others who for ethnic considerations feel more comfortable with the ethnolinguistic diversity represented among the Islamic Unity's leadership. The core of this camp forms around two men of recent prominence, both rural (at least non-Kabul) backgrounds and unrelated to any of the traditional ruling elites, either politically or religiously. These men, Professor Burhanuddin Rabbani of the Jam'iat-e Islami (Islamic Society) party and Engineer Gulbuddin Hekmatyar of the Hizb-e Islami (Islamic Party), spent some years at Kabul University and were particularly influenced by men at the Faculty of Islamic Studies. The personal charisma of these men, their personal piety, and their freedom from past blemished associations appear to have resulted in a larger following and better organization and cohesion among their coalition parties than that of the Islamic Alliance. A general summary of the political climate in which these relatively disciplined Islamic parties emerged will help to explain their success in the resistance.

Aggressive Islamic politics entered Afghan affairs quietly during the mid-1960s in the course of the hiatus between the two periods of Daoud's rule. From 1965 to 1973 Afghanistan experienced about eight years of chaotic and shifting constitutional government. It was a period in which many changes were taking place in the country, including educational expansion, economic development projects, and agricultural improvement attempts. But it was also a most important time politically both as many elements of rural power began to participate in the parliamentary aspects of government and as many political parties sprang up and languished. Although officially no legal channels existed for their establishment, parties in fact evolved, usually around a publication through which they made their views known. In fact, some groups formed whose sole purpose became the repudiation of the views of an opposing group. For example, *Mardum* (People), a newspaper founded in May 1966, voluntarily stopped publication after *Khalq* (Masses), which it opposed, was banned.[22] Of the early religiously oriented newspapers one may cite *Gahiz* (Morning), *Nida-yi-Haq* (Voice of Truth), and *Afkar-i Nau* (New Ideas), all three bilingual (Pashtu-Dari) weeklies.

The most significant of the religiously oriented political groups that emerged during the 1960s is the Jam'iat-e Islami-e Afghanistan (Islamic Society of Afghanistan, usually referred to in short as Jam'iat-e Islamic or Islamic Society), headed by Professor Rabbani since his election in 1972. Rabbani, a Dari speaker from Faizabad, had, as noted earlier, studied at al-Azhar in 1966–68 and then studied and taught at the Faculty of Islamic Studies of Kabul University. (The connections of the Jam'iat-e Islami with the Muslim Brotherhood [of Egypt, in particular] have been implied by the Marxist Kabul regimes but actual ties remain obscure, although similarities may be discerned.)

Active during the 1960s in the formation of the Jam'iat-e Islami were Professor Ghulam Muhammad Niazi (died in prison), Professor Abdul Rauof Sayyaf (first president of the first attempted unity of the exile groups and past president of Islamic Unity), and Professor Said M. Musa Tawana.[23] One of the students attracted to the Jam'iat-e Islami was Gulbuddin Hekmatyar, the current dynamic and controversial head of the Hizb-e Islami-ye Afghanistan (Islamic Party of Afghanistan, usually referred to as Hizb-e Islami or Islamic Party). Although Hekmatyar refused to remain in the first unity effort (1980-81) sponsored by Rabbani (mainly due to the presence of Gailani), relations between Rabbani's and Hekmatyar's groups have been close, especially since both had looked to Professor Sayyaf as the elder spokesman for the revolutionary Islamic ideological position. Cooperation in the field is carried on with some regularity.

To assess whether the Islamic revolutionary forces appeared as a response to Marxism and the Soviet invasion or whether they possess deeper roots that indicate greater strength, we need to examine who has joined this movement and what its origins have been, and then its current position. Just as Daoud's arrest of Marxists in April 1978 precipitated the coup of that month, so it may be argued, the Marxist attempts to control the country have hastened the politicization of the two elements that strengthen and uphold the Islamic revolutionary force. These elements are the educated youth of Kabul and their rural brothers and fathers. Afghan nationalism as a motivation for resistance was sparked mainly by the physical invasion of the country in late 1979 and has little altered the philosophy of the Islamic revolutionary groups, although it has changed them in other substantial ways. First, it has increased their active following by driving large numbers of Afghans into refugee camps where they take part in the institutions that support the Islamic revolutionary forces, i.e., schools, resistance forces, and information sources (newspapers, bulletins, and speeches). Second, the invasion drew world attention to the leadership of the Islamic revolution, forcing them into confrontation on the battlefield to maintain their credibility. Third, it has allowed all of the resistance to unequivocally identify the Kabul regime with atheism, thus strengthening the hands of the Islamic groups.

The date when the various resistance groups began their propaganda or armed struggle against Kabul is a fair indication of the degree to which they are committed to Islamizing the Afghan struggle. Rabbani and Hekmatyar were among the first to criticize the central government for its unwillingness to abide by a revitalized interpretation of Islam. Even as President Daoud took power in 1973 from his cousin, Zahir Shah, Rabbani, in an anonymously published booklet from Iran, condemned Daoud for selling out to the Russians.[24] Daoud in turn conducted a campaign to eliminate the Ikhwan ul-Muslimin (Muslim Brotherhood) and its Afghan sympathizers. Professor Sayyaf spent a number of years in Daoud's jails and Professor Niazi died there.

Hekmatyar, a student of Rabbani, became active in 1968 in a group calling itself Sazman-e Javanan-e Musalman (Organization of Young Muslims) which operated quite openly and attracted thousands of adherents. In early 1970 the two groups making progress among young Afghans were the Maoist Shu'lah-ye Javid (Eternal Flame) group and the Young Muslims. Among the latter were included Sunni as well as Shi'ite young men. Competition between the two groups, especially on the Kabul University campus, escalated to the point where Saidal, a member of the Shu'lah, was killed and another person badly wounded. The government rounded up members of both groups, although perhaps more of the Young Muslims.

Shortly thereafter, Menhajuddin Gahiz, editor of the Muslim weekly *Gahiz*, was found murdered in his home. Although many felt the act was committed by the Shu'lah members in revenge for the death of Saidal, leading members of the Jami'at lay the blame at the Russian Embassy. They argued that the Russians saw an opportunity to eliminate both camps of foes—the pro-Peking and Muslim groups—by inducing them to wage war. This did not occur. *Gahiz,* a publication which carried the writings of Egyptian and Iranian Islamic writers such as Said Qutb, Ab'ul Qasim Farzaneh, and Nasser Makarim Shirazi, continued publishing under Abdul Salim Ferghani.

After Daoud came to power in 1973, three political groups were accused of plotting against his government and eliminated. The best-known case concerns former Prime Minister Hashem Maiwandwal, the leader of the Musawat party (a secular centrist group), who was eliminated in prison. Then the government turned on the Maoist Shu'lah members. Finally, it directed its attention at the Muslim organizations and, accusing them of conspiracy, jailed many and shot a large number, while killing others in prison.[25] Members of both the Jami'at and the Muslim Youth went into hiding, fled into the countryside, or eventually attempted to overthrow the government by inciting revolt in the outlying areas. Such an effort, launched in the Panjshir Valley and a few other places during the summer of 1975, resulted in the arrest of a large number of Jami'at members. As many of them recall, including Ahmadshah Mas'ud, the now celebrated Jam'iat leader in the Panjshir Valley, the peasants refused to help them but rather turned them in to the government forces. In five years, events were to unite the same peasants and the matured Jami'at enthusiasts.

According to the Jami'at, Daoud took several steps to reduce the influence of the newly emerging revivalist Islamic groups in addition to executing their members. For example, he attempted to prevent Afghan religious students from continuing their education in Pakistani religious schools, a practice commonly followed for decades. To limit Afghan religious contact within the Muslim world the number of Afghans permitted to make the Hajj (pilgrimage to Mecca) was slashed by 70 percent in 1973. To decrease the influence that the young religious students might have, the number of students at religious training schools was cut by 30 percent, their stipends were either reduced or eliminated altogether, and graduates were not allowed to teach in the regular elementary and secondary schools.[26]

Finding themselves hunted and their channels for communication and indoctrination virtually eliminated, many of the Jami'at and Muslim Youth members fled to Pakistan and relative obscurity. Attempts to revive an active organization—Sazman-e Mujahidin-e Fada'yi Khalq-e Afghanistan (Organization of the Sacrificing Mujahidin of the People of Afghanistan)—and a publication—*'Idalat u jang* (Justice and Battle)—failed for lack of support.

Languishing in Pakistani exile, the revolutionary Islamic groups resuscitated themselves following the death of Daoud and the establishment of the Taraki regime in 1978. Suddenly, all the dire predictions that their leadership had made regarding Soviet plots and impiety came to pass. As the government of Taraki demonstrated itself less and less sensitive to the need to preserve a semblance of respect for Islamic values, general alarm began to spread throughout the countryside. The elimination of all Islamic symbolism from the Afghan flag (restored by Babrak Karmal in 1980), the arrest and execution of members of respected traditional religious leadership, and the rush to embrace and peddle Marxist jargon gradually led to the alienation of the majority of the Afghans in the countryside. The ranks of the revolutionary Muslim groups swelled, particularly in the absence of any other foci for opposition to the government.

Not until the spring of 1979 did men who had been closely aligned to the traditional ruling elites and/or the royal family stir into action. When they did arrive in Peshawar, with them came bureaucrats of the old regime of Daoud, sworn enemies of the now established Hizb and Jami'at. Gailani, viewed as part of this Kabul elite, at this time aimed his appeal chiefly to his followers in Paktya who revered him as a Sufi pir.

The traditional groups, such as Gailani's, gained momentum with the Soviet invasion of the country which profoundly shocked the nationalistic Afghans and provided them with a motive for resistance. Thus it is that the Soviet invasion has fostered resistance among both the traditional and revivalist leaders, but it has not, as noted above, appreciably altered the philosophical or even political position of the revolutionary Muslim camp regarding what is best for the Afghan people. Indeed, this position has been very similar for the past fifteen years. Daoud perceived the Islamic revolution as a threat; in the Taraki-Amin period that evaluation continued; and throughout its early months the Khalq regime attempted to discredit the Muslim Brotherhood (Ikhwan el-Muslimin) in many ways, including derisively referring to it as the Ikhwan al-Shayatin (Satanic Brotherhood).[27]

Eventually, Kabul has come to recognize the sympathy it has carelessly discarded by originally taking a secularist, indeed anti-Islamic, stand openly. The Karmal regime has attempted to amend this situation in a number of ways while at the same time continuing to project the resistance as nothing more than bandits. For example, very early on the regime organized a High Council of Ulama and

Religious Scholars and a Department of Islamic Affairs. These organizations conduct activities corresponding roughly to the Ecclesiastical Boards of Muslims in the Soviet Union. Following a 1981 visit by Mufti Babakhanov (d. 1982), the head of the Central Asian and Kazakh Ecclesiastical Board of Muslims, Babakhanov and Dr. Saed Afghani, his Kabul counterpart, signed a joint communiqué in which they condemned "the intrigues of imperialist countries . . . and [proclaimed] the consolidation of real Islam."[28] In effect, this message indicates the political function of Dr. Afghani (and Mufti Babakhanov) and the attempt to present Soviet Islam as the ideal.[29] Were Kabul and Moscow not faced with a relatively successful revolutionary Islamic resistance, it is highly unlikely that those clerics who remain in Kabul would have had any opportunity to be visible and therefore to possess some limited power to persuade. On the other side of the border, Soviet Muslims would not have gained the relative privilege they have gradually come to enjoy were it not for their growing usefulness to the state in its dealings with the Middle East, and particularly with African states on the periphery of Islam.

The Present Position of the Islamic Revolutionary Parties

When the first attempt at unity among the array of resistance forces, made in March 1980, failed in April 1981, the more natural alliances were formed: the old Kabul University coalition of bright, dedicated, rurally educated, and devout Muslims which characterized the Jami'at of the 1960s in effect regrouped in the Islamic Unity camp, joined by elements of various rural, particularly Pashtun, tribal groups, such as that of Yunus Khalis, and the many rural Pashtuns formerly led by Mawlavi Nabi, and by the more urban multiethnic elements that broke away from traditional Sufi leader, Sibghatullah Mujadidi; in the Islamic Alliance camp, the traditional religious and Sufi leadership closed ranks with Kabul elites, former bureaucrats, and nationalists. The protraction of the Afghan-Soviet struggle has resulted in certain modifications to these alignments. For example, certain Naqshbandiyya Sufi pirs, generally remnants of those older rural generations trained in the madrasah system, have become associated with the Islamic revolutionaries and have even attempted to revive the old madrasah system among the refugees in the North-West Frontier Province (NWFP) of Pakistan.[30] The best known of the Kabul Sufi leadership, however, continues to ally itself with the traditional religious and political elements. The Islamic Unity of Afghanistan Mujahidin, it must be noted, insists on being the party of the Islamic Revolution of Afghanistan. Its differences with the Islamic Alliance and with other exile groups such as Afghan Millat or the Free Afghanistan Union lie not in whether Afghanistan must be freed from Russian domination, but in what role should be assigned to the Islamic motivation for the struggle. The traditional groups such as Gailani's, while calling the struggle to drive the Russians out of the country a *jihad* (holy war), do not speak of revolution, certainly not in the sense of an Islamic revival. The secular groups prefer to play down religion or omit it altogether. Afghan Millat, at the head of its weekly bilingual newspaper *Istaqlal* (Independence), prints *"watan wa Islam"* (country and Islam), yet the contents of the six pages rarely, if ever, make further reference to anything Islamic.[31] A tract from the Ittihad-e Afghanistan- e Azad (The Free Afghanistan Union) states, "Briefly our views are that we want an independent Afghanistan free of Soviet imperialism, American imperialism, and Chinese reactionary domination."[32] This thought is echoed by both Hekmatyar and Rabbani. In a personal interview in the spring of 1980 Hekmatyar responded to the question of accepting aid from the United States by saying that he did not want Afghanistan to become the battlefield for two superpowers. Politely, he did not add that many of his followers view the United States as an enemy of Islam due to its perceived animosity toward the Arab people. With regard to financial aid from Muslim states, Hekmatyar said his help comes from private individuals in the Gulf states.

In the same vein, in the course of a speech delivered on the occasion of their graduation, Rabbani addressed the students and faculty of the Refugee School the Jami'at conducts as follows: "In the [schools] there was everything but no Islamic thought, Islamic training, Islamic culture. There existed Russian thought, American philosophy, unbridled Chinese [thought], European decadence, all manner of deceit, vileness, all . . . cultures, all kinds of wicked training. But the invigorating spirit of Islam, Islamic revolutionary training, tranquility-inducing Islam was not there."[33] Moreover, Rabbani and Hekmatyar exercise great caution in either accepting direct Saudi government aid or advocating the return of Zahir Shah as a figurehead for unity in a compromise government. For these reasons Hekmatyar specifically turned down the United States government's offer in 1981 by the Reagan Administration (upon the soliciation of Gailani) on the grounds that such assistance would violate the non-aligned nature of the Afghans and symbolize dependence on a country which is viewed as unfriendly to Islam. None of these Islamic revolutionary parties, however, reject aid from private persons or groups in the Arab world (indeed, they rely heavily on such aid) or in the West. It is suspected that part of this refusal of these leaders not to appear to work in tandem with the United States may relate to their desire to appear more acceptable to the Soviet government during discussions about a future Afghanistan following Soviet troop withdrawal. While this may be the motive for Hekmatyar, who is highly ambitious personally, it may be too cynical an assessment of Rabbani. The ambiguous position of the revolutionary Muslim groups regarding the United States and Western Europe is demonstrated by the pamphlet distributed by the Islamic Unity of Afghanistan Mujahidin on the occasion of Afghanistan Day (21 March 1982). Making no mention of any Western countries, the pamphlet makes a strong appeal for international acknowledgment of the trampling of Afghan human rights, maintains the integrity of Afghanistan and Islam, and warns of the threat to stability from leadership imposed by the outside. The tract states, "While directing the attention of all groups and nations to their human responsibilities, we strongly demand [from] them not to carve false and plastic guardians and leaders for the Afghan nation and its Jehad."[34]

In discussing the revolutionary Islamic parties and their formulation of an Islamic political philosophy, we speak mainly of positions stated by Professor Rabbani and Engineer Hekmatyar, the chief spokesman for the Islamic Unity. Too little attention has been given to these positions since all of the groups that claim Islam as their guiding motivation are frequently lumped under the facile term "fundamentalist."[35] As Olivier Roy has indicated, "the Islamic movement among the young is not a reaction of tradition faced with modernism, but on the contrary, it is a manner of modern thought."[36] Its foundations reject Marxism, Westernism, and the corruption of the ruling establishment. They have also stood against the political passivity and inertia of the body of ulama. This explains their dislike of Gailani and his establishment adherents and their scarce tolerance of Mujadidi and the entrenched ulama.

On many levels, the philosophical debate between the Marxists and the Islamic revolutionaries rises to the same lofty, idealistic levels. Both employ the vocabulary of revolutionary struggle against foreign imperialism, the power of the establishment, traditionalism and superstition, and maintenance of the status quo for the benefit of elites. Both groups recruited among the young, especially from the science institutions such as the Kabul Polytechnic and the faculties of Science, Engineering, Agriculture, and Medicine at Kabul University.

The Jami'at could even claim high-level army officers as members, although most of these suffered, and were virtually annihilated by Daoud.

Students at Kabul University during the 1960s recall that cells and political discussion, and, most important, translations of works by the theoreticians of the various ideologies comprised the activities of the Marxists and the partisans of Islam. In fact, when students of a strong religious leaning became disenchanted with the behavior and ideas of their Marxist mentors, they frequently made full turns into the arms of the Muslim revolutionaries. The materialism and licentiousness of the upper levels of the Parcham and Khalq appear to have particularly offended young village recruits who found the drinking, womanizing, and irreverence of Karmal, in particular, repulsive.

A major problem in discussing the politics of the Marxists and the Islamic revolutionaries lies in the lack of theoreticians on either side. While both groups have been led by charismatic leaders with good organizational ability—Hafizullah Amin, on the one hand, and Professor Rabbani, on the other—there are no real theoreticians able to readily justify action through theory or policy, certainly not in any depth. Thus, to understand the position of the Islamic revolutionaries, one must instead discover their attitude on important Afghan and regional issues in order to discern the pattern behind the point of view.

With regard to Afghan/Pakistan relations, the Islamic revolutionaries advocate and maintain close ties with the people of Pakistan and the religious leadership, particularly when it is like-minded, as in the case of the Jama'at-i Islami. Jama'at General Secretary Qazi Hussain Ahmad appears at important Afghan exile functions to demonstrate support. In the question of Pashtunistan, the Afghan Islamic camp avoids discussion of the matter. In the past, however, they have opposed the raising of the issue, regarding it as a Russian fabrication to divide Islamic countries in the region in order to gain access to the Indian Ocean. Rabbani has claimed that even the 1958 instigation of a confrontation with Pakistan by Daoud was part of Soviet machinations to gain access to the Shindand air base. Only the intervention of Zahir Shah prevented Daoud from signing an agreement giving the Soviets the rights they now fully enjoy. (In this regard, we should recall that about 70 percent of Soviet troop concentration after the invasion was in the Shindand area, on Iran's border.) Moreover, it is evident from the multiethnic composition of the revolutionary Islamic groups that ethnicity plays no major role in their ideological stand since they regard ethnic origin merely as an accident of birth. Rabbani himself prefers not to discuss his ethnic background. (Faizabad, his home, is in a predominantly Uzbek, but mixed, ethnic area on the borders of Soviet Tajikistan.) One hears several languages used among the Islamic revolutionaries: Persian appears to be intelligible to most since many of them are or were students. The Uzbek and Turkoman languages also may be heard. Among the Hizb members there appears to be a greater number of Pashtu speakers. However, this ethnic factor appears not to present any obstacle to the philosophical unity of the Islamic groups. Most publications of the Islamic Unity appear in Persian or they are bilingual. Radio Free Afghanistan, the French-funded radio station of the Islamic Unity, broadcasts in both languages of the country.

With regard to Iran and its revolution, not only the Islamic leaders but other factions in the Afghan resistance have also become silent. Whereas during the early period of the Iranian Revolution, statements by Iranian revolutionary leaders were often quoted and news of Iranian matters published, after 1981 this activity ceased. This may be partly explained by the Iran-Iraq war in which the Afghans do not wish to take sides. Although the sympathy of parts of the Afghan resistance remains with the elements that formed the religious opposition to the Pahlavi regime, alienating the wealthy Arab states and individuals who provide financial assistance to the political parties of the resistance seems to play an important role in this issue. Moreover, Iran's internal religious factions, especially the strong clerical faction and its insistence on backing mainly Shi'ite Afghan elements, may have created some nervousness on the part of the Islamic revolutionary camp of the Afghan resistance.

The execution of Sadegh Qotbzadeh, the former Iranian Foreign Minister, in itself a reflection of the internal friction among Iranian leaders, brought forth strong Afghan response in one Afghan publication, *Istiqlal*. Qotbzadeh was praised for many things in this eulogy, but particularly for his support of the Afghan resistance on the regional and international levels. Ominously, the author warned that Moscow's hand, extended through the Tudeh party, had snuffed out the life of a good Muslim, similar to the way that Moscow had rid itself of patriotic Afghans during the Daoud period through its Parcham lackeys.[37]

On a different level, however, the Iranian revolutionary fighter, viewed as faithful and brave, provides a model for success. The following short poem, written by a *shahid* (martyr), illustrates in the Persian that is used the close connection with Iranian revolutionary fighters.

> I am a *pasdar* [guard] of my *meyhan* [fatherland] and the death of
> my enemy,
> I am a revolutionary soldier and a man of iron,
> The Koran is the root of my motivation,
> Unafraid in battle, of death and dying I am.[38]

These four lines offer an idea of the fervor and dedication felt by the Afghan fighting model. The use of words like pasdar and meyhan, however, provides a clue to the fact that the Afghan *mujahid*'s (holy warrior, freedom fighter) self-view relates closely to the Iranian model. These worlds are commonly used in Iranian Persian but not in Dari. Pasdar, in particular, recalls revolutionary Iranian usage.

The Afghan Islamic revolutionary view of Soviet Muslims is difficult to discern in any detail. Awareness of their existence has always affected the rhetoric of some Afghan leaders. As far back as 1929, Bacha-i Saqao (Habibullah II) publicly called for the liberation of Bukhara. Individual men in the field continue to wistfully talk about freeing "Bukhara." No official statements from the leadership, however, have appeared. Hekmatyar has publicly announced that Soviet Tajiks are fighting within his ranks.[39]

The issue that explains the heart of the Islamic revolutionary position, and sets it apart from the traditional nationalist sections of the resistance, has to do with the vision of a future, Soviet-free Afghanistan. Rabbani's conception, published in a speech, gives some indication of these views.

> First, I should explain a common misunderstanding. When we say
> we want a government on the model of the early Islamic pattern,
> many people think we want to move history backward and have a
> living situation exactly as 14 centuries ago. They think a government
> based on that model cannot be compatible with the conditions of
> the electronic age. But the issue is not as simple as they think. We
> do not see any difficulty in implementing the principles and values
> which prevailed in the time of Prophet Mohammad (Peace be upon
> Him) in our society. We believe those principles are applicable no
> matter how much the world advances. I will give you an example.
> Justice is an Islamic principle. It was implemented in the time of the
> Prophet Mohammad (Peace be upon Him) to the extent that when a
> noble lady stole something and some gentlemen came to intercede,

the Prophet exclaimed: "by God! If my daughter Fatima steals, I will cut her hand!" Now the implementation of justice is as much applicable today as it was at that time. Or take another example. Islam enjoins seeking knowledge as a duty of every Muslim man and woman. Today, the form of seeking knowledge might be different. It is studied in schools and universities now and it was otherwise at that time. But seeking of knowledge is as much practical today as it was 14 centuries ago—and even more so. The same is true about national and international politics. Islam enjoins that the leader of Muslim Umma [community] should be chosen from among the people. This was done in case of the righteous Caliphs. And today election of the ruler is the most advanced form of government. Shoora [council] is an Islamic principle. It is the order of the Holy Qoran to Muslims to decide their affairs on the basis of consultation. This is almost the same thing you have as a parliament today.

In international affairs, Islam tells Muslims how to regulate their relations with the "people of the book" (i.e., Christians and Jews) and how to treat the non-believers. It orders Muslims: "But if the enemy incline towards peace, do thou (also) incline towards peace, and trust in God: for He is the One, the Hearer and Knower (of all things)." (Al-Qoran: VIII/61) Islam enjoins on its followers to have good and friendly relations with all the people until Islamic ideology is not suppressed, so that Islam has the freedom to present its ideology to all the people. And this is the right of freedom of speech, and no one can object to it today.[40]

It bears noting, with regard to the Afghan Islamic conception of government, the sympathetic reception of the ideas of Ali Shariati, the anticlerical ideologue of the Iranian Revolution in its early stages, by the Afghan revolutionary camp. Shariati, a Shi'ite, describes, in a more sophisticated vein, the same ideas that Rabbani expresses about the applicability of the early Islamic model to contemporary Islamic society.

Rabbani's statement leads to the following conclusions regarding his position: that Islamic revolutionary philosophy entails the unity of all Muslim people regardless of international boundaries or ethnolinguistic barriers; that although Iran's revolutionary success may provide a model for the fighter in the field, the situation of the Afghan revolutionary does not correspond to that of the Iranian clerics; that Marxism is equated with atheism and not with socioeconomic progress or equality of man. Thus, in the Soviet Union the Afghan revolutionary sees not only a colonial oppressor and the instigator of anti-Islamic actions in Afghanistan, but also the ultimate atheistic state. By extension, an atheistic state is not one that an Afghan Muslim is enjoined to accept.

Rabbani, as an activist Afghan Islamic revolutionary, has offered the general outline of the objective of the Islamic revolutionary wing of the Afghan resistance. Others in the Islamic revolutionary camp, representing the more radical trends, would prefer to dictate more explicitly the objectives of the movement. Nevertheless, the fact remains that the Islamic revolutionary group has been strengthened considerably by its reliance on Islam as a basic unifying force as well as by its comparatively long period of incubation and organizational formation. By contrast, the traditional conservative/bureaucratic coalition that includes traditional Sufi leadership and nascent urban nationalists, formed only as a response to the Marxist coup and the Soviet invasion, lacks both a convincing unifying ideology and vigorous organization. Perhaps more critical and crippling to the coalition is it unwillingness or inability to state objectives for a future free Afghanistan other than the restoration of the conditions prior to the events precipitating the crisis.

REVIVALIST ISLAM in the AFGHAN CRISIS

The relationship of government to religion has been affected by several factors in modern Afghan history. Included in these are a population that requires piety of its rulers and a religious establishment that has lacked the intellectual vigor to establish itself as the intermediary between the people and the government and is deficient as the guardian of Islam. Successive changes in the external situation—beginning in the sixteenth century when Shi'ism became the state religion of Iran and ending as British and Russian colonial encroachment aroused xenophobia in the Afghan people—isolated the Afghan religious establishment. While the religious institutions languished, the state began to emerge as a political entity capable of exerting a unifying influence on the countryside through the use of force primarily, but also through the gradual expansion of the infrastructure, in particular, through secular schools. From the late nineteenth-century period of Amir Abdur Rahman onward, we see the Afghan clergy, at least, gradually subjugated to the state and evolving into a mere sector of the paid government bureaucracy. This process by which the state infringed upon the areas exclusively reserved by the clergy for themselves in traditional Islamic society became formalized through the four constitutions in operation between 1923 and 1978.

In Afghanistan, however, the religious establishment does not consist of only the clergy, the maktab-madrasah educational system, the waqf, and the judiciary. There, as in much of Central Asia, the Sufi orders and their prominent leaders have frequently enjoyed great prestige and attracted a following whose loyalty to the pir can cut across not only ethnic lines but also supercede loyalty to the state, ruler, and region. Thus, the head of a leading Naqshbandiyya family, the Hazrat of Shor Bazar (Mujadidi), has exerted much political influence in twentieth-century Afghan history. Other Sufi pirs as well as local *mawlawis* (religious, sometimes Sufi, leaders belonging to a region and often tribally affiliated) have served and continue to serve as foci for large sections of the population, particularly in times of political stress and warfare.

The revivalist Islamic movement that has slowly gained in strength in the Middle East since the turn of the century began to have political impact within Afghanistan only since the 1960s. This movement, centered at the Faculty of Islamic Studies of Kabul University, appears to have established itself in rural areas, especially among young, rural, newly educated boys and young men. Professor Burhanuddin Rabbani, Engineer Gulbuddin Hekmatyar (and to some extent, Professor Abdul Raouf Sayyaf), are the leading exponents of the position of the revivalists. Although they were persecuted under Daoud, the 1978 Marxist coup offered them the advantage of preaching their position to a wide and receptive audience, particularly in the refugee camps in Pakistan. The Soviet invasion of 1979 catapulted these persons into greater prominence still and made popular the chief revolutionary Islamic criterion for resolution of the Afghan situation. The Afghan problem for them is rooted in the decay of Afghan-Islamic values, the introduction of secularism, and the subversive influence of Soviet Marxism. Past Afghan governments are held accountable for these problems and past officials are held responsible. Accordingly, the next state formed in Afghanistàn must be placed on a true Islamic path by men of strong religious instincts and background.

The Islamic revolutionaries are separated from the traditional religious leadership (including many Sufi leaders) and their sympathizers among nationalists and former bureaucrats by an ever-widening chasm caused by resentment of past cooperation with secular governments. The intellectual inclinations of the Islamic revolutionary leadership sets it apart from many Sufi elements who are despised for the literal adulation of some pirs, in particular, as encouraged by Sayyid Ahmad Gailani. The Islamic revolutionaries have relied heavily on allies in the Muslim world, usually individuals rather than governments, except in the case of Saudi Arabia and Pakistan, and intermittently, Iran. With the passage of time, the Afghan Islamic revolutionaries have become increasingly estranged from the mixture of tradition, revolution, and dogma that mark the Shi'ite clergy in power in Iran. As a model of Islamic fervor that successfully toppled a militarily superior force, however, Iran remains a source of inspiration for the ordinary fighting Afghan.

In the absence of legitimate government, the Islamic revolutionaries and the traditional conservative/bureaucratic coalition contribute the two major ideological trends for the Afghan people. The two camps, through their administrative structure, function also as quasi-governments to regulate Afghan society wherever conditions allow them to carry on. This may be in the refugee camps in Pakistan or in the hidden valleys in the interior. While the organization of the Islamic revolutionary groups remains loose and the chain of command is accepted by consensus rather than through force, nevertheless, their prestige appears to be growing in comparison to that of the traditional coalition. Young men join the former while the old bureaucrats tire of the latter and the arduous conditions in rural environments.

Without the crisis created by war it is hard to imagine that the Islamic revolutionaries would have had an opportunity to directly influence the Afghan population. In view of the desperate need of the Afghan resistance for an ideology that can bind the various ethnic groups together and at the same time offer a challenge to the proclaimed egalitarianism of Soviet Marxism, the Islamic revolutionaries will in all likelihood influence or even guide the region, including Soviet Central Asia, for some years to come.

NOTES

1. For a succinct discussion of this matter, see Alexandre Bennigsen and Marie Broxup, *The Islamic Threat to the Soviet Union* (New York: St. Martin's Press, 1983).

2. Canfield, for example, discusses the Hazaras's religion in light of social organization. See Robert Leroy Canfield, *Faction and Conversion in a Plural Society: Religious Alignments in the Hindu Kush*, Anthropological Papers, No. 50 (Ann Arbor: Mu-

seum of Anthropology, University of Michigan, 1973). The research of David Busby Edwards holds promise of detailed study of Islamic practice among Afghans. See his "The Evolution of Shi'i Political Dissent in Afghanistan," in *Shi'ism and Social Protest*, ed. by Juan R. I. Cole and Nikki R. Keddie (New Haven: Yale University Press, 1986) pp. 201–29.

3. The two major general Afghan histories by Westerners, Dupree and Gregorian, as well as the prominent Persian language modern history by Ghubar, treat the tension between religious leadership and secular authority simply on the level of modern versus reactionary. Often the distinction or interaction between religiously and ethnic/tribally inspired opposition to Kabul is blurred or glossed over as in the description of the Mangal uprising and the Qandahar protests of 1959. Hasan Kakar, in his meticulously documented monograph on Abdur Rahman's reign, does treat religious and intellectual institutions but provides limited analysis or comparison of the development of intellectual theory or religious institutions. See Louis Dupree, *Afghanistan*, 3rd ed. (Princeton, N.J.: Princeton University Press, 1980); Vartan Gregorian, *The Emergence of Modern Afghanistan: Politics of Reform and Modernization, 1880–1946* (Stanford, Calif.: Stanford University Press, 1969); Mir Ghulam Muhammad Ghuobar, *Afghanistan dar Masiir-i Tarikh* (Afghanistan's Path Through History) (in Persian) (Kabul: Duwlati Matha'a, 1346/1967); Hasan Kawun Kakar, *Government and Society in Afghanistan: The Reign of Amir 'Abd al-Rahman Khan* (Austin: University of Texas Press, 1979).

4. Raymond D. Gastil, ed., *Freedom in the World: Political Rights and Civil Liberties, 1981* (Westport, Ct.: Greenwood Press, 1981), p. 17.

5. Gerard Chaliand, *Report From Afghanistan*, trans. Tamar Jacoby (New York: Viking Press, 1982), p. 80.

6. Kakar refers to Brahman Hindus who were given high positions in the bureaucracy or military during the reign of Abdur Rahman. (Kakar, *Government and Society in Afghanistan*, p. 149.)

7. Leon B. Poullada, *Reform and Rebellion in Afghanistan, 1919–1929: King Amanullah's Failure to Modernize a Tribal Society* (Ithaca, N.Y.: Cornell University Press, 1973). Ghubar makes the same point in his work cited above. As ethnic minorities have begun to develop political aspirations beyond their own regions, they have started to voice the view that the opposition leading to the downfall of Habibullah II grew out of ethnic animosity toward the Tajik by the Pashtuns. Indigenous records are scarce from the brief period of Takij rule but a review of British and Soviet sources, as well as oral accounts, could provide materials for a more evenhanded study of this period.

8. Canfield, *Faction and Conversion in a Plural Society*, pp. 95–100.

9. Abdur Rahman attempted to upgrade the religioeducational system by establishing new *madrasahs* (advanced schools for Islamic learning) in Kabul and Kerat with geometry and mathematics added to their regular curriculum of Islamic theology, Arabic, and so forth. Afghan xenophobia made foreign-educated ulama suspect in that period. Kakar, *Government and Society in Afghanistan*, p. 261.

10. One or two Afghan Islamic judges who served in the early part of this century had studied in Bukharan schools. In more recent decades, Islamic scholars from Afghanistan, had begun to study at recognized foreign institutions such as al-Azhar.

11. Such mobility through education is demonstrated in the case of Sadriddin Aini (1878–1953), a poor Tajik peasant who attained some prestige even in the

Uzbek-dominated Bukhara of the pre-1920 era. His memoirs, *Yaddashtha* (Stalinabad, 1952–57), provide a detailed account of the role of traditional Muslim educational institutions at the turn of the century.

12. A succinct discussion of the first three Afghan Constitutions, 1923, 1931, and 1964, appears in M. E. Yapp's, "Afghanistan," in *Dustur: A Survey of the Constitutions of the Arab and Muslim States* (Leiden, 1966).

13. Gregorian, *The Emergence of Modern Afghanistan*, p. 250. The Sabi refers to the Sevener Shi'ites or Ismai'lis for whom parts of northeast Afghanistan have served as refuge since the tenth century. Zendiq is considered a general term in Muslim criminal law applied to any heretic whose teachings become a danger to the state. Zendiqs are liable for capital punishment. This is the only crime systematically punished by the Prophet Muhammad, and Hanafi law prosecutes as Zendiq those who dishonor the Prophet. Louis Massignon, "Zindik," *Encyclopedia of Islam*, Vol. 4 (1934), pp. 1228–29. Although Ottoman fatwas against Shi'ites are based on this interpretation, it is not clear whether Zendiq in the Afghan case refers to any one group or merely to individuals who are deemed heretically dangerous to the state. For further discussion of Islam and the 1923 constitution see Mohammad Hashim Kamali's *Law in Afghanistan: A Study of the Constitutions, Matrimonial Law and the Judiciary* (Leiden: E. J. Brill, 1985) p. 29.

A Qadyani (better known as Ahmadiyah, the controversial sect found in Pakistan, India, and West Africa) execution in 1924 led to protests on the subcontinent.

14. Gregorian, *The Emergence of Modern Afghanistan*, p. 249.

15. The Afghan Constitution of 1964, while stating that no law repugnant to Islam could be introduced, in fact made Shari'ah laws subservient to secular law. By 1976 a four-volume Civil Law, based on a compilation of Shari'ah and customary law further regulated the remaining juridical area of Islamic law, that of family law. (Dupree, *Afghanistan*, pp. 579, 765.)

16. Akbar S. Ahmed, *Pukhtun Economy and Society: Traditional Structure and Economic Development in a Tribal Society* (London: Routledge & Kegan Paul, 1980), p. 92.

17. Joseph Schact, *An Introduction to Islamic Law* (Oxford: Clarendon Press, 1964), p. 185.

18. The most important of the Afghan madrasahs at the beginning of this century were the Dar-ul-Ulum (Kabul) and the Najm-ul-Madaris (Jalalabad), where future *qazis* (religious judges) and teachers were trained. Other schools served in Qandahar, Herat, and Balkh/Mazar-i Sharif.

19. Kakar, *Government and Society in Afghanistan*, pp. 153–54.

20. Gregorian, *The Emergence of Modern Afghanistan*, p. 261.

21. *Mirror of Jehad* (Peshawar), May–June 1982, pp. 68–69, 15.

22. Dupree, *Afghanistan*, chart 23.

23. The influence of Professor Sayyaf continues to grow as his facility with Arabic, his experience with Arab cultures as a student at al-Azhar, and his long-standing position as an Islamic intellectual gain for him support from important patrons such as the Saudi Arabs. From the largely ceremonial presidency of the Islamic Unity he has created for himself an important focus for funds and support that may overshadow the positions of Rabbani and Hekmatyar.

24. The following booklet, attributed to Rabbani, describes events leading to the 1973 coup and provides a history of the formation of the Islamic revolutionary

forces: *Faji'eh-ye 26om Saratan va Sima-ye Zi'amat-e Da'ud Khan* (Belleville, Ill.: Nuhizat-e Azadi-ye Iran, 1355/1976).

25. Ibid., pp. 69–70.

26. Daoud appears to have been copying steps taken by Abdur Rahman to curb the power of the religious establishment. See Kakar, *Government and Society in Afghanistan*, pp. 147–63.

27. *Yulduz* (Star), an Uzbek language weekly published in Kabul, 13 September 1978, p. 1.

28. *The Kabul New Times*, 4 July 1961, p. 1.

29. The use of the official Muslim establishment of the Soviet Union to gain influence among Muslims in susceptible areas has formed part of Soviet practice since the 1940s. In the aftermath of the Arab-Israeli war of 1967, the effort has been expanded considerably.

30. An example is the very successful madrasah established in Barra by a Naqshbandiyya pir, Mawlawi Fazl Hadi Shinwari.

31. Eden Naby, "The Mujahidin Press," *Afghanistan Newsletter*, January 1983, pp. 23–24.

32. *Afghanistan Azad* (Free Afghanistan), undated pamphlet of the Ittihad-e Afghanistan-e Azadi.

33. *Shahid-e Zahdi* (Witness to Devotion), no. 6/7 (1361/1982), p. 4.

34. Mimeographed tract sent from Peshawar, Spring 1982.

35. For a discussion of Islamic "fundamentalism" as an outgrowth of the political philosophy espoused by Muslim thinkers of the turn of the century such as Jamal al-Din al-Afghani (Asadabadi) and Muhammad Rashid Rida, see Hamid Enayat, *Modern Islamic Political Thought* (Austin: University of Texas Press, 1982), pp. 69–110.

36. Olivier Roy, *L'Afghanistan: Islam et Modernité Politique* (Paris, Editions du Seuil, 1985) esp. chapter 4.

37. Naby, "The Mujahidin Press."

38. *Mithaq-e Khun* (Drop of Blood), nos. 17/18 (1360/1982), p. 35.

39. *Mirror of Jehad* (Peshawar), 1:1 (January–February 1982), p. 33.

40. *Mirror of Jehad* (Peshawar), 1:2 (March–April 1982), pp. 9–10.

II

IRAN

5

RELIGION, ETHNIC MINORITIES, and the STATE in IRAN
An Overview

NIKKI R. KEDDIE

EACH GENERATION has its own history and social science. The subjects covered in this book, reflected in the topics of the Iran
chapters—state formation, minority-state relations, and religion and
society—reflect key concerns of social scientists of the past two decades. These concepts are in part consequences of new social
realities—the attempts of an unprecedented number of nations to
form or reshape states since the colonial liberation and populist politics that followed World War II; the importance of ethnic and religious
conflicts within both new and old states; and the recent resurgence of
religion in politics, especially in the Muslim world.

Through much of this century, and especially between the
world wars, *class* would have been regarded by many social scientists
as the most important operative category behind the three major phenomena discussed here. These three might have been discussed as
subordinate or ideological expressions of a fundamental class struggle. This view of history and politics is still widely followed in the
world today, and if it appears only as a subordinate factor in these
chapters, it is likely that a future resurgence of clear-cut working class
or peasant struggles could once again bring class to the center of
social science and make other categories recede. There are still good
scholars who would argue the view, not represented herein, that
state formation is tied to the strength of new ruling classes that include modernized bourgeois, technocrats, and market-oriented landlords; that ethnic conflict is largely a conflict between a dominant

157

majority who represent the interests of privileged classes and the minorities who include especially oppressed classes; and that religious revival combines the interests of one sector of the premodern ruling classes with an ideological religious expression of the grievances of the oppressed classes. There is considerable truth in such views, however much some of their proponents may present them in absolute and oversimplified form.

To look at the issues discussed herein in a comparative light, one may note that Iran, a very old country but a new modern state, is neither a country whose modern state formation began before the twentieth century (countries which range from early modernizers like England and France to late ones like Turkey and Japan), nor one that gained independence after World War II, like Pakistan and many others. Instead, Iran began significant formation of a modern state after World War I as did, to a lesser degree and with more difficulties, Afghanistan. Iran had an advantage over other new states in that Iran as a political and cultural entity had roots in pre-Islamic times and especially in the Islamic Safavid, Zand, and Qajar dynasties, which ruled for most of the period between 1501 and 1921. The main unifying principle for most Iranians in Safavid and Qajar times was adherence to the Shi'i branch of Islam, even though some border ethnic minorities—Baluchis, Turkomans, most Kurds, and some Arabs— follow the Sunni branch of Islam, and other Iranians are Zoroastrian, Christian, Jewish, and Baha'i. A large majority of Iranians are Shi'i, but only about half are native Persian speakers, even though Persian is understood by many more than half the population today. Religion has been more central than language in most people's self-identification, at least until the 1920s and possibly thereafter.

The early Safavids, who conquered Iran and founded their dynasty in 1501 on the basis of a populist form of Shi'ism, used religion to unify the population and distinguish Iran from its hostile Sunni neighbors—the Ottomans and the Uzbeks. Iranians were, in part, forcibly converted to Shi'ism, but they came to identify with it, as is seen in the failure of Nadir Shah's mid–eighteenth-century efforts to transform Twelver Shi'ism into a fifth legal school of Sunni Islam. In the early Safavid period there was an elementary form of state formation into what might be called a patrimonial state, and Shi'i leaders, including some imported from Arab-speaking lands, were in part incorporated into the patrimonial structure. From the mid-sixteenth century on, however, documents indicate that one group of Shi'i leaders opposed the ties of their colleagues to the temporal state, and there continued to be ulama opponents to association with, or subservience to, rulers. Recent scholarship is showing that the relationship of religious leaders to the state has been variable, not only over time, but also at any given time. In the absence of any "pope" or even council to lay down dogma, it is possible to find individual figures in almost any period who were either friendly or hostile toward the temporal government. Sometimes these figures were associated with schools of thought or doctrine—the best known are the Akhbaris and the Usulis—but even these schools changed over time.

In the question most relevant to the chapters herein, the attitude of the ulama toward Iran's temporal government, men in or near the early Akhbari school, which opposed the power of *mujtahids* (men whom the Usulis considered empowered to interpret the law and doctrine), also opposed some Usulis' close ties to those in power. In the eighteenth century, however, there appears to have been a change in Usuli views, probably owing largely to the trauma of Nadir Shah's confiscation of Shi'i *waqfs* (endowments that benefited religious authorities) and his attempt to deinstitutionalize Shi'ism. Left without a government with which to identify, the Usulis took on some of the independence and skepticism toward government formerly associated more with the Akhbaris, and as the Usulis became by far the predominant school by the nineteenth century, in that century ulama conflicts with the government were mainly associated with men of Usuli belief.[1]

The main point of the above brief outline lies not in its details, which may be further modified, but in its providing one example, of which there are many others, of the variability of religious doctrine even among "orthodox" religious leaders both at one time and over time. Hence, in discussing clerical attitudes toward, and relations with, the state in Iran, it is important to note, more than most authors do, that there were diverse trends in time and space, and, to take a favorite question for scholars as an example, no absolute statements may now be made about views of all ulama on the legitimacy of temporal government.

Another consideration relevant to the subjects under discussion here is that scholars are usually, especially as regards the past, confined to written materials. Even though it is recognized that writers during most of the Pahlavi period and Islamic Republic had to remain silent, speak insincerely, or only hint indirectly regarding many questions, so that few take the publications of these periods as real expression of the range of views held in society, the same commonsense caution is often not followed regarding past clerical writings. Orally expressed views should not be discounted. For example, I often heard in pre-Khomeini Iran from Iranians who knew Shi'ism well, including Sayyid Hasan Taqizadeh and others with a good Shi'i education, that Shi'ism regards temporal rulers as illegitimate. Even Joseph Eliash, who argues against any early doctrinal basis for such a view of illegitimacy, wrote that it was widely held in Iran.[2] It is now becoming fashionable to attribute this view to a few Western scholars, but in fact it is an Iranian Shi'i view that long predates the Ayatollah Ruhollah Khomeini, however little it is found in published doctrinal works, and however little its possible revolutionary implications were worked out before Khomeini. It appears moot to argue that it is not part of Shi'i doctrine because it is not found in major Shi'i texts; many firmly believed ideas in various Iranian religions and other traditions have been taught orally, often through commentaries on texts, and oral evidence is often as important as are written texts.

It does appear, however, that the Shi'i ulama in Safavid and early Qajar times were primarily supportive of the dynasty. Some of them occupied state-appointed positions, and they were often active, in cooperation with the state, in putting down minority religious movements, particularly Sufism under the late Safavids, and Babism-Baha'ism since the mid-nineteenth century. Leading ulama were often landlords and/or merchants, and their domination of religious courts, schools, and welfare institutions gave them great control and influence over the other classes in society. Unlike the Egyptian and Turkish ulama, they were not brought under central government control until the late 1920s. Their longer independence resulted largely from the weakness of the Iranian state and their own power to cause trouble, deriving largely from their ideological and financial independence of the state. The decline in ulama power 1925–78 was a concomitant of the formation of a modern state by Reza Shah and of state building and other modernizing activities by the Pahlavis, supported by those of the middle and upper classes who were Western-oriented. Under Reza Shah the ulama had to give up control of the new courts, schools, and welfare institutions, to pass examinations to show their capacity for religious or judicial functions, and to confront an officially blessed burgeoning of secular nationalism, secular education, courts, and other institutions, and reforms even in such sensitive spheres as family law.

Beneath the surface, however, there were developments that enabled the ulama later to become a focus for organized opposition to the Pahlavis. First, the very retreat of the leading ulama from certain places, especially in Iraq, which became less hospitable than it had been under the Ottomans, gave them compact centers, especially in Qum and Mashhad, where there was closer contact than before among leaders of the ulama. Second, the divorce of many leading ulama from many activities like trade and general education and their need to take examinations brought on some professionalization of the ulama corps, which was accented by the law saying that only recognized ulama could wear long robes and turbans. Third, there was some change in the class character of most ulama; while formerly sons of leading ulama and upwardly mobile bazaaris got religious educations, increasingly ulama came from rural and especially small-town backgrounds, while sons of leading ulama were more liable to get Westernized educations and enter modern professions. The ulama who back Khomeini tend to come from such small-town origins, and such nonelite origins help explain the radicalism of Khomeini and those around him.[3]

The anticlericalism and secularism of the increasingly unpopular Pahlavis, the fading memory of the ills brought on by clerical power in earlier periods, and the continued independence of some clerical leaders, displayed notably in the antigovernment demonstrations led by Khomeini in 1963, made the clerics seem useful allies to many opponents of the Pahlavis. Many who by late 1978 threw in their lot with Khomeini were not part of a religious opposition, notably the secular National Front groups. Secularists saw both in 1963 and 1978 that Khomeini could influence the masses more than the National Front or Marxist groups, including the Fedayan guerrillas, the Tudeh party, and the Maoist Paykar. Revulsion against Pahlavi tyranny and Western incursions had also led to an anti-Western and pro-Islamic reaction among some liberals and leftists. This was most importantly represented by the guerrilla, and later mass, movement, the Mojahedin-e Khalq, but is also seen in a number of leftist and third world intellectuals, notably Jalal Al-e Ahmad, Ali Shariati, and Abolhasan Bani Sadr. It is surely no accident that all three had clerical fathers; such men, even more than average Iranians with similar views, no doubt felt a need to reconcile the apparently contradictory attractions of their religious upbringing with the secular radicalism they encountered during their later education.

The Khomeini-led revolution was able to appeal (1) to generalized anti-Shah and anti-American discontent, based on a variety of economic and social realities that have been analyzed elsewhere;[4] (2) to strong support for Khomeini among a large section of religious students and ulama, among rural-urban migrants who had been helped by clerics, and among bazaaris; and (3) to non-Khomeinist organized oppositionists, chiefly National Font and leftist, who saw that Khomeini was the opposition leader with the greatest mass popularity, and convinced themselves he would step aside for them once the shah was weakened or overthrown. The continued power of Iran's ulama and the appeal of an Islamic doctrine modified to meet mass populist demands gave to Khomeini and his followers more power than his temporary allies ever expected, however.

The Islamic Republic, even though its initial growing radicalism and later moves to the right and toward stability follow the general pattern of Brinton's *Anatomy of Revolution*,[5] is in many ways a unique historical phenomenon. In no other modern state have clerical leaders taken direct power and held the major positions of government. Nor does this position for clerics, despite Khomeini's writings since 1971, find support in earlier Shi'i doctrine. Only the Twelfth Imam returned as Mahdi has a claim to rule, and while leading clerics may claim to be the Imam's deputies and to interpret his will in matters of law and doctrine, this interpretation is specifically regarded as fallible, and past clerics have not, to our knowledge, spoken of direct rule by one or several clerical figures.

For all its uniqueness, however, Khomeini's government in practice incorporates many features known to other governments. Like most governments that emerge from great mass revolutions it is highly ideological—dividing the world into the virtuous and the evil—and carries out a war demanding great sacrifice in the name of its ideology. Again like many postrevolutionary governments, it has had to adopt and often intensify many of the practices of its prerevolutionary predecessor: in Khomeini's case including heightened terror against political opponents; the rebuilding of a strong central state with emphasis on internal and external security organizations; and even a return to stress on foreign trade, investment, and technical aid. The government has become even more heavily involved in the economy than before. There has been some redistribution of income, but no really new economic system. Along with these policies reminiscent of non-Islamic revolutionary governments have gone reinstitution of "Islamic" laws, practices, and punishments that especially affect women and are reminiscent of nonrevolutionary governments like those of Pakistan and Saudi Arabia.[6] But there has been no attempt at a return to a premodern past, and the government has been able to use technocrats in high- and second-level positions in order to bring the oil industry and economy back into reasonable functioning order, despite the very costly Iran-Iraq war.

The relation between religion and politics in Iran since the Safavids introduced Shi'ism in 1501 may thus be seen to have been one of uneasy alliance, criticized by a growing body of clerics, under the Safavids and early Qajars. The two attempts radically to cut the power and income of clerics—that of Nadir Shah and that of Reza Shah—are seen to have had ironically contradictory results. After Nadir Shah the clergy were more determined than ever to protect their power and independence, while the Pahlavi attacks on clerical power somewhat similarly strengthened the desire of some important clerics to stand up to the shahs. The changing doctrines of the Shi'i clerics were just one factor in their continuing power. Probably more important were their continuing control of religious taxes that in Sunni countries went to rulers, their ties to the bazaar (traditional merchant and artisan) classes, their role as an independent force in a country that was hard to centralize, and other factors that I and others have discussed elsewhere. In class terms, the modern struggles of the ulama in the rebellious and revolutionary movements 1890–1911 represented, even more than clerical interests, those of the bazaar middle classes, who participated heavily, and of some intellectuals and modernizing landlords and courtiers. In 1963–79 the Khomeinist movement represented religious and many secular students, often of rural, small-town, or lower bazaar background; much of the traditional bourgeoisie, petite bourgeoisie, and workers, generally referred to together as bazaaris; as well as rural-urban migrants. Given these different class backgrounds of the two revolutions, as well as a different main enemy (a traditional regime in 1906–11; a Westernizing pro-Western one in 1978–79), it is not surprising that the largely elite clericals who supported the 1906 revolution acquiesced in a Western-style constitution, while the nonelite Khomeinists of 1979 demanded a far more radical "Islamic Republic" and constitution.[7]

State formation in Iran began with Reza Shah (1925–41) and inevitably clashed both with religious power and with the claims of various ethnic, religious, and tribal groups. Modern state formation requires a homogeneity of basic law and administration and cannot tolerate groups with independent control over means of coercion, such as clerics with armed followers, or armed nomadic tribes. Hence the important homogenizing measures of Reza Shah included not only those noted above, which reduced the power of the clergy in areas that most modernizing rulers want to be government-controlled institutions—notably courts and schools—but also hospitals, orphanages, and the like. Reza Shah's centralizing measures also included a huge increase in the central bureaucracy and a modernized army with which he could and did suppress any possible revolt by tribes. Several successful antitribal campaigns were followed by the forced settlement of most nomads without any compensating means to enable ex-nomads to gain a living without enough pastures. Some migration resumed in 1941, but Muhammad Reza Shah's modernizing measures, including land reform and the nationalization of forests, were carried out so as to deprive tribes of land needed for grazing and migration. Although migration increased at the time of the Islamic Revolution, the present government is now concerned to control tribes.[8]

The tribal issue is related both to state formation and to the issue of minorities. The major tribal groups are non-Persian speaking, but in most historical periods their mode of life and production has been more important than their language in distinguishing them from the settled Persians. Among non-Persian speakers who include in their ethnic group migrating or formerly migrating tribes, two main categories may be distinguished. First are the large border groups, entirely or partly Sunni in religion, who have a related group across the border, which increases their possibilities of revolt. These are the Baluchis in the southeast, the Turkomans in the north, the Kurds in the west (partly Shi'i), and the Arabs in the southwest (mostly Shi'i). Before Reza Shah the ties of these to the central government were often weak, and they have been involved in various revolts before and since the 1979 revolution, particularly the Kurds, whose autonomist revolt continues. The second group, composed of smaller entities, sometimes organized into tribal confederations, mainly not located on borders, and Shi'i in religion, presents less danger to the state. It includes the Bakhtiari and Qashqa'i tribal federations, the Lurs, Afshars, and other tribes. These groups have been less rebellious, although the Qashqa'i have a history of rebellion and one section of them revolted after the 1979 revolution. The major ethnic minority, the Azerbaijan Turks, are not tribal (except for the Shahsevans) and many of them have long identified closely with the state.

Linguistic diversity was not an important problem in pre-twentieth century Iran, mainly because national education and communication were undeveloped, but religious minorities by contrast had more problems both before and after the Pahlavis than they did under the secular Pahlavi state. Islam decrees a recognized position for "People of the Book"—which in Iran came to mean Christians, Jews, Zoroastrians, and Sabeans. Muslims granted better treatment to religious minorities than did medieval Christians. Modern secular governments like that of the Pahlavis, however, preferred to end traditional religious segregation and the second-class status of certain religious groups, partly in order to make use of the talents of the minority groups, who often had the advantage of modern educations. Separate treatment has always been given the Baha'is, who were widely seen as heretics and allies of the West, and this has reached terrible proportions under the Islamic Republic. The Islamic Republic was willing to grant linguistic minorities some right to use their own languages (though it is unclear how far this has been carried out in practice), but it was much harder on religious minorities than were the Pahlavis, and even Sunnis have complained about a Shi'i monopoly of power.[9]

Iran, Afghanistan, and Pakistan have each experienced ethnic-linguistic minority problems and have had unstable and changing governments in recent years, but in all three many measures needed to set up a modern economy have been put into force. In none of the three is government stable, despite a considerable background in modern state formation, and in all three extraordinary coercive measures are utilized in different degrees to keep the government in power. Islam is a political force in all three countries, but it plays a very different role and is utilized ideologically by different groups in Iran, Pakistan, and Afghanistan.

Iran's unique experiment has yet to be imitated in any other country, though it has influenced many Muslims outside Iran. Only time will tell whether Iran's Islamic Republic will remain a unique and perhaps short-lived experiment, or whether it will continue well beyond the death of Khomeini and perhaps inspire imitators who can, however, hardly copy the Iranian model, given the unique role of the Iranian ulama.

NOTES

1. Important new conclusions about the Usulis and the Akhbaris will appear in the forthcoming UCLA dissertation by Andrew Newman, and in Juan R. I. Cole and Nikki R. Keddie, eds., *Shi'ism and Social Protest* (New Haven: Yale University Press, 1986).

2. Joseph Eliash, "Misconceptions regarding the Juridicial Status of the Iranian 'Ulama'," *International Journal of Middle East Studies*, 10:1 (February 1979), pp. 9–25.

3. Eric Hooglund, "Social Origins of the Revolutionary Clergy," in Nikki R. Keddie and Eric Hooglund, eds., *The Iranian Revolution and the Islamic Republic*, 2nd ed. (Syracuse: Syracuse University Press, 1986); and Michael M. J. Fischer, *Iran: From Religious Dispute to Revolution* (Cambridge, Mass.: Harvard University Press, 1980). Mangol Bayat is studying such factors as ulama professionalization under Reza Shah.

4. See especially Nikki R. Keddie, *Roots of Revolution: An Interpretive History of Modern Iran* (New Haven, Conn.: Yale University Press, 1981); Fred Halliday, *Iran: Dictatorship and Development* (New York: Penguin, 1979); Eric Hooglund, *Land and Revolution in Iran, 1960-1980* (Austin: University of Texas Press, 1982); Ervand Abrahamian, *Iran Between Two Revolutions* (Princeton, N.J.: Princeton University Press, 1982); Robert Graham, *Iran: The Illusion of Power*, rev. ed. (London: Croom Helm, 1979); Shaul Bakhash, *The Reign of the Ayatullahs* (New York: Basic Books, 1985).

5. Crane Brinton, *The Anatomy of Revolution* (1938; 1952; New York: Vintage Books, 1965).

6. On women in and since the revolution see Farah Azari, ed., *Women of Iran* (London: Ithaca Press, 1983); Azar Tabari and Nahid Yeganeh, eds., *In the Shadow of Islam* (London: Zed Press, 1982); and Guity Nashat, *Women and Revolution in Iran* (Boulder, Colo.: Westview Press, 1983).

7. For a comparison of the two Iranian revolutions on this and other points see Nikki R. Keddie, "Iranian Revolutions in Comparative Perspective," *American Historical Review*, 88:3 (June 1983), pp. 579-98. See also the discussions of both revolutions in Abrahamian, *Iran Between Two Revolutions*, and Keddie, *Roots of Revolution*.

8. See the chapter and bibliographical items in the Higgins chapter within, and Lois Beck, "Revolutionary Iran and Its Tribal Peoples," *Middle East Research and Information Project [MERIP] Reports* (No. 87), 10:4 (May 1980), pp. 14-20.

9. On minorities, in addition to the Higgins chapter within, see Nikki R. Keddie, "The Minorities Question in Iran," in Shirir Tahir-Kheli and Shaheer Ayubi, eds., *The Iran-Iraq War: Old Conflicts, New Weapons* (New York: Praeger, 1983); and Leonard M. Helfgott, "Tribalism as a Socioeconomic Formation in Iranian History," *Iranian Studies*, 10:1-2 (1977), pp. 36-61.

6

MINORITY-STATE RELATIONS in CONTEMPORARY IRAN

PATRICIA J. HIGGINS

B Y ALL ACCOUNTS the departure of the Shah from Iran in January 1979 was met by most Iranians with the expectation of greater freedom, individually and collectively. For a number of minority groups, this included the expectation of greater cultural and political autonomy. Initially the new Islamic Republic appeared to be sympathetic to such expectations, but by the summer of 1979 violent conflicts were erupting between the central government and members of several tribal, regional, and ethnic minority groups. While the central government appears to have contained the ethnic and regional autonomy movements, officials and analysts have continued to express concern over the possible fragmentation of Iran, and autonomy movements are viewed by some as a significant obstacle to the consolidation of the new regime and/or a threat to its stability.

Continued concern with such issues warrants a closer look at how the relationship between minority groups and the central government has changed in Iran since the revolution and the establishment of the Islamic Republic.[1] The subject has obvious practical implications for international politics as well as for the internal development of Iranian society. In addition, comparison of minority-state relations in the Pahlavi state (1925–79) and in the Islamic Republican state can contribute to our general understanding of contemporary nation building and of the nature of group formation, maintenance, and dissolution.

For these purposes the Iranian Revolution and the subsequent establishment of the Islamic Republic can be seen as a naturally occurring experiment in which the territorial and population boundaries of the state have remained (more or less) the same, while some changes in the organization of the state and in the relationship of the state to external forces have occurred. Structural changes which have influenced minority group consciousness, mobilization, and relationship to the state may be found to be examples of more generally occurring processes of group formation and not unique to contemporary Iranian society. Admittedly, a full analysis along these lines is not yet possible, due to the limited nature of the data available and due to the incomplete institutionalization of the Islamic Republic. Nevertheless, comparative analysis of minority-state relations in these two eras of Iranian history can be begun, and some tentative conclusions can be drawn.

Briefly stated, it is suggested here that changes in minority-state relations should be investigated along two dimensions: the ideological dimension, which concerns individual identification with the state and/or other social groups of lesser (or greater) inclusiveness; and the materialistic dimension, which concerns the degree and mode of individual or group access to the economic and political resources of the state. It is assumed that the state, which by definition has the greater power, sets the structural framework which bounds both ideological and materialistic dimensions for minority-state relations. Members of minority groups by and large adjust their response to this framework, though they may attempt to secure a redefinition of the framework as well. In applying this approach to the study of minority-state relations in contemporary Iran, the frameworks established by the Pahlavi and the Islamic Republican states are first compared. The type and degree of integration of various minority groups in the two states is "predicted" in view of the framework established by each. Then, actual changes in the situation and in the response of three groups—chosen because of their pivotal position theoretically as well as practically—are examined relative to these predictions.

This analysis reveals that the dramatic and significant shift in emphasis from the secular, language-based, Persian nationalism of the Pahlavi state to the Shi'ite Islamic religious focus of the Islamic Republic has been accompanied by relatively little change in other aspects of state organization relevant to minority-state relationships. Nevertheless, this shift in emphasis, in combination with actual and planned changes in the Iranian economy, has changed the situation of the various minority groups and generated predictable responses, and it may preface some longer-term readjustments in minority-state relations. The range of possible readjustment is limited, however, by the need for any central government of Iran, including that of the Islamic Republic as well as that of the Pahlavis, to maintain itself under basically similar internal and external conditions.

ETHNICITY AND THE STATE: THEORETICAL CONSIDERATIONS

A comparative analysis of minority-state relations in the Pahlavi and Islamic Republican periods need not begin in a conceptual vacuum, for it involves phenomena that have been widely studied by social scientists. A selective review of what is known about ethnic groups and ethnicity, on the one hand, and the contemporary state, on the other, provides initial guidelines for our understanding of this particular case.

For the purposes of this analysis I adopt with slight modification the definition of an ethnic group formulated by Talcott Parsons: it is a transgenerational and multifunctional group, "the members of which have, both with respect to their own sentiments and those of non-members, a distinctive identity" rooted in a sense of common history and, I would add, in a belief in common descent.[2] In addition to a sense of common history and ancestry, the distinct identity of an ethnic group may include other features. While the single most commonly recognized criterion of ethnic identity is language, religion is also often used as an ethnic marker. Features as diverse as common values and rituals, common written and/or oral literature, a common mode of economic adaptation, common elements of social organization, and a common aesthetic tradition have been associated with distinct ethnic identities. Viewed comparatively, however, no one of these features can be said to characterize ethnic identity in all cases, and many can also serve as mechanisms for identifying and uniting groups of other types.

Whatever the particular criterion for group identity, inquiry into the relationship of ethnic groups to the larger sociocultural systems of which they are a part ought to rest on the "situational" approach to ethnicity. As pioneered by Fredrik Barth, this approach is concerned with the "processes . . . involved in generating and maintaining ethnic groups." Barth argued that "the critical focus of investigation from this point of view becomes the ethnic *boundary* that defines the group, not the cultural stuff that it encloses." Cultural features characterizing different ethnic groups are significant primarily as "signals and emblems and of differences"—as markers that help maintain the boundaries and regulate interaction between ethnic groups.[3] Following Barth, ethnic groups will be viewed here not primarily as units rooted in ancient history or primordial identity and indelibly wedded to a distinctive cultural content, but rather as groups that exist in a dynamic functional relationship to one another and to the larger sociocultural system. This approach is particularly appropriate to an investigation of *change* in minority-state relations since the key questions involve the conditions under which ethnic markers might change, individuals might shift allegiances, and boundaries themselves might be altered.[4]

The situational approach tends to focus attention on the practical aspects of identity from the perspective of the individual. Changes in group boundaries and indeed society as a whole are viewed as the result of cumulative, individual, interest-based decisions. Individual decisions depend on the perception of economic, political, social, or even psychological interests, and they are necessarily made within a sociocultural context. That context includes fellow group members, members of other ethnic groups, and, in virtually all contemporary societies, a state bureaucratic structure.

As an organizational form that unites a number of local communities in a territorially based, sovereign political unit, the state tends to bring groups with divergent cultural histories into long-term, compulsory contact with one another. Claiming immunity from outside political forces and ultimate control over the legitimate use of force within their boundaries, states establish an "autonomous structure of public authority" and an "authoritative arena" within which individuals and groups act and interact.[5] It is increasingly recognized, moreover, that the organization of the state is not simply passive or at most responsive to existing ethnicity. The state can and often does have a part in creating and maintaining ethnicity as well as in its reorganization and redirection.[6]

Contemporary states share a number of additional features relevant to minority-state relationships by virtue of the fact that they coexist within a broadly common technological, economic, and international political environment. Compared to states of the nineteenth century and earlier, the boundaries of the contemporary state are more precisely defined, and the state more effectively occupies the entire territory. Technological advances, especially in the military and in transportation and communication, allow the state to penetrate all sectors of society. As state power and influence extend over the lives and affairs of peoples who consider themselves distinct from the dominant group, ethnic identity is often enhanced and politically mobilized ethnicity may result. If, on the other hand, a larger proportion of the population comes to identify with the state and/or the dominant group in the state, this geographic and sociopolitical extension of state power can occur more smoothly.

The management of ethnicity is of special concern to the contemporary state for another reason: the contemporary state generally "derives its legitimacy from its constituent population."[7] In contrast to earlier times, the rulers of virtually every state today justify their rule to some extent in terms of the will of the people. In practice, therefore, contemporary states attempt to establish and/or maintain a basis for identification between the government and the populace that can be extended to the entire population and that can be called upon as necessary to override other, often preexisting, identities and loyalties.

Contemporary states are also distinguished by a tendency to incorporate citizens into the state structure *individually*—to stress individual rights and duties with respect to the state rather than collective ones; to define individuals as equals in rights and duties; and to apply impersonal and universalistic principles in regulating relationships within their authoritative arenas. For a multiethnic state this generally involves encouraging acculturation to a common or core culture and the promise of assimilation (structural incorporation into any strata of society) to those who do acculturate. An alternative approach, common in preindustrial states, is to make that incorporation collective. In this case the state explicitly recognizes differences between constituent groups and to some extent defines the relationship of individuals to one another and to the state in terms of their group affiliation. Whether one group controls the state and positions of power or the ruling group is a coalition of elites from the constituent groups, neither assimilation nor extensive acculturation of the population is encouraged. If an ideology of equality is adopted, it is likely to focus on the proportional allocation of economic and political resources.[8] While most contemporary states rely primarily on individual incorporation of citizens, they often make some limited use of collective incorporation as well.

Contemporary states also play a more important role than did their predecessors in economic affairs and accept much responsibility for the material welfare of the population. Thus, the state "becomes a crucial and direct arbiter of economic well-being, as well as of political status,"[9] and changes in the structure of the state may affect both the economic and the political fortunes of large numbers of people. This in turn will affect the individual's definition and utilization of ethnic identity and boundaries.

IDEOLOGY and STRUCTURE of TWO IRANIAN STATES

Changes in minority-state relations precipitated by the 1978–79 revolution in Iran must be appreciated in the context of changes already effected by events of the twentieth century. The Iranian state is no longer weak and loosely integrated, governing through the representatives of semi-independent groups and threatened by territorial colonial expansion; rather, it has become a highly centralized, militarily powerful state whose boundaries are by and large supported by the world system of states and whose population has been partially integrated into a common socioeconomic and cultural order.[10] Comparison of the Pahlavi and the Islamic Republican states indicates that both display qualities characteristic of the contemporary state. Both have sought to maintain effective and pervasive control over the whole of their carefully demarcated territory and to enhance their powers vis-à-vis constituent groups, and in general both states have succeeded. Both cite the will of the people as one source of legitimacy and accept responsibility for their welfare. Both display a similar pattern of individual incorporation and the encouragement of acculturation and assimilation to a dominant sociocultural order. And both have tended to exert state control through highly centralized bureaucracies. Though the Islamic Republican regime has been accused of attempting to reinstitute a medieval social order in Iran, a study of the state structure and policies relevant to minority-state relations reveals rather, for better or worse, its twentieth-century character.

Although neither the Pahlavi nor the Islamic Republican state rest their claim to legitimacy on popular support alone, both do cite the will of the people as one source of legitimacy. This can be seen in the constitutions of the two states—the 1906 Constitution and the 1979 Constitution—both of which maintain that while ultimate sovereignty rests with God, the powers and sovereignty of the state are derived from the people.[11] While such formal declarations cannot be taken as accurate representations of state organization, they do constitute public expressions of some aspects of the ideological foundations of the state. In less formal documents leading political figures of both states have been portrayed or have portrayed themselves as ruling by both divine grace and the will of the people, and they and their followers have characterized their programs as recipients of both divine blessing and popular support.[12] The appeal to popular support as a basis of legitimacy, though combined with appeal to religious principles, increased the need to demonstrate a degree of identity between the state and the bulk of the population.

Both the Islamic Republican and the Pahlavi states also seek, on the whole, to incorporate citizens on an individual basis rather than collectively. Both constitutions guarantee equal rights before the law to all citizens, and citizens are expected to participate in the government individually by electing representatives to a national assembly.[13] Individual responsibility for the payment of taxes, for legal infractions, and for military service has been the norm in both states, in contrast to nineteenth-century Iran, in which relatively self-sufficient and quasi-independent local communities met many of these obligations to the state collectively.[14]

Like many contemporary states, both the Pahlavi and the Islamic Republican states do make partial exception to individual incorporation for some groups—Zoroastrian, Jewish, Armenian, and Assyrian Iranians. The 1979 Constitution guarantees these non-Muslim minorities religious freedom and limited autonomy with respect to personal status and family law, and the National Consultative Assembly includes representatives elected from and by each group.[15] Similar status was guaranteed the same groups under the 1909 Electoral Law and the Civil Code of the Pahlavi state (as adopted in 1935).[16] Concomitant with the collective incorporation of these religious minorities is their exclusion from ministerial status under the old constitution and from the office of president under the new one.[17] In these respects non-Muslims are not guaranteed the same rights as Muslims under either system.

Neither the Pahlavi nor the Islamic Republican state make any provision for the collective incorporation of any other minority group. Non-Shi'ite Muslims have no separate representation in the government; neither are they officially barred from any state positions. Members of linguistic minorities are also treated as individuals rather than as collectives in both states, and members of such minorities, provided they are Muslim, are theoretically eligible for any position in government and society.

A further similarity relevant to minority-state relations is the degree to which the two states are centralized polities. While the constitutions of both include provisions for some regional governance through elected local councils,[18] other policies have restricted the exercise of local governance. The Pahlavis centralized economics and politics in Tehran; redrew and renamed administrative units in an effort to eliminate feelings of regional distinctiveness; and named outsiders to key regional posts to weaken local elites.[19] The Islamic Republican government has considered plans for limited regional autonomy or decentralization, but proposals directed toward the establishment of a confederation were rejected in favor of a unitary state,[20] and, as in the Pahlavi state, discontent in provincial regions of the Islamic Republic has often focused on the dominance of outsiders in local affairs.[21] Both states also attempt to control economic affairs within the country and accept considerable responsibility for the economic well-being of the populace. In both cases, state control in the economic sphere is lodged in command of the oil income. State ownership of other mineral resources and of transportation, banking, and other large industries has continued under the Islamic Republic, and expansion of the state-controlled sector of the economy is planned.[22]

Like most contemporary states that seek to maintain a centralized unitary polity, that appeal to popular support for legitimacy, and that stress individual rather than collective incorporation of citizens, both the Pahlavi and the Islamic Republican states have attempted to establish and maintain a sense of identification between the state and the people, and both have encouraged acculturation to a common or core culture through universal education, the media, and other state institutions. While values directly supportive of the state are included, the common culture must also provide a basis for regular communication and interaction between individuals of diverse background; thus, it must consist of more than superficial state symbols and supportive propaganda. From this perspective it can be seen that, despite differences in state symbols, the common culture promoted in both the Pahlavi and the Islamic Republican states is essentially an urban, Persian, Shi'ite culture. Just as both states recognize Islam, and in particular the Twelver Ja'fari school of thought, as the state religion, both also recognize Persian (Farsi) as the official language. Though differing in emphasis, both also seek to spread more sophisticated urban versions of Persian literacy and literature and of Islamic values and theology.

The most striking and obvious contrast between the Pahlavi and Islamic Republican states is, of course, the difference in their use of Islam as an element in the common culture. Islam is taken as the focal symbol of identity between the state and the people in the Islamic Republic, and the primary bond uniting the populace; as such Islam permeates the common culture promoted by the state. That culture is promoted to a large extent through Persian (Farsi), the most widely used language in the country; but ideally Persian is simply the medium of communication and not itself a focal symbol of identity in the Islamic Republic. On the other hand, while the Pahlavis did identify themselves as Muslims and did make some claim to legitimacy on religious grounds, neither Reza Shah Pahlavi (1925–41) nor Muhammad Reza Shah Pahlavi (1941–79) stressed religion as a basis for identification with the state. They sought, rather, to develop and extend a sense of Persian identity, defined primarily in terms of language and literature and pre-Islamic history, as the basis for unity within the population and for identification with the state.[23]

The common culture fostered in schools of the Pahlavi era focused upon the secular literature and history of the Persian-speaking population, with more attention given to Euro-American culture than to variations in the cultures of Iran or the Islamic world. The tenets of Shi'ite Islam were taught, but as a separate subject, reinforcing the state-supported definition of religion as a realm apart from social and political affairs. Persian nationalism, the monarchical tradition, and modernization were further propagated as elements of the state-supported common culture through mass military conscription and a literacy corps and rural extension service. Radio, television, and film also portrayed models of modern, urbanized, secular lifestyles; glorified the monarchy and selected aspects of traditional Iranian culture; and denigrated village mullahs and other manifestations of backwardness.[24] As in many "modernizing" states, "modernity" itself was identified with secular nationalism and with the ethnicity of the core group—the Persians.[25]

Controversy continues over the content of the common culture to be fostered by the Islamic Republic and the particular interpretation of Shi'ite Islam to be supported by the state.[26] It is clear, however, that religious values and traditions are being emphasized rather than secular ones and that the Islamic rather than the Euro-American world is taken as the relevant international cultural context. Curriculum reform began almost immediately with the removal of materials glorifying the Pahlavis and the monarchical tradition and the substitution of Arabic for English as a second language, and plans called for "more religious instruction in the textbooks, along with . . . discussions of the role of Moslem clergymen in the building of Iranian society."[27] Analyses of television, radio, and the press in the

Islamic Republic also demonstrate the dominance of religious figures and religious values and the degree to which the Islamic world has become the focal international context.[28]

INTEGRATION of MINORITIES

The Pahlavi and the Islamic Republican policies of individual incorporation of citizens, of nonrecognition of minorities (other than selected religious minorities), and of encouragement of acculturation to a common culture, in combination with the guarantee of equal rights, imply an ideal of assimilation. Individuals should have equal access to resources, power, and all social positions, whatever their ancestry; this is particularly true to the extent that they learn the common culture, can operate effectively according to the common rules, and can identify with the unifying principles of the state. Differences in unifying principles, state symbols, and the common culture supported by the state are likely, however, to affect the ease of acculturation and assimilation for various minorities. In particular, to the extent that the structural framework of each state reflects its principle of unity, one might expect individuals of Persian-speaking non-Shi'ite background to have been integrated into the Pahlavi state more easily than those of non-Persian Shi'ite background. Conversely, individuals of non-Persian Shi'ite background should find integration into the Islamic Republican state easier than should Persian-speaking non-Shi'ites (see Table 6.1).

The potential importance of this change in the state-supported principle of unity and the associated shift it implies from language to religion as the dominant criterion of mainstream or minority status can be seen in any computation of the sizes of religious and linguistic groups in Iran (see Table 6.2). While population estimates of the several linguistic groups vary widely, it is generally accepted that native speakers of Persian (Farsi), strictly defined, make up no more than half of the population of Iran. Broadly defined to include the native speakers of all Indo-European languages, Iranian linguistic identification can be extended to include some 65 percent of the population. In contrast, Shi'ite Muslims make up 90 percent of the population, and if all Muslims are included the total primary identification group climbs to 97 percent of the population.

In the Pahlavi state the ideal of acculturation and assimilation was extended in effect to both religious and linguistic minorities, despite formal recognition of Shi'ite Islam as the state religion and of the special status of select religious minorities. In practice, however,

TABLE 6.1   DIMENSIONS OF UNITY

	Religion			
Language*	Shi'ite Islam	Sunni Islam	Recognized Religions	Others
Persian (Farsi)	Persians		Jews	Baha'is
			Zoroastrians	
	Bakhtiaris			
	Lurs			
Other Indo-Iranian	Kurds	Kurds	Jews (Kurdish	
		Baluchi	speaking)	
Other Indo-European			Armenian	
Arabic	Arabs	Arabs		
Other Semitic			Assyrians	
Turkish	Azeris	Turkoman		
	Qashqa'i			

*Language classification is based on Nyrop, ed., *Iran: A Country Study,* pp. 140–43; and Herbert H. Vreeland, ed., *Iran* (New Haven, Conn.: Human Relations Area Files, 1957), pp. 48–51.

assimilation was only partially achieved, and by and large minorities did not have equal access to positions of power and authority. During the late 1960s, for example, the political elite was found to be almost exclusively Tehran-based and the only linguistic minority from which any number achieved high government positions was the Azerbaijani.[29] A review of the background of cabinet members during the late Pahlavi era suggests that the underrepresentation of linguistic minorities among the political elite had not changed.[30] On the other hand, religious minorities may have been overrepresented in government, given their very small numbers in the population, and efforts were made toward the end of the Pahlavi era to remove some of the legal and social disabilities faced by religious minorities in government service.[31]

Economically, too, the regionally based linguistic minorities did not have equal access to resources, while religious minorities reportedly enjoyed a somewhat higher standard of living under the Pahlavis than did the average Iranian.[32] Regional development projects often siphoned more wealth out of the provinces than they returned and provincial areas did not receive equitable services. The relative neglect of rural and regional areas in favor of centralized urban development was felt more strongly by the linguistic minorities than by the largely urban, religious minorities.

TABLE 6.2   ETHNOLINGUISTIC GROUPS of IRAN

Group	Language	Religion	Population Estimates* (1977)	Location
Persians	Farsi	Shi'ite Islam	17,000,000	Central plateau; major cities
Azeris	Azeri Turkish	Shi'ite Islam	9,000,000	Northwest; major cities
Kurds	Kurdish	Sunni and Shi'ite Islam	3,500,000	Western mountain areas
Arabs	Arabic	Shi'ite and Sunni Islam	600,000	South; Persian Gulf littoral
Baluchis	Baluchi	Sunni Islam	600,000	Southeast
Qashqa'i	Turkish dialect	Shi'ite Islam	400,000	Southern Zagros
Turkoman	Turkish dialect	Sunni Islam	500,000	Northeast
Bakhtiaris	Bakhtiari	Shi'ite Islam	570,000	Zagros
Lurs	Luri	Shi'ite Islam	500,000	Zagros
Armenians	Armenian	Christian	270,000	Northwest; major cities
Assyrians	Assyrian	Christian	32,000	Northwest; major cities
Jews	Farsi	Jewish	85,000	Isfahan; Tehran; major cities
Zoroastrians	Farsi	Zoroastrian	36,000	Yazd; Kerman; Tehran
Baha'is	Farsi	Baha'i	300,000	Major cities
			34,000,000	

*Population estimates are based primarily upon Nyrop, ed., *Iran: A Country Study*, pp. 143–54; Eden Naby, "The Iranian Frontier Nationalities," p. 84; and Beck, "Revolutionary Iran and Its Tribal Peoples," p. 16. Adjustments have been made in light of other, often contradictory, estimates found in the literature. Since the censuses of 1956, 1966, and 1976 did not record ethnicity or first language, and there have been no other statistically sound studies of language distribution in Iran, these figures must be considered highly tentative.

In contrast, assimilation of religious minorities is neither officially nor unofficially considered a desirable goal by the Islamic Republican state. Besides the Council of Guardians and the Supreme
Judicial Council, two institutions constitutionally established to insure the religious acceptability of government actions,[33] the National
Consultative Assembly, the Presidency, and many ministerial posts
have come to be dominated by religious figures.[34] This has been associated with efforts to insure that religious minorities fill only those
political roles formally allotted to them. The recognized religious minorities occupy a special status which no amount of acculturation
(short of conversion) is expected to modify.

In the economic sphere, too, changes since the revolution
effectively restrict the access of religious minorities to material goods
and positions of power and wealth. The decline in the service sector,
in foreign trade, and in enterprises based on foreign investment and
the high unemployment rates among white-collar workers must affect the religious minorities disproportionately, as they have tended
to specialize in such business activities. The proposed expansion of
the state-controlled sector of the economy is also likely to be disadvantageous for religious minorities since they are now restricted from
many types of government positions which, as well-educated,
middle-class, urban residents, a number formerly held.

On the other hand, the emphasis on religion rather than on
language as the basis for unity within Iran may allow linguistic minorities to be more easily integrated and better assimilated into the
Islamic Republic than they were into the Pahlavi state. The 1979 Constitution makes Persian the official language of Iran, but adds that
"the use of regional and national languages in the press and the mass
media, however, as well as for teaching in schools the literatures written in them is permitted in addition to Persian"[35]—rights which minorities sometimes exercised but which were never guaranteed under
the Pahlavis. At least in principle, therefore, linguistic minorities are
not required to forsake the key feature of their ethnic affiliation as the
price of assimilation.

Other political and economic changes hold some promise of
increased access to positions of power and authority in the state for
members of linguistic minorities. The state recognizes an obligation
to strengthen the economic base of the provinces and to provide comparable economic opportunities and services for regional populations,[36] and new plans for regional investment have been drawn up.
The greater emphasis on agriculture and rural development in general may benefit the linguistic minorities, many of whom are concentrated in rural and previously underdeveloped regions.[37]

Furthermore, despite centralizing tendencies, power continues to be more dispersed and decentralized than it was during the Pahlavi era.[38]

Both the economic and the political situation in Iran are in considerable flux. Nevertheless, the shift in emphasis in state ideology from a linguistic to a religious basis for unity appears to have been accompanied by a restructuring of the authoritative arena and economic sphere along parallel lines. As a result, religious minorities are likely to be less well integrated individually in the Islamic Republic than they were in the Pahlavi state, while linguistic minorities may eventually be better integrated economically and politically than they were formerly.

MINORITY RESPONSES: BAHA'IS, KURDS, and AZERBAIJANIS

On the basis of the preceding analysis, one might expect to see some predictable variation in the responses of different minority groups to changes in the authoritative arena affected by the Islamic Republic, limited as these changes are. Religion ought to be a sharper boundary marker and language a less pronounced boundary marker than formerly—not only in the classification of individuals and groups by the state, but also in the individual's own sense of identity, display of cultural markers, boundary-crossing behavior, and classification of others.

The relationship of the major ethnic groups of Iran to the alternative principles of unity has been illustrated in Table 6.1. The official cultures promoted by both the Islamic Republic and the Pahlavi states, and most of the leading figures of both regimes, are contained within the same category—that of Persian-speaking Shi-'ites. The revolution resulted not in the transfer of state control from one ethnic group to another, but rather in its transfer between portions of this same dominant group. Persian-speaking non-Shi'ite Iranians, who are expected to have been more easily integrated into the Pahlavi than into the Islamic Republican state, include Jews, Zoroastrians, and Baha'is,[39] while non-Persian-speaking Shi'ites, for whom the situation is reversed, include Azeris, Qashqa'i, and some Arabs. Baluchi and some Kurds—Sunni Muslims whose languages are related to Persian—are in a marginal position with respect to the state and the dominant ethnic group by either principle of unity, and in this sense their position has not changed. One might expect, however, that their identity within the Islamic Republic would focus more sharply on the religious factor than it did in the Pahlavi state and that linguistic differences would be a less prominent focus of any conflicts between these groups and the state than they were previously.

As a test of these expectations the following sections compare the actual situation of three minority groups—the Baha'is, the Kurds, and the Azeris—and their response to that situation within the Pahlavi and Islamic Republican states. These particular groups have been chosen because each is in a distinctly different relationship vis-à-vis the alternative principles of unity and because there exists for each a reasonable (though by no means exhaustive) body of data covering the time period in question. While both the ideological and the materialistic dimensions of ethnic identity and minority-state relations have been considered in the analysis of each case, the relative importance of these two dimensions has not been tested, as might be done by comparing groups in similar relationship to the state ideologically (Kurds with Baluchi, for example, or Jews with Zoroastrians) or by comparing individuals or subgroups in different materialistic situations within ethnic groups. In comparing the situations and responses of these three groups within the two states, it must be borne in mind as well that the groups vary considerably in size, in degree of geographic concentration, and in historical depth of group identity. These are all variables which can be expected to affect the situation and the response of particular ethnic groups, somewhat independently of their relationship to one or another principle of unity.

The Baha'is: An Unrecognized Religious Minority

An outgrowth of the nineteenth-century Babi movement, the Baha'i religion has clear historical roots in Iran and in Shi'ite Islam.[40] The founder of the religion, Baha'ullah, was exiled from Iran and eventually settled near Acre, then part of the Ottoman Empire, later under British control, and now part of Israel. Baha'ullah's successors lectured widely and Baha'i texts were translated into many languages, so that by the mid-twentieth century the Baha'i religion had an estimated three million adherents in over a hundred countries.

Baha'i teachings reflect both the Islamic and Iranian roots of the faith and the extensive contacts of its early leaders with Western intellectual traditions. All major religions are believed to share a common foundation, and the prophets of Judaism, Christianity, and Islam are recognized (as are those of Buddhism and Zoroastrianism). The message of these prophets has been superseded, however, by that of Baha'ullah—a message uniquely suited for the present age.

Any adult can become a Baha'i by professing faith in Baha'ullah, and no one becomes a Baha'i simply by descent from Baha'is; each individual must independently investigate religious truth. Baha'i teachings stress the oneness of humanity, and universal education, sexual equality, world peace, and an auxiliary international language are advocated. A peacefully established world government is anticipated for the future, but in the meantime Baha'is are expected to obey the laws of the state in which they reside and to refrain from participation in politics.

From the perspective of the Shi'ite clergy and many Iranian Muslims, however, Baha'ism is considered not a religion but an Islamic heresy or a British and/or Zionist-backed subversive political movement. Because Baha'is have not been a recognized religious minority in either the Pahlavi or the Islamic Republican state, facts and figures concerning Iranian Baha'is are particularly scarce. Though estimates of their number vary from less than 100,000 to 500,000, they are commonly thought to be the largest single non-Muslim group in the country.[41] Baha'is appear to be geographically dispersed in small numbers throughout the country, though they are primarily urban based with major concentrations in Tehran and Shiraz. They most often speak Persian as a native language and are not readily distinguishable from the dominant population.

The secular tone of the Pahlavi state and its efforts to contain the power of the religious leaders generally made the incorporation of the Baha'is into the state and the society as a whole relatively smooth. Lack of recognition did make it difficult for Baha'is to register marriages and births, publish religious literature, or run their own schools, and they were subject to discrimination on an individual basis. More seriously, the Pahlavis were willing, on occasion, to sacrifice Baha'i interests in order to mollify Islamic leaders, as in the 1955–56 anti-Baha'i riots led by religious leaders with implicit government acquiescence.[42] On the whole, however, the Pahlavi government protected the rights of Baha'is as citizens, and the Baha'is, in accordance with their policy of nonparticipation in political affairs, in effect supported the Pahlavis.

In the Pahlavi state, Baha'is could be seen as particularly good citizens. In addition to speaking Persian and implicitly supporting the government in power, they combined in their beliefs and traditions elements from both Islamic Iranian civilization and other progressive and Western-style ideas. Their beliefs in universal education, sexual equality, and service to humanity, for example, correspond to policies supported by the Pahlavis in their efforts to modernize Iran. The practice of these beliefs made Baha'is, on the whole, better educated than the average Iranian, and they probably have been overrepresented among Iranian professionals. Thus, they could be seen as filling useful economic as well as political niches.

As long as Iran was becoming a more secular state, that Baha'is were not a recognized religious minority could be advantageous in that they could rise to positions in the government formally forbidden to non-Muslims. The extent to which they took advantage of this opportunity is difficult to judge. Several cabinet ministers of the late Pahlavi era were rumored to be Baha'i, and their Baha'i parentage is acknowledged, though they considered themselves and were considered by the government to be Muslims.[43] Baha'is agree that these high government officials were not Baha'i, though some had Baha'i relatives, and in at least one case when an acknowledged Baha'i accepted a position in the cabinet he was expelled by Baha'is.[44] Nevertheless, many Baha'is were employed by the state at less prominent ranks, in contradiction to the letter of the law, and in the private sphere a number of prosperous businessmen and several top industrialists and financiers were Baha'i.[45] Overall, it seems that, despite some official restrictions, incidents of individual discrimination, and the underlying threat of religiously sanctioned attacks, Baha'is were fairly well integrated into the Pahlavi state and were able to take advantage of their de facto equality to achieve at least moderate economic success and material prosperity. At the same time, the history of persecution and the shared sense of the precariousness of their situation as an unrecognized religious minority and one actively opposed by many religious leaders insured that the Baha'is remained a distinct group within Iranian society.

Under the Islamic Republic the situation of the Baha'is has changed dramatically. Their implicit cooperation with the Pahlavis, their Western-style teachings, and their international orientation, in combination with their heretical religious beliefs, have caused them to be seen as internal enemies of the state. Individually they have been subjected to numerous attacks on their property and their persons, and for the most part the government has not taken action against attackers. Rather, the government itself has arrested, tried, and executed a number of Baha'i leaders (generally on charges of spying for the United States and Israel) and has confiscated Baha'i community property. It has also encouraged the enforcement of regulations prohibiting employment of Baha'is by the state in any capacity and forbidding the issuance of identity cards (necessary for many transactions of normal life) to any but those of recognized religions. Moreover, by reordering national priorities in the economic sphere, the government has, in effect, made it less rewarding economically as well as politically to be a Baha'i in Iran. In sum, the Baha'is, who by virtue of their beliefs and practices could be respected and even prominent citizens in the secular Pahlavi state, are now being pressured to change their religious identification as the minimal price for citizenship in the Islamic Republic.

The response of Iranian Baha'is has been flight and/or appeals to international bodies to pressure the Iranian government to change its policies. The most favorable outcome for the Baha'is as a group within the Islamic Republican state would seem to be to gain recognition as a religious minority. This appears unlikely, however, given the existence of many Muslim Iranians with similar skills, the decline in those sectors of the economy in which Baha'is were concentrated, and the high degree of doctrinal inflexibility displayed by Shi'ite leaders with respect to the Baha'is over the past century. While the Baha'is—relatively few in number and geographically dispersed—are hardly a threat to the state, they play a symbolic role in the ideology of the Islamic Republican state which makes any official change in the position of the state difficult to imagine.

In the meantime, some Baha'is who remain in Iran may be, if not converting, then quietly passing as Muslims.[46] Their lack of distinguishing physical, linguistic, or behavioral features and their tenet that one becomes a Baha'i by choice as an adult and not by virtue of being born into a Baha'i family facilitate this process. Obviously, if a significant number of Iranian Baha'is choose either to convert, pass as Muslim, or leave the country, group boundaries will be affected and the Baha'is could cease to be a relevant Iranian minority group.

The Kurds: Marginal Linguistically, Religiously, and Economically

In contrast to the Baha'is, the Kurdish population is both large and regionally concentrated. Numbering some two to six million, depending on the source of population estimates, Iranian Kurds live primarily in the mountainous western portion of the country, and large numbers of co-ethnics live across the borders in Iraq and Turkey.[47] Occupied in agriculture, pastoralism, and production for subsistence and localized markets, Kurds have been somewhat buffered from and marginal to the national economy. They speak an Indo-European language related to Persian and are primarily Sunni Muslims; thus, whether language or religion is chosen as the major basis for state unity, the Kurds find themselves in a marginal position.

Under the Pahlavis acculturation of the Kurds was encouraged. While the Pahlavi emphasis on the cultural affinity of Kurds and Persians may have eased the assimilation of some into mainstream Persian society, most Kurds resented the cultural restrictions placed upon them.[48] Publication in Kurdish was banned (though some works were published clandestinely), and all teaching of Kurdish was forbidden. While there were radio broadcasts in Kurdish, these were controlled by the central government and directed as much or more toward Kurds in neighboring Iraq as toward Iranian Kurds.

Kurdish resistance to Pahlavi policies sometimes took a very active form. During the first several years of his reign, Reza Shah Pahlavi was involved in an intermittent campaign against rebellious tribal leaders. During World War II Kurdish nationalists established semi-independent regimes, culminating with the Mahabad Republic (1945-46); the Republic is believed to have had considerable popular support and to be indicative of the failure of Reza Shah's acculturation policies in Kurdistan. At the end of the war the Iranian army reasserted state control over the region. Renewed efforts to encourage acculturation followed, accompanied by tight military and security control.[49]

Kurdish nationalists maintain that the Pahlavi government, while denying Kurds both cultural rights and political autonomy, also denied them an equal share of the country's resources. Schools were few and ill equipped, illiteracy high, medical care inadequate, and per capita income and standards of living low. The economy of the region had, in fact, declined by some measures, due to some undermining of the local economy by imports, the poorly developed communication networks, and the lack of industrialization.[50] While grounds for complaint in a state that professes to treat all citizens equally and to promote assimilation, this economic marginality has also helped to maintain the cultural distinctiveness and ethnic boundaries which Kurdish nationalists are to some extent defending.

For several (sometimes contradictory) reasons, therefore, many Kurds felt they were not receiving their just due within the Pahlavi state, and in 1978 they joined actively in the revolution. Demonstrations and violent clashes with government forces were especially pronounced in the urban centers of Kurdistan and the Kurdish Democratic Party, revived some years earlier by a group of Kurdish intellectuals, took a leadership role.[51] With the revolution's success, Kurdish forces, in de facto control of their own region, pressed their claims for greater autonomy under the new regime. The new central government refused to recognize this autonomy, however, and clashes between representatives of the central government and Kurds have continued intermittently to the present. While negotiations have also continued intermittently, Kurdish leaders are reportedly fearful that the end of hostilities between Iran and Iraq will allow a strengthened central military to be turned against them.[52]

Politically, therefore, Kurds find themselves in a relationship vis-à-vis the Islamic Republic similar to their relationship with the Pahlavi state. Many are resisting incorporation into a state system with which they fail to identify. Of special interest for present purposes is whether the changes that have occurred in the central government and/or those that have occurred in the economy are reflected in the formulation of Kurdish identity.

In the Pahlavi-era literature on and by the Kurds, Kurds are identified and identify themselves primarily in terms of descent from ancient Indo-European tribes, demonstrated in practice through the use of the Kurdish language.[53] Prior to the 1920s identity and loyalty focused on smaller tribal groups and on individual leaders, and some chieftains and whole tribes prided themselves on Arabic (rather than Indo-European) descent.[54] The latter suggests that not only was the gradual transformation of identity from tribal to an ethnic basis a product of twentieth-century socioeconomic changes—as it was for many other Iranians[55]—but also that the choice of language as the basic criterion of ethnicity occurred in response to the Pahlavi focus on linguistically based ethnicity.

While most Kurds are Sunni Muslims, religion was not generally considered a crucial criterion of Kurdish ethnic identity during the Pahlavi era. Religious distinctions between Kurds had been important earlier because of the Safavid-Ottoman rivalries, but post-World War I nationalist movements included both Sunni and Shi'ite Kurds.[56] Writers even refer to Christian and Yazidi Kurds,[57] although the latter are not considered Kurds by all.

Since the revolution, however, there have been several indications of increased consciousness among Kurds as among Persians of the religious factor. While practical leadership of Kurdish political organizations has remained in secular hands, a Sunni religious figure, Shaykh Ezzeddin Hosseini, has been widely acknowledged as the most prestigious contemporary Kurdish leader.[58] Kurdish leaders claim that by 1981 Shi'ite-dominated sections of Kurdistan were also resisting the central government, but early resistance was greater in the Sunni areas, and the rank and file of the Sunni Kurdish religious leaders has been supportive of the Kurdish cause.[59] Concern focused initially on references to Iran as a Shi'ite state and on the central government's attempts to place Shi'ite religious leaders in charge of revolutionary organizations in Kurdistan. The demands of the Kurds now include that religious freedom be guaranteed, a demand not made in earlier autonomy movements under the Pahlavi state.[60] The continuing hostility and active conflict between large portions of the Kurdish population and the Islamic Republic appears to have promoted not only heightened ethnic consciousness but also an increased emphasis on religion as a significant aspect of Kurdish identity.

Nevertheless, Kurdish leaders are not calling for a Sunni Kurdish region or state but rather for autonomy within a secular state. In the program of the Kurdish Democratic Party, the largest and most influential organization presuming to represent the Kurds in Iran, the central government would "retain control over long term planning, the armed forces, foreign policy and the monetary system," while other affairs, including internal security, would be in the hands of elected Kurdish officials. Kurdish would be the official language, with Persian as a second language. Minorities would be allowed to teach and publish in their own languages, and equal rights and religious freedom would be guaranteed to all.[61]

Little attention is given in current Kurdish demands to economic questions beyond the general desire for more economic development and better services and facilities. If the Islamic Republic carries out its plans to strengthen domestic agriculture, promote small-scale technology, and foster regional economic development, the Kurds could be in a better economic position than they were in the Pahlavi state. The economic philosophy of the Islamic Republic appears to be more supportive of the type of small-scale regional self-sufficiency that has characterized the economy of Kurdistan.

Kurdish leaders stress that "no political force in Iranian Kurdistan wants to secede from Iran,"[62] and other observers agree that there has been no talk of secession or separation. Their demands can only be met, however, within a state framework rather different from the current one, and they have proposed that Iran be constituted as a federation of internally autonomous regions.[63] From the perspective of the central government, the Kurds are more threatening than the Baha'is not only because they are more numerous, geographically concentrated, and a border minority, but also because they are demanding not a slight readjustment of the state framework but a major reorganization. Should they be joined by similarly situated minorities and/or by Shi'ite Persian forces desirous of a secular state and agreeable to a confederacy, the balance of support for the Islamic Republic could be severely undermined.

The Azerbaijanis: A Well-Integrated Linguistic Minority

Clearly the largest of Iran's minorities, Azerbaijanis are esti-mated to number from six to fourteen million—up to one-third of the population of Iran—with large numbers living in Tehran and other Iranian cities as well as in the northwestern region of the country.[64] Like the Kurds, they are a border minority, with many co-ethnics living in neighboring regions of the Soviet Union. Though they speak a form of Turkish, the overwhelming majority of Azerbaijanis are Shi'ite Muslims, and many leading Shi'ite religious figures are and have been Azerbaijanis. Economically, Azerbaijanis have been rela-tively well integrated into the national system (and on a roughly equal basis with Persians) since well before the Pahlavi era.[65] Com-pared to other minorities Azerbaijanis have been better assimilated socially as well, with representatives at all levels of the political, mili-tary, and intellectual hierarchies, as well as the religious hierarchy.[66] Since their language has been their primary source of identity and sense of distinction vis-à-vis the dominant Persians, a change in the ideology and structure of government to emphasize religion rather than language as the focus of unity should make their identification with the Iranian state even easier than it has been in the past.

There is notable agreement in the literature that Azerbaijanis do not see themselves as a separate nation but rather identify closely with Iran.[67] There were strong provincial leaders in the 1917-25 period and an Autonomous Government of Azerbaijan was established un-der the protection of the Soviet Union in 1945. But lack of local sup-port can be seen as a major reason for the demise of both the post-World War I and World War II movements.[68] That no separatist movements occurred during the relatively free era of the early 1950s and that Azerbaijani garrisons were staffed with local officers and men during the later Pahlavi era are also considered evidence of the lack of separatist sentiment.[69]

Nevertheless, it is recognized that the Azerbaijanis were un-happy with many aspects of Pahlavi policies. In the nineteenth and early twentieth centuries Azerbaijan had been among the wealthiest of Iranian provinces and Tabriz a center of international trade. This preeminence was gradually lost as the Pahlavi program of economic modernization, initially based on revenue generated from the agricul-turally strong provinces like Azerbaijan, concentrated new industries in the Central province. The shift to dependence on oil income as a source of development funds and the rapid pace of economic growth in the 1960s and 1970s led to even greater economic centralization, so

that the provinces of East and West Azerbaijan fell even farther behind the average for the country on several socioeconomic indicators.[70] This decline in the relative importance of the province was
offset to some extent for the people of Azerbaijan by heavy migration
to Tehran and other areas in central Iran where many were able to
better their economic situation.

Azerbaijanis were discontent as well with the political centralization inherent in Pahlavi policies and practices, and more local
control of provincial government had long been desired. Suppression
of the use of Turkish in local government, in the schools, and in the
press was particularly resented,[71] and bilingual literate Azerbaijani
intellectuals were among the most critical of the monolingual and
monolithic educational program of the late Pahlavi era. Azerbaijan
and Azerbaijanis had played leading roles in the turn-of-the-century
constitutional movement; later they were among the staunchest supporters of Muhammad Mossadeq and his National Front (1950-53).[72]
And still later they were among the most active in the struggles to
overthrow the Pahlavi regime.

The tendency for Azerbaijanis to cast their lot with Iran as a
whole can also be seen in postrevolutionary events.[73] Early conflicts
in Azerbaijan were between leftists and followers of the Ayatollah
Ruhollah Khomeini, rather than between representatives of the central government and Azerbaijani nationalists; as such, they paralled
struggles going on in Tehran and other Persian-dominated cities
rather than those occurring in Kurdistan and other ethnically distinct
regions. Later conflicts between the Islamic Republican People's
Party, the membership of which was largely Azeri, and the Islamic
Republican Party concerned primarily national-level politics or local
manifestations of national power struggles.[74] In the years since 1981,
when the Islamic Republican Party solidified its control over the government, there have been few reports of disturbances in Azerbaijan,
particularly in comparison to those reported for Kurdistan where the
struggle for greater autonomy clearly continues.[75]

Even the events of December 1979—during which the Islamic
Republican People's Party and their backers, with the support of local
police, army, and air force units, effectively prevented the central
government from exercising its sovereignty in Azerbaijan for several
weeks—occurred as a result of national issues. Ayatollah Kazem Shariatmadari's criticisms of the proposed constitution and the resulting
boycott of the constitutional referendum by some 80 percent of Azerbaijani voters marked the beginning of this incident. While both Shariatmadari and the Islamic Republican People's Party advocated

somewhat greater regional autonomy, their basic demand—that the constitution be revised to encourage more secular participation in government—was supported by other elements of the population, and Shariatmadari's criticism of government efforts to destroy all opposition parties was not limited to the defense of Azerbaijani interests. Furthermore, their demand that the religious leader followed by most Azerbaijanis have the right to name officials to the Azerbaijan government suggests that they were not advocating a completely secular state. The conflict is probably better seen as one between two interpretations of the role religious leaders should play in government than as an Azerbaijani autonomy movement.[76]

Because of their numbers, their physical and social dispersal throughout Iranian society simultaneous with their maintenance of a provincial home base, and the wealth of their province, Azerbaijanis have the potential to shift the balance within the state itself. Thus, it has been in their interest to participate fully in Iranian states (including their formation and dissolution) rather than to seek autonomous status or collective recognition and collective incorporation by the state. The Islamic Republic's stated intentions to strengthen domestic agriculture and spread the benefits of economic development more evenly should be advantageous for the province of Azerbaijan. Moreover, Azerbaijanis' long sense of identity with the Iranian state is likely to be reinforced by the Islamic Republican state's emphasis on Shi'ism as the principle basis of unity and its concurrent relaxation of restrictions on the use of local languages. For Azerbaijanis, more than any other minority group in Iran, ethnic identity and group boundaries may well become increasingly less important.

SITUATIONAL CHANGE and ETHNICITY

Theoretical models of ethnic groups and ethnicity, on the one hand, and of contemporary states, on the other, call attention to both ideological and materialistic bases of identity and of group formation, maintenance, and dissolution. Ethnic groups, in addition to being historical units with which the state must cope, are also functional units which change in accordance with changing circumstances. Among those changing circumstances can be features of the state itself.

Comparison of the structural frameworks established by the Pahlavi and Islamic Republican states highlights the dramatic shift from Persian language and history to Shi'ism as the focus for identity between the state and its constituent population and the basis of unity within the population. In addition, concurrent changes in the political and economic structure have made it less advantageous than previously to be a member of a religious minority and relatively more advantageous to be a member of a linguistic minority. Comparison of the two state structures also reveals, however, several basic similarities relevant to minority-state relations, including a tendency toward centralization of state power; citation of the will of the people as one source of legitimacy; acceptance of responsibility for material welfare and economic affairs; a preference for individual incorporation of citizens (save for select religious minorities); and the encouragement of acculturation to a common urban Persian Shi'ite culture. These similarities are to some extent indicative of the limits imposed on even revolutionary change by the need to maintain the state under similar internal and external conditions; their extensiveness casts doubt on any expectation of imminent and massive reorganization of minority-state relations in Iran.

Analysis of the situation of three key minority groups illustrates some changes in the relationship of religious and linguistic minorities to the state. Baha'is, as members of an unrecognized religious minority, find themselves in a much more disadvantageous position politically and economically in the Islamic Republic than they were in the Pahlavi state, and the Baha'i group in Iran may well contract as individual Baha'is withdraw from their situation. The Kurds, marginal to the dominant ethnic group whether the boundary markers are linguistic or religious and marginal as well to the national economy, find their situation little changed under the Islamic Republic. While they may stress their religious distinctiveness somewhat more than in the past, they continue, as under the Pahlavis, to attempt to change the framework for minority-state relations in Iran. The Azerbaijanis, in contrast, share with the dominant ethnic group the current criterion for identification with the state; they also occupy a more or less parallel range of economic and political positions. Individually and collectively, they have been more involved in efforts to effect minor readjustments in the state structure than to claim a protected or autonomous status for themselves or to produce a major reorganization of the state. The comparison of these three groups, in the context of a comparison of the Pahlavi and Islamic Republican states, suggests that a situational analysis of ethnicity can help to illuminate contemporary problems in minority-state relations in Iran.

NOTES

1. The research on which this chapter is based was carried out as part of a National Endowment for the Humanities Summer Seminar (1981) on Muslim Ethnic Minorities in the Middle East and the USSR. Seminar directors Richard Frye and Eden Naby have made helpful comments on previous drafts of this paper. An abbreviated version was presented at the Sixteenth Annual Meeting of the Middle East Studies Association, November 1982. This study has also appeared, with modifications, in *Iranian Studies* 17:1 (Winter 1984), pp. 37-71.

2. Talcott Parsons, "Some Theoretical Considerations on the Nature and Trends of Change of Ethnicity," in Nathan Glazer and Daniel P. Moynihan, eds., *Ethnicity: Theory and Experience* (Cambridge, Mass.: Harvard University Press, 1975), pp. 53-83, esp. p. 56. This definition shares with most the notion that an ethnic group is a (self-) ascriptive biosocial group which exists within a larger sociocultural system and which is united by a sense of shared and distinctive customs. Though Parsons, like many social scientists, ignores the question of common descent in discussing ethnicity, a belief in common descent, bolstered by a tendency to marry within the group, does set apart those groups usually considered ethnic groups from other groups with a common history. For a good introduction to the conceptual parameters of ethnicity see James H. Dorman, "Ethnic Groups and 'Ethnicity': Some Theoretical Considerations," *Journal of Ethnic Studies*, 7:4 (Winter 1980), pp. 23-36.

3. Fredrik Barth, "Introduction," in Fredrik Barth, ed., *Ethnic Groups and Boundaries: The Social Organization of Culture Difference* (Boston: Little, Brown, 1969), pp. 9-38, esp. pp. 10, 15, 14.

4. For a recent theoretical discussion of ethnicity which parallels the approach taken here see Jeffrey C. Alexander, "Core Solidarity, Ethnic Outgroups, and Social Differentiation: A Multidimensional Model of Inclusion in Modern Societies," in Jacques Dofny and Akinsola Akiwowo, eds., *National and Ethnic Movements* (Beverly Hills, Calif.: Sage Publications, 1980), pp. 5-28.

5. The former is the terminology of Cynthia H. Enloe, *Ethnic Soldiers: State Security in Divided Societies* (Athens: University of Georgia Press, 1980), p. 12; the latter is the phrase used by Crawford Young, *The Politics of Cultural Pluralism* (Madison: University of Wisconsin Press, 1976), p. 67.

6. For examples of the active use of ethnicity by the state in Iran see Ervand Abrahamian's discussion of Qajar manipulation of communal conflicts in *Iran Between Two Revolutions* (Princeton, N.J.: Princeton University Press, 1982), pp. 42-49. Pahlavi development policies also resulted in significant changes in the relationship between ethnic groups, whether or not this was intentional. See Akbar Aghajanian, "Ethnic Inequality in Iran: An Overview," *International Journal of Middle East Studies*, 15:2 (May 1983), pp. 211-24.

7. Young, *Politics of Cultural Pluralism*, p. 70.

8. For discussions of collective incorporation in contemporary states see Pierre L. van den Berghe, *The Ethnic Phenomenon* (New York: Elsevier, 1981); and Milton M. Gordon, "Toward a General Theory of Racial and Ethnic Group Relations," in Glazer and Moynihan, eds., *Ethnicity*, pp. 84-110.

9. Nathan Glazer and Daniel P. Moynihan, "Introduction," in Glazer and Moynihan, eds., *Ethnicity*, pp. 1-26, esp. p. 8.

10. For recent accounts of this transition see Abrahamian, *Iran Between Two Revolutions*, pp. 9–165; and Leonard M. Helfgott, "The Structural Foundations of the National Minority Problem in Revolutionary Iran," *Iranian Studies*, 13:1–4 (1980), pp. 195–204.

11. Constitution of 1906, Supplement, art. 26 and art. 35; Constitution of 1979, art. 6 and art. 56. The copy of the 1906 Constitution used is the translation by Ali Pasha Saleh in *Constitutions of Nations*, rev. 3d ed., vol. 2 (The Hague: Martinus Nijoff, 1966), pp. 452–70. Quotations from the 1979 Constitution are from the translation by Hamid Algar, *Constitution of the Islamic Republic of Iran* (Berkeley, Calif.: Mizan Press, 1980). See also the copy edited and introduced by Rouhollah K. Ramazani, *Middle East Journal*, 34:2 (Spring 1980), pp. 181–204.

12. Reconciling the notion that sovereignty derives from God with the principle that sovereignty resides with the people is a problem faced by religious scholars since the first constitutional movement and one which has received renewed attention since the establishment of the Islamic Republic. See Said Amir Arjomand, "The State and Khomeini's Islamic Order," *Iranian Studies*, 13:1–4 (1980), pp. 147–64; and Shahrough Akhavi, "Clerical Politics in Iran Since 1979," in Nikki R. Keddie and Eric Hooglund, eds., *The Iranian Revolution and the Islamic Republic* (Washington, D.C.: Middle East Institute/Woodrow Wilson International Center for Scholars, 1982), pp. 17–28.

13. Constitution of 1906, art. 2, art. 3, and Supplement, art. 8; Constitution of 1979, art. 19, art. 20, and art. 62.

14. See, for example, Ahmad Ashraf, "The Roots of Emerging Dual Class Structure in Nineteenth-Century Iran," *Iranian Studies*, 14:1–2 (Winter–Spring 1981), pp. 5–27; Michael E. Bonine, "Shops and Shopkeepers: Dynamics of an Iranian Provincial Bazaar," in Michael E. Bonine and Nikki R. Keddie, eds., *Continuity and Change in Modern Iran* (Albany: State University of New York Press, 1981), pp. 203–28; and Gene R. Garthwaite, "Khans and Kings: The Dialectics of Power in Bakhtiyari History," in Bonine and Keddie, eds., *Continuity and Change in Modern Iran*, pp. 129–42.

15. Constitution of 1979, art. 13, art. 14, and art. 64.

16. Richard F. Nyrop, ed., *Iran: A Country Study*, 3d ed. (Washington, D.C.: American University, 1978), p. 189; Sayyid Ali Reza Naqavi, *Family Laws of Iran* (Islamabad: Islamic Research Institute, 1971), pp. 14–15.

17. Constitution of 1906, Supplement, art. 58; Constitution of 1979, art. 115.

18. Constitution of 1906, Supplement, art. 91; Constitution of 1979, art. 100.

19. On the centralization policies and practices of the Pahlavis, see Amin Banani, *The Modernization of Iran: 1921–1941* (Stanford, Calif.: Stanford University Press, 1961), esp. pp. 58–61; Richard W. Cottam, *Nationalism in Iran. Updated Through 1978* (Pittsburgh, Penn.: University of Pittsburgh Press, 1979), esp. pp. 20–22, 98–101, and 286–311; Mary-Jo DelVecchio Good, "The Changing Status and Composition of an Iranian Provincial Elite," in Bonine and Keddie, eds., *Continuity and Change in Modern Iran*, pp. 229–48; and Nyrop, ed., *Iran: A Country Study*, pp. 181–98.

20. Richard Falk, "Balance Sheet on a Revolution," *The Nation* 232:2 (17 January 1981), pp. 39–42; Fred Halliday, "Iran's Revolution: The First Year," *Middle East Research and Information Project* [hereafter *MERIP*] *Reports* (No. 88), 10:5 (June 1980), pp. 3–5; and Helfgott, "The Structural Foundations of the National Minority Problem," p. 212.

21. Lois Beck, "Revolutionary Iran and Its Tribal Peoples," *MERIP Reports* (No. 87), 10:4 (May 1980), pp. 14–20; Good, "The Changing Status and Composition of an Iranian Provincial Elite," pp. 238, 246–48.

22. On the economic policies of the Islamic Republic see Homa Katouzian, *The Political Economy of Modern Iran: Despotism and Pseudo-Modernism, 1926–1979* (New York: New York University Press, 1981); Patrick Clawson, "Iran's Economy: Between Crisis and Collapse," *MERIP Reports* (No. 98), 11:6 (July–August 1981), pp. 11–15; and the Constitution of 1979, art. 43.

23. Beck, "Revolutionary Iran and Its Tribal Peoples," p. 16; Cottam, *Nationalism in Iran*, esp. pp. 26–32 and 146–57; Helfgott, "The Structural Foundations of the National Minority Problem," pp. 204–209; and Richard N. Frye, *Persia*, rev. ed. (New York: Schocken, 1969), p. 94.

24. Hamid Naficy, "Cinema as a Political Instrument," in Bonine and Keddie, eds., *Continuity and Change in Modern Iran*, pp. 265–83; Majid Tehranian, "Communication and Revolution in Iran: The Passing of a Paradigm," *Iranian Studies*, 13:1–4 (1980), pp. 5–30.

25. This is discussed as a widespread characteristic of modernizing societies in Tonu Parming and L. Mu-Yan Cheung, "Modernization and Ethnicity," in Dofny and Akiwowo, eds., *National and Ethnic Movements*, pp. 131–41.

26. See Richard Falk, "Iran Revisited: The Sidetracking of a Revolution," *The Nation*, 234:4 (30 January 1982), pp. 102–8; Michael M. J. Fischer, "Becoming Mollah: Reflections on Iranian Clerics in a Revolutionary Age," *Iranian Studies*, 13:1–4 (1980), pp. 83–117; and Rouhollah K. Ramazani, "Iran: The 'Islamic Cultural Revolution,' " in P. H. Stoddard, P. C. Cuthell, and M. W. Sullivan, eds., *Change and the Muslim World* (Syracuse, N.Y.: Syracuse University Press, 1981), pp. 40–48.

27. Mohamad Parsa, "A Qualitative Study of Public and Guidance Cycle Education in Iran," *International Education*, 9 (Fall 1979), pp. 7–11, esp. p. 11.

28. Hossein Keyvan, "Domestic Media in Iran: Radio and Television," *Frontier*, 1:29 (15 September 1982), pp. 7–8; and Hossein Keyvan, "Domestic Media in Iran: Newspapers," *Frontier*, 1:31 (13 October 1982), pp. 8–9.

29. Marvin Zonis, *The Political Elite of Iran* (Princeton, N.J.: Princeton University Press, 1971), pp. 179–80.

30. Farhang Mehr, personal communication, 1982.

31. Mehr, personal communication, 1982.

32. On the economic status of linguistic minorities under the Pahlavis, see Abrahamian, *Iran Between Two Revolutions*, p. 449; Aghajanian, "Ethnic Inequality in Iran," pp. 214–19; Beck, "Revolutionary Iran and Its Tribal Peoples," p. 15; A. R. Ghassamlou, "Kurdistan in Iran," in Gerard Chaliand, ed., *People Without a Country: The Kurds and Kurdistan*, trans. Michael Pallis (London: Zed Press, 1980), pp. 107–34; Helfgott, "The Structural Foundations of the National Minority Problem," p. 209; and Martin Short and Anthony McDermott, *The Kurds*, 4th rev. ed. (London: Minority Rights Group Ltd., Report No. 23, 1981). On the economic status of religious minorities under the Pahlavis, see Leonard Binder, *Iran: Political Development in a Changing Society* (Berkeley: University of California Press, 1962), p. 162–63.

33. Constitution of 1979, art. 91, art. 96, art. 107, and art. 110.

34. James A. Bill, "Power and Religion in Revolutionary Iran," *Middle East Journal*, 36:1 (Winter 1982), pp. 22–47. See also Arjomand, "The State and Khomeini's Islamic Order"; Eric Hooglund, "Social Origins of the Revolutionary Clergy," in Ked-

die and Hooglund, eds., *The Iranian Revolution and the Islamic Republic*, pp. 29–37; and Ramazani, "Iran: The 'Islamic Cultural Revolution.' "

35. Constitution of 1979, art. 15.

36. Constitution of 1979, art. 48.

37. For a recent study of rural development projects actually implemented see Reinhold Loeffler, "Economic Changes in a Rural Area Since 1979," in Keddie and Hooglund, eds., *The Iranian Revolution and the Islamic Republic*, pp. 59–66. See also Beck, "Revolutionary Iran and Its Tribal Peoples," esp. pp. 18–19; and Lois Beck, "Economic Transformations Among the Qashqa'i Nomads, 1962–1978," in Bonine and Keddie, eds., *Continuity and Change in Modern Iran*, pp. 85–108.

38. See Akhavi, "Clerical Politics in Iran Since 1979," p. 18; and William Green Miller, "The Possibility for a New United States-Iranian Relationship," in Keddie and Hooglund, eds., *The Iranian Revolution and the Islamic Republic*, pp. 132–39.

39. For the purposes of this study, and by the definition used here, Iranian Baha'is can be considered an ethnic group. They have a distinct identity, marked primarily by their religion, and though Baha'is have existed for less than 150 years they do have a sense of common history. Because conversions often follow family lines and because, like many ethnic groups, they tend to marry endogamously, there are bonds of common descent as well. While Baha'is see their religion as a universal one, their very minority status within Iran fosters intragroup cohesiveness.

40. The information included here is derived primarily from Roger Cooper, *The Baha'is of Iran* (London: Minority Rights Group Ltd., Report No. 51, 1982). See also Geoffrey Nash, *Iran's Secret Pogrom: The Conspiracy to Wipe Out the Baha'is* (Suffolk, Eng.: Neville Spearman, 1982); and the series of articles by Firuz Kazemzadeh, "For Baha'is in Iran—A Threat of Extinction," *New York Times*, 6 August 1981, p. A23; "The Terror Facing the Baha'is," *New York Review of Books*, 29:8 (13 May 1982), pp. 43–44; and "The Persecution of the 'Infidels'—Attack on the Baha'is," *New Republic*, 186:24 (16 June 1982), pp. 16–18.

41. For population figures see Cooper, *The Baha'is of Iran*, p. 7; Nash, *Iran's Secret Pogrom*, p. 7; and Kazemzadeh, "The Terror Facing The Baha'is," p. 43.

42. Shahrough Akhavi, *Religion and Politics in Contemporary Iran: Clergy-State Relations in the Pahlavi Period* (Albany: State University of New York Press, 1980), pp. xvii, 77–78; Michael M. J. Fischer, *Iran: From Religious Dispute to Revolution* (Cambridge, Mass.: Harvard University Press, 1979), p. 187.

43. Mehr, personal communication, 1982.

44. Nash, *Iran's Secret Pogrom*, p. 45.

45. Cooper, *The Baha'is of Iran*, p. 14. Nash cites a number of such prominent individuals (*Iran's Secret Pogrom*, pp. 45–46).

46. Among *Kayhan* classifieds one finds ads placed by "ordinary people who either announce that they do not belong to the Baha'i faith, or that they have been enlightened and abandoned faith in Baha'ism and have converted to Islam." See Keyvan, "Domestic Media in Iran: Newspapers," p. 8. See also Nash, *Iran's Secret Pogrom*, pp. 94–95, 126.

47. For population estimates see George S. Harris, "Ethnic Conflict and the Kurds," *Annals of The American Academy of Political and Social Science*, 433 (September 1977), pp. 112–24; "Kurds on the Move," *Middle East*, 55 (May 1979), pp. 47–52; Joane Nagel, "The Conditions of Ethnic Separatism: The Kurds in Turkey, Iran, and Iraq," *Ethnicity*, 7:3 (September 1980), pp. 279–97; Short and McDermott, *The Kurds*, p. 5;

Martin van Bruinessen, *Agha, Sheik and State: On the Social and Political Organization of Kurdistan* (Utrecht: Rijksuniversiteit, 1978), p. 21; and Omran Yahya Feili and Arlene R. Fromchuck, "The Kurdish Struggle for Independence," *Middle East Review*, 9:1 (Fall 1976), pp. 47–59.

48. Eden Naby, "The Iranian Frontier Nationalities: The Kurds, the Assyrians, the Baluchis, and the Turkmens," in William O. McCagg, Jr., and Brian Silver, eds., *Soviet Asian Ethnic Frontiers* (New York: Pergamon Press, 1979), pp. 83–114.

49. See Hassan Arfa, *The Kurds: An Historical and Political Study* (London: Oxford University Press, 1966); Cottam, *Nationalism in Iran*, pp. 65–74; Ghassemlou, "Kurdistan in Iran"; William Eagleton, Jr., *The Kurdish Republic of 1946* (London: Oxford University Press, 1963); and Archie Roosevelt, Jr., "The Kurdish Republic of Mahabad," in Chaliand, ed., *People Without a Country*, pp. 135–52.

50. Van Bruinessen, *Agha, Sheik and State*, pp. 22–28; Aghajanian, "Ethnic Inequality in Iran," p. 212–13.

51. Data on Kurdish involvement in the revolution and on the relationship between the Kurds and the postrevolutionary central government has been obtained primarily from the *New York Times*. For a summary of these events see Gerard Chaliand, "Postscript, 1979," in Chaliand, ed., *People Without a Country*, pp. 229–32.

52. Short and McDermott, *The Kurds*, p. 8; Shirin Tehrani, interview by Fred Halliday, "Eyewitness From Iran: 'Signs of Civil War,' " *MERIP Reports* (No. 98), 11:6 (July–August 1981), pp. 8–11.

53. Arfa, *The Kurds*, p. 1; Short and McDermott, *The Kurds*, p. 5.

54. Van Bruinessen, *Agha, Sheik and State*, pp. 357–59.

55. Abrahamian, *Iran Between Two Revolutions*, p. 428.

56. Van Bruinessen, *Agha, Sheik and State*, p. 374.

57. Arfa, *The Kurds*, p. 5; Cottam, *Nationalism in Iran*, p. 67; Short and McDermott, *The Kurds*, p. 5; and van Bruinessen, *Agha, Sheik and State*, p. 134.

58. "Kurds on the Move," p. 50; and 'Abdul-Rahman Qassemlu, interview by Fred Halliday, "KDP's Qassemlu: 'The Clergy Have Confiscated the Revolution,' " *MERIP Reports* (No. 98), 11:6 (July–August 1981), pp. 17–19; accounts of earlier eras indicate, however, that the prominence of Kurdish religious leaders in autonomy efforts is not entirely new. See Eagleton, *The Kurdish Republic of 1946*, p. 29; Ghassemlou, "Kurdistan in Iran," p. 110; and van Bruinessen, *Agha, Sheik and State*, pp. 251, 357–58.

59. Qassemlu, "The Clergy Have Confiscated the Revolution," p. 18; Ghassemlou, "Kurdistan in Iran," p. 110.

60. Compare Ghassemlou, "Kurdistan in Iran," p. 132, with Eagleton, *The Kurdish Republic of 1946*, p. 57, and Roosevelt, "The Kurdish Republic of Mahabad," pp. 140–41.

61. Qassemlu, "The Clergy Have Confiscated the Revolution," pp. 17–18; Ghassemlou, "Kurdistan in Iran," p. 132.

62. Qassemlu, "The Clergy Have Confiscated the Revolution," p. 17; see also "Interview: 'Everything Positive Has Come from the Masses Below," *MERIP Reports* (No. 88), 10:5 (June 1980), pp. 10–14.

63. Short and McDermott, *The Kurds*, p. 8.

64. Akhavi, *Religion and the Politics in Contemporary Iran*, p. 168; Binder, *Iran*, p. 160; and Helfgott, "The Structural Foundations of the National Minority Problem," pp. 205–6.

65. Helfgott, "The Structural Foundations of the National Minority Problem," p. 205.

66. S. Enders Wimbush, "Divided Azerbaijan: Nation Building, Assimilation, and Mobilization Between Three States," in McCagg and Silver, eds., *Soviet Asian Ethnic Frontiers*, pp. 61–81.

67. Binder, *Iran*, pp. 160–61; Cottam, *Nationalism in Iran*, p. 27, 119, 131; Katouzian, *The Political Economy of Modern Iran*, p. 149; and Wimbush, "Divided Azerbaijan," pp. 74, 76.

68. Binder, *Iran*, p. 160; Cottam, *Nationalism in Iran*, p. 128; and Robert Rossow, Jr., "The Battle of Azerbaijan, 1946," *Middle East Journal*, 10:1 (Winter 1956), pp. 17–32.

69. Cottam, *Nationalism in Iran*, pp. 123, 130.

70. Aghajanian, "Ethnic Inequality in Iran," pp. 215–20.

71. Abrahamian, *Iran Between Two Revolutions*, p. 163; Cottam, *Nationalism in Iran*, p. 131; and Helfgott, "The Structural Foundations of the National Minority Problem," pp. 206–207.

72. Abrahamian, *Iran*, pp. 87, 97; and Cottam, *Nationalism in Iran*, pp. 119–29.

73. Information on this period is derived primarily from U.S. newspapers and periodicals.

74. Circumstances surrounding the establishment of the Islamic Republican People's Party are discussed by Akhavi, *Religion and Politics in Contemporary Iran*, p. 175.

75. See, for example, the *New York Times Index* for 1982–84 or the *Middle East Journal*'s quarterly chronology for this period.

76. For a discussion of the ideological differences between Ayatollah Khomeini and Ayatollah Shariatmadari see David Menashri, "Shi'ite Leadership: In the Shadow of Conflicting Ideologies," *Iranian Studies*, 13:1–4 (1980), pp. 119–45.

7

STATE FORMATION and CONSOLIDATION in TWENTIETH-CENTURY IRAN
The Reza Shah Period and the Islamic Republic

SHAHROUGH AKHAVI

To THE OBSERVER of the Iranian state it rapidly becomes clear that state formation has proceeded further than in a number of surrounding areas, such as Afghanistan, Pakistan, or Iraq. However, in the twentieth century two important historical periods have seen the serious weakening of the Iranian state, raising in some minds the possibility of a reversion to a "proto-" or even non-state situation. These two periods are respectively the period following the end of World War I and lasting until perhaps the late 1930s; and the period following the Iranian Revolution of 1978–79. Upon each of these occasions, the task of state formation and/or state consolidation became an imperative for newly emergent elites. The twentieth-century experience in Iran, then, provides a good opportunity to compare and contrast the mechanism, resources, and policies of state leaders faced with the requirements of either building virtually new institutions or at least modifying existing ones in rather drastic ways. (While the state-building process had to be resumed after 1941, when the second Pahlavi shah came to the throne, and thus it could be argued that yet a third period of state formation might validly be investigated, the present chapter assumes a greater degree of continuity of the post-1941 state with its predecessor than is the case in the other two instances mentioned.)

Unlike some neighboring countries such as Pakistan and Iraq, Iran is an "old new state," meaning that if one views it as a member of the third-world societies, it nevertheless has an ancient tradition and history within roughly the same frontiers as those of today. After the Arab conquest in the seventh century, the country became a region of the Islamic caliphate, but before that time state-centralizing dynasties ruled the territory on behalf of a power structure, the masses of the population, and a religioideological system which distinguished it from other political systems. It is important to bear this in mind, given the revolutionary regime's current stress on the purely Islamic aspects of Iran's historical experience.

SOME PRELIMINARY OBSERVATIONS on the IRANIAN STATE

Sasanid Iran (A.D. 224–651), the political system at the time of the Arab conquest, was ruled by a "militantly Iranian dynasty" that deliberately used the state for major economic projects. Cultural unity was maintained on the basis of an official religion promoted by a priestly stratum known as the Magi. Allegiance to the ruler stemmed from the traditional view that called for an absolute ruler standing above petty quarrels and ambitions and providing justice for his people. This ruler presided over a stratified society in which each stratum accepted its role and place as a natural expression of good and righteousness. Sasanid society lauded government and the priestly art as these were respectively spelled out by the ruler and his administrative staff, on the one hand, and the Magi, on the other. Very large-scale irrigation in the Tigris-Euphrates River Valley and mercantile trade formed the backbone of the Sasanid economy. Sasanid patrimonial administration rested upon agricultural extractions taken as surplus from the peasantry. The latter held an "honoured" place in society's social mythos due to the value placed upon their role in growing crops to feed the people. There is no doubt that Sasanid patrimonialism evinced a symbiotic relationship between monarch and priests and even periods of parity in the authority of the shah and nobles. Yet, the classic Sasanid state, epitomized by the reign of Anushirvan (A.D. 540–89), was one in which the ruler controlled society through his administration and his military, both of which he regarded as his economic assets.[1]

The onset of Islam and its expansion in Iranian areas led to new developments. Conceptions about the state henceforth require examining the relationship between *ummah* and *khilafah*, Islamic terms referring respectively to the community of believers and its leadership.[2] Ummah is the overarching concept denoting the spiritual-political body whose life and organization are sustained by the khilafah. This distinction is to some extent artificial, since it has frequently been noted that the spiritual and temporal realms are fused in Islam—at least in theory.

Analytically, though, it is probably helpful to separate the two concepts. The caliph, the head of the ummah, is one who, with the help of others, interprets the law of Islam and implements it in the real world. His functions transcend strictly spiritual or pietistic concerns. They include matters of resource extraction and allocation, order, social justice, taxation, defense. In the broadest terms, he is charged with bringing both harmony and prosperity to his community in accordance with the holy law. In the early Islamic period (622–61), insurrections broke out and the rule of particular caliphs came under challenge. But basically a consensus existed as to the appropriateness of the caliph in principle representing both the spiritual and the political interests of the community. Over time, a transition occurred in the relationship between ummah and khilafah. Whereas in earlier times khilafah stood in natural relationship to ummah in the theory of Islamic legists, later on it came to stand in unnatural relationship to it in practice. At this juncture, *mulk*, or kingship, became a concomitant factor. Thus, in the *Kitab al-taj*, attributed to the ninth-century author, al-Jahiz (d. 869), mulk is a central topic of discussion. By the time of ibn Khaldun (d. 1406), who was a major historian of Islam, it is clear that conceptions of secular rule by sultans and shahs had come to be accepted as a fact. Ibn Khaldun had little difficulty with the reality of secular rule by sultans, though he did advocate tempering it by religious constraints.

In the period between the mid-seventh century until the Mongol conquest (661–1258) temporal rulers steadily usurped the political and socioeconomic powers of caliphs. Constitutional theorists accepted the reality of sultans wielding effective political power by arguing the necessity of acquiescence to seizures of power lest the unity of the ummah be destroyed. Hence, Buyid princes in the mid-tenth century affixed the sobriquet of "al-Dawlah" (the state) to their names. The three brothers of the Buyid house, Imad al-Dawlah, Muizz al-Dawlah, and Rukn al-Dawlah, exercised temporal rule over Shiraz, Isfahan, and Baghdad while acknowledging the spiritual authority of the caliph. A parallel development had been taking place with the title of "al-Mulk" (the kingdom), best exemplified by the name of the famous Saljuq vizier, Nizam al-Mulk (d. 1092).

Originally, *dawlah* meant to wander around aimlessly. Later, it came to mean to go in turn, to alternate; then, to have one's turn in success, especially in exercising rule over a group. In the Safavid period (1501–1722), "the term *dawlat* [the Persian for the Arabic *dawlah*] meant 'bliss,' 'felicity,' an abstract term just beginning . . . to be used in the concrete sense of 'the state'."³ Current use of the word in Persian is not without ambiguity, as it is not clear, sometimes even in context, whether by dawlat is meant the Iranian state or the government of the day.

In short, the word for state today is relatively recent and to a large extent the product of contact and conflict with the West. This is not to say that some kind of state did not exist prior to the modern period in Iran. But the state in the early period of Islam was considered by Muslims to be a theocracy. In a development more particular to Iran than perhaps other Islamic areas, pre-Islamic conceptions of state and monarchy had now come to be transferred to the sultans.

> With the disappearance of the last imam in 260/873–4 the divine light [of the imams] became, in theory, stationary, political authority being meanwhile wielded by others who were presumed to be under the guidance of the agents of the Hidden Imam. Just as concepts belonging to the theory of the caliph had been transferred to the theory of the sultan, so also there stemmed from the conception of the infallibility of the imam an assumption of perfection in the temporal order. . . . The ruler ruled by divine right and the only duty of his subjects was to pray for his welfare.⁴

It must be admitted that in practice, often tribal power rivalries underlay the actual success or failure of ruling groups to seize power at this time, but the point Lambton is making here is that on the theoretical side notions of divine right of kings began to emerge in pre-Safavid times. These considerations apply all the more in the Safavid period itself, as the earlier doctrine of the ruler as *zillullah* (the Shadow of God) elaborated by Batini and Sufi-oriented Shi'ite writers came to inhere. The Safavids succeeded in propagating the additional doctrine of their descent from the imams. Thus, "if the Safavid ruler was not himself the perfect man he was as the representative of the Hidden Imam at least closer to the possession of absolute truth than any of his fellow men. As such he was entitled to absolute rule."⁵

What is notable about the early Safavid state was the subordination of the interests of ummah to the interest of dawlah, something that carried through into the later Safavid period as well. This fact was reinforced by the willingness of the clergy to accept posts in the state administration, an administration featuring a four-tiered stratification system in which the clergy occupied the second level.[6]

But decline set in after the mid-seventeenth century, and the state appears to have vanished for nearly a century following the Afghan invasion in 1722. Though it was reconstituted by the Qajars, for most of the period of their rule (1796-1925) the state seemed to be becoming progressively weaker to the point that its very existence became endangered by the onset of the first world war. For most of the late Qajar period (about 1875-1925) the monarch was hard pressed to successfully extend his authority outside his own capital without the sufferance of provincial elites.[7]

Reza Shah's successful restoration of the Iranian state may be seen in the light of certain generally necessary conditions for the emergence of any state: "specialization of governmental roles, centralization of enforceable authority; permanence, or at least more than ephemeral stability, of structure; and emancipation from real or fictive kinship as the basis of relations between the occupants of governmental roles and those whom they govern."[8] Reasons for the particular appearance of a specific state at a given time, however, vary widely. No categorical statement can be made, since it will always be an empirical question as to why an individual state has come into being at a certain historical moment. Among the *basic* factors leading to the formation of new states or the revitalization of ones in serious decline are: demographic pressures; long-distance or foreign trade; warfare or military pressures; internal violence; efforts by elites to protect their privileges, in the face of overwhelming challenge by counterelites and social forces; religious movements of a millenarian sort; organizational needs, innovations, or pressures. When a number of these factors combine in a context of consolidation of administrative, legal, and military structures at the expense of categorical local autonomy, a state is likely to be formed.[9]

State formation in societies such as the Iranian results from a complex interplay of phenomena. At the most general level, external warfare leads to conquest and the capture of slaves by a warrior group that evolves in a framework of fighting. Herding, pastoral nomadism, and irrigation agriculture generate distributional and redistributional mechanisms (the market and tax systems). The latter requires the creation of a managerial cadre of specialists and officials. Alongside the warriors, nomads, and agriculturists develops a priestly caste which both has ties to the military and mediates between it and the common people. The slaves captured in military campaigns participate in increased craft production, while the development of irrigation agriculture results in increasing social differentiation in the rural sector and the concentration of wealth in the hands of a landed stratum. Social interaction and marital alignments among the landed elite, the religious leaders, and the managerial officials generate the so-called "thousand families" who render service to the state as its officials. The monarchs are generally assessed in terms of an archetypical charismatic predecessor, and individual rulers combine his "aura" with their own background in the priestly and/or warrior groups. As a consequence, authority comes to feature sacral principles of kingship which are typical of traditional forms of domination as discussed by Weber.[10]

This somewhat ahistorical summary of state formation may be specified more in terms of the different Iranian states. The state in Iranian history has alternated between a centralized bureaucratic system and one based on decentralized tribal structures. In both cases, monarchs have ruled over society in arbitrary and despotic ways. If by Oriental despotism one means arbitrary rule by a ruler through an elite bureaucracy based on the latter's control over the water system, then Iran should probably not be viewed in these terms, as can ancient Egypt and China. In fact, Iran is not essentially a riverine society, and the irrigation networks of canals crucial to the nation's agriculture were historically regulated and supervised in a decentralized manner by local officials.[11] The Achaemenid (559–330 B.C.), Sasanid (A.D. 224–651), and Pahlavi (1925–79) states formed strong central bureaucracies. It was the bureaucracy that processed transformations in demographic patterns, agricultural output, craft production, market exchanges, and social ceremonies. The Safavid (1501–1722) and Qajar (1796–1925) states, by contrast, originated in religio-tribal movements which in some measure retained their primary, tribal characteristics as time passed. It is true that the Safavid dynasty later on marginalized the tribal component, and so it is in a somewhat separate class. But in the case of the Qajars, the state resembled more a confederation of ministates loosely joined by whatever symbolic allegiance the shah could generate toward his *dawlat-i 'aliyyah-yi shah-in-shahi* (eminent imperial state). The Islamic Republic, for its part, is a state created by antibureaucratic, nontribal, urban-based clerics with paramilitary support given it by the lower and lower middle classes.

STATE FORMATION and CONSOLIDATION UNDER REZA SHAH

"By 1920 the situation in Iran had sunk to its lowest level for over a century."[12] The period before 1921 was one of "total economic and financial, as well as socio-political, chaos."[13] These observations imply that Iran had come perilously close to the threshold of total state collapse, facing a situation of foreign domination, internal immobilism, notoriously corrupt elite behavior, the complete absence of central authority, and tribal assertiveness among Turkomans, Bakhtiaris, Qashqa'is, Baluchis, Kurds, Lurs, and Arabs. In 1919 the British seized the chance to create a protectorate in all but name out of the country.

In the face of these trends the key mechanisms of state formation employed by Reza Shah (r. 1925–41) included a standing army, a central bureaucracy, a national bank, state investment policies in social overhead capital and infrastructure, and far-reaching legal and educational reforms.[14] Linking these mechanisms together was an ideology of nationalism that bordered on chauvinism and particularly stressed ties to the pre-Islamic period.[15]

Sources differ on the contribution that the oil sector made to state building under Reza Shah. According to one scholar, in the late Reza Shah period oil revenues "accounted for only 13 percent of total government receipts."[16] On the other hand, a recent estimation is that in the 1933–41 period oil revenues "provided over 20 percent of budgetary *allocations*; but, given the fact that actual expenditures almost invariably fell short of planned allocations, it is certain that the share of oil revenues in state *expenditures* was higher than this."[17] A third authority holds that "in the mid-1920s the direct royalties [from the Anglo-Persian Oil Company (APOC)] represented about 10 per cent of the government's general budget. This figure increased to about 30 per cent between 1929 and 1932, and, inclusive of petrol taxes, settled to about 25 per cent during 1934–8."[18] It would appear, then, that oil was a major ingredient in the state formation policies of Reza Shah. More specifically, revenue from the operations of the APOC apparently went virtually entirely into the development of the Iranian army.[19]

The state invested heavily in infrastructure, especially roads, railways, telecommunications, and physical plant (notably school construction). Such investment increased by fivefold the length of the gravel road system between 1925 and 1938. And the Trans-Iranian Railway, linking the Caspian Sea to the Persian Gulf, was completed in the period between 1927 and 1938. The growth of infrastructure evidenced by the extension of such networks can operate both to enhance the reach of the state into the periphery and promote opportunities for extending linkages from the outlying areas to the center. The point here is that integration[20] is a two-way process if it is to be successfully achieved. Reza Shah appeared to approach the integration process, however, from the point of view of absorbing the periphery into a centralized bureaucratic state. For example, among the supports that masses might be expected to extend to the state and its government are compliance with regulations on taxation, loyalty, to the state's constitution, and national service. But Reza Shah failed to elicit the ethos which could have served such purposes, not to mention the linkages for initiatives "from below." In short, he slighted the process of having regionally or locally based groups establishing organic ties to the center, thus fostering a rather brittle state-society relationship that became unraveled upon his departure from the scene.

This pattern may be noted from the fact that for the bulk of the Reza Shah period little net rural-to-urban migration seemed to take place but then between 1935 and 1940 the annual compound rate of population growth in the urban areas was 2.3, whereas for rural areas it was only 1.3.[21] These figures reflect the fact that Reza Shah's policies were inducing the rural population to abandon their villages and tribes and migrate to the urban areas which were the focus of his state investment activities and expansion of the oil industry. Ultimately, Reza Shah's integration policies led to overcentralization. A point of comparison may be made with the Achaemenid dynasty, with which Reza Shah consciously wished to identify but the stability of which exemplified an interesting symbiosis of centralized rule and regional autonomy.[22]

Another factor that facilitates the process of state formation is the creation of national, financial, commodity, and labor markets. Reza Shah's government paid significant, albeit unsystematic, attention to industry and foreign trade to the neglect of agriculture. In essence, the agricultural market remained very much untouched as a local or at best regional barter system. In general, then, the following comment applies, mutatis mutandis, for Iran in the Reza Shah period: "Markets [were no] more than accessories of economic life. As a rule, the economic system was absorbed in the social system . . . The principle of barter or exchange, which underlies this pattern, revealed no tendency to expand at the expense of the rest."[23]

The government tried to encourage private industry through a program of tax exemptions, rebates, and credits, but, in fact, its policies of creating state monopolies in industry and foreign trade led to a decline in the rate of growth of gross domestic fixed capital formation throughout the 1931–38 period.[24] Such a decline does not deny that the commodity market under Reza Shah spread its grid beyond the situation in the early 1920s. But in fact, as Bharier observes, the 1920s featured tendencies toward state monopolies that "discourag[ed] industrial activity in the private sector."[25] In the 1930s such tendencies became even more pronounced. Consequently, the growth in the commodity market at the national level was due basically to government investment in the light industry sector, including enterprises in glass, textiles, soap, sugar, matches, and the like. The impact of public expenditure in this sector led to a modest movement of light industrial operations from periphery to center. "There is qualitative evidence that some rural and semi-rural industries, such as soap manufacture and some textile and footwear production, had begun to move to towns."[26]

Rationalization and centralization of the financial markets, which previously had been fragmented among a number of quasi-medieval *sarrafis* (moneylenders) in the bazaar, began in 1922. This was the period of the first Millspaugh financial mission (1922–27), and it culminated in 1927 with the creation of the National Bank, which in 1931 acquired the right to issue legal tender. However, a combination of bureaucratic red tape, nepotistic lending policies, and tight credit hampered a measured development of the financial market.[27] It seems that the key advance in the financial/monetary areas was the annual promulgation of budgets for government departments. Although the government achieved tariff autonomy in 1928 and sought to use levies to protect domestic infant industries, it has already been indicated that this did not have the desired effect in the private sector. Essentially, then, Reza Shah pursued etatist policies, which may have been unavoidable in any case. But in his autocratic behavior toward private businessmen, he compounded the problems associated with attracting private sector capital formation and investment in industry, construction, and technology.

Evidence for this remains anecdotal rather than systematic. For example, the first Iranian company created in the Reza Shah period—the Joint Stock Trading Company of Iran—was formed through royal fiat. The story of its creation is as follows. All the leading merchants were summoned to a meeting organized by Abd al-Husayn Taymurtash, a chief aide of Reza Shah. They were persuaded into capitalizing the company out of their own pockets. Although a managing board was hastily selected, none wanted to be Director-

General out of fear of being held legally accountable in the event of adversity. Finally, the choice fell to one of the assembled, and the total subscribed capital came to something less than 1 million tumans (probably equal to about U.S. $250,000 in those times). After two years of desultory activity, a telegram came from Reza Shah, ordering that no annual meeting of the stockholders take place and effectively blocking the distribution of the meager dividends to the owners.

Although the meeting was in fact held, Reza Shah put in an appearance. Characteristically blunt, he warned the company officials: "Give me results or I'll burn you alive." An official later lamented: "What a job we've made of it! They force us to give money from our own pockets and then say they'll burn us alive if we don't produce results!!"[28]

This story typifies Reza Shah's efforts to create a national commodity market by forcing entrepreneurs to create factories. In general it is difficult to disagree with the comment that a "lack of integration in the Iranian economy before the mid-1930's" prevailed.[29] This was not for want of investments, which totaled about $520 million during Reza Shah's rule. Of this figure, about half was in railroads and the remainder in industry, of which some $130 million has been estimated to have come from the private sector.[30] If this latter figure is reliable, it means that private sector investment totaled about $8 million a year—not a great deal considering that it is for the whole country.

The growth in the labor market was chiefly associated with the oil sector and the state monopolies. Because the oil sector was essentially not an integral part of the economy—revenues from this sector represented a pure form of economic rent[31]—it did not provide for forward and backward linkages and especially required virtually no input factors of production from the Iranian economy. Another potential spin-off, in terms of mobility of oil workers to other enterprises in the industrial sector, remained quite limited. Politically, moreover, the growth of the labor market had serious repercussions, most notably for the 1941-47 period when political parties proliferated and industrial strikes became more frequent.[32]

It is also appropriate to note some social consequences of Reza Shah's economic policies. They helped put an end to whatever remnants existed of the old communal city wards. "By 1941 [even earlier, perhaps] in most towns the Ni'mati, Haydari, Karimkhani, Shaykhi, and Mutashar'i mahallahs [quarters] ha[d] passed into history."[33]

To summarize, market development under Reza Shah was

not an important mechanism and concomitant of state formation and consolidation. Reza Shah's restitution of the Iranian state proceeded more on the basis of legal, administrative, social, and military reforms, rather than economic ones. Departing from the tradition of creating an army out of tribal levies, Reza Shah molded his military from the Cossack Brigade and the Swedish gendarmerie, undertaking tactical alliances with tribal groups against which he subsequently turned—especially the Bakhtiari.[34] The centerpiece of his military reforms was the military conscription law of 1925, which permitted the recruitment of individuals throughout the country into a new national service organization, the standing army.

The bureaucratic changes initiated by Reza Shah were of fundamental importance and are always cited by those discussing his policies. By decree, he centralized the ministerial departments, instituted a pattern of provincial and local government that was patterned on the French prefecture system, and placed budgetary authority in the central state agencies. In the effort to enforce these changes major efforts were made in public finance administration and a program was instituted to subsidize the training of Iranian students in economics, law, education, and other fields in foreign institutions. These efforts, when combined with the enforcement of decisions by the army, created the foundations for a bureaucratic state not all that different from the Turkish Republic of Kemal Ataturk.

The clergy have sometimes acted in a manner that has helped state centralization of authority and power. However, at other times their behavior has abetted localism and regionalism. The classic examples, respectively, of these different roles are provided by the Safavid and Qajar states. Reza Shah's systematic campaign after 1925 against the religious institution shattered his earlier alliance with the clergy and severely weakened another important base of localism in the country. In systematic fashion, the Pahlavi state declassed the clergy by striking at the heart of its resource base: administration of shrines, endowed properties, judicial appointments, magistracies, theological seminaries, mosques. Whole areas of social legislation touching upon land tenure, education, personnel policies in government departments and the courts lost their religious underpinnings. Instead, a "secularization of the shari'ah" (the sacred Law of Islam) occurred.[35] Thus, Reza Shah's policies toward the clergy drove them into opposition to the bureaucratization of the state's power, and they came to represent one of the major centrifugal forces in the society. The importance of these actions can hardly be overemphasized, since they amounted to a forcible disjuncture between the religious and temporal realms that previous Iranian monarchs had not attempted. In other words, Reza Shah was abandoning the time-honored Achaemenid, Sasanid, and Safavid patrimonial practice of anchoring the state in the religious institution, and thereby created a yawning gap between the Iranian state and its society.

If the clergy were subdued, what of the other two main forces contending against a centralizing state: the landed aristocracy and the tribal groups? The gentry's fortunes generally improved under Reza Shah, although it is true that he eliminated the most unreconstructed Qajar noblemen and he expropriated the lands of those landowners whose property he coveted. Those whom he trusted, however, he rewarded with land and positions in the state.

One of Reza Shah's own wives was a Qajar noblewoman; his older daughter's first husband was a scion of the well-known Qavam al-Mulk family from Shiraz. Although he abolished titles, he generally protected the privileges of the aristocracy. Undoubtedly there were variations in different parts of the country, but in those regions which still adhered to the practice of villager appointment of headmen, Reza Shah ended this practice and gave the landlord the right to make such appointments.[36] A number of the conservative landowners, though their land was not threatened, nonetheless opposed Reza Shah's military reforms. Represented in the Reformers' Party, they feared that conscription would lead to a drain on peasant labor on their estates. Reza Shah, who had earlier achieved an alliance with this group, found little trouble in terminating their parliamentary influence.[37] In sum, then, he was careful to promote the interests of the landlords so as to get their support for his state, but he permitted them no autonomy. This contrasts with Achaemenid practice (see note 22) of loose centralization.

As for the tribes, they suffered greatly under his policies. "Even before Reza Khan was crowned as Reza Shah, the great [Bakhtiari] khans—especially Khosrau Khan Sardar Zafar—perceived him and his policies as a threat to their autonomy and power."[38] Among the Basseri of the Khamseh confederation Reza Shah's antitribal policies meant that "only a small faction . . . were able to continue their nomadic habit, and most were sedentary for some years, suffering a considerable loss of flocks and people."[39] That such adversity did not beset all tribes may be seen in the observation about the Yarahmadzai Baluch during the 1928–35 pacification campaigns that they came to enjoy "limited access to previously unavailable labor and goods markets and to national government resources."[40]

One suspects that if any gains were made in the prospects of any Iranian tribes during the 1920s and 1930s these were registered basically by smaller clans. By contrast, among the Yomut Turkomans a decline in fortunes set in and forced them, after the autumn of 1925, to flee across the Soviet frontier. However, increasingly antitribal policies pursued by the Soviet regime led to their reentry into Iran, where they in effect became virtual vassals of the monarch: "During the decade of the 1930s, most of the territory of the Yomut became a part of the king's personal estates . . . The[y] . . . paid a rent for agricultural land and a grass tax for pasture . . . , were forced to build permanent dwellings, and migrations were forbidden in some areas and in other areas were allowed only under careful regulation at certain times of the year."[41]

A tactic Reza Shah used against the tribes was to lure their leaders to the capital and then imprison them. Some tribes rebelled rather than retreat, as occurred for the Qashqa'i in 1929 and again in 1932. Following the second uprising, "which proved even more disastrous for the Qashqa'i [t]he government instituted a brutal policy of forced sedentarization."[42] On the whole, as the state continued its encapsulation of the periphery, the "major tribes . . . experienced unprecedented economic hardship and disorganization due to the policy of forced sedentarization."[43]

Government repression of the tribes was a product of a number of considerations. These included the relative size of the tribes, their ideological orientation, their access to resources in competition with the state, and, possibly, their political structure.[44] In any case developments in the rural areas in the Reza Shah period seemed to represent policies for the systematic enclosure of lands. Good data for all regions of the country on the particular patterns of confiscations of land and resources and of restriction of mobility by the state are not presently available. But it is clear that its instrument was the army. The interaction between the military and the rural masses did not include attempts by officers and noncommissioned officers to become involved in the daily lives of the people. Unlike the situation in Mexico earlier in this century or in China during the 1920s and 1940s, the Iranian army in the 1920s and 1930s essentially played the role of enforcer of the King's writ. The Mexican and Chinese examples, as well as that of the neighboring Turkish army, show that the military provided what Wolf calls "tactical power" to rural masses to emerge from subjugation.[45] By contrast, the Iranian army's relations with the local populations in the periphery were rooted in the authoritarian and elitist principles of its leader.

One means by which monarchs seek to promote the legitimacy of their authority historically has been the "royal progress," a term that refers to the monarch's ceremonial movement throughout his realm to establish or reinforce his claims to state power.[46] Arab monarchs have secured the oath of fealty (*bay'ah*) from supporting tribes on an annual or periodical basis. In Reza Shah's case, this process of touring his territories was in the form of harsh military campaigns, interspersed with public appearances at ceremonies, particularly those in connection with the opening of an industrial enterprise or inauguration of infrastructure facilities. Reza Shah's particular form of royal progress was intended to generate support from a new bureaucratic and professional middle stratum, choosing to ignore the bulk of the population. If Reza Shah's state had its structural foundations in this particular social force (and the army), the narrowness of its social basis must be strongly underscored.[47]

STATE FORMATION and CONSOLIDATION
in the REVOLUTIONARY PERIOD

In the nearly four decades intervening between the abdication of Reza Shah and the clerical seizure of power in the revolution, the Iranian state had become transformed through policies that had made it the dominant force in the villages and the leading investor in the economy. In the process, the traditional bazaar had been displaced as the center of commerce at the national level, and a series of central plans (especially the third through the fifth, 1962–79) were utilized for the purpose of rationalizing market relations on behalf of state supremacy. If Reza Shah had relied upon oil revenues for economic development, his son Muhammad Reza Shah Pahlavi (r. 1941–79) had consummated this process to the point that Iran had become classic rentier economy.

After the departure of this Shah in January 1979 and the return of Ayatollah Ruhollah Khomeini in the next month, the clergy and their allies tried to establish a theocratic state. In his book, originally entitled *Islamic Government, or Rule By The Jurisconsult* 1971, Khomeini denounces monarchy and seeks to justify on doctrinal grounds the legitimacy of a theocratic state. In doing so he totally rejects the old Safavid concept of zillullah—that the shah is God's

Shadow on Earth—a doctrine claimed by the weaker Qajars and implicitly pressed by the Pahlavis.

How did Khomeini and his clerical allies seek to accomplish the task of creating an Islamic state? In some respects, the process was the inverse of the state formation process under Reza Shah, who imposed the state by main force and bureaucratic power. In the revolution society "imposed itself" upon the state, as it were. The revolution, in short, represents a popular reconstruction of the state, as opposed to an elitist one. However, during seven years of revolutionary construction, new elitist tendencies have emerged.

The stages that followed the return of Ayatollah Khomeini in the first fifteen months of the revolution by and large enjoyed mass support. These included the referendum on the Islamic Republic in March 1979, elections to the Council of Experts to draft a constitution in August, the plebiscite on the constitution in November, presidential elections in January 1980, and parliamentary elections in March and May.

Nevertheless, by October 1980 disillusion had set in among the merchants of the bazaar, a key ally of the clerical regime. The bazaar thus joined a series of disaffected groups, certain religious-minded but nonclerical officials of the regime, distinguished *mujtahids* (the highest-ranking scholars and teachers of religious law), tribal leaders, women, and elements of the armed forces. However, the urban poor apparently continued to lend their support, and therefore the Islamic state became clearly petit bourgeois in nature with extensive support from the migrant poor in the cities.[48]

In view of the narrowing of the social base of the revolutionary regime, what prospects are there for state consolidation? The answer must remain ambiguous. On the one hand, new institutions have been established—the *faqih* (supreme Muslim jurisprudent), the Council of Guardians, the Supreme Judicial Council, and the Ministry of Justice and its network of courts. A republic has replaced the monarchy, judicial organizations have acquired great power, the constitution vests sovereignty ambiguously in both the faqih (Khomeini) and the nation, but thus far it is clear that the former supervenes in any conflict between the two. Apart from new institutions, the clergy seem to have succeeded reasonably well in preventing economic collapse during a protracted war with Iraq. The population continues to be fed, despite serious shortages, very high inflation rates, and severe manpower deficiencies.[49] Khomeini has basically employed his charisma and the social mythos of Shi'ism to undergird clerical organizations (the *imam-jum'ah*-preacher-judge network). On the other hand, if a centralized repressive bureaucratic/military organization has not existed to impose the state's writ, repression has nevertheless been exercised through "parastate" agencies. The latter consist mainly of the Islamic Revolutionary Guards and Revolutionary Committees and Revolutionary Courts that have spread especially in the urban centers. Repression has also been applied via an informal network of rowdies known as *hizbullahis* (those of the party of God). The Islamic Republican Party (IRP) has served as one mobilizing organization, but it would be a mistake to consider it a disciplined cadre party.

A long list of shortcomings has also been cited by revolutionary officials in the course of the seven years of the revolution. Clearly, establishing the theocratic state and sustaining it with systematic policies are very different things. Chaotic conditions in state offices have been created by continuing purges. For some, such as the Qum Friday Mosque prayer leader, Ayatollah Husayn Mishkini and the designated heir of Khomeini, Ayatollah Husayn Ali Muntaziri, such purges must be continued in the interests of ideological purity. For others, such as the Chief Justice of the Supreme Court, Ayatollah Abd al-Karim Musavi Ardabili, coercive measures such as purges have gone too far, requiring regime officials to mount campaigns to persuade disaffected specialists to return to their jobs.[50]

A continuing battle has raged between those advocating continued independence for revolutionary organs and those urging their consolidation in the official state apparatus. Probably at the center of this controversy has been the issue of the Revolutionary Courts, which proliferated both at the national, provincial, city, and district levels and also functionally, becoming attached to the army, the guilds, and so on. Relatively early in the revolutionary period, Ayatollah Ardabili and the State prosecutor-General, Ayatollah Rabani Amlashi, issued a report advocating the merger of the Revolutionary Courts with those in the Ministry of Justice. Ayatollah Khomenini overruled them, however.[51] But recently, the issue has emerged once again, and this time it would appear that proponents of state consolidation have won out. Presumably, the difference is that Khomeini tends to perceive the debates swirling around him and seeks to hold the middle ground. Whatever utility independent Revolutionary Courts may have had earlier presumably had lapsed for a majority of the clerical power elite, so that continued independence for these courts had come to jeopardize their interests.

Symptomatic of the problems that exist for the revolutionary regime despite its creation of new state institutions are a series of public policy issues touching upon land and trade. Attempts upon the part of the so called *maktabis* (those faithful to Khomeini's line) to nationalize foreign trade and expropriate large landholdings from their owners irrespective of the legality of acquisition of such lands have foundered. Again, Khomeini may be seen to be cleaving to the center. For example, in 1981 the Majlis (parliament) passed a land law permitting the government to confiscate large landholders' property for the purpose of redistribution to landless or small holder peasants. The Guardian Council, which the constitution has vested with the power of judicial review over legislative enactments, declared the bill null and void. The Speaker of Parliament, Hujjat al-Islam Ali Akbar Hashimi Rafsanjani, thereby importuned Khomeini for assistance. Probably sensing widespread support for legislation of the sort just vetoed, Khomeini agreed to the idea of vesting some of his powers as faqih in the parliament. The legal justification for this attempt at override was that Islamic law permits "secondary principles" (*qavanin va ahkam-i saniviyah-yi Islam*) to take precedence over primary principles in circumstances that require innovation. Despite this transfer of power, the land question remained unresolved. In early 1983 Rafsanjani again announced that Khomeini had given parliament extraordinary powers, this time specifying that a two-thirds majority in that body would have to request it (in contrast to 1981, when only a majority was specified). But still nothing has been done, and Khomeini, sensing significant opposition now, has criticized the deputies for passing legislation they know the Guardian Council will veto. "If the Guardian Council says something is against Islam, then it is against Islam," he admonished. Moreover, he bluntly asserted that "there is no connection between the secondary decrees [principles] and the implementation of *velayat-i faqih* [rule by the jurisprudent]."[52]

The same thing has happened with regard to nationalization of foreign trade. In November 1981 the Majlis enacted legislation vesting complete control of foreign trade in the state. However, in May 1982 the Guardian Council vetoed this act. In December 1982 parliament once again was debating a trade nationalization bill, leading Guardian Council member, Ayatollah Muhammad Riza Mahdavi Kani, to declare it in advance to be "an annulment of people's property ownership." He urged the parliament to compromise by only nationalizing that part of foreign trade which has to do with the heavy industries that the state has taken over.[53] But his comment begs the question as to why the Guardian Council did not object to state ownership of heavy industry enterprises in the first place.

Attempts by the revolutionary regime to integrate the periphery have proven difficult. As is to be expected, wide variations may be seen in different parts of the country. In Boir Ahmad and in Kuhgiluye province the authorities undertook road and irrigation projects which went further than those implemented under the Pahlavi state.[54] The emphasis has been upon small-scale mechanization of agriculture as a means of creating strong regional commodity markets. Decentralization is thus promoted, but it is difficult to know whether this has proven beneficial or not. In the Fars region, generally speaking, productivity has not increased since the revolution, and popular discontent is high: "There are no effectual programs . . . for a comprehensive land consolidation . . . the introduction of high yield crops . . . protection and regeneration of pasture land . . . modernization of animal husbandry . . . an organized marketing system, or a reliable price structure."[55]

Additionally, neglect of certain industrial projects of the Pahlavi state, such as oil drilling, has resulted in the inability of villagers to supplement their income by wage labor. In Fars and Boir Ahmad the chance to work both at industrial sites and on the land had benefited some rurals in the past. Now, due to the revolution and the war with Iraq, rapid rates of increase in inflation and widespread shortages have led to a drastic decline in the standard of living for many in southern Iran. The regime thus faces increasingly alienated groups in the countryside. One wonders whether for this regime the same situation is not being created as under Reza Shah in which the state tries to penetrate the periphery but the masses there refuse to extend it their active support.

The Islamic state's ideal in encouraging small-scale mechanization of agriculture and paced industrialization derives from Khomenini's definition of social justice. Economic projects in the past, large-scale as they were, tended to aggrandize the state, its ruler, and prebendary officials. It is this state of affairs that constitutes true injustice (*zulm*) in the eyes of the clerical elite. The administrative state that underwrites its existence by extracting a surplus from the peasantry is by its very nature an oppressive state according to this outlook. Yet, it seems that despite the smashing of the Pahlavi bureaucratic state, the clerical elite has succeeded in creating its own elite-mass integration problems.

In the Kurdish regions the Islamic state has found natural allies in the landlords and not the poor rurals (except in Shi'ite areas). Sunni Kurds have been labeled Communists, according to one authority. "Immediately after the fall of Tehran landlords at several places established "Islamic Revolutionary Committees," showing a clear understanding of how to best protect their interests . . . landlords started to expel peasants from their land [and] . . . invoked and received external support, at first from the (Azari) Revolutionary Committee of Urmia, later from revolutionary guards."[56]

Because the formal mechanisms and representatives of the clergy never extended into the more rural areas, less-educated and less prestigious agents of the religious leaders had to serve in this capacity. These mullahs established rapport with only a small fraction of Iranian villagers, and then mainly with the landlords. For these alone had the resources to maintain the mullahs' upkeep. Thus, "typically, the poor majority identified the village *mullahs* as allies of the very group they believed were oppressing them by means of land expropriations, inequitable sharecropping arrangements and usurious lending practices."[57] Initially, the younger villagers welcomed the revolution, but the failure of the regime to enact land reforms has led to the return of the former anticlerical biases in the villages. The peasants appreciate the infrastructure projects (such as repair of roads, bathhouses, silos) in areas such as the Shiraz district. But the state is perceived as unwilling to deliver on land, employment, and such, leading to villager perceptions of the state as "at best incompetent, and in its worst aspects a travesty of the very Shi'i ideals it should uphold."[58]

But the state's impact in other areas has been more mixed. At least in the early months after the revolution exploitative moneylending vanished in certain tribal areas. Tribals in some cases recouped a lost market in meat and dairy products as a result of early policies banning the importation of frozen meat and dairy products.[59] But this has since changed, and the regime has been importing large amounts of frozen meat again, and meat is now so scarce that it has reached the staggering price of about $15 per kilogram on the black market and as high as $10 for those fortunate to be able to buy it in the regular market.[60]

Can the revolutionary state reintegrate the rural areas into a new Iranian state? It is too early to tell for certain, but it is worth noting that in virtually every case the state has rejected ethnolinguistic demands for autonomy. The most notable groups that have registered such demands are the Kurds, the Arabs, the Qashqa'is, and the Turkomans. Apart from sending its military contingents to suppress tribal uprisings, the state has denied parliamentary seats to elected tribal khans, captured and imprisoned them, or executed them. This has been the lot of individuals such as the Arab shaykh, Muhammad Khaqani, and Qashqa'i chief, Khusrau Khan. In some respects, different agencies of the state seem to be operating at cross-purposes in tribal and rural areas, as the Revolutionary Guards and Revolutionary Committees have acted in high-handed fashion in a number of districts, whereas the Reconstruction Corps (Jihad-i Sazandagi) has won approval.

Labor has been mobilized by the revolutionary regime but it has refused to grant workers any autonomy in the form of syndicates and unions. The Labor Minister and other state officials have publicly proclaimed the "un-Islamic nature" of labor unions and admonished the proletariat not to expect such unions under pain of sanction.[61] Thus far, based on impressionistic evidence, it is possible to say that the rich-poor gap has marginally lessened under the current regime. But all is not well in the affairs of the state. For example, the Majlis deputy from Tehran, Fakhr al-Din Hijazi, attacked the labor bill for lack of any provisions pertaining to unionization, insurance, retirement, and child protection.[62] At a more general level, regime leaders have been forced publicly to deny that things have gotten worse under the clerical state than they were in the Pahlavi period on the questions of social justice and egalitarianism. Thus, for example, parliament speaker Rafsanjani indignantly rebutted charges that in fact nothing had been done for the "deprived" masses (mustaz'afan) or that in the last four years the poor have gotten poorer and the rich richer. "Then what about all these large factories and companies that have been seized?" he asked.[63] But to some in the regime, he picked the wrong issue. For the Minister of Heavy Industry, Behzad Nabavi, has accused state-owned industries of having lost untold billions of dollars, singling out the Industrial Development and Research Organization—a state agency—for having lost by itself $3.6 billion.[64] Ayatollah Khomeini has labeled such interpretations as "heretical" (kufr amiz) and noted that they implied that monarchy is better than Islam.[65]

Relations of the revolutionary state with the bazaar are critical because of the historic alliance between clerics and the bazaar in previous cases of collective protest and rebellion in Iran. The more well-to-do bazaar merchants have been hurt by the regime's attempt to control foreign trade, and although this issue still has not been resolved, government manipulation of foreign exchange controls has adversely affected this group, as well as the middle bazaar stratum. A series of strikes in the bazaars of Tehran and Qum must have alarmed the revolutionary elite in late 1980.

Although the revolution was in large measure directed against the bureaucratic state, the Islamic Republic clearly required some cadres from the old regime to carry on at least essential services. Yet, bureaucrats have either fled or been purged or laid off as the state increasingly found it difficult to pay salaries in a period of severe inflation and the war with Iraq. One source suggests that salaried bureaucrats and labor have been very adversely affected by "cutbacks in government salaries and layoffs."[66]

Disaffection among the mujtahids has deepened as well. Many of the distinguished mujtahids have bitterly criticized a wide variety of violations of law and coercive behavior on the part of those identifying themselves explicitly with maktabi positions. The most famous example of mujtahid dissidence is Ayatollah Kazim Shariatmadari, but denunciations have been leveled by other leading theologians as well.[67] It is true that they have remained largely silent since early 1982, but this could change if the regime begins losing support among the urban poor. Their criticisms have ranged from such fundamental points as the lack of doctrinal basis in Shi'ism for vilayat-i faqih (rule by the jurisprudent) to loss of civil rights.

The politically articulate members of the women's movement, who originally strongly supported the revolution, have also gone over to the opposition. Originally, the clerical leadership was faced with a united movement that forced the regime to demur on its early requirement that women appearing in public be veiled. But women supporters of the clergy then began to circulate petitions in state offices and places of employment urging employers to require the veil anyway. The women's movement became polarized, so that by the end of 1979 and early 1980, veiling had become standard for those employed in the public and private sectors.[68]

The foregoing suggests that the theocratic state has been able to act with remarkable independence from its social base of support. Given all the defections, discussed above, from the Islamic Republic, how has it managed to survive? The consensus seems to be that its survival has been a function of the fragmentation of the opposition. One must not underrate the role of Ayatollah Khomeini and the force of his charismatic personality, either. At a particularly vulnerable moment for the revolutionary state, when the bazaar had struck in late 1980, Khomeini alternated between sharp condemnation and lamentation. When bazaaris began chanting that the clergy must return to the mosques, Khomeini branded this an "imperialist plot" to separate religion and politics as the Shah tried to do. He complained: "I regret that this plot is working in Qum. If a bazaari in Qum or Tehran accepts this, then things are in extremely bad shape."[69] The bazaar opened its doors after this reaction by the faqih. Other regime leaders have threatened the bazaar with exemplary punishment by the Revolutionary Courts for "economic terrorism," meaning hoarding, price gouging, and deliberate sabotage.[70] Recently, Ayatollah Khomeini tried to reassure the bazaar when he made a speech insisting on the need for the bazaar to play a central role in the economy despite the growing tendency of the public sector to dominate it.[71]

To be sure, the state's autonomy from its social base does not mean that this state is strong in the rural areas. The contrast with the late Pahlavi state is striking in this regard. Localist tendencies in socioeconomic matters will challenge the government for some time to come, as the state will be hard pressed to implement its tax legislation outside the urban areas.[72] Although seven years is a very short time, it is clear that the state formation and consolidation process has been very difficult so far in the case of the Islamic Republic.

CONCLUSIONS

Theda Skocpol cites Lenin as having stated: "the basic question of every revolution is that of state power."[73] Although himself not a revolutionary, Reza Shah lived in a period of quasi-revolutionary protest and chaos. His goal was certainly the conquest of state power. The crisis that had brought about these anarchic conditions was largely one centered in the Qajar state, the feeble remnants of which were toppled and then replaced by a bureaucratic state machinery.

What may one say about the Islamic revolutionaries? They too, as legal experts above all else, have insisted upon a constituted state, albeit an Islamic one. The Islamic revolutionaries have succeeded in smashing the old state and replacing it with a new one that is weaker in its administrative power, but one that aspires to penetrate the lives of the people more extensively. Its chief institutions include the faqih, the Guardian Council, the Supreme Judicial Council, and the Ministry of Justice and its extensive network of courts. There is, too, the informal judicial network which we may term the imam-jum'ah/Society of Combatant Clergymen/Qum seminary network. Taken together, these elements can wield significant moral power, especially in their ability to mobilize urban masses through the intermediary of gang leaders. The cabinet and parliament exist, too, as state agencies as they did in the old regime. But in the Islamic

Republic the members of these bodies seem to be acting as mere commissioners of the clerical leaders. Of course, one must not forget that although the Revolutionary Courts have been formally absorbed by the Ministry of Justice, the Revolutionary Committees and Revolutionary Guards continue to operate. And in some respects, they enjoy autonomy to the point of criticism by Khomeini, Ardabili, and others in the very top leadership positions.[74] Thus, so far this state is fundamentally different from that of Reza Shah or of his successor in at least certain structural aspects.

Khomeini has sought to prevent a premature effort to consolidate the state (premature from his point of view). His problem is similar to that of most revolutionary leaders who try to maintain a high level of revolutionary elan for a long period after the revolution. This has conflicted with the desire of apparatchiks and political leaders eager for a breathing spell and consolidation. Thus, consider the guarded criticism of permanent revolutionary ardor by the Deputy Prime Minister for Revolutionary Institutions, condemning duplication and even sabotage of professional work by state officials. Integrating the revolutionary organs into the state agencies "would in no way be correct," he conceded; but the relationship between them needed to be "regularized" through the issue of laws and regulations.[75]

The migrant poor and urban lumpenproletariat will probably exert pressure against too rapid a consolidation of the state as long as they feel conservative clergymen—especially in the Guardian Council and the Supreme Judicial Council—will continue to deny them squatting rights, confiscations of wealth, and social mobility. Routinization, after all, could not only lead to a loss of certain gains in the revolution but ultimately result in taxation and conscription policies similar to those to which the previous state had subjected them.

It is ironic that, despite its ideal policy of small-scale mechanization of agriculture, self-sufficiency in food, and paced industrialization to integrate traditional and larger industrial development, the revolutionary state seems to be repeating the rentier experience of the past. Although a "rentier absolutist state"[76] will probably not be the pattern because it is based on a thoroughgoing bureaucratization of power that seems unlikely under the clerics, efforts at state centralization will continue. A dialectical relationship is likely to exist between the revolutionary organs and the state apparatus as such, with periodical purges a likely concomitant.

Perhaps one similarity between the state under Reza Shah and the Islamic Republic that needs to be accentuated is that in each case the state entered into tactical alignments with social groups but then turned upon them. Reza Shah's tactical alignments with the clergy, for example, and also with the members of the Reformers' Party and the Revival Party[77] were rapidly followed up by attacks against them. The same situation prevailed in the Islamic Republic, as the foregoing analysis has shown. This has been so pronounced that the clerical state has been able to dispense even with what might otherwise be considered its most vital support—high-ranking clergymen. Factionalism within the ruling Islamic Republican Party has been significant, but not so much that it has led to immobilism.

In summary, the two cases analyzed in this chapter well exemplify the variations in the emergence and growth of the Iranian state over time. At certain historical periods this state has been a sharply hierarchical and bureaucratic structure with strong centralizing tendencies based on patrimonial forms. At other times, the state has been more in the nature of personal rulership and charismatic authority, with structures rooted in tribal or populist origins. In terms of the relationship between state and society, the first type of state seems to succeed in imposing itself upon society but has difficulty in truly integrating society into the state. In the second type, society is more autonomous in the interrelationship and seems more capable, at the same time, of being organically integrated into the state. Yet, the state is itself unable to extend its machinery and symbols into the periphery effectively due to as yet weak structures or inappropriate policies.

NOTES

I would like to thank Ali Banuazizi and Nikki Keddie for their careful reading of an earlier draft and for their very helpful comments, many of which I have incorporated.

1. Marshall G. S. Hodgson, *The Venture of Islam: Conscience and History in a World Civilization*, vol. 1 (Chicago: University of Chicago Press, 1974), pp. 44, 138–44.

2. Erwin I. J. Rosenthal, *Islam in the Modern National State* (London: Cambridge University Press, 1965), p. 12.

3. Roger Savory, *Iran under the Safavids* (New York: Cambridge University Press, 1980), p. 177.

4. Ann K. S. Lambton, "Quis custodiet custodes? Some Reflections on the Persian Theory of Government," *Studia Islamica*, pt. 1, 5 (1955), p. 137.

5. Lambton, "Quis custodiet custodes?," pt. 2, 6 (1956), p. 129.

6. Ibid., pp. 136–37.

7. Ervand Abrahamian, "Oriental Despotism: The Case of Qajar Iran," *International Journal of Middle East Studies*, 5:1 (January 1974), p. 13.

8. W. G. Runciman, "Origins of States: The Case of Archaic Greece," *Comparative Studies in Society and History*, 24:3 (July 1982), p. 351.

9. Adapted from Ronald Cohen, "Introduction," in *Origins of the State: The Anthropology of Political Evolution*, ed. Ronald Cohen and Elman R. Service (Philadelphia: Institute for the Study of Human Issues, 1978), p. 8.

10. Henry T. Wright, "Toward an Explanation of the Origin of the State," in Cohen and Service, eds., *Origin of the State*, fig. 4 from Robert McC. Adams, *The Evolution of Urban Society: Early Mesopotamia and Prehispanic Mexico* (Chicago: Aldine, 1966), p. 54.

11. Karl A. Wittfogel, *Oriental Despotism: A Comparative Study of Total Power* (New Haven, Conn.: Yale University Press, 1957), p. 53, refers to "the care with which the available water was assigned" in Eastern Iran in the pre-Islamic period. He comments upon the "clock-like cooperation between the 'water master' (*mirab*), his subordinate officials and aides, and the village heads." But it is clear that water control was local. It is true that the Sasanid state organized large irrigation works in the Mesopotamian (i.e., non-Iranian) region. But Iran proper was another matter.

In ancient Egypt and China, by contrast—classic hydraulic societies—large-scale irrigation necessitated systematic scheduling of the use of water, planning for the construction of new works or repair of existing ones, extensive coordination of workers employed on the dams, ditches, dikes, and the like. Success in these areas led to sustained agricultural production, but breakdowns eventuated in social unrest and famine. As a consequence of control over these processes, the leadership became wealthier and stratification patterns differentiating it from the masses became increasingly articulated. However, class conflict in the sense of politically conscious collective action by individuals defining their interests in terms of economic, political, and social commitments was held to a minimum by the elites. At least part of the explanation for low levels in the magnitude of *class* conflict lies in the fact that the elite fulfilled sacral priestly functions. This did not make them immune from social protest, since many examples of conflict in the countryside may be cited in the history of these states. But since the main lines of stratification there had historically been vertical rather than horizontal, conflicts mainly affiliated around ethnic, religious, linguistic, or other non-class loyalties. Discrepancies of wealth, therefore, could be rationalized by the state officials on religious grounds.

12. L. P. Elwell-Sutton, "Reza Shah the Great: Founder of the Pahlavi Dynasty," in *Iran Under the Pahlavis*, ed. George Lenczowski (Stanford, Calif.: Hoover Institution Press, Stanford University, 1981), p. 8.

13. Homa Katouzian, *The Political Economy of Modern Iran: Despotism and Pseudo-Modernism, 1926–1979* (New York: New York University Press, 1981), p. 92.

14. Amin Banani, *The Modernization of Iran: 1921–1941* (Stanford, Calif.: Stanford University Press, 1961), passim.

15. While it was not Reza Shah who added "Aryamehr" (light of the Aryans) to his titles but rather his son, it is clear that he laid the groundwork for the aryanization of Iran's ideology of modernization. The very choice of the dynasty name, Pahlavi (an ancient Iranian language), is indicative. For a laudatory presentation of themes embedded in the Iranian monarchical ideology, including divine light, "aure-

ola of saints and kings," the "victorious halo of glory," etc., see Pio Filippani-Ronconi, "The Tradition of Sacred Kingship in Iran," in Lenczowski, ed., *Iran Under the Pahlavis*, pp. 51–83.

16. Charles Issawi, "The Iranian Economy: Fifty Years of Economic Development," in Lenczowski, ed., *Iran Under the Pahlavis*, p. 131.

17. Katouzian, *Political Economy of Modern Iran*, p. 129. Emphasis Katouzian's.

18. Julian Bharier, *Economic Development in Iran 1900–1970* (London: Oxford University Press, 1971), p. 159.

19. Issawi, "The Iranian Economy," p. 131.

20. For a classification scheme of integration featuring five types—national, territorial, value, elite-mass, and integrative behavior—see Myron Weiner, "Political Integration and Political Development," *Annals of The American Academy of Political and Social Science*, 358 (March 1965), pp. 52–64.

21. Bharier, *Economic Development in Iran*, p. 28.

22. Wittfogel, *Oriental Despotism*, pp. 308–9. Here, Wittfogel is arguing that, faced with the heterogeneous nature of his empire, the Achaemenid ruler exercised authority through grants of "unusual freedom" to regional administrators. The king even permitted the latter to acquire a "quasiroyal status." Yet, "a central system of communication and intelligence, inspection by metropolitan officials, and the maintenance of Persian garrisons at strategic points prevented the satrap from attaining military or fiscal independence." Stability of the ancient Iranian state, therefore, seemed to be embedded in the network of central administration and regional enclaves that were enmeshed in the Achaemenid state by appropriate financial, trade, and bureaucratic ties.

23. Karl Polanyi, *The Great Transformation: The Political and Economic Origins of Our Time* (Boston: Beacon Press, 1957), p. 68.

24. Bharier, *Economic Development in Iran*, p. 52.

25. Ibid., p. 53.

26. Katouzian, *Political Economy of Modern Iran*, p. 95.

27. Ibid, p. 53.

28. A. Khvajah Nuri, *Bazigaran'i 'Asr-i Tala'i* (The Play Actors of the Gilded Age) (Tehran: Chap, 1323 H. Sh.?/1944?), pp. 50–57.

29. Bharier, *Economic Development in Iran*, p. 45.

30. Issawi, "The Iranian Economy," p. 132. Issawi maintains that private sector investment under Reza Shah was "very high," although most sources disagree with such an assessment, including Bharier, *Economic Development in Iran*; George B. Baldwin, *Planning and Development in Iran* (Baltimore, Md.: Johns Hopkins Press, 1967); Robert E. Looney, *Economic Origins of the Iranian Revolution* (New York: Pergamon Press, 1982); and Katouzian, *Political Economy of Modern Iran*.

31. Hossein Mahdavy, "The Patterns and Problems of Economic Development in Rentier States: The Case of Iran," in *Studies in the Economic History of the Middle East from the Rise of Islam to the Present Day*, ed. M. A. Cook (London: Oxford University Press, 1970), pp. 428–67.

32. Ervand Abrahamian, *Iran Between Two Revolutions* (Princeton, N.J.: Princeton University Press, 1982), p. 351; also Fred Halliday, *Iran: Dictatorship and Development* (Baltimore, Md.: Penguin Books, 1979), pp. 177–78.

33. Abrahamian, *Iran Between Two Revolutions*, p. 147.

34. Farhad Kazemi, "The Military and Politics in Iran: The Uneasy Symbiosis," in *Towards a Modern Iran: Studies in Thought, Politics and Society*," ed. Elie Kedourie and Sylvia G. Haim (London: Frank Cass, 1980), p. 220; Abrahamian, *Iran Between Two Revolutions*, pp. 141–42.

35. Banani, *The Modernization of Iran*, p. 71; Shahrough Akhavi, *Religion and Politics in Contemporary Iran: Clergy-State Relations in the Pahlavi Period* (Albany: State University of New York Press, 1980), pp. 37–59.

36. Abrahamian, *Iran Between Two Revolutions*, p. 149.

37. Ibid., pp. 131–32.

38. Gene R. Garthwaite, "Khans and Kings: The Dialectics of Power in Bakhtiyari History," in *Modern Iran: The Dialectics of Continuity and Change*, ed. Michael E. Bonine and Nikki R. Keddie (Albany: State University of New York Press, 1981), p. 171.

39. Frederik Barth, *Nomads of South Persia: The Basseri Tribe of the Khamseh Confederacy* (Boston: Little, Brown, 1961), p. 3.

40. Philip Carl Salzman, "Continuity and Change in Baluchi Tribal Leadership," *International Journal of Middle East Studies*, 4:4 (October 1973), p. 428.

41. William Irons, "Nomadism as a Political Adaptation: The Case of the Yomut Turkomen," *American Ethnologist*, 1:4 (November 1974), p. 650.

42. Paul Barker, "Tent Schools of the Qashqa'i: A Paradox of Local Initiative and State Control," in Bonine and Keddie, eds., *Modern Iran*, p. 143; also Pierre Oberling, *The Qashqa'i Nomads of Fars* (The Hague: Mouton, 1974), p. 153.

43. G. Reza Fazel, "The Encapsulation of Nomadic Societies in Iran," in *The Desert and the Sown: Nomads in the Wider Society*, ed. Cynthia Nelson (Berkeley: Institute of International Studies, University of California, Berkeley, 1973), p. 135.

44. Philip Carl Salzman, "The Study of 'Complex Society' in the Middle East: A Review Essay," *International Journal of Middle East Studies*, 9:4 (November 1978), p. 544–45.

45. Eric R. Wolf, "Peasant Rebellion and Revolution," in *National Liberation: Revolution in the Third World*, ed. Norman Miller and Roderick Aya (New York: Free Press, 1971), pp. 54–55; Wolf, *Peasant Wars of the Twentieth Century* (New York: Harper & Row, 1969), pp. 37, 41, 151–53.

46. Clifford Geertz, "Centers, Kings, and Charisma: Reflections on the Symbolics of Power," in *Culture and Its Creators: Essays in Honor of Edward Shils*, ed. Joseph Ben-David and Terry Nichols Clark (Chicago: University of Chicago Press, 1977), pp. 150–71.

47. Abrahamian, *Iran Between Two Revolutions*, p. 149, goes as far as to say that Reza Shah's state "hovered somewhat precariously, without class foundations, over Iran's society." See also Nikki R. Keddie, *Roots of Revolution: An Interpretative History of Modern Iran* (New Haven, Conn.: Yale University Press, 1981), pp. 111–12.

48. Michael M. J. Fischer, "Islam and the Revolt of the Petit[e] Bourgeoisie," *Daedalus*, 111:1 (Winter 1982), pp. 115–20; Farhad Kazemi, *Poverty and Revolution in Iran: The Migrant Poor, Urban Marginality and Politics* (New York: New York University Press, 1981).

49. In a remarkable admission, Ayatollah Khomeini has recently said that chaos and starvation (*qahti*) will prevail for a long time to come because revolutions

tend to create such circumstances. See *Iran Times* (Washington, D.C.), 29 Bahman 1361 H. Sh./18 February 1983. All references to this sources hereafter will be abbreviated as *IT* and also indicate Persian language articles unless otherwise noted.

50. *IT,* 9 Bahman 1360 H. Sh./29 January 1982; *IT,* 28 Isfand 1360 H. Sh./19 March 1982; *Ittila'at* (Tehran), 26 Khurdad 1358 H. Sh./17 June 1979; *IT,* 6 Khurdad 1362 H. Sh./27 May 1983; *IT,* 13 Khurdad 1362 H. Sh./3 June 1983; *IT,* 30 Urdibihisht 1362/20 May 1983.

51. *IT,* 7 Khurdad 1361 H. Sh./28 May 1982; *IT,* 30 Urdibihisht 1362 H. Sh./ 20 May 1983. Note that the Constitution, in its articles pertaining to the courts (156– 174), does not mention revolutionary tribunals.

52. *IT,* 1 Aban 1360 H. Sh./23 October 1981; *IT,* 15, 22 Bahman 1361/4, 11 February 1983; FBIS-SAS-83-032, 15 February 1983.

53. *IT,* 19 Azar 1361/10 December 1983.

54. Reinhold Loeffler, "Economic Changes in a Rural Area Since 1979," in *The Iranian Revolution and the Islamic Republic,* ed. Nikki R. Keddie and Eric Hooglund (Washington, D. C.: Middle East Institute/Woodrow Wilson International Center for Scholars, 1982), p. 62.

55. Ibid., pp. 62–63.

56. Martin van Bruinessen, "Nationalismus und religiöser Konflikt: Der kurdische Widerstand im Iran," in *Religion und Politik im Iran: Mardomnameh—Jahrbuch zur Geschichte und Gesellschaft des Mittleren Orients,* ed. Kurt Greussing (Frankfurt am Main: Syndikat Verlag, 1981), pp. 400–401. See also Jim Paul, "Iran's Peasants and the Revolution: An Introduction," *Middle East Research and Information Project* (hereafter *MERIP) Reports* (No. 104), 12:3 (March–April 1982), pp. 22–23; and the anonymous "Report from an Iranian Village," in ibid., pp. 26–29.

57. Eric Hooglund, "Rural Iran and the Clerics," *MERIP Reports* (No. 104), 12:3 (March–April 1982), p. 24.

58. Ibid., p. 25.

59. Lois Beck, "Revolutionary Iran and Its Tribal Peoples," *MERIP Reports* (No. 87), 10:4 (May 1980), p. 19.

60. Of 200,000 tons of imported meat, in 1982, only about 6 percent was fresh—the rest being frozen meat. The state has announced that the quota of imported meat in 1983–84 will decline to 152,000 tons. See *IT,* 15 Bahman 1361/4 February 1983.

61. *IT,* 27 Azar 1360 H. Sh./18 December 1981. The Minister of Labor has argued that "in Islam rights are given to every individual."

62. *IT,* 19 Farvardin 1362 H. Sh./8 April 1983.

63. *IT,* 6 Khurdad 1362 H. Sh./27 May 1983.

64. *IT,* 13 Khurdad 1362 H. Sh./3 June 1983.

65. *IT,* 6 Khurdad 1362 H. Sh./27 May 1983.

66. Patrick Clawson, "Iran's Economy: Between Crisis and Collapse," *MERIP Reports* (No. 98), 11:6 (July–August 1981), p. 14.

67. Shahrough Akhavi, "The Ideology and Praxis of Shi'ism in the Iranian Revolution," *Comparative Studies in Society and History,* 25:2 (April 1983), pp. 211–19.

68. Azar Tabari, "The Enigma of the Veiled Iranian Woman," *MERIP Reports* (No. 103), 12:2 (February 1982), pp. 22–27.

69. *IT*, 30 Aban 1359 H. Sh./21 November 1980; 7 Azar 1359 H. Sh./28 November 1980; 19 Day 1359 H. Sh./9 January 1981.

70. These officials include Ayatollah Ardabili and Hujjat al-Islam Rafsanjani. See, for example, *IT*, 6 Azar 1360 H. Sh./4 December 1981; and *IT*, 2 Urdibihisht 1362/ 22 April 1983.

71. *IT*, 9 Shahrivar 1363 H. Sh./31 August 1984.

72. Even in Tehran, things are in a parlous state. According to the Deputy Mayor, citizens have failed in great numbers to pay automobile, business, and property taxes. The Minister of Treasury announced that 1982–83 brought in about $1.1 billion more in taxes than was the case in 1981–82, so matters are improving. However, Prime Minister Mir Husayn Musavi has revealed that there will be a budget deficit of $8.4 billion in 1983–84. See *IT*, 22 Bahman 1361 H. Sh./11 February 1983; *IT*, 27 Isfand 1361 H. Sh./18 March 1983; *IT*, 30 Urdibihisht 1362 H. Sh./20 May 1983.

73. Skocpol, *States and Social Revolutions: A Comparative Analysis of France, Russia, and China* (New York: Cambridge University Press, 1979), p. 284.

74. For example, see the eight-point "reform program" promulgated by Khomeini in December 1982 in which he ordered strict legality in the behavior of state agencies. And Ardabili's and Prime Minister Musavi's letter complaining about the behavior of certain judges (*hukkam-i shar'*) in illegally seizing people's property in contravention of the Khomeini program. Cf. *IT*, 3 Day 1361 H. Sh./24 December 1982; *IT*, 29 Bahman 1361 H. Sh./18 February 1983.

75. *IT*, 31 Urdibihisht 1361 H. Sh./21 May 1982.

76. Theda Skocpol, "Rentier State and Shi'a Islam in the Iranian Revolution," *Theory and Society*, 11:3 (May 1982), p. 268.

77. For these alignments, see Abrahamian, *Iran Between Two Revolutions*, pp. 120–26; Akhavi, *Religion and Politics in Contemporary Iran*, pp. 28–32.

8

From RELIGIOUS ACCOMMODATION to RELIGIOUS REVOLUTION

The Transformation of Shi'ism in Iran

ALI REZA SHEIKHOLESLAMI

ALL SOCIETIES NEED TO AFFIRM, through ritualized processes, holidays, or parades, their collective personality, or, as Durkheim called it, their "collective sentiments."[1] Such rituals indicate the depth and breadth of internal agreements which hold the society together. In the case of Iran such rituals are predominantly religious.

Neither political rituals nor the central political authority in Iran came to serve as a link between the sacred and the secular, helping to recreate common bonds and common ideals and to enhance sensibilities and sensitivities toward civic obligation. While coronations in many societies function to elevate the ruler from the realm of the profane to that of the divine, rendering the king into a symbol of solidarity,[2] the attempts by Iranian court historians and panegyrists to call the king *zillullah* (the Shadow of God) failed. There is no evidence that coronation in Islamic Iran performed a sacred function, transforming the monarch from an actual power holder to the symbol of divinity. While the practice was taken more seriously during the Safavids (1501–1722), it was practically ignored by the Qajars (1794–1921). The Pahlavi (1925–79) attempt to revive it harked back to pre-Islamic Iran, and the coronation of the late Shah in 1968 seemed empty and at best an afterthought, leaving most of the population unaffected. Actual control of political power in Islamic Iran has generally been recognized by the minting and inscription of coinage and in the recitation of the *khutbah* (Friday sermon). But no intense celebrations, bringing the various segments of the population

227

together, accompanied these occasions. The absence of political rituals (with the exception of *Naw-Ruz* [the New Year], a symbol of
Iranian national solidarity, presently beseiged by the regime) is striking when contrasted with the plethora of religious rituals and symbols. It is, in fact, sacred symbolism which establishes paradigms for
social action and models for political behavior.

Throughout the post-Sassanian period in Iran, a period
which began in mid-seventh century, law, as the external indicator of
the "collective sentiments" of the society, remained Islamic or was
Islamized, particularly in personal matters such as marriage, divorce,
inheritance, and relations between husband and wife. To behave according to the Islamic law and to be ruled by it was a collective ideal.
Adherence to the same general legal framework which included attitudes, practices, behavior, ideals, and ideas, was the fundamental
pillar of the Islamic community. In fact, through this general sense of
solidarity the rule of successive waves of Turkish tribes became more
palatable and perhaps less oppressive and antagonistic.

In addition to embodying symbolic unity through law, Islam
consists of devotional acts which help to integrate the individual with
the community and thus strengthen the spirit of the collectivity.[3] The
Islamic rites are regular events which methodically separate the believer from the ordinary and everyday attempt to earn a livelihood,
generating in him social awareness. The important five pillars of Islam, such as *shihadah* (testifying that no god exists but God and the
truthfulness of Muhammad's mission), daily prayers, payment of religious taxes, fasting during Ramadan, and finally the *hajj* (pilgrimage
to Mecca), are rites which frequently bring the individual out into the
community and impress him with the idea of his unity with fellow
believers. During Ramadan, the month of fasting, food, drink, and
sex are shunned, and individual pursuit of self-gratification is replaced with the search for collective ideals. During the pilgrimage to
Mecca one's identity becomes Islamic. In the aftermath of this collective effervescence the sense of the symbol of collectivity, namely Allah, becomes most pronounced. The intensity of the emotions
aroused by the assembled group of pilgrims goes beyond the cumulative intensities of the individual believers. Fervor, religious or political, is expressed more strongly in crowds than individually. The
created event, which brings men together, sharing similar sentiments, is, in the words of Durkheim, "the only way of renewing the
collective representations."[4] Even for a nonbeliever like Richard Burton, the experience of the hajj was a moving one. Writing of his
unusual journey to Mecca in the middle of the nineteenth century, he

observed, "I may truly say that of all the worshipers, who clung weeping to the curtain, or who pressed their beating hearts to the stone, none felt for the moment a deeper emotion than did [I]."[5]

The *Id al-Adha* (Feast of Sacrifices) ceremony, when families sacrifice a lamb to commemorate God's granting Abraham permission to sacrifice a lamb instead of his son, is another case in point. The Id and the slaughtering of a lamb set into motion a flurry of interaction among the believers. The Id represents the danger to the solidarity of the community and its deflection through God's mercy. The sacramental meal, the lamb, is sacred in itself, and thus creates a tight bond among its consumers, tantamount to a relation of kinship. Commensality in this sense, however, has more of a social function than a religious one, as it primarily brings the individuals together as a group and only subsequently imprints that group with a religious identity. The Iranian custom of *sufrah* (serving food in the name of a particular Shi'ite saint) functions in the same manner. The food is to be shared with the poor and thus it is a social leveling device to preserve the welfare of the society rather than a means of saving souls.[6]

The most moving rituals in Iran, however, have been the rituals associated with the dead, which are, ironically, celebrations of life. The symbolism associated with them makes the society deeply conscious of itself. The commemoration of the deceased emphasizes the historical continuity of the community, and the social sentiment which the ritual arouses is more than sufficient to compensate for the death, i.e., the breach of solidarity. All these mourning rituals are associated with commensality which brings the community together, and the partaking of the food in particular brings life, contrasted with death, into a clearer focus.

The activities which take place on Tasu'a and Ashura, the ninth and tenth days of the lunar month of Muharram, marking the martyrdom of Husayn, the third Shi'i Imam in 680 are probably the most important of such rituals. These organized activities symbolically draw the attention of the participants to real anxieties men have about death. By bringing Husayn back to life every year, they feel a sense of victory over death. Indeed, in the aftermath of these rituals, the participants express a sense of well-being.[7] The celebrations which follow the death of a Shi'ite Muslim on the third, the seventh, and the fortieth days and thereafter on the anniversary of the death annually function in the same manner, albeit on a smaller scale. Finally, the concept of *ma'ad* (resurrection) is an assurance from God that the community will survive individually and collectively.[8]

It is thus important to ask what elements in the society prescribed these rituals, defined their messages, and held them to be
significant. It is also important to identify the symbols which are
absent and their relevance.

The Shi'i rituals have been mass-based and mass-oriented.
The high *ulama* (Islamic clergy; literally, "learned men"), by and
large, either ignored the mass hysteria or were plainly contemptuous
of it. The populace, on the other hand, required an identity other
than that of a subject population. None was provided by the successive military rulers in Iran who developed few organic links with the
population, and, in the final analysis, whose rule was based on
power and the population's preference for order, rather than any
popular sense of political legitimacy. Still, since 1694, only four Iranian monarchs have not been murdered or forced to abdicate. In
view of this history of political instability, it is not surprising that no
symbols of secular solidarity[9] or secular nationalism binding the state
and nation developed and that the collective identity of Iranians is as
Shi'i Muslims. The absence of political rituals intensified the need for
religious ones.

Shi'ism became the identity of the nation. For the believer
Husayn's martyrdom came to symbolize his own. The victory of the
military forces of the Umayyads and the establishment of the caliphate (600–750) over the legitimate claims of Husain was a replay of the
history of military domination. The belief in the occultation of the
Twelfth Imam and his messianic advent as the Mahdi presented hope
which permitted the believer to continue with life. These beliefs were
taken so seriously that the medieval Islamic historian, Yaqut Hamawi,
recalls that the inhabitants of Kashan used to take a white horse to
the outskirts of the city at dawn every Friday expecting the advent of
the Mahdi.[10] Behind all these symbols and rituals lay social reality.

Historically, the higher ulama adhered to strict scriptualism,
avoiding most popular rituals. Fearful that symbolic interpretations of
these mass rituals would lead to freedom of thought, eventually alter-
ing the character and framework of Islam, they sought refuge in rigidity. The lower ranks of the religious classes, the *rawdhah khvan*
(religious chanters) and the dervishes, had no such inhibitions.
Moreover, in contrast to the higher ulama, who were members of the
ruling class and often served as the intellectuals of the regime, the
lesser clergy had an affinity with the populace. They eagerly involved
themselves in the passionate acts of rituals and so strengthened their
own links with the populace. Thus it is not surprising that in the

process of the destruction of the Pahlavi regime in the name of Islam it was the lower-ranking clergyman who came to power, and the learned high clergy was either silenced or discredited. This social transformation, as we shall see, is paralleled by a symbolic reinterpretation of Islam, which, as crude as it may be, reflects the new social reality.

MILITARY RULE and SHI'I PASSIVITY

In spite of the prevalence of religiosity among the populace as evidenced by their high level of collective ritual activity, the state was until recently only superficially affected by Islam. The poetry composed by Shah Isma'il, who founded the Safavid dynasty in 1501 and restored internal order in Iran, is even sacrilegious in Islamic terms, giving evidence that he considered himself divine as a godhead and that his soldiers accepted him as such.[11] The pledges given by tribal leaders and other lords of the valleys to the reigning monarchs were not couched in religious terms. Rather, they recognized the de facto power of the monarchy, although the authority of the king, in the final analysis, depended on his military.[12] That power alone was the basis of the state had a long tradition, alluded to by Kai Kavus, advising his son. This minor medieval king wrote: "In the course of your kingship, never permit your commands to be treated with indifference. The king's solace and pleasure lie in giving commands; in other respects the king is like his subjects, and the difference between them is that the king issues commands while the subjects obey."[13]

A serious theoretical attempt, however, was made to associate the office of kingship with divinity. The great eleventh-century Saljuq minister, Nizam al-Mulk, trying to revive the ancient Persian concept of kingship, argued that, "God, most high, in every epoch chooses someone from among the people and adorns him with royal virtues and delegates to him the affairs of the world and the peace of his servants."[14] Not long after the minister's death, Sultan Sanjar (1118–57), bestowing the government of Farah to the prince of Nimruz, declared himself directly appointed by God. Making no reference to the religious authority of the caliph, he wrote to the prince that "God . . . entrusted the key of the climes of the world into the hand to our government and power."[15] Abu Hamid al-Ghazali (d. 1111) had earlier tried to set up the theoretical foundation for this claim by arguing for the absolute power of the ruler and holding him accountable only to God. Under these conditions no legitimate basis for rebellion existed.[16]

Others, before and after al-Ghazali, argued the same point. Jalal al-Din Dawwani, the late fifteenth-century thinker, also argued that sovereignty was a gift from God and consequently the sovereign's authority was absolute and his power did not need any justification.[17] The court historians went even further.[18] Such claims to appointment by God, while seemingly giving a religious legitimacy to the state, were in fact supra-religious and put the office of the king and that of the Prophet on par. They justified the royal actions beyond the framework set by the Prophet. Ann Lambton argues that during the Great Saljuq period (1050–1157) the justification for the king's authority was not the recreation of the perfect community of Muhammad, but the maintenance of order and justice to provide the political and social stability under which the religious institution could flourish and the various classes fulfill their different functions.[19]

The state in Islamic Iran was conceived of as the property of the ruler, who controlled it by the right of conquest. Officials served as personal retainers of the king. The royal authority over his subjects was the king's personal possession which he exploited in such a manner as one exploits economic advantages. Indeed, as Weber points out, "in the patrimonial state the most fundamental obligation of the subjects is the material maintenance of the ruler."[20] The tendency to reduce political obligations to economic ones, and the need to pay for a large army, made the sanctity of private property questionable. This process was further accentuated by the need of the patrimonial lord to hold his subjects not individually but collectively responsible for the payments of special dues and taxes. Much of the land, therefore, as permanent and immobile units of income production, seemed to be state property. By the seventeenth century, for instance, much of the land was certainly in this category. The holdings which were directly related to the crown, such as the endowments of the Safavid family shrine in Ardabil, were enormous. In 1671 the endowments of the shrine included forty villages in southern Azerbaijan, and in Ardabil, two hundred houses, nine public bathhouses, eight caravansarais, the bazaar in the main square, all of the covered bazaar, one hundred individual shops, and road dues collected from the merchants entering or leaving Ardabil. The shrine's other vast endowments were scattered from Gorgan to Qazvin and Tabriz, stretching across the northern border of Iran. The district of Kazirun with its annual income of 13,917,200 dinars was given in the form of *tuyul* (approximately equivalent to a limited fief) to the commander of the irregular forces. The chief of the Royal Guard similarly controlled Abarqu and its annual income of 7,115,300 dinars.[21]

Given the preponderance of the crown's military and economic power, it is not surprising that the ulama filled a secondary role and were forced to accept the monarch's hegemony. The Sunni theologian al-Ghazali admitted that in his day the only way of appointing the caliph was through designation by the holder of actual power.[22] His Shi'i counterpart, Fakhr al-Din Razi (d. 1209), recognized that ability takes precedence over knowledge (meaning knowledge of theology and Islamic jurisprudence) in choosing a ruler. According to Lambton, Fakhr al-Din argued that "if disputes arose the dominant party was to be preferred and the evil done to the other party ignored. Unjust kings were not to be abused because security was achieved through them; however tyrannical the king, the good achieved through his existence was greater than the evil which came through him."[23]

In short, the high clergy, faced with the choice between anarchy or power based on the control of the means of violence, developed a theory of state which legitimized any existing pattern of rulership.

The absoluteness of the center and the inability of the fragmented periphery to generate sustained opposition and present an alternative forced the greatest Shi'i theologians to reconcile themselves to the prevailing political reality. One of the earliest and prominent Shi'i ulama, Sharif al-Murtada (d. 1044), for instance, condoned cooperation with illegitimate governments. "If the unjust ruler has gained control of the religion," the Sharif wrote, "it is inevitable for everyone who is in his country and belongs in appearance to be his subject, that he extol him, display reverence to him, and submit to his orders as if obedience to him were a religious duty." He continued that it does not help a Shi'ite to avoid holding an office, because he will have to display "all kinds of reverence which we have mentioned out of precaution (*taqiyya*) and fear." Thus while isolation does not save the Shi'ite, participation in the government may enable him to do some good.[24] The great Shi'i theologian, Muhammad al-Hasan al-Tusi (d. 1067), concurred with this opinion and considered the agents of an unjust sultan obligated to carry out his edicts as if they were under the command of the true sultan.[25] Other major shi'i thinkers have argued very much in the same manner, condoning cooperation with unjust sultans and the necessity for *taqiyyah* (dissimultation).[26] Many specifically legitimated the payment of dues to an unjust government,[27] although some remained silent on the issue, but none urged believers to withhold taxes from the government.

None of the major ulama supported rebellion against the state, while many went so far as to accept positions as public officials and hence to rely on the machinery of the state to enforce their religious findings, particularly in the Safavid period. In consolidating their power in the sixteenth century Safavid rulers needed the ulama "to carry through their religious policy and relied on them to maintain, for reasons of political expediency, religious conformity," Lambton observed. "Shi'ism was, to this extent, absorbed into the state and, because of the circumstances in which this happened, the religious institution was, from the beginning, subordinate to the political."[28] The Shi'i ulama who had served under earlier Sunni rulers found it easier to serve a Shi'i dynasty. They were present during the coronations of the Safavid monarchs. On one such occasion Mirza Ali Rida, Shaykh al-Islam of the capital, attested to the letter by the grandees giving Shah Sulayman (1666–94) support and then presented a sword and a dagger and placed the crown on the monarch's head. In the religious sermon read by another high clerical figure the king was declared the Shadow of God, the caliph of God (*janishin*), sitting in God's place on earth. "In regard that in submitting to their [kings'] commands we submit at the same time to the Holy Books in all things." The sermon continued to say, "though they seem contrary to our Reason and Understanding." The royal commands, even when they seemed unjust, had to be followed as a religious duty.[29]

The ideological content of Shi'ism until the contemporary period has been mostly conservative. Unable to change social reality, the higher ulama had to come to an accommodation. The process of depoliticization of the religion was a direct response to the futility of political challenge. The stronger the state and the less capable the society in mobilizing against it, the more the religion became pacified and the less it was concerned with the secular world. The theory developed soon after the occultation of the Twelfth Imam in 873–74 that in his absence, *jihad* (holy war) could not be declared. In fact, jihad was not to be declared when an imam existed either. "The imam [the legatee of the Prophet] was not expected to revolt against the existing government," Madelung writes, "and rebellion without his authorization was unlawful."[30] Instead of rebellion, the believer was advised to practice dissimulation of his true beliefs. Gradually the idea was put forward that the injustice of the ruler was God's punishment for the subjects' sins and depravity. By relating social injustice to divine origins rather than tracing it to the hierarchy of power relations, the theologians helped to avert rebellion.[31]

Other concepts, which might have been associated with social protest, such as *amr bi al-ma'ruf wa nahi an al-munkar* (enjoining the good and forbidding the evil) were downgraded. Al-Tusi recommends that one may protest outwardly only when it does not pose any personal harm to oneself or to others. Otherwise, one should do it in one's heart.[32]

The final hope of the oppressed was the expected advent of the Hidden Imam, which kept the chialiastic fervor alive. But the Mahdi's messianic advent, as with the advent of any prophet, would have negated the authority and the position of the ulama. Priesthood, as Weber observed, finds any prophecy challenging.[33] While the populace eagerly expected deliverance through the Mahdi, the theological writings anticipated such an improbable set of conditions to be fulfilled before he could appear that his advent was made practically impossible. In fact, the advent of the Mahdi was relegated to the realm of the other world (*akhir-i zaman*), and thus it was made innocuous as a serious alternative to the existing rulership.

Not all Shi'i theologians participated avidly in the affairs of the state and reconciled themselves to existing social and political conditions. Many withdrew from the world of wickedness into quietism, which also deflected conflict with the state. Finding refuge in the world of religiosity, they systematized beliefs and practices into canonical writings. Sacred knowledge became the symbol of membership in the community, and the ulama became the guardians of the holy doctrine. Although they were a major status group, their attitudes were otherworldly and consequently posed no threat to the existing power relations. The most important example here is Imam Ja'far al-Sadiq (d. 765), the sixth Shi'i Imam and the founder of Imami Shi'ism, whose teachings were purely religious and divorced from political meanings.[34] The theological questions raised by the major Shi'i writers and the esoteric manner in which they discussed them left much of the population baffled instead of educated. Even in current times the popularity of Ali Shariati's attack on many classical Shi'i theologians and the elevation of Ayatollah Ruhollah Khomeini to the position of infallibility as an imam indicate that much of the present population of Iran implicitly rejects the traditional scholarship of Shi'ism as irrelevant. Nor can one expect that in earlier Iranian society, with its predominantly nonliterate peasant and tribal social structure, the scholarly discussion of religion without its popularization by the lower-ranking clergymen had much effect.

Whether worldly or otherworldly, the Shi'i writings have presented a conservative world view which was a reflection of the existing social relations. Even *Nahj al-Balghah*, the collected sermons, letters, and sayings attributed to Imam Ali (Muhammad's cousin and son-in-law (d. 661), which at present is interpreted by many in contemporary Iran as a revolutionary commentary on social justice, and indeed is humane in its tone, presents a Hobbesian view of man's nature, arguing that men are given to greed, selfishness, conceit, haste, and persistence in error. This leads to the justification for the authoritarian exercise of power. The concept of the class structure it presents is similar to that of the *Mirror for Princes* in which the classes are parts of an inviolable cosmic order. Merchants in particular are glorified as "a gentleness from which there is no fear of calamity and a pacificity from which there is no worry of disruption."[35]

Other Shi'i theologians deified the existing social relations. The greatest Safavid theologian, Muhammad Baqir Majlisi (d. 1699–1700), referred to the prevailing structure of power and status as "a God-given hierarchy of authority" and went on to present a conservative argument that everyone had authority over someone and thus an interest in maintaining existing social relations. Rebellion, therefore, was condemned.[36]

Historically, the ulama encouraged such values as patience, resignation, humility, and passivity in the subject population. Not only were these values politically realistic for the subjects in the historical circumstances when rulership was a military phenomenon and society was fragmented, but they also supported the concept of an ethical God and the positions of the ulama themselves. The religious virtues advocated for the patrimonial rulers were, however, rather different. They were to be generous and magnanimous, and not as a social obligation but as a way of pleasing the ethical God.[37]

The development of the Safavid state permitted close cooperation between the state and the ulama. As noted earlier, many clerics became part of the administrative apparatus. The *imam jum'ahs* (leaders of Friday congregational prayers) and *shaykh al-islams* (presidents of religious courts in major cities) were directly appointed by the shah, and in many cases the appointments became hereditary. The *divan-baygi*, often a military official, executed the religious decisions and the *sadr*, in charge of religious institutions, was a court official. The ulama had no authority over tribes, whose legal conflicts were settled according to common law under the supervision of the divan-baygi.[38] The *qadis* (religious judges) were also gradually absorbed by the state from Seljuq times on.[39] Appointed by the king, they were dependent on him. Consequently, by the Safavid period, they had ceased to be leaders of the communities in which they resided. Their decline paralleled the ascendency of local notables such as the *kalantars* and the *kadkhudas*[40] (respectively, the mayors and district chiefs). Too closely identified with the government, the clergy's link with the populace had become weakened. As a result, when Nadir Shah (1736–47), before his coronation in 1736, forced the recognition of the four Sunni legal schools, reduced the infallible position of Imam Ja-'far al-Sadiq to that of other founders of legal schools, and recognized the legitimacy of the three Sunni caliphs who preceded Ali and were considered by the Shi'is as usurpers, there was no opposition from the ranks of the ulama. The chief cleric, Mirza Abd al-Husayn Mulla-Bashi, who privately expressed displeasure, was strangled.[41] Mulla Ali Akbar, Nadir's Mulla-Bashi (chief of the religious establishment), worked obediently under him as a political functionary. The clergy was so weak, the society was so fragmented, and Nadir's military power was so well-established that when he confiscated most of the religious endowments in Isfahan, claiming that his soldiers were more effective in expelling the Afghans than the ulama's prayers, no one challenged him.[42] Nor was he contested when he declared that he could produce a work superior to the Qur'an, committing the most serious sacrilege in Islam.[43]

Karim Khan Zand (1750–79), another military chief who established a measure of stability during a period of anarchy, in his simple style declared the religious strata as worthless. The state treasury was to be spent on "the army, the defense of the frontiers, and the administration of the country." Therefore, there was no money for anyone who did not perform some essential function. Karim Khan then went on to discuss his mode of legitimation, which was fundamentally secular. "We have public obligations towards all of the people of Persia. We have fulfilled them by ordering that food, items of clothing, and the necessities of life be traded at very low prices." At the end, Karim Khan indirectly suggests that the ulama join the productive forces. "The sensible thing for all the people is to belong to one of the four classes involved in agriculture, trade, craft, and government services."[44]

During the Qajar period (1794–1921) the clergy is presumed by recent analysts to have become the antithesis of the state. The participation of the clergy in the events which led to the cancellation of the Reuter Concession in 1872 and of the Tobacco Regie in 1892 are well-known. So is the participation of the clergy in the Constitutional Revolution of 1905–11. But the clerical participation in these widespread social protests was not to establish a new order, but to restore the past. In each of these three protest movements the ulama were not acting alone, but were allied with major sectors of the ruling class as well as with a major foreign power. Rather than social revolutions, these were conflicts over the shaping and sharing of power within the governing establishment. The consequences of any such conflict are the weakening of the top, the opening of avenues for the populace to register dissent, and the search for allies among the hitherto politically nonparticipant members of the society by the weaker sector of the elite. The Iranian social protests were no exception to this general rule. The mass mobilization which accompanied them, and the radical political changes which followed them, were unintended and incidental.

In the case of the Constitutional Revolution, the clergy at first simply sought an *adalat khanah* (house of justice) over which they would have had control and which would have insured their stake in the sharing of power with the rest of the political elite. When this modest demand opened a Pandora's box and the embryonic Iranian bourgeoisie demanded the restructuring of the patrimonial state along a constitutional model, the clergy did its best to retain for its own leadership the control of the Majlis or representative assembly by assigning to itself veto power over all legislation. The electoral regulations for the first parliament symbolized the new social reality, to the extent that they publicly recognized the position of the clergy as a major partner in government and they also recognized the political rights of merchants, guild craftsmen and tradesmen, and property holders, i.e., the bourgeoisie. Landowners whose property was valued at less than 1,000 tumans (which was a substantial amount) and shopkeepers whose rentals for their shops were below the median remained disenfranchised.[45] The conservative role of the clergy in the Constitutional Revolution became clearer in the conflicts which followed the declaration of the Constitution (1906–7) and the formation of political parties. Even Muhammad Husayn Na'ini, one of the most radical clerical figures of the early twentieth century, did not advocate a mass-oriented and mass-based political system, but the establishment of a system of rules and right guidance as opposed to the prevailing patrimonial arbitrariness; a progressive idea for the times, but hardly a revolutionary one.[46]

The clergy did not question the legitimacy of the apex of the social system, the shah. During the height of the conflict between the Qajar state and the ulama, one no less than Mulla Ali Kani, the most outspoken and effective leader of the movement which forced the dismissal of Mirza Husayn Khan as the grand vizier and the abrogation of the Reuter Concession, wrote in a letter: "Absolute kingship is the expression of God's power and belongs to the king who is the shadow of God on earth, in the same manner that the ulama are the expression of the religion. Thus they are both successors to the Hidden Imam, may God accelerate his advent. The unity of the ulama and the king is derived from the fact that they are both fruits of the same tree."[47]

During the Regie crisis the *marja'-i taqlid*, Muhammad Hasan Shirazi, acclaimed at the time the highest living authority in Shi'ism and the man who eventually issued the *fatwa* (formal legal opinion) in opposition to the tobacco monopoly, wrote to Nasir al-Din Shah that

> these improper actions [such as the banishment of the clergyman, Haji Sayyid Ali Akbar Fal-i Asiri, from Shiraz] have, of course, not been presented to your most holiness. Otherwise, your Majesty's dedication to the progress of the state and the people would not have allowed that they be carried out. This well-wisher, as a supporter of the state, cannot permit that after all these good deeds that such evils . . . God forbid, destroy the good name of the state. May God bless your majesty with glorious victories and strength and glorious and secure kingship.[48]

At another time, during the reign of Nasir al-Din Shah, an incident of rebellion occurred in Qazvin and the leaders of the insurrection took *bast* (refuge) in the houses of the ulama. The Shah had to send a special emissary, who reported to the Shah that his "orders were communicated to the ulama that bast was forbidden and if any of them gave bast his house would be destroyed over his head. They all said that, "The house of none of us is a bast and we do not desire it to be either, and we will not let anybody in." They sent away the people who had taken bast in their houses."[49]

The recognition that the religious establishment gave to the monarchical state makes questionable the fashionable theory that Shi'ism and the state were diametrically opposed to each other. In spite of the claims of much recent scholarship, it seems that a political theory to accommodate the state within the religious belief system had finally been developed.[50] The ulama accepted the legitimacy of the Shah's secular authority, and he in turn gave recognition to the ulama by financing them through endowments, by performing external acts of religiosity, and by being accessible to their requests. Often a major prince was in charge of relations between the monarch and the ulama. The ideal-typical model of the power structure of the ulama, based on the utterances of some ulama, ignores the actual structural, ideological, and characterological components which bound the state and the clergy together. These are overlooked so much so that the heuristic model bears no resemblance to such developments as the integration of the clergy within the ruling class.

The cooperation between the state and the ulama was assured by the latter's social prominence. The place of the ulama as members of the ruling class is attested to in a reorganization order by Nasir al-Din Shah regarding titles, in which the highest three ranks of the ulama are referred to as "excellency," along with ministers of the state, and the two lowest-ranking ulama are called "honorable," along with important merchants.[51] In other local histories the ulama are included as an important sector of the ruling class.[52] The symbolic recognition of the ulama's social position is supported by the fact that they contributed to the makeup of the Qajar political elite numerically as much as the princes and tribal leaders combined. Moreover, with respect to the clerical elite for whom there is information, 82 percent inherited their positions. Compared to most other members of the ruling class, there was a stronger tendency for the ulama to inherit their positions.[53] This, to a large extent, explains the conservative nature of the clergy as a status group.

The conservative nature of the clergy fitted the conservative social structure as long as the political elite was firmly in control of the society's basic means of production and could defend its control with the help of formidable means of violence. The otherworldly ideology of society, rooted in its inability to resist the ruling class, further facilitated the dominance of conservatism.[54] Khomeini accurately summarized the historical role of the clergy in his 1943 book *Revealing the Secrets:* "Bad government is better than no government. We have never attacked the sultanate; if we criticized, it was a particular king and not kingship that we criticized. History shows that *mujtaheds* [theologians] have aided kings, even kings who did wrong."[55] In fact, Khomeini himself, as late as 1963, in a critical letter to the late Shah which was widely distributed by opposition forces at the time, still recognized the authority of the Shah.

SHI'ISM and RADICAL POLITICS

Clerical conservatism and the close relationship between the establishment clergy and the state was gradually being questioned by lower-ranking clergymen in the Qajar period. The ability of the lower clergy to challenge the state as well as the religious establishment is closely linked to the gradual emergence of new patterns of social stratification. The expansion of the middle sector in the Iranian population (consisting of merchants, traders, artisans, bazaar shopkeepers, workshop owners, and bureaucrats) and increasing urbanization provided a social basis upon which some clergymen came to depend. The continuous integration of Iran into the world capitalist market system meant the weakening of traditional social formations, such as tribe, and precapitalist economic relations, such as direct state ownership of the land. The state's increasing need for cash in order to pay for imports burdened the productive strata with higher taxes, little of which could be paid in kind. Patrimonial rulership, as a consequence, became more oppressive and anachronistic at the same time. The weakening of the conservative social structure, the need for specialized technical and administrative training brought about by increasing interaction between Iran and the capitalist world, and the development of a nascent bourgeoisie substantially affected the composition of the servants of the state in the latter part of the Qajar period.

In contrast to the patrimonial system where ascriptive norms prevailed and political offices were limited to loyal members of the Shah's household and were later bought, sold, or inherited, governmental positions were increasingly given on the basis of nonprescriptive values. For instance, while 66.8 percent of the Qajar officeholders inherited their positions in the first fifty years of Qajar rule, only 38.3 percent did so in the last fifty years. The new structural forms and processes which came into existence during Nasir al-Din's attempts at institution building necessitated a change in the social composition of the bureaucracy, which in turn contradicted the patrimonial authority of the king.[56] The extension of capitalist relations, political centralization, and improvement in communication systems accelerated the process of social cohesion and transformed the Asiatic society, in Marxian terms, into one which was increasingly class-based. The change which was advocated by the constitutionalists in the early part of the twentieth century was fundamentally different from the earlier patterns of political change. It was not as much a demand for the change of the ruler as it was for change in the nature of rulership.

The ideology of protest represented not support for a particular primordial sentiment, but a new class, namely, the bourgeoisie. Consequently, it was fundamentally capitalistic. Security of individual liberty and private property and rationalization of rule making and rule application are the basic themes which are repeated not only in the writings of a Westernizer like Malkam Khan (d. 1908) in his newspaper, *Oanun*, but also by clerics such as Jamal al-Din al-Afghani (d. 1897) and Ayatollah Na'ini, among others. The popularity of the carriers of the new ideas signaled the chasm between the upperclass clergymen and the emerging class structure. The nonaristocratic clergymen, on the other hand, found themselves able to forge new alliances.

In the middle of the nineteenth century many such clergymen completely broke with the religious and political establishment and joined the ranks of the Babis. Of Ali Muhammad Bab's first eighteen disciples, known as Letters of the Living, at least twelve were Shi'i clerics and no less than three others were sons of clergymen. Many of the Babi rebellions in the mid-nineteenth century, such as those in Nayriz and Zanjan, were led by the clergymen. Many of the Babi rebellions in the mid-nineteenth century, such as those in Nairiz and Zanjan, were led by the clergymen. Many of those who fought alongside the Babis in Shaykh Tabarsi were also clergymen.[57] Revivalist movements, such as the one led by Sayyid Alamadar in Kalardasht, engaged the army from time to time. Some lower-ranking ulama, acting within the traditional framework of Shi'ism, considered the payment of taxes to the state as impermissible.[58]

During the latter part of the Qajar rule, therefore, there is already an attempt by the lower clergy, mostly in association with the embryonic bourgeoisie which was threatened by Western imperial expansion and the discretionary nature of patrimonialism, to establish a new pattern of rulership. Other clerics were affected by the process of centralization and secularization. The partnership between the religious establishment and the state was continuously being changed in favor of the state. This transformation set in motion the process of separation between the state and religion. The final result of the clerics' loss of status and power was to turn them from elite into counterelites.

The rise of the Pahlavi rule and the rapid development of modern structural forms, both civil and military, made the sovereignty of the state complete. The state control of education, its expansion and secularization, a plethora of legal enactments, and the control of the judiciary by the state and the increasing control of the

religious endowments seriously undermined the pillars of the ulama's high social standing.[59] At the same time, change in the symbiotic relationship between the clergy and the state changed the
sociological makeup of the former. No longer an upper-class institution, the clerical ranks did not attract the sons of establishment
ulama. Many of them joined the state bureaucracy, while others entered various professions since bureaucrats and professionals came to
constitute the prestigious stratum. Consequently, most of the new
clerical recruits came from the villages or from the lower strata of the
city.[60] Not only did the rule of the Pahlavis affect the composition of
the clerics but it accelerated the process of societal change, particularly during the last fifteen years of the Pahlavi reign. In fact, societal
development was well ahead of political development, and, for the
first time in the course of Iranian history, there was a conflict between
the social structure and the political structure. The state which appeared modern and was manned by a technocratic stratum was still,
in 1978, essentially patrimonial, while the society had finally become
class-based. The predominantly peasant and tribal society, atomized
through its medieval subsystems, was rapidly transformed into an
integrated society in which the peasant was replaced by the urban
worker as the dominant segment.

As Table 8.1 indicates, in merely two decades the makeup of
the Iranian society changed from a fundamentally agrarian one to
one in which modern class lines differentiated the population. Between 1956 and 1976 the relative share of the labor force in agriculture dropped from 55 percent of the work force to 33.4 percent. In
contrast, the size of the work force involved in production, transportation, and services almost doubled during the same period, and its
relative share of the employed population increased from 35.5 percent to 47.7 percent. Finally, it is of interest to note that the bourgeoisie, namely, those who hired the labor of others, was not significantly
enlarged, and, in fact, their relative share dropped by 0.1 percent in
the decade before the Revolution. What is significant in the new social structure is the rise of the petit bourgeois elements, including
clerical workers, the self-employed, managers, and professionals. Islamic ideology, with its emphasis on self-orientation, appealed to
most members of this class, as the dependent and Western-oriented
capitalist system in Iran was far more receptive to large industrialists
and traders who maintained connections with the multinational corporations. The capital-intensive Iranian industry, monopolization,
and the open-door policy did not permit many members of the petite
bourgeoisie to seek further upward mobility.

TABLE 8.1   EMPLOYED POPULATION ACCORDING to OCCUPATION and EMPLOYMENT STATUS

	Thousand Persons			Percent or Total		
	1956	1966	1976	1956	1966	1976
1. Employers	69	153	186	1.2	2.2	2.1
2. Professional, Managerial, and Clerical Workers	272	404	2,006	4.6	5.9	11.4
3. Production, Transportation, Sales, and Service Workers	2,095	2,946	4,191	35.5	43.0	47.7
a) Wage Earners	(1,441)	(1,959)	(2,674)	(24.4)	(28.6)	(30.4)
b) Self-Employed and Unpaid Family Workers	(654)	(987)	(1,517)	(11.1)	(14.4)	(17.3)
4. Agricultural Workers	3,247	3,093	2,933	55.0	45.1	33.4
5. Workers Not Classified by Occupation and Status	225	262	472	3.8	3.8	5.4
Total	5,908	6,858	8,788	100.1	100.0	100.0

Sources: Statistical Center of Iran, *Statistical Yearbook of Iran, 1969* (Tehran, 1970), pp. 90, 91; and Statistical Center of Iran, *National Census of Population and Housing, November 1976, Total Country* (based on 5 percent sample) (Tehran, 1976), p. 67.

The Pahlavis' success in the destruction of conservative intermediary elites such as the ulama, the landowners, and the tribal chiefs to a large extent reduced the level of the conflict to a dichotomy, as one between the royal household, consisting of the royal family and the small class which depended on them, and the populace at large. Within the new class structure patrimonialism, as an atavistic mode, lost its social appeal. The patrimonial, albeit weak, form of traditional solidarity rooted in the social and economic stagnation of society virtually disappeared, replaced by the new form of solidarity which manifested itself in the form of the aspirations of the Islamic Revolution of 1978-79. Although the village structure upon which patrimonialism was historically based did not participate in the Revolution, and although at times villagers allowed themselves to be used, albeit ineffectively, as counterdemonstrators,[61] the urban strata, on the other hand, joined the revolutionary forces in large numbers.

Within the urban population the industrial work force itself was a small one. Only 5 percent of the labor force worked in industrial units which employed ten or more workers.[62] Others involved in production worked in small shops, utilizing few modern techniques. They were displaced, but not modernized, and they regarded the Shah's Western-oriented vision for Iran as a negation of themselves. Politicized and radicalized Shi'ism, on the other hand, provided them with the security of the familiar and an explanation for the unfamiliar. Displacing the Western-oriented elite, it also provided them with an opportunity to improve their social and economic positions. The smallness of the industrial working class, on the other hand, made a revolution of the Marxist variety less probable. The relatively large petite bourgeoisie and the traditional work force, on the other hand, constituted a dominant force and their aspirations were crystallized in the new Shi'ism.

Peasants, contrary to modern assumptions, are not easily swayed by religion. Generally speaking, religion, Islam as well as early Christianity, has not been a peasant but an urban phenomenon. Adherence to Islam requires knowledge of many intricate ways in which one relates to the Deity, known as *ibadat*, and the manner in which one deals with fellow men, known as *mu'amalat*. Not only can religious information not easily be disseminated among nonliterate groups, but compliance with religious regulations is frequently difficult in nonurban settings.[63] The Qur'an itself is replete with denunciations of the tribal elements for their faithlessness. And the peasant, in much of Persian literature, is portrayed as both ignorant and divorced from religious practices. "The lot of the peasants," Weber argues, "is so strongly tied to nature, so dependent on organic processes of natural events, and economically so little oriented to rational systematization that in general the peasantry will become a carrier of religion only when it is threatened by enslavement or by proletarianization."[64]

Moreover, one can argue that religion entails the structuring of society on the basis of faith. This, of necessity, contradicts solidarity on the basis of blood groupings such as the clan. The former, therefore, can emerge as dominant only if the latter recedes. Consequently, it is not surprising that urbanization, much to the surprise of theorists of modernization, should be accompanied by religious activism and that the recently proletarianized and urbanized peasants should express themselves religiously. Medieval Europe went through the same process. Areas which experienced rapid social change, and where population, commerce, and industry were increasing, accompanied by a decline in premodern group ties, experienced millenarian movements.[65] The ranks of the revolutionary messianism, Norman Cohn argues, were filled by men who "lacked the material and emotional support afforded by traditional social groups; . . . [whose] kinship-groups had disintegrated and . . . [who] were not effectively organized in village communities or in guilds; . . . [and for whom] there existed no regular, institutionalized methods of voicing their grievances or pressing their claims."[66] During such periods of social discontinuity the habitual and passive religiosity of the uprooted becomes transformed into a reflective and dynamic one. In the words of Clifford Geertz, religion becomes a "cultural map," enabling man to relate the new social elements to the past, thus rendering them comprehensible.[67]

Durkheim's argument that as a society becomes more differentiated, social conformity can no longer be simply based on "passive resignation" but should be replaced by "enlightened allegiance" follows the same line of discussion.[68] The change from one mode of solidarity to another is, however, a problematic one. The confusion brought about by social change and the loss of cognitive reference may result in anomic behavior, as pointed out by Durkheim and earlier by his compatriot, de Tocqueville.[69] Some elements of the Iranian society, mostly those whose break with the past was more serious, manifested such behavior. Many others, on the other hand, formed a new synthesis between the sacred symbols of the past and the social realities of the present. The reinterpreted sacred symbols presented a new way of behavior, a new morality, a new world view which seemed to answer the anxieties of the loss of innocence, unreflecting allegiance, and the illusiveness of reasoned adherence. As sources of information, they enabled the ordinary man to intellectually relate to his surroundings.

The sacred symbols put the world in proper order. To do so they must be made to correspond to social reality. In a way, as Goody points out, sacred symbols essentially affirm that God does not act irrationally.[70] The symbols attributed to Allah do just that. He is the guardian of social order and sees to it that man's life has meaning and that his actions are to be compensated for on the Day of Resurrection. Man constantly seeks escape from chaos. The symbolic interpretation of the world, most importantly religious symbolism, presents him with an orderly world. The symbols, as paradigms of the macrocosm, should continuously be open to reinterpretation if they are to continue to make sense of the world around us. The ossification and rigidity of symbols will inevitably lead to a chasm between social reality and symbolic representation of that reality. This will bring about not only cognitive confusion in the short run, but eventual withering away of the symbolic patterns.

The success of Shi'ism in imprinting the Islamic Revolution with its own stamp is related to two outstanding facts. Firstly, most symbols, rituals, and holidays in Iran were historically either completely religious or were affected by religiosity. Secondly, the new Shi'ism were able to reinterpret the sacred symbols in such a way that they could be used to explain contemporary issues. The new religious status group was not the continuation of the old one. Because it was not bound to the material or conventional interests of the former status group, it could look at the religion anew. The original, albeit simplistic, attitudes of the ideologues of the new Shi'ism were much more relevant to the aspirations and conceptual framework of contemporary Iranians than the thoughts of much more scholarly and established divines such as Ayatollah Kazam Shariatmadari of Qum, Ayatollah Ahmad Musavi Khunsari of Tehran, or, for that matter, even Ayatollah Abu al-Qasim Kho'i of Najaf, all of whom represented traditional and scriptual Shi'ism. It is significant that the high clergy has lost out. Given the absence of church organization to depend on, the Shi'i clergy needed to relate its ideas to those of the laity in order to survive and it did so.

As a consequence of the transition from a peasant society to an increasingly urban one, the conception that laity has of cause and effect has become increasingly rationalized. As more causes are now believed to be of social origin, and not divinely ordained, the new religion has to a greater degree become worldly. In traditional Islam, unconditional reliance on God meant that men attributed to him the consequences of their own actions. This passive reliance on God is replaced in the new theology by holding man responsible. In traditional Islam, particularly among mystic groups, man was presumed to be a vessel of God. The close association between man and God, described by Weber as a characteristic of agrarian societies,[71] is replaced by an ascetic concept of a distant and powerful God which corresponds to the complex urban society where authority is hierarchial, distant, and unforgiving.[72] It is interesting that while, with the exception of one, all chapters of the Qur'an begin with "In the Name of God who is Kind and Forgiving," the new clerical order often refers to the exception, in which God is described as determinant and vengeful. In the new conceptualization, man is no longer a vessel of God, but a tool in his powerful and disciplinarian hands. Man's failure does not warrant forgiveness anymore, but harsh punishment. Salvation cannot be achieved simply through prayers, intermediaries, and reliance on God's kindness, but only through the accomplishment of what God has intended for man to accomplish on earth.

In the same manner, martyrs have changed meanings as sacred symbols. While in the past martyrs were celestial and comforting figures, who functioned as intermediaries between God and man, granting wishes, now they have become agitating symbols who demand revolutionary political action. Martyrs enter the daily life of men as examples to be emulated. The continuous message is that the dead sacrificed for the living. The living should keep their memories alive by sacrificing their individual purposes for the collective one, which entails the good of the community. Many streets in Iran have been renamed after those who are declared martyrs by the Islamic Republic and many days of the calendar have been set aside to commemorate them. The contemporary cult of the dead in Iran, through a system of symbols and rituals, has attempted to bring the dead and living together, charging the symbol of the dead with political meanings, relating the dead to the living, and consequently bringing the living together. The living individuals become an association and are related to the other world. Subsequently, the society as a whole becomes sacred. The individuals become symbolically united through this effervescent experience. Thus, the references to the "nation of Iran" by officials of the Islamic Republic of Iran and the official press are always qualified by the adjective "martyr-producing."

Deeply ingrained in this scene of martyrology is the belief of the underprivileged that their social and economic inferiority is caused by the sinfulness of the privileged strata. The general Islamic orientation that God will compensate men for earthly activities imbues the quest to correct the profane social inequality with a religious fervor. Loss of one's life in the process of eradicating the perceived sinfulness becomes a meritorious act which will eventually be rewarded by God. "In this theodicy of the disprivileged," Weber argues, "the moralist quest serves as a device for compensating a conscious or unconscious desire for vengeance."[73]

The lonely and peaceful Shi'i martyr who was wronged is transformed into a strident and vengeful one. The passive acceptance of one's fate is replaced by heroic demand for change. From a conservative figure, the martyr is transformed into an angry revolutionary figure. In the process, he becomes more closely associated with the social conception of a contemporary Iranian than the sad figure of yesteryear. Furthermore, the symbol, it can be argued, has become democratized. To the Shi'i, the martyr used to represent the house of the Prophet. Now the Islamic Republic assures all that such status as a martyr can be attained by any Muslim zealot.

Other passive Shi'i concepts such as *intizar* (expecting the Mahdi's advent) are also reinterpreted by the new theology in a fundamentally secular and politically meaningful manner. Expectation is no longer simply a hope that one day justice will rule supreme and that men will be delivered through divine intervention. Rather, expectation comes to mean man's deliverance through his own actions.

Ali Shariati, for instance, defines expectation as "spiritual, material, and ideological readiness for revolutionary action, belief in the universal change and certainty that justice will become victorious over oppression, that the pauperized and enslaved classes will inherit the earth."[74] Thus, idle expectation is replaced by active and hopeful participation.

Shi'ism itself becomes, above all, a political pursuit. To Shari'ati, it is primarily "a revolutionary political party, in possession of systematic ideology, clear goals and demands, organized and well disciplined, leading the liberating movements and the tyrannized and oppressed masses, seeking justice."[75] Even Khomeini, an established theologian, also sees the political dimension of Islam as its primary characteristic.[76] The ascendency of the political criterion has necessarily meant increasing the worldliness of the religion.

Thus, the soteriology of the new faith radically departs from the older conception. Salvation has come to depend on political action and collective orientation. Acts of external religiosity, prayer, and pilgrimage may not save those who do not manifest public con-

sciousness. "We have no choice," Khomeini maintains, "but to destroy the corrupt and corrupting system." He continues to argue that
acts of religious worship do not save one, as it is impossible to remain
moral within an immoral political system.[77] The new Shi'ism has so
far successfully utilized religious symbols as cognitive dimensions of
social control, by interpreting them within the framework of the new
class-structured society. "Ritual symbolism," Steven Lukes points
out, "can provide a source of creativity and improvisation, a counter-
cultural and anti-structural force, engendering new social, cultural
and political forms."[78] Whether it does so or not depends on the composition of the status group which is recognized as the carrier of
ideas. It also depends on the constellation of social forces within the
society at large. This social arrangement in Iran was such that the
transformation from conservative Shi'ism to radical Shi'ism was possible.

NOTES

1. Emile Durkheim, *The Elementary Forms of Religious Life: A Study in Religious
Sociology,* trans. Joseph Ward Swain (London: George Allen & Unwin, 1915), p. 427.

2. See Edward Shils and Michael Young's discussion of the function of coronation in England in "The Meaning of the Coronation," *Sociological Review,* 1;2 (December 1953), pp. 67–80.

3. See Durkheim's comments on religion as a whole in his own review of
the *Elementary Forms of Religious Life* in Emile Durkheim, "Les Formes elementaires de
la vie religieuse," *L'Annee sociologigue,* 12 (1913), pp. 91–98.

4. Durkheim, *Elementary Forms of Religious Life,* p. 346.

5. Richard Burton, *Personal Narrative of a Pilgrimage to al-Madinah and Meccah,*
2 vols. (1855; New York: Dover, 1964), vol. 2, p. 160. For an Islamic and symbolic
interpretation of hajj see Ali Shari`ati, *Hajj* (Tehran, 1979).

6. Robert Smith whose contribution to sociology of religion influenced
Durkheim observed that rituals of sacrifice are periodical reassertions of the unity of
the community, "binding its members to each other and to their God, and revitalized
itself at this communal sacrifice." Cited in Steven Lukes, *Emile Durkheim: His Life and
Work, A Historical and Critical Study* (New York: Harper & Row, 1972), p. 450.

7. James Bassett, a missionary who spent many years in Iran, gives a description of the rituals associated with the death of Husayn in the nineteenth century
in his *Persia: The Land of the Imams, A Narrative of Travel and Residence, 1871–1885* (New
York, 1886), pp. 303–6.

8. W. Lloyd Warner in his *The Living and the Dead: A Study of the Symbolic Life
of Americans* (New Haven, Conn.: Yale University Press, 1959), and *American Life:
Dream and Reality,* rev. ed. (Chicago: University of Chicago Press, 1962), extensively

discusses the importance of the Memorial Day as a symbol of victory over death and the continuation of collective life.

9. The rituals have historically ignored the non-Shi'i bases for an Iranian identity and consequently have had an adverse effect on the development of secular nationalism in Iran. This has gone so far that in postrevolutionary Iran nationalism is officially debased and one would search in vain in the government newspapers for any mention of Iran. The solidarity that these rituals represented was an extraterritorial Shi'i one. While the existence of a sense of nationalism is undeniable, the ability of the present government to combat it and the desire to do so indicate the inherent weakness of Iranian secular nationalism, so much so that the collective identity of the Iranians today, at least officially, is as Shi'i Muslims.

10. Cited in N. V. Pigoulevskaya, et al., *Tarikh-i Iran az Dawre-yi Bastan ta Payan-i Sadah-yi Hizhdahum*, 2 vols., trans. from the Russian by Karim Kechaverz (Tehran, 1967), vol. 2, pp. 430–32.

11. V. Minorsky, "The Poetry of Shah Isma`il I," *Bulletin of the School of Oriental and African Studies* (University of London), 10:4 (1942), pp. 1006a–53a. The account left by an unnamed Venetian merchant who spent the years 1511–20 in Iran gives further evidence of the early Safavid claims to divinity. See *A Narrative of Italian Travels in Persia* (London, 1872), pp. 206–23.

12. The standing army was often very large and took precedence over other institutions. During the reign of Nasir al-Din Shah (1848–96), not one of the epochs known for military power and expansionism, the Shah relied on a sixty-thousand-man army. Given the size of the population this was a formidable force. See anonymous, *Juzvah dar Nazm-i Afvaj* (Tehran: The National Library, n.d.), Ms. No. 338, folios 3–4. The manuscript is not dated but it is written for Nasir al-Din Shah; Al-Ma`i, *Karrasah-i al-Ma`i*, 4 vols., Majlis Collection, folios 2735–37. In a letter to the Shah, Mirza Husayn estimates the size of the army as 100,000. See Ibrahim Safa'i, ed., *Bargha-yi Tarikh* (Tehran, 1971), p. 35. The army was used effectively to break several religiously inspired or supported rebellions. Other dynasties which preceded the Qajars were also military-based, often depending on their tribal base for martial support. See Mirza Ja`far Khan Haqayiq Nigar, *Haqayiq-i Akhbar-i Nasiri* (Tehran, 1867–68), pp. 44, 87.

13. Kai Kavus ibn Iskandar, *A Mirror for Princes: The Oabus Nama*, trans. Reuben Levy (New York: E. P. Dutton, 1951), pp. 226.

14. Nizam al-Mulk, *Siyast-Namah*, ed. Ch. Schefer (Paris, 1891–93), p. 5.

15. Cited in Ann K. S. Lambton, "Quis custodiet custodes? Some Reflections on the Persian Theory of Government," *Studia Islamica*, pt. 1, 5 (1955), p. 130.

16. Imam Muhammad al-Ghazali, *Nasihat al-Muluk*, ed. Jalal Huma'i (Tehran, 1972).

17. Jalal al-Din Dawwani, *Practical Philosophy of the Muhammedan People, Being a Translation of the Akhlaq-i, Jalali*, trans. W. F. Thompson (London, 1839), pp. 377–78, 417–18.

18. See, for example, Khavnd Mir, *Habib al-Siyar*, 4 vols. (Tehran, 1954–55), vol. 4, p. 467; Iskandar Munshi, *Alam-Aray-i Abbasi* (Tehran, 1955–56), vol. 2, p. 377.

19. Lambton, "Quis custodiet custodes?," pt. 1, p. 132.

20. Max Weber, *Economy and Society: An Outline of Interpretive Sociology*, ed. Guenther Roth and Claus Wittich, trans. Ephraim Fischoff, et al., vol. 3 (New York: Bedminster Press, 1968), p. 1014.

21. Pigoulevskaya, et al., *Tarikh-i Iran*, vol. 2, pp. 557-59; Ahmad Ashraf, "Historical Obstacles to the Development of a Bourgeoisie in Iran," in M. A. Cook, ed., *Studies in the Economic History of the Middle East, from the Rise of Islam to the Present Day* (London: Oxford University Press, 1970), pp. 308-32, relates the monopolization of economic activity by the crown to the absence of capitalistic development in the Safavid Iran.

22. Leonard Binder, "Al-Ghazali's Theory of Islamic Government," *Muslim World*, 45:3 (July 1955), pp. 230-39.

23. Lambton, "Quis custodiet custodes?," pt. 1, pp. 140.

24. W. Madelung, "A Treatise of the Sharif al-Murtada on the Legality of Working for the Government, mas' ala fi'l 'amal ma`a 'l-sultan," *Bulletin of the School of Oriental and African Studies* (University of London), 43:1 (1980), pp. 26-27, 30.

25. Muhammad Ibn al-Hasan al-Tusi, *al-Nihayah fi Mujarrad al-Fiqh wa al-Fatwa*, Persian text, ed. Muhammad Baqir Sabzavari, 2 vols. (Tehran, 1954-56), vol. 1, p. 301.

26. Najm al-Din Ja`far Ibn Yahya, *Al-Muhaqqiq al-Hilli, al-Mukhtasar al-Nafi*, translated from the Arabic into Persian, ed. Muhammad Taqi Danishpazhuh (Tehran, 1964), pp. 149-50.

27. For example, the most major figure in the early Safavid religious structure, Shaykh Ali Ibn Husayn Ibn Abd al-Ali al-Karaki, in *Qata`at al-lajaj fi hill al-kharaj*, cited in Ann K. S. Lambton, *State and Government in Medieval Islam* (Oxford: Oxford University Press, 1981), p. 271.

28. Lambton, *State and Government in Medieval Islam*, p. 267.

29. Sir John Chardin, *The Travels of Sir John Chardin into Persia and the East Indies Through the Black Sea and the Country of Colchis to Which is Added the Coronation of This Present King of Persia, Solyman the III* (London, 1691), pp. 14-15.

30. W. Madelung, "Hisham b. al-Hakam Abu Muhammad," *Encyclopaedia of Islam*, ed. H. A. R. Gill, et al., new ed. (Leiden: E. J. Brill, 1971), vol. 3, p. 497.

31. Barrington Moore in his *Injustice: The Social Bases of Obedience and Revolt* (White Plains, N.Y.: M. E. Sharpe Inc., 1978), pp. 3-31, forcefully argues that so long as it is assumed that God rather than man is responsible for inequality and injustice, no rebellion can be expected to take place.

32. Al-Tusi, *al-Nihayah fi Mujarrad al-Fiqh wa al-Fatwa*, pp. 199-200.

33. Weber, *Economy and Society*, vol. 2, pp. 439-42.

34. Lambton, *State and Government in Medieval Islam*, pp. 228-29.

35. Sharif al-Radi, *Nahj al-Balaghah*, ed. Muhammad Abduh al-Misri (Beirut, 1889-90), pp. 71-72, 74, 76.

36. Muhammad Baqir Majlisi, *Ayn al-Hayat* (Tehran, 1962-63), pp. 178, 487-92, 499.

37. See Weber's discussion of the conservative role of the priesthood, *Economy and Society*, vol. 2, p. 591.

38. Pigoulevskaya, et al., *Tarikh-i Iran*, vol. 2, p. 583.

39. Lambton, "Quis custodiet custodes?," pt. 1, pp. 133-35.

40. During the eighteenth century at times of crisis, A. K. S. Lambton points out, it was not the qadi or other religious leaders anymore who led the populace, but the local chiefs such as the kadkhudas and the kalantars. See her "The Tribal

Resurgence and the Decline of the Bureaucracy in Eighteenth Century Persia," in Thomas Naff and Roger Owen, eds., *Studies in Eighteenth Century Islamic History* (Carbondale: Southern Illinois University Press, 1977), pp. 120–21.

41. Mirza Mahdi Khan Astar-Abadi, *Jahan-Gusha-yi Nadiri* (Tehran, 1962), p. 270; Muhammad Kazim, *Tarikh-i 'Alam-Aray-i Nadiri*, ed. N. D. Miklukho-Maklai (Moscow, 1965), 3 vols., vol. 2, p. 31.

42. Muhammad Mahdi Isfahani, *Nisf-i Jihan fi Ta` rif-i Isfahan* (Tehran, 1961), p. 257.

43. Laurence Lockhart, *Nadir Shah* (London: Luzoc and Co., 1938), pp. 280–81.

44. Muhammad Hashim Rustam al-Hukama, *Rustam al-Tavarikh*, ed. Muhammad Mushiri (Tehran, 1969), p. 309.

45. *Nizam-Namah-yi Intikhabat-i Avvalin Majlis-i Dar al-Shura-i Milli*, articles 1 and 6.

46. Muhammad Husayn Na'ini, *Tanbih al-Ummah va Tanzih al-Millah dar Asas va Usul-i Mashrutiyat: Ya Hukumat az Nazar-i Islam*, ed. Mahmud Taliqani (Tehran, n.d.), pp. 40–47, 69–70. Na'ini during the latter part of his life actually supported Reza Shah.

47. Mulla Ali Kani to Mirza Ali Khan Amin al-Mulk, telegram, n.d., Persian Foreign Office Archives, Ms. No. 173, no folio number. The letter, intended to be seen by the Shah, must have been written between 1874 and 1883, as it was at this time that Mirza Ali Khan had the title of Amin al-Mulk.

48. Cited in Shaykh Hasan Karbala'i, *Tarikh al-Dukhaniyah*, ed. Ibrahim Dehqan (Arak, 1954), pp. 36–37.

49. Sa`id al-Mulk to Nasir al-Din Shah, Qazvin, 23 August 1862, Persian Foreign Office Archives, Ms. No. 6268, section XVII, no folio number.

50. See, for instance, Hamid Algar, *Religion and State in Iran 1785–1906: The Role of the Ulama in the Qajar Period* (Berkeley: University of California Press, 1969), p. 21, claiming that "Shi'i Islam denied legitimacy to secular power."

51. Nasir al-Din Shah, "Kitabchah-i Dastur al-`Amal-i Tashkhis va Tarqim-i Alqab," *Farhang-i Iran Zamin*, 19 (1973), pp. 49–61.

52. Abd al Rahim Kalantar Dharrabi, *Tarikh-i Kashan*, ed. Iraj Afshar (Tehran, 1962), p. 251; Mirza Husayn Khan Tahvildar, *Jughrafia-i Isphahan*, ed. Manuchehr Sutudah (Tehran, 1973), pp. 64–80.

53. Ahmad Ashraf, "Maratib-i Ijtima'i dar Dawran-i Qajariyah," *Kitab-i Agah*, 1 (1981), pp. 88–92.

54. See, for instance, Farhad Kazemi and Ervand Abrahamian's analysis of the passivity of the peasantry in "The Nonrevolutionary Peasantry of Modern Iran," *Iranian Studies*, 11 (1978), pp. 259–304.

55. Cited in Michael M. J. Fischer, "Islam and the Revolt of the Petit Bourgeoisie," *Daedalus*, 111:1 (Winter 1982), p. 116.

56. Ashraf, "Maratib-i Ijtima'i," p. 90, see the discussion of new bureaucratic forms and norms, particularly the emergence of technically oriented ministries such as post and telegraph and rationalization of administrative behavior in A. Reza Sheikholeslami, "The Patrimonial Structure of Iranian Bureaucracy in the Late Nineteenth Century," *Iranian Studies*, 11 (1978), pp. 199–258.

57. Firuz Kazemzadeh, "The Muslim Clergy and the Peacock Throne," *World Order*, 5:4 (Summer 1971), p. 47.

SHEIKHOLESLAMI

58. Mirza Muhammad Zaman Khan to Mirza Yusuf (Finance Minister), Telegraph, Simnan, 25 January 1884, Persian Foreign Office Archives, Ms. No. 111, no folio number.

59. For a discussion of the relationship between the state and religion in this period see Shahrough Akhavi, *Religion and Politics in Contemporary Iran: Clergy-State Relations in the Pahlavi Period* (Albany: State University of New York Press, 1980), pp. 23–59. For a study of bureaucratic developments in this period see A. R. Sheikholeslami, "Administration in Iran: ii. The Pahlavi Period (1925–79)," *Encyclopaedia Iranica*, ed. Ehsan Yarshater (London: Routledge & Kegan Paul, 1982–84), vol. 1 (1983), pp. 466–70.

60. See, for example, the occupational background of the theology students in Golpaygani School in Michael M. J. Fischer, *Iran: From Religious Dispute to Revolution* (Cambridge, Mass.: Harvard University Press, 1980), p. 80.

61. Rasoul Nafisi, "The Genesis of the Clerical State in Iran," *Telos*, 51 (Spring 1982), pp. 200–201.

62. Estimated from the data in Government of Iran, Ministry of Industry and Mines, *Iran Industrial Statistics* (Tehran, 1972), p. 38, Bank Markazi Iran, *Annual Report and Balance Sheet* (Tehran, 1974), p. 195; Bank Markazi Iran, *Annual Report and Balance Sheet;* (Tehran, 1977), p. 198; Statistical Center of Iran, *National Census of Population and Housing, November 1976, Total Country* (based on 5 percent sample) (Tehran, 1976), p. 82.

63. See, for instance, Fredrik Barth's observations regarding the absence of religiosity among the Basseri tribe in *Nomads of South Persia: The Basseri Tribe of the Khamseh Confederacy* (Boston: Little, Brown, 1961), pp. 135–38.

64. Weber, *Economy and Society*, vol. 2, p. 468.

65. Guenter Lewy, *Religion and Revolution* (New York: Oxford University Press, 1974), p. 248.

66. Norman Cohn, *The Pursuit of the Millennium: Revolutionary Millenarians and Mystical Anarchists of the Middle Ages*, rev. ed. (New York: Oxford University Press, 1970), p. 282.

67. Clifford Geertz, *The Interpretation of Cultures* (New York: Basic Books, 1973), p. 216.

68. Emile Durkheim, *Moral Education: A Study in the Theory and Application of the Sociology of Education*, trans. Everett K. Wilson and Herman Schnurer; ed. Everett K. Wilson (New York: Free Press of Glencoe, 1961), p. 115.

69. Alexis de Tocqueville, *Democracy in America*, 2 vols., trans. Henry Reeve (New York: Alfred A. Knopf, 1956), vol. 2, pp. 311–12.

70. Jack Goody, "Religion and Ritual: The Definition Problem," *British Journal of Sociology*, 12 (1961), pp. 142–64.

71. Weber, *Economy and Society*, vol. 2, pp. 544–56.

72. Weber relates the Protestant concept of God to the development of modern organization, essential to capitalist mode of production. See Max Weber, *The Protestant Ethic and the Spirit of Capitalism*, trans. Talcott Parsons (New York: Charles Scribners' Sons, 1958), pp. 79–92.

73. Weber, *Economy and Society*, vol. 2, p. 494.

74. Ali Shari'ati, *Tashayu`-i Alavi va Tashayu`-i Safavi* (Tehran, 1971), p. 249.

75. Ibid., p. 11.

76. Ayatollah Khomeini, *Hukumat-i Islami: Wilayat-i-Faqih* (n.p., 1971), pp. 174, 179.

77. Ibid., pp. 24, 41.

78. Steven Lukes, *Essays in Social Theory* (New York: Columbia University Press, 1977), p. 69.

III

PAKISTAN

9

ISLAM, ETHNICITY, and the STATE in PAKISTAN
An Overview

LEONARD BINDER

In Pakistan the state is controlled by the military, traditional legalistic Islam has reasserted itself, and the largest ethnic community prevails over all the others. It is not apparent that this system is unusually exploitative or that any other feasible arrangement could be more effective. Nevertheless, Pakistan is not a democratic state; Islam is not, in Pakistan, a driving moral force; and neither political nor religious institutions have succeeded in diminishing interethnic conflict.

   Despite a good deal of political unrest and ideological disagreement, the Zia regime appears to be stable or at least capable of maintaining power for the time being. Even should something happen to General Zia al-Haq himself, it is likely that the same sort of political arrangement will continue in Pakistan. The strength of the regime, even in the face of considerable popular opposition, is based upon a number of domestic and international "structural" elements. Foremost among these is the demographic, geographical, cultural, economic, and sociological predominance of the Punjab. More specifically, as pointed out in the following chapters, a small number of Punjabi districts supply a disproportionately large number of the Pakistani military elite. This group is sustained in its position by a tacit alliance based on economic interests shared with the Punjabi landed elite. But the Punjabi military elite is also in alliance with a smaller but politically highly significant group of Pashtun officers whom they patronize. On the other side, there is a fairly dependable alliance between Punjabi landowners and Muhajir entrepreneurs. The final element which has solidified the position of the current regime was the remarkably easy integration of the traditional and fundamentalist Sunni Muslim elites.

The Zia regime is further sustained by a number of foreign powers because of the ways which Pakistan's support can serve their interests. Always disappointed in the level of support it received from other Muslim countries and from the United States in its repeated confrontations and competition with India, Pakistan long ago determined to end its isolation at all cost. The war between India and China and subsequent Soviet support of India permitted an important strengthening of Pakistan-Chinese relations. The resultant military and political cooperation determined that Pakistan would play a major role in the Afghan resistance to Soviet domination as much as did Islamic solidarity and the fear of communism. But Pakistan was also able to improve relations with the Arab states after the 1967 Middle East war and especially after the explosion of petroleum prices in 1973–74. Saudi Arabia's effort to counterpose Islam to the Nasserist Arab nationalism of the day and the Saudi's need for both a reliable labor force and a dependable Muslim security force opened the Gulf region to Pakistani guest workers and to more or less permanent military missions. The more Pakistan seemed to be playing a "positive" role in the Gulf, in Afghanistan, and even in Islamic politics, the more did the United States support the Zia regime.

While many foreign observers have expressed apprehension regarding Pakistan's efforts to develop a nuclear weapons capability, particularly regarding the possibility that Pakistan might make nuclear weapons available to other Muslim states or groups in order to consolidate its place among the Muslim nations, others have indicated that they fear that Pakistan only lends halfhearted support to the Afghan "rebels" and that given a chance Zia would strike a deal with the Soviets that would leave the United States high and dry. Pakistan thus appears to have gained some room for international maneuver and to have become less vulnerable to international pressure. As a consequence the Zia regime is more self-confident and manages to elicit various kinds of supportive responses from its allies, all of which tend to sustain the domestic legitimacy of the regime.

The bureaucratic elite of the Pakistani state was from its inception in 1947 alien to the political orientation of the leadership of the Muslim League. Yet the bureaucratic elite was unable to assert itself definitively against the party elite except through the intervention of the military. While the level of cooperation between the two has varied over time, and even though some changes have occurred in the social origins of both groups, it may fairly well be said that the bureaucracy and the military in Pakistan have grown into a deep mutual interdependence. As a result, the apparatus of the Pakistani state closely resembles a traditional patrimonial system in which the goals of governing are defined by institutional interests thinly covered by references to some form of trusteeship. The twin organizations are identified with an ideal of rationality—though that is more justified with regard to organization than with regard to policy making.

The Pakistani state is therefore, in the parlance of development theory, "autonomous" in the sense that it is insulated from most forms of pressure from nonofficial groups. Even its dependence upon the military does not necessarily make of it a praetorian state, because there is little evidence that the state works in the sole interest of the military. Rather it was the military that intervened in order to prevent the breakdown of the patrimonial system and the opening of that system by means of expanding political participation. In this sense, the level of institutionalization of the system has been maintained, political participation has been curbed, and the autonomy of the state apparatus has been preserved. This presumed prerequisite of political development has not resulted in a gradual extension of the franchise, nor any diminution of ethnic hostilities. Perhaps the development process has not gone on long enough. Nevertheless there is little evidence that Pakistan's particular form of bureaucratic authoritarianism is leading to a social and economic restructuring that will allow the growth of a liberal political movement. The Punjab and Muhajir bourgeoisie seems content with the degree of responsiveness they now find in the Islamabad government.

The most remarkable achievement of the Zia government has been the co-optation and the diversion of the Islamic movement in Pakistan. In the early days of the Muslim League governments, despite the frequent reaffirmations of Islamic identity only a small group of Muhajir ulama strongly supported the authorities, and the fundamentalist Jama'at-i Islami, led by Abu'l-Ala Mawdudi, posed a formidable challenge. Later when the "politicians" or the party elite was ousted from power by Ayub Khan, working alliances were formed between the ulama and the lay political leaders. But these were generally ad hoc arrangements which involved a good deal of mutual exploitation. The ulama, and even the Jama'at, were strongly tempted to enter electoral politics directly. The politicians, for their part, wished to arouse the population of the cities against the regime, hoping to portray it as not only un-Islamic but also alien in culture. The politicians and the religious leaders were alike restrained in their attacks on the government by a strong apprehension that advocacy of political and economic radicalism would open the floodgates of mass politics. While they demanded access and influence for themselves and threatened to arouse the masses, they really did not wish to open effective participation to all classes. The ulama were even more conservative than many of the politicians, and it turned out that the Jama'at was to become one of the most conservative forces in Pakistan when it came to social and economic policy.

The transformation of the image of the Jama'at from that of religious radical to arch-conservative contains a lesson for all those trying to fathom the meaning and political consequences of the rise of Islamic fundamentalism. The Pakistani experience is of particular relevance, also, because of the enormous popularity enjoyed by the works of the late Mawdudi among Egypt's fundamentalist youth.

In any case, the most radical movement of all turned out to be the largely secular, quasi-collectivist movement led by Zulfiqar Ali Bhutto, the flamboyant, wealthy, Western-educated Sindhi landowner and entrepreneur. Bhutto emerged into prominence during the national crisis and humiliation of the secession of Bangladesh—and he was in no small measure responsible for the hard line taken by the Pakistan authorities at the time. Both the military and the clergy were partially and temporarily discredited at the time because neither military force nor Islamic appeals succeeded in preventing the secession. Bhutto tried and almost succeeded in creating a new political force based on an appeal to the material interests of urban lower-middle-class segments. The later formation of an alliance between the religious elites and the military-bureaucratic establishment—which is an important element in the present regime—was the dialectical result of the sometimes radical, sometimes dictatorial threat posed by Bhutto.

While the ulama and the Jama'at have been somewhat disappointed by Zia's reluctance to turn power over to them, they still find themselves more in favor of than against this regime. That the regime is both socially conservative and Islamic in orientation pleases them. Yet a further lesson regarding the Islamic resurgence and the character of fundamentalism, the major manifestation of the Islamic character of the government in Pakistan is the return to legalism. It is instructive and important to note that the Islamic movements do not propose some form of Islamic policy to solve the many problems facing Muslim states. They rather urge the implementation of the sacred law for its own sake and in the pious expectation that such implementation will either be an efficient solution or bring some divine favor. Thus, through the reaffirmation of Islamic law, Zia has won over the conservative religious leadership and he has denied religious legitimacy to his opponents (except for the Shi'a). Official Islam is once again closely identified with the state, and its function, as of old, remains the maintenance and enhancement of social control.

The politicization of religion, generally considered a form of hypocrisy or a form of discrimination in the "liberal" West, has a quite different sense among believing Muslims. If the most frequently repeated theme of contemporary Muslim thought is rejection of assimilation and the reassertion of an authentic Islamic cultural identity, that identity is most often linked to the belief that Islam requires the unity of religion and politics, indeed the unity of all aspects of life in a single cultural whole. Hence the politicization of religion, far from being taken as an abuse of religion or of the naive faith of the masses, is the central demand of the fundamentalists, and it has been adopted as well by many of the traditional ulama. Pakistan has moved from the anomaly of an Islamic democracy which tried to keep religion and politics separate, despite the establishment of Islam, to a theocentric state. The Shari'ah has not only been declared to be the law of the land, but the current ruler has embarked upon a policy of claiming personal credit for the politicization of Islam. Despite the obvious elements of exploitation involved in this policy, there is little evidence of organized and vigorous religious opposition to Zia's abuse of Islamic symbols. Traditional Sunni Islam has often been accused of being too cautious and too willing to make prudent compromises with illegitimate power in order to maintain the establishment of Islam. It is not, therefore, so surprising to find the ulama falling into line behind Zia. It is, rather, more surprising to find the fundamentalists willing to swallow their misgivings regarding the legitimacy of the Zia regime in return for the establishment of Shari'ah courts.

Political judgments of ethnicity are even more beset by ambivalence than are questions of the politicization of religion. Normally, the aspiration for political development leads to the conclusion that ethnicity is an obstacle to progress. On the other hand, even the demand for cultural integration as a prerequisite of modernization often entails a flat rejection of Western culture as both alien and divisive. Developmental failure and conflict which is defined in terms of "center and periphery" is often attributed to the misguided adoption of alien values by ruling elites. But when cultural authenticity is insisted upon as both materially and spiritually necessary for development, every ethnic group as well as every religious community in a developing country may reasonably demand recognition for its own cultural particularities. Similarly, the politicization of ethnicity in the form of nationalism conflicts with a similar politicization of ethnicity in the form of demands for consociational institutions.

In Pakistan it was early thought that "provincialism" would not long continue to place burdens on the new state because of the availability of Islamic universalism and because of the political domination of Muhajir leaders. Moreover, even the elite military and administrative services were considered to be above regional, sectarian, and ethnic loyalties. Though ethnicity itself has never been sanctioned in Pakistan, and though it was the major accusation hurled at the Bengali leaders, with time, the Pakistani state and its military, religious, bureaucratic, and economic establishments have succumbed to ethnic politics.

The irony of all this is that Punjabi ethnic feeling is not as deep or all-pervading as is sometimes suggested. Fate and fortune have favored the educated Punjabi classes. West Pakistan was a peripheral part of India, but West Punjab was virtually an integral part of the North Indian heartland. Consequently, we have a greatly reduced heartland—with its own peripheral challenges, ringed about by far less advanced regions demanding to be treated with Islamic equality.

It would be unfair to argue that Punjabi ethnic dominance is the "real" raison d'être of the Pakistani regime. It is just as misleading to argue that Zia's regime is but a facade for the interests of either Muhajir capitalism or the interests of the precapitalist zamindars of the Punjab. Nor is it wholly correct to say that the Islamic character of the regime is merely an ideological justification for the dominance of either the bourgeoisie of Lahore and Karachi or the self-sustaining patrimonial elite. Yet each of these interpretations of the nature of the Pakistani regime contains part of the truth, and all are sustained by the existential character and dimensions of Punjabi ethnicity.

Democracy, equality, justice are all related to interethnic rather than class or religious differences in Pakistan. The interethnic balance is sought at the level of parliaments, representation, or positions in the bureaucracy and the military. A form of collective affirmative action is demanded by the subordinate and peripheral ethnic communities, but it is expected to be manifested in provincial institutional arrangements. The result would be a great diminution in the individual rights of Punjabis and it would limit the impact of Punjabi mass politics to the one province. There is much truth in the accusation that the Punjabi elite lacks political generosity, but there is also truth in the argument that settling the ethnic question by giving in to the minority demands will greatly diminish the political capabilities of the Pakistani state. It is one of those cases where we have to conclude that life, or geography, or history has just been unfair. The Punjabis have much more of what Pakistan needs. Nevertheless, the problem of ethnic inequality might well be mitigated were it not for the fact that it is so closely integrated with other economic, social, and ideological elements of power in Pakistan.

The government of Pakistan has consistently denied the legitimacy of politicized ethnicity, and it has attempted to use the twin instruments of Islam and the state to overcome this subversive force. Ethnicity is subversive in Pakistan because as long as it exists as a separate state Pakistan will have to face the continuing challenge of its coexistence with a larger, more successful, and more widely respected India. India has attained only limited success in its struggle with multiple ethnicities in addition to its continuing difficulties with religious pluralism. India with its flawed federal democracy and its rejection of consociational solutions has not resolved all the problems of a developing and plural society, but it has been able to cope with ethnicity and communalism without denying their legitimacy entirely. Even India's limited success is a challenge to Pakistan, for wherever India does not threaten to support a separatist movement as it did in Bengal, its example encourages the formulation of political demands on a regional-ethnic basis. Obviously consociationalism has its strongest appeals where the territorial basis of ethnicity is either absent or must be denied. Federalism has its own territorial dimensions, but since Pakistan has been traumatized by the fear of loss of territory, federalism has its own terrors for the Pakistani authorities.

A variety of circumstances has converged to place Pakistan in the impossible position of denying the political legitimacy of ethnicity even while the state is itself dominated by a segment of a single ethnic community. This form of elite structure is neither unique nor widely recognized in developing countries, but little comparative research has been devoted to exploring the various patterns of interconnection between elite structures and the larger ethnic context from which they are drawn. In any case, Pakistan has had to cope with the problem of a highly politicized but illegitimate multiethnicity. The alternative solutions have been to give in to ethnic demands, to strengthen the penetrative and coercive capabilities of the state, to transform the class structure of the more backward ethnic territories, and to offer more than lip service to the idea of an Islamic polity.

The Zia regime has not yet found a solution to the problem, though it has embarked on a number of policies at once, all calculated to control, if not reduce the ethnic problem. Yet Zia has not indicated that he is completely serious about any of these policies. His Islamic reforms are superficial, the developmental pressures in Baluchistan and the North-West Frontier Province (NWFP) are attenuated, the restoration of democratic federalism is still remote, and even institutional reform of the apparatus of the state is mostly window dressing.

From the example of Pakistan we learn much of the problems posed by ethnicity, but little in the way of creative solutions. There are, it seems to me, two major issues in the politics of ethnicity, and these are only indirectly related to the question of modernization. These two issues are the consequence of the logical distinction between two demographic situations: where there is a single, overwhelmingly dominant ethnicity and where there is not. In the first case, the main problem is how to give distinctive institutional expression to the political dimensions of the dominant culture. In the second case, it is how to provide for justice, equality, and cooperation without expunging the freedom of ethnic organization and cultural expression. In both cases, ethnicity is translated from political tribalism into some sort of cultural expression; and in both cases the politicization of ethnicity is distinguished from the need to offer ideological justifications for the exercise of political power. Unfortunately, Pakistan is not one of those countries from whom we can learn how such solutions are produced.

10

ETHNICITY and the POLITICAL STALEMATE in PAKISTAN

SELIG S. HARRISON

Thirty-nine years after Partition, Pakistan had yet to establish a stable polity based on a broadly accepted constitutional consensus. Among the many factors that have contributed to this conspicuous political failure, the most sensitive and intractable has been the built-in conflict between dominant Punjabi and Muhajir (immigrant) elites and the non-Punjabi ethnic groups indigenous to the areas that have made up Pakistan. During the fifties and sixties the challenge to Punjabi-Muhajir dominance by the Bengali majority in East Pakistan, working in concert with its Baluch, Pashtun, and Sindhi allies in the west, was the overriding factor that prompted the Punjabi-dominated armed forces to take over political power.[1] More recently, with the Bengalis removed from the equation, Punjabi-Muhajir dominance has been more firmly established than ever under the aegis of the armed forces. The fact that centralized authoritarian military rule serves to reinforce the control of the dominant ethnic group has aggravated ethnic tensions that would be difficult to manage even within a more representative political system allowing greater scope for accommodation between central and local authority. By the same token, the persistence of these tensions provides a rationale for continued military rule, especially in the context of intermittent Soviet efforts to manipulate ethnic unrest.

Pakistan's ethnic arithmetic is difficult to establish in precise terms because the official census has not contained a specific question concerning the mother tongue of individual respondents since 1961, and even this data was subject to controversy. (See Figure 10.1 and Table 10.1.) However, the 1981 Census did contain what it de-

FIGURE 10.1   MAJOR ETHNOLINGUISTIC GROUPS in PAKISTAN

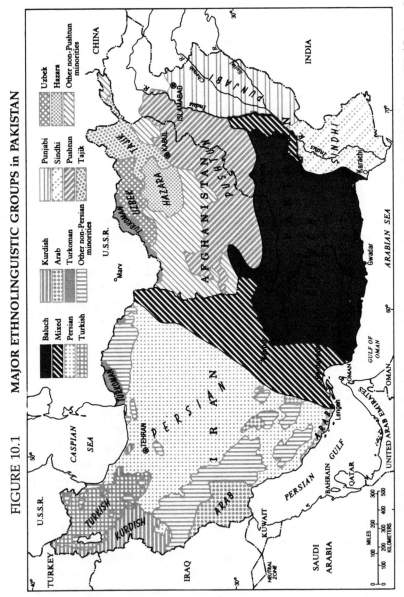

From Selig S. Harrison, *In Afghanistan's Shadow: Baluch Nationalism and Soviet Temptations* (New York: Carnegie Endowment for International Peace, 1981), following p. 84.

TABLE 10.1   MAJOR ETHNOLINGUISTIC GROUPS of PAKISTAN

Group	Language	Major Religion	Population (1961) (*millions*)	Percent of Total‡ (1961) (%)	Population (1981) (*millions*)	Percent of Total (1981) (%)	Location
Punjabis	Punjabi	Sunni and Shi'a Islam	28.53	66.39	40.31	48.17	Northeast
Sindhis	Sindhi	Sunni Islam	5.41	12.59	9.85	11.77	Southeast
Pashtuns	Pashtu	Sunni Islam	3.64	8.47	10.99	13.14	Northwest
Seraikis*	Seraiki	Sunni Islam	—	—	8.22	9.83	Central Indus Valley
Muhajirs†	Urdu	Sunni and Shi'a Islam	3.25	7.58	6.36	7.60	All Regions
Baluch	Baluchi and Brahui	Sunni and Zikri Islam	1.46	3.42	3.52	4.21	Southwest
Other			.66	1.55	4.38	5.24	All Regions

Sources: This table is based on Pakistan government Census data. For 1981, see *Main Findings of 1981 Population Census* (Islamabad: Population Census Organization, Statistical Division, Government of Pakistan, December 6, 1983), table 4(c), p. 13. For 1961 data, covering the areas then constituting West Pakistan, see *Census of Pakistan: Population 1961*, vol. 3 (Karachi: Ministry of Home and Kashmir Affairs), Statement 7-B, p. IV-46.

*Seraiki speakers, centered in Bahawalpur, Multan, and Dera Ghazi Khan divisions of Punjab state, adjacent to Sind, have a mixed Punjabi and Sindhi cultural heritage. While disavowing a Punjabi identity, they do not have a sense of territorially defined separate identity comparable in strength to that of the Punjabis, Baluch, Sindhis, and Pashtuns. Seraikis were treated as Punjabis in the 1961 census.

†This term is a catchall for Muslim refugees who migrated after 1947 from various parts of undivided India to the areas that constituted Pakistan. As such, they do not identify themselves historically with ethnic homelands, as do the Baluch, Sindhis, Pashtuns, and Punjabis. However, the Muhajirs constitute a distinct group in the interplay of social forces within Pakistan and share a common Urdu linguistic and cultural heritage not shared as widely by the other four groups.

‡In 1961 Pakistan included the Bengali areas now constituting Bangladesh. For purposes of comparison with 1981, this total covers only what was then West Pakistan.

scribed as "a family question on 'language usually spoken in the household.' "[2] A United Nations report stated that this question was presented to a random sample of 10 percent of the Census respondents.[3] The 1981 random sample would suggest that the Punjabis constitute 48.17 percent of the population (40.31 million), as against 11.77 percent for the Sindhis (9.85 million), 13.14 percent for the Pashtuns (10.99 million), and 4.21 percent for the Baluch (3.52 million).[4] In addition to these clearly defined ethnolinguistic groups, the 1981 Census reported that 9.83 percent of the population spoke Seraiki (8.22 million), a blend of Punjabi and Sindhi spoken in the border districts of Punjab, adjacent to Sind, and that Urdu-speaking refugees (Muhajirs) who migrated to Pakistan from India after Partition number 7.60 percent (6.36 million). Another 5.24 percent spoke miscellaneous minor languages. Given the inclusion of Seraiki as a separate language, for the first time, the 1981 Census does not treat the Punjabis as a majority.[5]

Significantly, while the Baluch, Sindhis, and Pashtuns comprise less than 30 percent of the population, they identify themselves historically with ethnic homelands that make up 72 percent of Pakistan's territory. To the ideologists of Pakistani nationalism, it is infuriating that the minorities should assert proprietary claims over such large areas of the country despite their numerical inferiority, and Islamabad consciously seeks to obliterate regional and ethnic identities in order to pursue modernization programs addressed to what is viewed as the greatest good for the greatest number of Pakistanis. But to most members of the minorities, the disparity between their population and their territorial claims is irrelevant, since "Pakistan," i.e., the Punjabis and Muhajirs, is perceived as having occupied and annexed their territories forcibly as an imperial power.

It is no accident that the smallest of the minorities, the Baluch, who see no hope for achieving significant power in Pakistani politics even under a democratic dispensation as a result of their numerical weakness, is the most alienated from Islamabad and the most responsive to secessionist appeals. Only the Baluch have waged significant armed insurgencies against successive Pakistani central governments, and only the Baluch have thrown up a broadly accepted leadership that is openly committed to achieving independence from Pakistan. By contrast, the Sindhis, while seriously disaffected from most regimes in Islamabad, have not yet produced an effective separatist movement, and the more calculating Pashtuns are content, for the moment, to use separatism as a thinly veiled bargaining weapon to win provincial autonomy and to exact economic and political concessions from the Punjabi-Muhajir elites.

This chapter does not seek to deal comprehensively with ethnic groups in Pakistan but focuses deliberately on the minorities. It examines the growing assertion of ethnic identity on the part of the Baluch, Sindhis, and Pashtuns as dynamic phenomena worthy of attention in their own right rather than as subordinate aspects of the larger effort to forge an overarching Pakistani nationalism. It also explores why Islamabad has generally failed in its efforts to utilize Islamic appeals to dilute ethnic consciousness. Finally, it assesses Punjabi and Muhajir attitudes relating specifically to the minorities and their demands, especially with respect to the appropriate type of constitutional setup for Pakistan as a multiethnic state.

THE ROOTS of BALUCH ALIENATION

In seeking to mobilize a nationalist movement today, Baluch leaders can manipulate the powerful historical symbolism of a tortuous struggle for survival stretching back for more than two thousand years.[6] According to the most widely accepted Baluch legends, the Baluch and the Kurds were kindred branches of a tribe that migrated northward from Aleppo in what is now Syria shortly before the time of Christ in search of fresh pasture lands and water sources. One school of Baluch historians attempts to link this tribe ethnically with the original Chaldean rulers of Babylon; another with the early Arabs.[7] In any case, there is agreement that the Kurds headed toward Iraq, Turkey, and Northwest Persia, while the Baluch moved into the coastal areas along the southern shores of the Caspian Sea, later migrating into what are now Iranian Baluchistan and Pakistani Baluchistan between the sixth and fourteenth centuries.

Western historians regard the Aleppo legends as unsubstantiated, but scholars in Baluchistan and the West generally agree that the Baluch were living along the southern shores of the Caspian at the time of Christ. This consensus is based largely on linguistic evidence showing that the Baluchi language originated in a lost language linked with the Parthian or Medean civilizations which flourished in the Caspian and adjacent areas in the pre-Christian era.[8] As one of the older living languages, Baluchi is a subject of endless fascination and controversy for linguists. While it is classified as a member of the Iranian group of the Indo-European language family, consisting of Persian, Pashtu, Baluchi, and Kurdish, Baluchi is a separate language and is closely related only to one of the members of the Iranian group, Kurdish. In its modern form, it has incorporated borrowings from Persian, Sindhi, Arabic, and other languages, but it has retained striking peculiarities of its own.

J. H. Elfenbein, the most authoritative student of the Baluchi language, divides Baluchi into six regional dialects: the Eastern Hill, Rakshani, Sarawani, Kachhi, Lotuni, and Coastal. While there is "no doubt that all dialects are more or less mutually intelligible," Elfenbein stresses, "what differences do exist are deeply rooted" and complicate the development of a standard literary language.[9] The problems of standardization are aggravated by the lack of a universally accepted alphabet for Baluchi. There is a rich and ancient Baluchi folklore that has been handed down orally from generation to generation, but the first attempts to develop a Baluchi script were not made until about 150 years ago. By 1969, when a Baluchi textbook was prepared at McGill University, a distinctive Baluchi alphabet consisting of thirty-seven letters plus diacritics and special symbols, had evolved as an outgrowth of the nationalist movement. The authors of the textbook described it as a modified form of the Persianized Nastaliq style of the Arabic alphabet, which has been adapted to the sounds of Baluchi and contains a number of new letters.[10] But the Nastaliq script is not universally accepted by Baluch writers, and many Baluch nationalist works have been written in Urdu or English.

The Baluch have been remarkably successful in preserving their separate cultural identity in the face of continual pressures from strong cultures in neighboring areas. Despite the isolation of the scattered pastoral communities in Baluchistan, the Baluchi language, for all of its dialect difference, together with a widely shaped folklore tradition and value system, have provided a unifying common denominator for some five million people in seventeen major Baluch tribal groupings native to the 207,000 square-mile areas reaching from the Indus River in the east to the Persian province of Kerman in the west. This tradition has been strong enough to subsume and absorb the Brahui linguistic subgroup within Baluch society.[11] Politically, however, the Baluch record is a mixed one, marked heretofore by relatively brief interludes of unity and strong leadership among centuries of fragmentation and tribal strife.

The most impressive demonstration of Baluch political unity came in the eighteenth century when several successive rulers of the Baluch principality of Kalat succeeded in expanding their domain to bring most of the Baluch areas under one political umbrella. Mir Nasir Khan, who ruled Kalat for forty-four years beginning in 1749, set up a loose bureaucratic structure embracing most of Baluchistan for the first time and got the principal Baluch tribes to adopt an agreed system of military organization and recruitment.

During the early years of Nasir Khan's reign, Kalat was a tributary of the newly established state of Afghanistan, a salient historical fact which is cited by Afghan nationalists today as a justification for including Baluchistan in a "greater Afghanistan." Once he had established his army on a solid basis, however, Nasir Khan took on the Afghans militarily, fighting Ahmad Shah Durrani's forces to a standstill in 1758. Thereafter, Kalat enjoyed sovereign status until the arrival of the British, though it remained a military ally of Afghanistan.

Prior to the Nasir Khan period, the early Kalat rulers had paid tribute to Iran, and Nasir Khan himself was installed on his throne with the backing of the Persian Emperor Nadir Shah. But Nasir Khan rejected his tributary status following the assassination of Nadir Shah and the decline of centralized authority of Iran. He even made nominal claims of sovereignty for Kalat over the freewheeling Iranian Baluch areas. For their part, the Iranian Baluch never produced a unified kingdom of their own comparable to Kalat, though they consistently resisted Persian and Afghan incursions. Certain strong chieftains were able to establish localized confederacies covering much of Iranian Baluchistan, notably Dost Muhammad, who was beginning to forge a coherent kingdom in southeastern Iran when Reza Shah Pahlavi subdued his forces in 1928.

For Baluch nationalists today, Nasir Khan's achievements remain an important symbol, providing some semblance of historical precedent for the concept of a unified Baluch political identity. Indeed, Ghaus Bux Bizenjo, former Governor of Pakistani Baluchistan and a leading nationalist, argued in an interview with the author that Nasir Khan's successors would have succeeded in creating an enduring polity if it has not been for the deliberate manipulation of the internal divisions in Baluch society by the British Raj. Playing off rival chiefs against each other in the half century after Nasir Khan's death, Britain systematically divided the Baluch area into seven parts. In the far west, the Goldsmid Line gave roughly one-fourth to Persia in 1871; in the north, the Durand Line assigned a small strip to Afghanistan in 1893; and in British India, the Baluch areas were divided into a centrally administered entity, British Baluchistan, a truncated remnant of Kalat, and three other smaller puppet principalities.

In Bizenjo's view, the Baluch suffered this unhappy fate simply because they happened to live in an area of vital military importance to the British, in contrast to the more fortunately situated Afghans. It was historical accident, he explained, that gave the Afghans the opportunity for independent statehood denied to the Baluch. Thus, it served the interests of the British to foster a unified Afghanistan under their tutelage as a buffer state that would shield their Indian Empire from Russia. Conversely, it was necessary to divide the Baluch in order to assure unimpeded control of the resulting imperial frontier with this Afghan buffer. Nasir Khan's Baluchistan might have emerged in a buffer state role instead, Bizenjo contended, if the Russians had moved southward sooner than they did and if they had swallowed up Afghanistan before Britain embarked on its nineteenth-century "forward policy."[12]

It should be remembered that the nineteenth and twentieth centuries marked a major watershed for the Baluch, who had never lost their freedom before their conquest by the modern armies of Britain, Iran, and Pakistan. The Baluch bitterly resisted their forcible incorporation into Iran by Reza Shah in 1928 and later into the new state of Pakistan left behind by the British Raj in 1947. In the case of Iran, the Shah's iron repression kept the Baluch largely under control with the exception of a brief, Iraqi-supported insurgency until the Khomeini revolution led to a weakening of the central authority in 1979 and an outpouring of long-suppressed nationalist feeling. In Pakistan, by contrast, Baluch insurgents have waged an on-again, off-again guerrilla struggle ever since the departure of the British, culminating in a brutal confrontation with 80,000 or more Pakistani troops from 1973 to 1977 in which some 55,000 Baluch were involved, 11,500 of them as organized combatants. Casualty estimates during this little-known war ran as high as 3,300 Pakistani soldiers and 5,300 Baluch guerrillas killed, not to mention hundreds of women and children caught in the crossfire. At the height of the fighting in late 1974, United States-supplied Iranian combat helicopters, some manned by Iranian pilots, joined the Pakistani Air Force in raids on Baluch camps. The Baluch, for their part, did not receive substantial foreign help and were armed only with bolt-action rifles, homemade grenades, and captured weaponry.

Significantly, when they started their poorly prepared insurgency in 1973, the Pakistani Baluch were not fighting for independence but rather for regional autonomy within a radically restructured, confederal Pakistani constitutional framework. They were seeking the creation of a Baluch-majority province[13] as part of a larger redemarcation of provinces to be followed by a division of powers within which Islamabad would retain control over defense, foreign affairs, communications, and currency, while the provinces would have unfettered local authority over everything else, including the exploitation of natural resources and the allocation of development funds.

By the time the shooting subsided in 1977, however, separatist feeling had greatly intensified. The wanton use of superior firepower by the Pakistani and Iranian forces, especially the indiscriminate air attacks on Baluch villages, had left a legacy of bitter and enduring hatred. Since nearly all Baluch felt the impact of Pakistani repression, the Baluch populace has been politicized to an unprecedented degree.

There is now a widespread Baluch nationalist consciousness that cuts across tribal divisions. Islamabad, however, ignoring this emergence of nationalism, tends to think of Baluch society solely in terms of its traditional tribal character and organizational patterns. Baluch discontent is artificially stimulated by the tribal sardars (landholding tribal chiefs) to protect their feudal privileges, it is argued, and economic modernization will alleviate Baluch unrest by gradually eroding the sardari system. This argument is undercut by the fact that the central government has been more than willing to protect and extend the privileges of cooperative sardars. Most sardars have attempted to safeguard their privileges by avoiding direct identification with the nationalist movement, while keeping the door open for supporting the nationalist cause in time of confrontation between the Baluch and the central government, as in the case of the 1973–77 insurgency. The only exceptions are the chieftains of the two largest tribes, Ataullah Mengal and Khair Bux Marri, who are the principal leaders of the underground organizations working for independence.[14] Mengal and Marri, now in exile in London and Kabul respectively, have followers and allies in all of the major tribes.

To be sure, it is important to recognize the strength of tribal loyalties and the monolithic power of the sardar in the hierarchical Baluch social structure to mobilize and discipline his tribes. It was the unified support of nearly every tribe, acting on a tribal basis, that made the Baluch insurgency during the 1973–77 period so effective. At the same time, it would be a mistake to underestimate the significance of the ongoing process of urbanization and education that is taking place as a result of the slow but steady impact of economic change. By conservative estimates, out of a total Baluch population of some five million in Pakistan, Iran, and the Persian Gulf, there are

300,000 to 450,000 literates[15] who are providing volatile raw material and politically conscious leadership for the Baluch independence movement.

The inability of the Punjabi-Muhajir establishment to neutralize ethnic self-assertion with Islamic appeals has been particularly evident in the case of the Baluch. The Jama'at-i Islami and other Islamic fundamentalist groups in Pakistan are generally viewed by the minorities as agents of the Punjabi-Muhajir establishment. Jama'at leaders preach a pan-Islamic doctrine in which ethnicity—and nationalism—are explicitly repudiated as incompatible with Islam. For this reason Jama'at leaders enjoy less influence among the minorities than local Islamic dignitaries who consciously seek to minimize the potential for conflict between the claims of Islam and the claims of ethnic identity. In tribally based societies such as those of the Baluch and the Pashtuns, the Muslim divine stands apart from the tribal power structure and depends on varying degrees of partnership with the tribal chief. In certain parts of Iranian Baluchistan, as Philip Salzman has explained,[16] the *mawlawi* (religious scholar) has been able to challenge the power of the sardar, but the mullah (religious leader) in Pakistani Baluchistan is generally kept in a junior partnership role.

The great majority of the Baluch are Sunnis of the Hanafi rite. However, there is a cleavage between the Sunni majority and an estimated 500,000 to 700,000 Zikri Baluch, who live in the coastal Makran area and in Karachi. The Zikris believe in the Messiah Nur Pak, whose teachings supercede those of the Prophet Muhammad himself. This heresy has led to intermittent Sunni repression of the Zikris ever since the sect originated during the fifteenth century. The Zikris have generally been allied with the Baluch nationalist cause in contemporary Pakistani politics, except for a significant segment in Karachi, where the late Zulfiqar Ali Bhutto's Pakistan People's Party (PPP) has enjoyed substantial Zikri support.

One of the most significant indicators of the vitality of Baluch nationalism is likely to be the extent to which the Baluch are able to develop a standardized language rendered in a commonly accepted script. Although a lively literature has developed as an adjunct of the nationalist movement, Baluchi books, magazines, and newspapers reflect a widespread linguistic confusion rooted in the existence of six regional dialects.

The 1973–77 insurgency aroused unprecedented political awareness in Baluchistan, and the degree of psychological alienation from Islamabad now evident in Baluchistan is strikingly reminiscent of the angry climate that was developing in East Pakistan during the late 1960s.[17] In particular, the Baluch nationalist movement, like the Bangladesh movement, is fueled to a great extent by economic grievances.[18] Ever since the secession of Bengali East Pakistan in 1971, many observers have blithely compared Baluchistan to Bangladesh, predicting the inevitable emergence of an independent Baluchistan sooner or later. This comparison is valid up to a point, but on closer examination, it is apparent that there are important differences between the two cases. Baluch nationalism has not yet acquired the cohesion and momentum that Bengali nationalism had achieved in 1971. Baluch leaders are seeking to build a nationalist movement on the uncertain social and cultural foundations of a fragmented tribal society with a minuscule middle class; low literacy levels; a relatively undeveloped literature with three competing systems of transliteration; a narrow, albeit growing, base of nationalist activists; and a relatively recent tradition of mass participation in political life. By contrast, the Awami League, which led the Bengalis to independence, operated in a relatively homogeneous society with a significant middle class; a well-established cultural and literary life; a vital, standardized language; a broad base of nationalist activists; and a heritage of mass politicization dating back to the struggle against the British Raj. Moreover, the dispersion of the Baluch population poses peculiarly complex and intractable problems for Baluch nationalists. Bengali leaders faced some demographic adjustments in dealing with their Hindu and Bihari Muslim minorities, but these problems were of a lesser magnitude than those presented by the Baluch diaspora.

In military terms, the Bangladesh independence forces were not only protected by the physical separation of East Pakistan from West Pakistan by more than 1,000 miles of Indian territory, but they also received substantial assistance from the Indian Army in the critical stages of their struggle. Baluchistan is directly exposed to the adjacent provinces of Pakistan and Iran, and the Baluch had not yet found a foreign mentor in late 1984. To be sure, it is possible that the Baluch will receive Soviet or other foreign support at some point in the future, which might well enable them to overcome their handicaps. But in 1984 the prospects for achieving an independent Baluchistan remained uncertain, and slender possibilities thus still existed for political settlements between the Baluch and the Pakistani and Iranian central governments.

"SINDHU DESH" or CONFEDERATION?

Demographic factors have closely linked the destiny of the Baluch in Pakistan with that of the neighboring Sindhis. Out of a total population of 19 million in Sind in the 1981 Census, only 8.5 million were "original" Sindhis,[19] with the remainder divided between some 6 million Muhajirs and Punjabis, 4 million Baluch and 500,000 Pashtuns. The Baluch subdivide, in turn, into some 2 million relatively recent Baluchi-speaking migrants, centered in Karachi, and 2 million earlier migrants who have come over the centuries. Some of the earlier migrants, such as the Talpurs, established Baluch dynasties that ruled Sind. Most of these 2 million earlier migrants have melted into Sindhi life and can speak Sindhi (thus the 9.85 million estimate for Sindhi speakers in the 1981 sample). While they speak Baluchi at home and function as a tightly knit ethnic bloc in local politics, this Baluch bloc has generally been allied with the "original" Sindhis in ongoing intraprovincial struggles with the Muhajirs. The earlier Baluch migrants are generally sympathetic to the Baluch nationalist movement, but are less actively involved in it than the more recent migrants in the industrial slums of Karachi.

The presence of such a large Baluch population in Sind has led to intermittent collaboration between Sindhi and Baluch nationalist leaders. Mir Ali Ahmed Talpur, who later served as Defense Minister in the Zia ul-Haq regime, told me in an August 1978 interview that "if worst should ever come to worst and Pakistan should disintegrate, the Baluch and the Sindhis would be together. They like each other and might well create a federated state of Sind and Baluchistan. But of course, we want Pakistan to survive." Two of Talpur's sons fought with Baluch guerrilla groups during the 1973–77 insurgency. In Baluch eyes, many Sindhis proved to be fair-weather friends during the insurgency. Nevertheless, the idea of a Sindhi-Baluch federation has a strong latent appeal for Baluch and Sindhis alike, especially on economic grounds. With an already existing industrial base and a thriving, established port in Karachi, such a state would be much more viable economically than a separate Baluchistan. Similarly, with the natural resources of Baluchistan, it would be more viable than the independent Sind advocated by Sindhi nationalists. Interviewed in 1981, Ataullah Mengal said that he was "in close touch" with Sindhi nationalist exiles and that "we have always been very interested in consulting closely with the Sindhis to explore a possible federation."

In the absence of a Sindhi-Baluch federation, the existence of ethnically overlapping populations in border districts could lead to serious frictions. Jacobabad, now in Sind, and Las Bela, now in Baluchistan, are the major focal points of potential controversy. The 1961 Census showed a Sindhi-speaking majority of 56.42 percent in Jacobabad and a Baluchi-speaking minority of 31.51 percent. In Las Bela, 66.58 percent claimed Sindhi as their mother tongue, as against 23.67 percent for Baluchi.[20] However, Baluch nationalists claim that many ethnic Baluch in these districts are bilingual. Should an independent Baluchistan ever be established, or even an autonomous Baluch state affiliated with a redesigned Pakistani federation, these Baluch nationalists envisage the retention of ethnically mixed border areas now in Baluchistan, specifically Las Bela, Kachhi, Sibi, and Nasirabad, as well as the accession of Jacobabad. By the same token, Sindhi nationalists would resist such demands, not only because Sindhis claim to be a majority in some of the areas concerned but also because many of these areas are economically oriented to Sind. A particular bone of contention could be the Guddur Barrage in Jacobabad district, which provides water to Sindhi and Baluch farm areas.

Advocates of a Sindhi-Baluch federation base their case primarily on the overlap of Sindhi and Baluch populations in the border districts and the resulting interdependence of the two groups. Moreover, pointing to the heavy admixture of Baluch throughout Sind and Sindhi reliance on the local Baluch to counter Mujahir power, proponents of a federation argue that the concept of a separate Sindhi political identity is extremely artificial. In this view, it would be even more difficult in practical terms to establish a Sindhi-majority province within Pakistan, or an independent Sindhi-majority state, than it would be to create a separate Baluch-majority state in the complex, multiethnic environment of Baluchistan with its continuing influx of Pashtun and Punjabi settlers. The federation idea is presented as a way for Sindhis and Baluch alike to neutralize the power of their ethnic adversaries in some form of common legislature. The idea has significant support among both the Baluch in Sind and the "original" Sindhis, but there is also a strong, parallel movement led by Sindhi nationalists who emphasize the separateness of Sindhi historic and cultural identity and the need for some form of political recognition of this distinctive identity.

Sindhi nationalist writings[21] contend that there has been a continuous Sindhi identity in the Indus Valley for more than five thousand years, dating back to the Mohenjodaro and Harappa civilizations. Sindhis have continually fought to preserve this identity, it is said, resisting the incursions of stronger Greek, Arab, Moghul and British invaders who annexed Sind to their empires. Nationalist writings stress that Sind has been ruled, for the most part, by independent local Muslim dynasties except for the period of Arab rule from the eighth through the tenth centuries, a brief interlude under Mahmud of Ghazni in the eleventh century, and Moghul rule during the seventeenth and early eighteenth centuries. The Sindhi golden ages highlighted in nationalist works were the eleventh-century Soomro dynasty and the period of Kalhora rule that lasted for more than a century between the ouster of the Moghuls in 1738 and the British conquest of Sind in 1843. Sindhi nationalists have their own folk heroes, notably Doda Soomro and Shah Bilawal, and a national "poet-saint," Shah Abdul Latif (1690–1750), who chronicled Sindhi history in *Shahajo Risalo* (Book of Kings) and patriotic epics such as *Umar Marin* (The Prince and the Shepherdess) and *Morero Mangar Machh* (Morero and the Crocodile). Latif's work marked the beginning of the development of a Sindhi literature, though a Sindhi folklore had existed for many centuries. Nationalists emphasize that the Sindhi language has retained its own special character despite the efforts of the Arabs and the Moghuls to supplant it with Arabic and Persian. Much of the energy of the nationalist movement has been devoted to the defense of Sindhi as the medium of local education and government in the face of pressures for the introduction of Urdu, and to parallel efforts for the development of a pristine Sindhi free from Arabic and Persian influences.

The modern Sindhi nationalist movement began during the latter years of British rule with a successful campaign for the separation of Sind from the Bombay Presidency. Initially, Hindus participated in the Sindhi movement, which is based on a regional linguistic and cultural heritage in which Hindus have shared. Sind is a stronghold of Sufism, the mystical brand of Islam that has long attracted Hindu as well as Muslim followers. The creation of a separate Sind in 1936, with Karachi as its capital, gave the Sindhi Muslims a majority in their province, but the Sindhi Hindus continued to control most of the business and professional life of Sind. Thus, in 1939, Sindhi Muslim leaders decided to support the Muslim League demand for Pakistan, hoping to extend their power by driving out the Sindhi Hindus.

As G. M. Sayed and some of the other Muslim leaders involved were to recall later,[22] they failed to foresee that the majority of Muslim Muhajirs from Hindu-majority areas of India would settle in

Sind following Partition, and that the Muhajirs would combine politically with a newly dominant Punjabi bureaucratic and military elite to impose their control on Sind at the expense of long-established local Sindhi and Baluch elites.

Soon after Partition, the Pakistan government, under the leadership of the Muslim League leader, "Quaid-i-Azam" (Founder of the Nation) Muhammad Ali Jinnah, aroused widespread Sindhi resentment by detaching the city of Karachi and its environs from Sind and making it a federal district. In the eyes of Sindhi Muslims who had supported the Pakistan movement, this "dismemberment" of the province symbolized the advent of Punjabi-Muhajir dominance at the expense of the minorities. A Sindhi journalist charged that it was deliberately designed to "make Karachi a springboard for Urdu politics with all of its octopus tentacles." He pointed to the fact that it had led to the abolition of Sindhi in city governmental affairs, the wholesale replacement of Sindhis in city jobs with Urdu-speaking employees, the shutdown of the Sindhi Department in Karachi University, and a ban on the use of Sindhi in the university as an examination medium.[23] Some of these measures were later reversed, but the memory lingered on. One of Pakistan's leading political journalists, M. B. Naqvi, himself a Muhajir resident of Karachi, wrote in 1972 that "Karachi's first separation from Sind by no less a person than Quaid-i-Azam left an unhealable wound in Sindhi hearts."[24] Another Muhajir journalist, seeking to explain "the defeatism and despair which have prevailed among a large section of the Sindhis over the last 25 years or so," concluded in a 1978 *Dawn* article that "the beginnings of this feeling can be traced to Pakistan's early days when Karachi was separated from Sind." This malaise became "more and more pronounced," he added, when Sind and other provinces were subsumed under "One Unit" embracing all of West Pakistan, and it was during this "One Unit" period that "a large group of the intellectuals and scholars of Sind came under the influence of G. M. Sayed,"[25] who advocated a sovereign and independent "Sindhu Desh" (Sindhi Homeland).

To some extent, the termination of "One Unit" by Yahya Khan in 1970 and the reestablishment of the provinces tempered Sindhi discontent, especially when a Sindhi, Zulfiqar Ali Bhutto, took over the leadership of what was left of Pakistan following the secession of Bangladesh. Bhutto's alliance with some elements of the Punjabi-Muhajir establishment alienated the more militant Sindhi nationalists, but he skillfully played on the divisions in nationalist ranks, winning over some of Sayed's lieutenants to his governing

Pakistan People's Party with various forms of patronage. In 1972 the PPP pushed through legislation in the provincial Assembly making Sindhi the official language of Sind, which provoked violent Muhajir-led riots and renewed demands for the separation of Karachi. Ironically, in view of the Punjabi-Muhajir support that had brought him to power, Bhutto's ouster at the hands of the military and his execution in 1979 made him a martyr to the Sindhi cause.

Despite the depth of Sindhi discontent, the Sindhi nationalist movement was weak and divided at the time of Bhutto's death. Analyzing the difficulties confronting the movement, one of its principal leaders, Rasul Bux Palejo, underlined a variety of structural peculiarities in Sindhi society. Palejo pointed, in particular, to the fact that the pre-Partition Sindhi middle class was entirely Hindu, and that a Sindhi Muslim middle class has yet to take its place. Even more important, he said, is the bitterness of the confrontation between an unusually rapacious group of Sindhi *waderas*, or absentee big landlords, and the *haris*, a rural lumpenproletariat of some three million landless, nomadic farm workers. This conflict has driven the landlords into intermittent alliances with the Punjabis and Muhajirs, leaving the Sindhi nationalist movement mainly in the hands of a variety of leftist factions. As the leader of the most important of these groups, Palejo bemoaned the non-Sindhi character of the industrial work force in Sind, which consists primarily of Pashtuns, Baluch, and Bihari refugees from Bangladesh. Charging that the Punjabis and Muhajirs have deliberately stimulated non-Sindhi migration to the province, he said that "we are deprived, as a consequence, of the possibility of developing our own proletariat, and all progressive thinkers are united on the proposition that no national liberation movement can be successful unless it is led by the proletariat of that nationality."[26]

Other observers, viewing Sind through non-Marxist lenses, have emphasized the "gentleness of the Sindhi soul"[27] resulting from the impact of Sufism. The Sufi tradition accounts, in part, for the fact that in Sind, as in Baluchistan, Islamic fundamentalist groups have had relatively little success in exploiting Islamic sentiment to counter regional loyalties. Utilizing economic as well as religious appeals, Islamabad has been able to make alliances with some of the tightly organized local Muslim sects that have grown up under the leadership of powerful pirs (saints) in the feudal environment of rural Sind. For example, the Pir of Pagaro, leader of the Hurs, who commands vast landholdings, has long been allied with the Muslim League in Pakistan-wide politics. This has been primarily explained by the

League's role as a champion of landed interests throughout Pakistan rather than by its religious appeal.

The Zia ul-Haq regime, like its predecessors, has relied heavily on alliances with waderas and pirs in seeking to impose its grip on Sind during the years of intermittent turbulence there following Bhutto's execution. Significantly, however, many of the waderas and pirs retain their hold over an increasingly militant local populace. Zia's heavy-handed military administration of rural Sind during the post-Bhutto period has provoked continuing unrest that burst into the open in mid-1983 in bitter clashes between makeshift Sindhi guerrilla bands and some 45,000 Punjabi troops. In many areas waderas and pirs led or joined this ill-prepared uprising, which was gradually crushed by Zia's forces after six months of sporadic conflict. The Pir of Hala Sharif, Talib ul Maula, led the anti-Zia forces in his corner of southern Sind; the Pir of Ranipur in his stronghold in the north. The Pir of Pagaro gave his nominal support to Islamabad, but his 8,000-man private army kept aloof from the fighting.

The 1983 clashes, in which at least 300 Sindhis were killed, have led to a consolidation of Sindhi nationalist sentiment and a rapid growth in underground political activity, reflected in the fact that 36 Sindhi periodicals were banned in late 1984. Sampling this underground literature, one finds vacillation between demands for a sovereign "Sindhu Desh" and a restructuring of Pakistan as a loose confederation in which a Sindhi-majority province, or a Sindhi-Baluch grouping, would enjoy the type of autonomy envisaged in Mujibur Rahman's 1970 "Six Point" manifesto. Moderates in nationalist ranks argue that confederal autonomy would enable Sindhis to achieve many of their demands, notably greater access to civil service and educational opportunities, and that independence could only be attained at the cost of enormous bloodshed. Advocates of independence respond that Sindhis can only win economic control of their province from the Muhajirs, develop the economic potential of Sind fully, and end the exploitation of Sind by other provinces by struggling for full sovereignty with help from India, the Soviet Union, or both. One of the major concrete arguments advanced by independence advocates is that Sind would gain increased bargaining power in dealing with the Punjab over the key issue of the Indus River waters. As part of Pakistan, it is argued, Sind is helplessly dependent and has been cheated of its fair share of the Indus waters, while as a sovereign state, controlling Punjab's outlet to the sea, it would be able to insist on its rights more effectively.

The demand for independence has clearly grown much

stronger since the 1983 clashes, and the possibility of Indian support for separatist adventures in Pakistan cannot be completely discounted in the context of the continuing tensions in Indo-Pakistan relations. Nevertheless, the immediate significance of the 1983 confrontation is that it has greatly stimulated sentiment for provincial autonomy, especially among prominent Sindhi politicians identified with Bhutto's Pakistan People's Party. Bhutto's daughter Benazir, eyeing PPP supporters in the Punjab, has been relatively cautious in her autonomy demands, but his cousin, Mumtaz, and his former Law Minister, Hafiz Pirzada, who drafted the 1973 Pakistan constitution, have called for restructuring Pakistan as a loose confederation. Pirzada has given voice to the new, post-1983 militance in Sind by advocating an independent "Confederation of the Indus," embracing Baluchistan, if Islamabad should refuse to accept a confederation.

PASHTUNS DIVIDED

Like the Baluch, who blame the British Raj for frustrating their achievement of a national identity, the Pashtuns, too, feel that colonialism cheated them out of their birthright. Until the advent of the Raj, the Pashtuns, or Pakhtuns, were politically united for nearly a century under the banner of an Afghan empire that stretched eastward as far as the Indus River. It was bad enough, in Pashtun eyes, that the British annexed forty thousand square miles of ancestral Pashtun territory between the Indus and the Khyber Pass containing half of the Pashtun population. It was adding insult to injury when the British imposed the Durand Line in 1893, formalizing their conquest, and then proceeded to hand over their ill-gotten territorial gains to the new, Punjabi-dominated government of Pakistan in 1947. By dividing the Pashtuns as they did, the British bequeathed an explosive irredentist issue that has perennially dominated the rhetoric of Pashtun-dominated Afghan regimes and has poisoned the relations between Afghanistan and Pakistan. At various times, Zahir Shah's monarchy, Muhammad Daoud's republic, and post-1978 Communist governments in Kabul have all challenged Pakistan's right to rule over its Pashtun areas, alternately espousing the goal of an autonomous Pashtun state to be created within Pakistan, an independent "Pashtunistan" to be carved out of Pakistan, or a "Greater Afghanistan" directly incorporating the lost territories.

The Pashtuns today paint an unabashedly romanticized and oversimplified version of their history, conveniently overlooking the internecine strife within the newly established Afghan monarchy that opened the way for the intervention of the British and their allies in the early nineteenth century. Looking at the broad picture, however, there is more than enough evidence in the historical record to account for the depth and power of Pashtun nationalism. Long before the British arrived on the scene, the Pashtuns were fighting to preserve their identity against the onslaughts of advancing Moghul emperors who ruled precariously over the areas west of the Indus from their capital in Delhi. The ideologists of Pakistani nationalism exalt the memory of Akbar and Aurangzeb as the symbols of a lost Islamic grandeur in South Asia. For the Pashtuns, however, the Moghuls are remembered primarily as the symbols of past oppression.

Pashtuns on both sides of the Durand Line share an ancient social and cultural identity dating back at least to the "Pakti" kingdom mentioned in the writings of Herodotus and possibly earlier. When a Punjabi critic asked him in 1975 whether he was "a Muslim, a Pakistani, or a Pashtun first," Khan Abdul Wali Khan, one of the principal Pashtun nationalist figures in Pakistan, made a much-quoted reply that he was "a six-thousand-year-old Pashtun, a thousand-year-old Muslim, and a 27-year-old Pakistani."[28] Eighth-century A.D. inscriptions have been found in a precursor of the Pashtu language. By the eleventh and twelfth centuries Rahman Baba and other poets were writing Pashtu folk ballads that are still popular today;[29] by the sixteenth century, Arwand Darweza had written *Makhzan* (Anthology), the first significant collection of Pashtu prose, and by the mid-seventeenth century Khushal Khan Khattak had begun to develop what is now treasured as the classic style of Pashtun poetry. The works of Khushal Khan, who immortalized Pashtun resistance to the Moghuls, have a special meaning for contemporary nationalists because he often appealed for Pashtu political and military unity in the face of external challenges. One of his best-remembered poems recalled that

> In days gone by Pakhtuns were kings of Hind
> And still in deeds the Moghul they outdo,
> but concord they know not, and they have stirred
> Against God's unity, so come to rue;
> Ah, God! Khushal would rise, a youth again
> Could'st thou but grant them concord, sweet refrain![30]

In addition to their recorded classical literature, popular ballads rendered by wandering troubadours, such as the romantic *Zakhmi Dil* (Bleeding Heart), and distinctively Pashtun dances such as the Khattak, Pashtuns also derive their sense of identity from the Pashtunwali, their common code of social values.

A rough estimate of the Pashtun population in 1984 would be 20 million, consisting of some 10.99 million native to the Pakistan side of the Durand Line and 9 million native to Afghanistan, some 2 million of whom are currently living in Pakistan as refugees. There are from two to three dozen Pashtun tribes, depending on how one categorizes them, generally classified into four major groupings, the Durranis and Ghilzais, centered in Afghanistan; the so-called "independent" tribes straddling the Durand Line; and several tribes, such as the Khattaks and Bannuchis, centered in the North-West Frontier Province of Pakistan. Several hundred thousand of the Pashtuns who have long been settled in urban or semiurban areas have become detribalized, but the tribal hold is still powerful throughout Pashtun society.

Although physically dispersed from western Afghanistan to the Indus, the Pashtun tribes regard themselves as members of a single, interrelated kinship group. As Richard Tapper writes, "in spite of endemic conflict among different Pashtun groups, the notion of the ethnic and cultural unity of all Pashtuns has long been familiar to them as a symbolic complex of great potential for political unity. Of all tribal groups in Iran or Afghanistan, the Pashtuns have had perhaps the most pervasive and explicit segmentary lineage ideology on the classic pattern, expressed not only in written genealogies but in territorial distribution."[31] However, in contrast to Baluch society, with its hierarchical structure and its all-powerful sardars, Pashtun culture has an egalitarian ethos symbolized by the role of the *jirgah* (assembly). Moreover, as Akbar Ahmed has pointed out, while the tribal *malik* (village headman) is the most powerful single figure in tribal affairs per se, the malik shares local power with the mullah in a complex, symbiotic relationship that differs conspicuously from the case of the Baluch.[32]

Ever since the British conquest of the trans-Durand territories, the Pashtuns have been frustrated in their continuing efforts to translate their sense of ethnic and cultural unity into what they regarded as a satisfactory political form. The Afghan state that Ahmad Shah Durrani founded in 1747 was unabashedly Pashtun in character. It was a Pashtun tribal confederacy established for the express purpose of uniting the Pashtuns and defending their interests and integrity in the face of non-Pashtun rivals. To be sure, the peoples encompassed by the new state, even at its inception, were not entirely homogeneous ethnically, but Afghanistan had an overwhelming Pashtun majority in the early nineteenth century. The fact that it was the only homeland of the Pashtuns reinforced its character as the political embodiment of Pashtun identity. By contrast, the loss of the trans-Durand territories in 1823 and the consequent division of the Pashtuns left a truncated Afghanistan with a more complex ethnic makeup. As the "Great Game" between Britain and Russia progressed during the nineteenth century, the British encouraged successive Afghan rulers to push the borders of Afghanistan northward to the Oxus River. The British objective was to make Afghanistan a buffer state, and the Pashtun rulers in Kabul had imperialist ambitions of their own. Vast areas populated by Hazaras, Tajiks, Uzbeks, and other non-Pashtun ethnic groups were gradually subjugated by Kabul after bitter and protracted struggles. But in the new, multiethnic Afghanistan that resulted, the Pashtuns have been increasingly unable to assert the position of unchallengeable dominance to which they feel entitled as the "true" Afghans.

Non-Pashtuns constituted at least 35 percent of the population of Afghanistan during the decades preceding the Soviet occupation—possibly as much as 45 percent—and their relative strength has grown in the wake of the large-scale Pashtun refugee movement to Pakistan. This built-in ethnic impasse has given the Pashtuns in Afghanistan a solid motive for seeking to reestablish some form of political unity with the Pashtuns in Pakistan that would make possible a restoration of Pashtun dominance in Afghanistan. To be sure, the "Pashtun-ness" of the Dari-speaking Muhammadzais was called into question by many Pashtuns, but it was precisely because the desire for Pashtun identity is so deep-rooted that various forms of Pashtun populism grew up during the Muhammadzai period, not the least of them being Hafizullah Amin's Khalq wing of the Afghan Communist movement.[33]

Given the responsibility of the British for the division of the Pashtuns, it is not surprising that anti-British sentiment during the twenties and thirties sparked the emergence of the Pashtun nationalist movement on what was to become the Pakistan side of the Durand Line. Stephen Rittenberg, analyzing the origins of Khan Abdul Ghaffar Khan's "Red Shirts," has shown that this anti-British sentiment was directly reinforced by the economic conflict between the wealthy khans who were allied with the Raj and a coalition of Pashtun tenants, small landholders, and artisans.[34] At the same time, Ghaffar

Khan consciously exploited the emotional bonds that link the Pashtuns of the North-West Frontier with their brethren in Afghanistan, calling explicitly on the eve of Partition for an independent "Pashtunistan." It is not germane here to review the tangled history of the pre-partition years that led up to Ghaffar Khan's Bannu Declaration of 22 June 1947, in which he demanded that the Pashtuns be given a choice between joining Pakistan or establishing an independent "Pashtunistan," rather than a choice limited to Pakistan or India. What is relevant is that the "Red Shirts" boycotted the referendum that was used by the departing British as their legal rationale for handling over the North-West Frontier Province and the adjacent Tribal Areas to the new Pakistani state. As a consequence, when it has suited their purposes, Ghaffar Khan and his son, Wali Khan, have been able to cast doubt on the legitimacy of the incorporation of these Pashtun-majority areas into Pakistan. For their part, Pakistani leaders, dismissing protestations of loyalty to Pakistan by Ghaffar Khan and Wali Khan, have periodically pointed to the Bannu Declaration.

Even though the two Pashtun leaders have reformulated the "Pashtunistan" demand since 1947 as a demand for provincial autonomy within Pakistan, Islamabad has continued to suspect their intentions. This distrust is rooted not only in suspicions of collusion with Afghanistan but also in the fact that Ghaffar Khan was explicitly opposed to the creation of Pakistan and was actively identified with the Indian National Congress in its struggle against the British. Ghaffar Khan recognized more clearly than Sindhi leaders did that the Pakistan movement was promoted mainly by Muslims in those provinces of undivided India where Hindus were in a majority. He argued openly that the formation of Pakistan would not serve the interests of the North-West Frontier Province, with its Muslim majority, since the new Pakistani state would be dominated by the Punjabis and Muhajirs. When Wali Khan and three leading Baluch nationalists were put on trial on treason charges in 1974, Islamabad's case against them was replete with allusions to their earlier "treachery" to the Pakistan cause dating back to the pre-Partition period.[35]

Compared to the demands for complete independence and sweeping confederal powers made by various Baluch leaders, Wali Khan's National Awami Party (NAP), heir to the "Red Shirt" tradition in the North-West Frontier, has made relatively moderate demands for regional autonomy. When opposition leaders formed the National Democratic Party in 1979 to succeed the outlawed NAP, Wali Khan objected to moderate Baluch leader Ghaus Bux Bizenjo's proposed use of the word "nationalities" in the party platform to describe the provinces of Pakistan, urging instead that they be characterized as "distinctive cultural and linguistic entities." On the key issue of provincial autonomy, Bizenjo insisted that the central government should control only defense, foreign affairs, communications, and currency, while Wali Khan favored a modified version of Bhutto's 1973 Constitution, which gave Islamabad more extensive powers.

The basic differences over strategy and tactics alike that continue to divide Baluch and Pashtun leaders reflect the fact that the Baluch feel much more alienated from the Punjabi-Muhajir establishment than the Pashtuns. At the psychological level the Baluch feel that the Punjabis view them with condescension and contempt as "primitive," in contrast to a more ambivalent Punjabi attitude toward the Pashtuns, especially toward the Pashtun aristocracy. More important, the Baluch have been almost completely excluded from the economic and political power structure in Pakistan, while the Pashtuns, albeit bitterly resentful of Punjabi-Muhajir dominance, do not feel a comparable sense of complete exclusion. Under the British, Pashtuns from the more aristocratic, urbanized families were given important posts in the army and bureaucracy. Pashtun officers constituted a potent bloc in the upper echelons of the army following Partition until many of them were forced out, in the late fifties, when the Punjabis consolidated their position. Even today, however, there are still a significant number of Pashtuns in high places in Pakistan, and the expansion of Punjabi influence in the military and the bureaucracy during the Zia ul-Haq regime has not been at the expense of Pashtun members of the establishment.

For the most part, the Pashtun areas are not as isolated geographically from other parts of Pakistan as the Baluch areas, which partly explains why there is greater economic integration of the Pashtun areas than the Baluch areas with the overall Pakistani economy. In Pashtun eyes, this integration is not an unmixed blessing, since it brings what is viewed as excessive dependence on the Punjab and exposes the Pashtun areas to exploitation by big-business interests centered in Karachi and Lahore. Pashtun nationalism focuses in large part on alleged economic discrimination against the North West Frontier Province in allocations of development expenditures both in industry and agriculture. One of the perennial charges leveled by Pashtun leaders is that Islamabad deliberately holds back on electrification of the Pashtun areas because it does not want them to become industrialized and that even the electricity produced there goes primarily to the Punjab. For example, Wali Khan repeatedly points to the fact that most of the tobacco and cotton grown in the NWFP is used to supply cigarette and textile factories located in other provinces. Islamabad even discriminates against the Pashtuns in agricultural development, nationalist spokesmen argue, channeling funds for the expansion of irrigation primarily to the Punjab or to areas in other provinces where Punjabi settlers will benefit most. The acceleration of work on the Chasma Right Bank Canal during the Zia ul-Haq period has dulled this argument to some extent, but the Kalabaqh Dam controversy rekindled bitter charges of pro-Punjab development policies.

"Basically, the Pushtuns want a bigger share of the cake," observed the Sindhi political scientist, Hamida Khuhro. "The Baluch want something more—identity, self-respect, real autonomy." This distinction is undoubtedly valid, but it does not necessarily follow that the possibility of a recrudescence of Pashtun separatism can be entirely written off. Even if one could assume that Islamabad will make the economic gestures necessary to alleviate Pashtun discontent, there is likely to be a growing undercurrent of resentment in Pashtun areas if Punjabi civil servants continue to play a dominant role in provincial administration and if Islamabad continues to resist Pashtun nationalist efforts to upgrade the Pashtu language in education. At present, Pashtu is the medium of instruction only up to the age of ten. Thereafter, Pashtun children must not only attend classes conducted in Urdu and use textbooks written in Urdu but most also use Urdu when competing in civil service examinations as well as in university and graduate school entrance examinations. The language issue is important in Baluchistan, Sind, and the North-West Frontier Province alike, but it is more important in the Sindhi and Pashtun areas than in Baluchistan because Sindhi and Pashtu are more standardized and better developed as literary languages than Baluchi and thus more readily adaptable for educational purposes.

Given the upsurge in Islamic consciousness among the Pashtuns resulting from the Soviet occupation of Afghanistan, the Jama'at-i Islami and other Islamic fundamentalist groups have been able to strengthen their position somewhat in the Pashtun areas since 1979. However, this growth in support for the Jama'at has been a compartmentalized phenomenon, centered largely in Jama'at-oriented Afghan resistance groups. It has not modified Pashtun antagonism toward what is viewed as a hostile, Punjabi-dominated government in Islamabad. Anti-Jama'at Pashtun groups identified with the veteran Pashtun leader Abdul Ghaffar Khan and his son,

Wali Khan, continue to claim widespread support among many of the same Afghan refugees who have been responsive to the Jama'at. It was Ghaffar Khan's success in mobilizing anti-Jama'at sentiment in the villages that has led to his periodic detention by the Zia ul-Haq regime. When electoral political activity has been permitted in Pakistan, Ghaffar Khan and Wali Khan have been allied with the late Mufti Mahmud's Jami'at ul-Ulama-i Islam (JUI), a Pashtun-based religious party that has successfully harmonized its appeals to the Islamic and ethnic aspects of Pashtun identity.

Against the background of the Soviet occupation and the resulting disarray of Pashtun society, the idea of a unified "Pashtunistan" linking the Pashtuns on both sides of the Durand Line is likely to be quiescent for the foreseeable future. By the same token, however, should the Pashtun refugees remain in Pakistan, pressures are likely to grow for an autonomous "Pashtunistan" within the framework of Pakistan. This is why many Punjabis want to resettle as many of the refugees as possible in Baluchistan, and it also explains why many Punjabis would welcome a political settlement of the Afghanistan conflict that would permit the gradual repatriation of Pashtun refugees to Afghanistan.

The PATH to CONSTITUTIONAL COMPROMISE

What are some of the critical preconditions for a moderation of ethnic tensions in Pakistan and for movement toward a more stable constitutional order?

Even moderates among the leaders of the ethnic minorities emphasize that a return to participatory politics under the 1973 Constitution would not, in itself, bring political stability, unless the Constitution were amended to incorporate safeguards barring the central government from forcibly ousting an elected provincial government unilaterally, as Bhutto did in 1973.

Ghaus Bux Bizenjo's Pakistan National Party (PNP) made a significant compromise proposal in 1980 that attempted to define the minimum safeguards sought by the minorities. In a memorandum to the Zia government the PNP called for reinforcement of the articles providing for equal representation of the four provinces in the Senate, and a concomitant strengthening of the Senate's powers, as the key to successful federalism in Pakistan. By offsetting the control wielded by the more populous provinces in the lower chamber of the

National Assembly, the memorandum said, such a reform would make central intervention acceptable under certain circumstances. It suggested that Islamabad could then be empowered to take over a province if "expressly authorized to do so for a specified and limited purpose, and for a specified and limited period of time" by a two-thirds Senate majority.

In my view, safeguards against arbitrary central government intervention are more critical to the minorities than the much-discussed issue of the division of powers between Islamabad and the provinces. The minorities are concerned not only with the substance of autonomy but also with the feeling of autonomy. This psychological factor explains why they attach so much importance to the safeguards issue.

The ethnic minorities emphasize the need for a linguistic re-demarcation of provincial boundaries that would give each of them majority control over a specific territory, together with explicit constitutional recognition of their distinctive ethnic identities. As to the precise form that recognition of separate ethnic identities should take, there is considerable disagreement among the minorities themselves, but these differences do not appear to be irreconcilable. At present, most Baluch leaders demand recognition of four distinct "nationalities" in Pakistan—Baluch, Sindhi, Pashtun, and Punjabi—a concept which is anathema to many Pakistanis who believe in a monolithic Pakistani nationality. Some Baluch leaders, notably Bizenjo, link the "four nationalities" concept with a companion demand that the constitution include the right of secession. Thus, Bizenjo proposed a joint declaration with the Tehriq Istiqlal (Movement for Integrity) in 1980 calling for the right of secession in the event that the central government violated rights guaranteed to the provinces in the Constitution. Conceivably, Baluch leaders would not insist on the right of secession if enough of their other major demands were met by Islamabad. However, that remains to be seen, since Bizenjo and others contend that a meaningful sense of autonomy requires acknowledgment of the residual right to secede. These Baluch leaders seek to legitimize the secession demand by citing language of the 1940 Lahore Resolution in which the Muslim League had foreshadowed its demand for Pakistan. Envisaging two Muslim states in the subcontinent following the departure of the British, the resolution called for a regrouping of "geographically contiguous . . . areas in which the Moslems are numerically in a majority, as in the northwestern and eastern zones of India . . . to constitute independent states *in which the constituent units shall be autonomous and sovereign"* (italics added).[36]

The concept of four coequal nationalities is paralleled by Ataullah Mengal's demand for complete parity for Baluch, Pashtuns, Sindhis, and Punjabis in both chambers of the National Assembly as well as in civil service and military recruitment, irrespective of population disparities. Pointedly withholding support for this position, Bizenjo's PNP has specifically limited its demand for parity in the National Assembly to the upper chamber, which suggests that Mengal's approach to the parity issue may prove to be negotiable. At the same time, all factions among the minorities are united in seeking radically upgraded representation in the civil service and the armed forces, and they regard the Pakistani concessions made in this sphere to date as inconsequential. Similarly, all factions believe that the minorities are economically victimized. They charge that central allocations of development funds are inequitable, arguing that the less developed provinces should receive greatly increased allocations in order to overcome economic disparities with the Punjab. They seek to impose restrictions on economic incursions in their provinces by Punjabi and other outside business interests. Most important, in the eyes of Islamabad planners, they demand local control over the economic resources in their provinces.

Turning to an examination of the attitudes of Pakistani leaders, it is important to distinguish between General Zia and like-minded allies, who see little need for compromise, and others in the Pakistani power structure who would like to find a basis for accommodation but regard minority demands as extortionate. What if Zia were to be replaced by a more moderate, albeit Punjabi-dominated, regime as the result of another military coup or a successful popular agitation spearheaded by Bhutto's People's Party or other opposition groups? Would it make a significant difference? How much room for compromise would exist if one assumed a liberalizing trend in Pakistani politics?

For many Punjabi and Muhajir moderates, minority demands for greater representation in the civil service, the armed forces, and the National Assembly would not be too difficult to swallow. Some influential Punjabi lawyers, judges, and bureaucrats have confided to me that they would welcome a Baluch, Pashtun, or Sindhi prime minister as a symbol of national unity in the event of a return to civilian rule. Many of these moderates are also cautiously optimistic concerning the possibilities for working out a constitutional settlement that would provide for increased autonomy to the provinces and for safeguards against arbitrary central intervention. With regard to the terms for such a settlement, however, even moderates are greatly disturbed by the extent of minority demands for economic autonomy. It is in the economic sphere that a constitutional compromise is likely to be most elusive, regardless of Pakistan's future political coloration.

Economic issues are likely to be peculiarly intractable because the same moderates who respect Western democratic values—and are thus sympathetic to minority pleas for greater equity—also tend to be the most avid proponents of economic modernization in Pakistan. These relatively Westernized, development-minded Pakistanis want to see rising living standards in Pakistan as a whole. They are just as disturbed by poverty in the Punjab as by poverty in the Baluch, Sindhi, and Pashtun areas, and their liberal instincts are just as offended by the ethnocentric attitudes of some minority leaders on issues relating to development as by the ethnic arrogance of many Punjabis and Muhajirs. They favor development programs and policies that take fully into account the economic interdependence of the different regions of Pakistan. This approach makes them extremely unsympathetic to minority demands for exclusive control over the natural resources that happen to lie beneath the soil of their ethnic homelands.

As for Zia himself, he made clear in interviews with the author on 29 July 1978 and 8 March 1980 that he has no sympathy for the concept of a "multinational" Pakistan in which Baluch, Pashtuns, Sindhis, and Punjabis are entitled to local self-rule. "I simply cannot understand this type of thinking," he said earnestly, pausing to reflect on the matter. "We want to build a strong country, a unified country. Why should we talk in these small-minded terms? We should talk in terms of one Pakistan, one united, Islamic Pakistan." If circumstances should ever permit, he commented at one point in our 1978 conversation, he would "ideally" like to break up the existing provinces and replace them with fifty-three small provinces, erasing ethnic identities from the map of Pakistan altogether. President Ayub Khan's One Unit concept was a valid one, he stated, and it was "unfortunate for the country" that Yahya Khan had "surrendered to pressures" and created the existing provinces. Nevertheless, "what is done is done," he emphasized, and for the sake of national unity he would adhere to the constitution adopted in 1973, which defines a "very liberal" type of federation in which the provinces enjoy "much more power than they do in the United States or in most federations."

Zia said flatly that he would "not consider for one moment" proposals for amendments to the 1973 Constitution that would rule out central intervention to dismiss an elected state regime. "We won't go beyond the 1973 Constitution," Zia declared. "There was a national consensus on this constitution, more of a consensus than we have ever had before. We would be opening a Pandora's box if we were to admit the possibility of changing it by one iota." Given Pakistan's record of political instability, Zia added, it would be "suicidal" for Islamabad to relinquish its right to intervene in politically disturbed provinces. Indeed, if there is a need to alter the Constitution, he went on, "it would be in the direction of strengthening it rather than weakening it." For example, he speculated, "it might be appropriate" for Pakistan to emulate the Turkish Constitution, which explicitly empowers the army to take over political power when it deems such intervention necessary in the national interest.

Until taking power from Zulfiqar Ali Bhutto in July 1977, Zia reflected, "I had never met a politician, and I must confess that I am continually amazed at the way they think." He questioned the meaning of the 1970 elections held by Bhutto, in which Ghaus Bux Bizenjo, Ataullah Mengal, and Khair Bux Marri emerged as the preeminent leaders of the Baluch and Wali Khan as the principal spokesman of the Pashtuns. These elections were "based on emotional grounds, on ethnic appeals, on the politics of negation," he explained, "rather than on reason and national considerations." thus, they produced "a certain group of leaders who had a particular trend of mind" and were not representative of the Baluch and Pashtuns as a whole.

Zia distinguished between Baluchistan, which he regards as important, and the "Baluch problem," which he believes has been greatly exaggerated by foreign observers. Referring to Baluchistan as "the most sensitive area of Pakistan," he warned that "if the Russians come there, it will be by naked aggression, and that is the only 'Baluch problem' we have to worry about." Given the military importance of Baluchistan, he declared, "we obviously cannot think of it as having something in particular to do with the Baluch. They have a provincial population equal to one third of the population of one city in the Punjab, Lahore. They have coal, gas, and oil that the whole country needs. We are one country, and the Baluch are part of our country. They can go anywhere to work. Why do you Americans and other foreigners make so much of this sort of thing? Many countries have problems like this and they deal with them in the necessary way. People don't talk about their breaking up. Look at the Irish, Welsh, and Scotch in Britain. Look at Canada. Look at your own country. It may be a crude example, but take the case of your South Carolina. It is a depressed state, while California is a developed state. What would you think if the demand should be raised that Carolina should have the same status as California?"

NOTES

1. For a further discussion of the relationship between ethnic conflict and the rise of military authoritarianism in Pakistan, see Selig S. Harrison, *The Widening Gulf: Asian Nationalism and American Policy* (New York: The Free Press, 1978), pp. 262–77, especially pp. 274–76; and Selig S. Harrison, *In Afghanistan's Shadow: Baluch Nationalism and Soviet Temptations* (New York: Carnegie Endowment for International Peace, 1981), especially pp. 33–40, 88–90, and 150–58.

2. *Main Findings of 1981 Population Census* (Islamabad: Population Census Organization, Statistical Division, Government of Pakistan, December 6, 1983), p. 12.

3. *Pakistan: Report of Mission on Needs Assessment for Population Assistance*, Report No. 23, United Nations Fund for Population Assistance, November 1979, p. 26. The author wishes to thank Pakistani demographer Feroz Ahmed for making this report available.

4. *Main Findings of 1981 Population Census*, Table 4(c), p. 13.

5. However, if Hindko, a dialect of Punjabi spoken in parts of the North-West Frontier Province, is lumped together with Punjabi, the Punjabi total would be 50.60 percent. Comparative state population figures in the 1981 Census show Punjab with a majority of 56 percent. The overall population of Pakistan in the 1981 Census is 84.25 million, including 47.29 million in Punjab; 13.25 million in the North-West Frontier Province and the Tribal Areas; 19.02 million in Sind; and 4.33 million in Baluchistan. *Main Findings of 1981 Population Census*, Table 1, p. 5.

6. For a detailed discussion of Baluch nationalism, past and present, see Harrison, *In Afghanistan's Shadow.*

7. For example, see Sardar Mohammed Khan Baluch, *History of the Baluch Race and Baluchistan*, rev. ed. (Quetta: Gosha-e-Adab, 1977), pp. 5, 16–17; and Ma'an Shana al-Ajli Al-Hakkami, *Baluchistan Dival Al-'Arab* (Baluchistan: The Home of Arabs) (Bahrain, 1979).

8. J. H. Elfenbein, "Baluchi," in *Encyclopaedia of Islam*, vol. 1: A-B (Leiden: E. J. Brill, 1960), p. 1006. See also J. H. Elfenbein, *The Baluchi Language: A Dialectology With Text*, Vol. 27 (London: Royal Asiatic Society, Monographs, 1966), pp. 41–45; and Richard N. Frye, "Remarks on Baluchi History," *Central Asiatic Journal*, 6:1 (1961), p. 49.

9. Elfenbein, *The Baluchi Language*, pp. 3, 10.

10. M. Longworth Dames, *Popular Poetry of the Baloches*, vol. 2 (London: Royal Asiatic Society, 1907), p. 201. M. A. R. Barker and A. K. Mengal in *A Course in Baluchi*, vol. 2 (Montreal: Institute of Islamic Studies, McGill University, 1969), p. 1, describe the Baluchi alphabet. The author is indebted to Richard N. Frye for a clarification of the relationship between Baluchi and the Arabic alphabet.

11. Harrison, *In Afghanistan's Shadow*, pp. 183–85.

12. For a differing interpretation of Baluch history, see Brian Spooner, "Tribal Ideal and Political Reality in a Cultural Borderland: Ethnohistorical Problems in Baluchistan" (Paper presented at the Ethnohistory workshop, University of Pennsylvania, Philadelphia, 10 April 1978), especially pp. 8, 15–16.

13. For a discussion of the continuing controversy over the size of the Baluch population in Pakistan and the population balance in the province of Baluchistan, see Harrison, *In Afghanistan's Shadow*, pp. 175–82, especially p. 181. In recent decades Baluch preponderance in Baluchistan province has been threatened by a growing influx of Pashtuns and Punjabis, and ethnic tensions in the province have been aggravated by the influx of Pashtun refugees from Afghanistan since 1978.

14. See Harrison, *In Afghanistan's Shadow*, pp. 40–91, for a discussion of Mengal, Marri, and the principal Baluch nationalist organizations.

15. This estimate refers to literacy in all languages among Baluch in Pakistan, Iran, and the Persian Gulf. Robert G. Wirsing found that the highest literacy rate in eight of the nine districts in Pakistani Baluchistan was 7.7 percent. "South Asia: The Baluch Frontier Tribes of Pakistan," in *Protection of Ethnic Minorities: Comparative Perspectives*, ed. Robert G. Wirsing (New York: Pergamon, 1982), p. 18. Alvin Moore, South Asia specialist of the Library of Congress, estimated that there were 123,000 literates in Baluchi in 1981. "Publishing in Pushto, Baluchi and Brahui, Part 2," in *South Asia: Library Notes and Queries* (Chicago: South Asia Reference Center, University of Chicago Library, March 1980), p. 3. The *Census of Pakistan: Population 1961*, vol. 2 (Karachi, West Pakistan: Ministry of Home and Kashmir Affairs, 1961), p. IV–94, reported 87,000 literates in Baluchistan province. The 1972 census did not contain comparable tables.

16. Philip Carl Salzman, "The Proto-State in Iranian Baluchistan," in *Origins of the State: The Anthropology of Political Evolution*, ed. Ronald Cohen and Elman R. Service (Philadelphia: Institute for the Study of Human Issues, 1978), pp. 125–40. See also Salzman, "Continuity and Change in Baluchi Tribal Leadership," *International Journal of Middle Eastern Studies*, 4:4 (1973), pp. 428–39, and "Adaptation and Political Organization in Iranian Baluchistan," *Ethnology*, 10:4 (October 1971), pp. 433–44.

17. For an analysis of this climate two years before the secession of Bangladesh, see Selig S. Harrison, "East Pakistanis Resent Army Takeover," a two-part series from Dacca, *Washington Post*, 30 March and 1 April 1969.

18. Baluch economic grievances and the economic viability of an independent Baluchistan are examined in my book, *In Afghanistan's Shadow*, pp. 161–75.

19. Together with Sindhi-speaking Baluch, domiciled in Sind for centuries and largely absorbed into a composite Sindhi bloc socially and politically, this figure becomes 9.85 million, i.e., 11.77 percent of the total population of Pakistan cited at the beginning of this chapter.

20. *Census of Pakistan: Population 1961*, vol. 3, Statement 7-A, pp. IV–42, IV–43.

21. An example in English is G. M. Sayed, *Sindhu Desh: A Nation in Chains*, a 254-page underground tract issued on 16 September 1974. For a recent scholarly

volume on the history of Sind, see Hamida Khuhro, ed., *Sind Through the Centuries* (Karachi: Oxford University Press, 1982).

22. Sayed, *Sindhu Desh: A Nation In Chains*, p. 5.

23. Fazul Sulleman, "Sind's Agony," *Frontier Guardian* (Peshawar), 26 August 1972, p. 15.

24. Naqvi, a veteran *Dawn* political columnist, made this observation in a column prepared for *Dawn's* issue of 10 July 1972. It was withheld under prepublication censorship procedures but was published by the weekly *Frontier Guardian*, subsequently banned. "Defusing the Situation," *Frontier Guardian* (Peshawar) 29 July 1972, pp. 12–13.

25. Mazhar Yusuf, "Political Undercurrents in Sind Today," *Dawn*, 22 November 1978.

26. *Third World Forum* (London), 2:4 (1975), p. 36. For a discussion of leftist activity in Sind, see *Pakistan Commentary* (Hamburg), Bulletin No. 30 (January 1980), pp. 1–3, which contains a translation of an article in *Bhagwat*, a leftist, Urdu-language Karachi weekly, December 1979.

27. A. K. Brohi, "The Soul of Sind," in Khuhro, ed., *Sind Through the Centuries*, p. 24. See also A. Z. Khan, "The Role of the Qadiri Sufis in the Religious Life of Sind," in ibid., pp. 118–23.

28. Affidavit to the Supreme Court of Pakistan, 1975, p. 133.

29. A. R. Pazhwak, *Pushtunistan* (Kabul: Foreign Ministry, 1956), pp. 48, 50.

30. Ibid., p. 49.

31. Richard Tapper, "Tribal Society and Its Enemies," *Royal Anthropological Institute News* (London), October 1979, p. 6.

32. Akbar S. Ahmed, *Millennium and Charisma Among Pathans: A Critical Essay in Social Anthropology* (London: Routledge and Kegan Paul, 1976), pp. 52–55. This is addressed in part to Frederik Barth, *Political Leadership Among Swat Pathans* (London: University of London, The Athlone Press, 1959); see especially pp. 18–28 and 133–34.

33. Amin's manipulation of Pashtun patriotism is discussed in Harrison, *In Afghanistan's Shadow*, pp. 141–47.

34. Stephen Rittenberg, "Agrarian Change and the Rise of Nationalism in the Peshawar Valley" (Paper submitted to the Southern Asia Seminar, Columbia University, New York, 10 March 1981).

35. State (through Secretary, Minister of Interior) vs. Abdul Wali Khan and Others, a complaint filed by the Government of Pakistan, Islamabad, Before the Special Court, Hyderabad, 15 April 1976 (Notification F44 [1] 76-A 20 February 1976).

36. Significantly, this was cited in Zulfiqar Ali Bhutto, "Pakistan Builds Anew," *Foreign Affairs*, 51:3 (1973), p. 545. See also Muhammad Iqbal's 1930 proposal for a "loose federation of all India" in Sir Reginald Coupland, *India: A Restatement* (London: Oxford University Press, 1945), p. 189.

11

STATE BUILDING IN PAKISTAN

STEPHEN P. COHEN

Pakistan remains a state on the verge of disorder despite the fact that it inherited a coherent set of administrative institutions from British India, that the idea of Pakistan was quite firmly held before the state was created, and that Pakistan has always had adequate material and human resources to sustain itself. Contemporary Pakistan is the complex product of historical invasion, colonial rule, communal strife, forcible partition, and civil war. In this chapter we shall focus on this "new" Pakistan, the state that once constituted Pakistan's West Wing, and primarily on those institutions in Pakistan normally associated with "the state,"[1] such as the bureaucracy, the political party system, the courts, and the armed forces. We make several assumptions about the role of such institutions in the state.

First, the contribution of these institutions to state building is not necessarily positive. Some political institutions can corrode and destroy the very structure which gives them purpose.[2] Neither the "state" nor its constituent institutions are value-free. States and their institutions everywhere serve some interests better (or worse) than others. They also influence and shape perceptions of what these separate and common interests are. As Aristotle argued—and as President Zia ul-Haq firmly believes—the state and its apparatus have a duty to and mold its citizens.

Second, politics everywhere—but perhaps more visibly in Pakistan—rests upon a mix of consent and coercion. This may take the form of the threat of withdrawal of consent—or the threat of the application of force—but the two are omnipresent. When consent is absent, coercion shows its face, usually in the form of the application or threat of military power. The military or police forces are only faintly removed from the center of political life in any state. As Katherine Chorley wrote, "the position of the army in almost any society is the pivot on which that society swings," a statement that is unquestionably true for a Pakistan which has been under military rule for more years than civilian.[3]

Third, the institutions of the state are not autonomous but rest on a broader political culture. When that political culture is mixed or is changing, then institutions may come into conflict or become ineffective. This is so because a change of the structure of state power will usually favor one institution over another, and important ideological, ethnic, regional, religious, or other groups are linked to particular institutions in the pursuit of their interests. In a multiethnic society such as Pakistan it has proven impossible to manage the relative power of state institutions—especially the military versus parliamentary structures. Pakistan was unable to function as a British-style parliamentary democracy because interwing and interethnic conflicts were too powerful to be contained in polite structures; it was later unable to maintain even a halfway-house "consociational" democracy, in which linked elites governed in concord.[4] But the ensuing military rule carries with it imbalances and may have the further consequence of damaging the military itself as an institution.

Finally, it is important to note the Janus-faced nature of the state itself. States "always exist in determinant geopolitical environments, in interaction with other actual or potential states," and this can be—and in Pakistan repeatedly is—a crucial factor in domestic politics.[5] State rulers use external threats (real or imagined) to shore up their own position or, as in the case of the Pakistani military leadership in 1971, to prevent the coming to power of groups (such as the Awami League in East Pakistan) which are thought to be soft toward hostile neighbors (such as India). Nowhere is this factor more striking than in Pakistan, whose military, police, and bureaucratic elites have been united in their concern over internal weakness vis-à-vis external threat and over external involvement in internal affairs. These state bureaucracies have generally been opposed on these issues by other important institutions, such as the parties, the courts, and the educational establishment. A more complex issue is whether particular state institutions, which were created to serve one end and which reflect one national value or goal such as security, can be adapted to serve another. Or can such institutions survive when sister institutions decline or disappear? This question was particularly pressing in a state ruled by military professionals who seemed to be dismantling those very professions and political and administrative institutions which give the modern state its purpose and direction.

COMPARATIVE PERSPECTIVES

In comparative terms, Pakistan is unique in certain ways, and it shares certain qualities with other countries. We shall return to some of the shared qualities below, but it is important to note three special features of the Pakistani state: its ideological underpinning, its physical integrity, and its traumatic truncation in 1971.

Islamic Pakistan

Islam is potentially an important unifying force in any largely Muslim society. Muslims gather for organized prayer, assemble in Mecca during pilgrimage, and partake in a holy war against unbelievers or enemies of the faith. Islam, more than other religions, is a religion of what Elias Canetti calls crowds, which unite the just in opposition to the unjust, the saved against the damned, the believer against the unbeliever.[6]

Though Pakistan is the only country explicitly formed as an "Islamic" state, modern Pakistan is not a throwback to the caliphate or even a religious state run by clergy. In Pakistan, Islam as an ordering principle of state structure is fostered by men who are themselves the product of Western secular institutions. Yet many who fought for Pakistan were not themselves orthodox Muslims. They did not want to see Pakistan guided and structured according to Islamic principles, but saw Pakistan as a state where they would be free from the domination of their more numerous Hindu neighbors. Others opposed the idea of Pakistan, in particular, the conservative and orthodox Jama'at-i Islami.[7] The Jama'at's leader, Mawlana Mawdudi, argued that an independent Pakistan would be incomplete as it would leave millions of Muslims within a largely Hindu India. After Partition in 1947, however, Mawdudi changed his mind and migrated to Pakistan. His Jama'at movement has generally supported the recent wave of Islamization in Pakistan.

The shift from the concept of a state run largely along British Indian secular principles to a Pakistan serving as a laboratory of Islam occurred after Independence. This renewed concern with Islam as an organizing principle of state structure has led to the same problems faced by analogous states. While Israel is the most interesting contemporary example, Pakistan officials point out the difficulties faced by the Catholic states of Europe. Like Pakistan, the Catholic states had to adjust the relationship between church, religion, and state apparatus; they had to deal with the problem of nonterritoriality; and they had to face the phenomenon of two or more religion-based states pursuing different policies with different state structures. Pakistanis, for example, are aware that their "Islamic" practices are often at variance with those of Saudi Arabia or Iran.

A considerable amount of state-supported research is now devoted to the problem of creating an Islamic state in Pakistan. If earlier efforts in Pakistan are any guide and if the experience of the Catholic states and Israel is relevant, this research will be inconclusive on major issues. Islamic law itself is divided in some matters by the Shi'a-Sunni schism, and in other areas it is unlikely to displace well-established and effective codes derived from British Indian practice. Nor does Islam provide many clues to structural changes which would allow Pakistan's many and unequal ethnic groups to achieve elite consensus. We shall return to this issue below.

Territory and Destiny

Not only is Pakistan unique among states in its explicitly Islamic origins, it is practically unique in its territorial configuration. The "old" Pakistan was for many years divided into two disparate and physically separated parts. Paraphrasing Freud, territory is destiny, and had a hostile India not been interposed between East and West Pakistan, it is unlikely that the breakup of 1971 would have occurred even though there were severe stresses. Pakistan's Eastern wing, which subsequently became Bangladesh, was relatively homogeneous ethnically. Although predominantly Bengali, East Pakistan did have a small non-Bengali immigrant community known as the Biharis (although not all were from the Indian state of Bihar), who generally allied themselves with West Pakistan against Bengali demands for greater autonomy within Pakistan.[8] Further, there was an important Hindu minority in East Pakistan, a minority viewed with great suspicion by West Pakistani elites. But East Pakistan tended to vote and act en bloc, whereas Pakistan's West Wing was more diverse, composed as it was of four major language groups (Punjabi—spoken by 60 percent of the West's population—Sindhi, Pashtu, and

Baluchi). In the old, two-wing Pakistan, Bengalis generally had their share of administrative positions and made an active contribution to Pakistan's intellectual life. They were, however, underrepresented in the military and complained bitterly that their own relatively under-developed economy was being exploited by West Pakistani firms. While Bengalis were not at the center of power in Pakistan and while they occupied only 15 percent of the territory, they were close enough to sense their relative powerlessness compared with their numbers—for they constituted just over 50 percent of the entire population. East Bengal *was* part of Pakistan—a majority of the state, in fact, not an appendage. Bengalis felt less than equal when they were more than half.

Ethnicity and Rebellion

Ultimately, accumulated grievances and mismanagement led to the separation of 1971. Physical separation multiplied the impact of ethnic diversity on the state. More crudely stated, the Pakistan government was unable to apply the necessary force to suppress Bengali discontent simply because of the distances involved; there is no doubt that it would have done so if Bengal had been contiguous to West Pakistan or if Bengal could have been insulated from Indian influence.

The geopolitics of the "new" Pakistan is quite different from the old. Ethnic divergences which seemed minor when East Bengal stood as a counterweight to the entire West Wing are not new, but are newly important. The example of Bangladesh is now available as a precedent for the non-Punjabi groups,[9] even perhaps for other states with troubled ethnic or religious groups.[10] This precedent cannot be exaggerated: before the formation of Bangladesh, separatism for the North-West Frontier Province (NWFP), Sind, or Baluchistan (which did not even become a province until 1971) was thought to be highly improbable. Bangladesh showed that Pakistan's neighbors could and would support separatist movements if the opportunity were there.

Yet, history has a way of foreclosing certain opportunities as well as creating them. The lessons of Bengal are deeply imprinted on the minds of those who have ruled Pakistan since 1972. By sensitizing the new Pakistan's leadership to the possibility of regional, ethnic, or linguistic separatism, Bangladesh has also made it harder for such a movement to succeed. Although not a military man, Zulfiqar Ali Bhutto applied brutal force against the Baluch armed rebels in the mid-seventies (too much force—he and his military advisers could not forget Bangladesh, where some thought that not enough force had been applied). Bhutto's successor, Zia, has adopted a more conciliatory approach, although some Baluch leaders regard this as merely a tactical difference and argue that the ultimate end is Punjabi dominance (as some Bengali leaders argued that Yahya Khan's regime was merely serving West Pakistani and Punjabi interests). These internal linguistic, ethnic, and cultural divisions still present a challenge to the integrity and very survival of the new Pakistan. Such divisions can still be exploited by surrounding states, and the combination of internal dissent and external support could once again be a fatal blow to the physical integrity of the Pakistani state.

Commonalities

If Pakistan presents some striking features in its ideological and physical makeup, it shares certain qualities with other important states. In terms of religion, Pakistan now has an almost entirely Muslim population, but, as in other Muslim countries, the differences between Sunni and Shi'a have an impact. while Sunnis dominate in Pakistan, there is a large Shi'a community. Various problems have arisen with regard to the enforcement of Islamic laws of taxation since Sunni and Shi'a legal codes differ in several important respects. The small non-Muslim communities have been relatively unaffected and in fact have usually found representation in cabinet and parliament,[11] although the presidency of Pakistan has been constitutionally reserved for a Muslim. More problematical has been the treatment of the Ahmediyas, a sect that has been declared non-Muslim.

As a multiethnic and multilingual state Pakistan also shares a number of characteristics with Iran, India, and other states in the region. Each major grouping in Pakistan (Punjabi, Pashtun, Sindhi, and Baluch) has its own provincial assembly, governor, educational system, and administrative cadre. However, the imbalance between the Punjab and the other three groups is more akin to Persian dominance in Iran than anything found in India; this Punjabi dominance is exacerbated by a predominantly Punjabi military establishment.

Further, many of Pakistan's ethnic groups spill over across state frontiers. Pashtuns, Baluchis, Kashmiris, and Punjabis are found in Afghanistan, in Iran, and in India, and subnationalist movements are not far beneath the surface in the case of the first three groups. This ethnic overlap has one overwhelming implication for the Pakistani state: its foreign policy, especially vis-à-vis its neighbors, is to a great degree a function of domestic politics. Similarly, Pakistan's treatment of its own population (especially in Kashmir, Baluchistan, and the North-West Frontier Province) is necessarily a concern to its neighbors.

Finally, Pakistan shares with several states a British legacy of constitutionalism and civilian rule despite functioning as a state without a constitution for most of its history and having been run by the military more often than not. While there are those who argue that Pakistan is destined to be like Iran, Iraq, or Syria—oscillating between bondage to the military and chaos—one critical difference is that among those institutions still functioning in Pakistan (including the military) there remains a deep commitment to constitutional civilian government.

The repeated displacement of civilian institutions by a military bureaucracy again raises the question as to whether an institution which has been established and organized to fulfill one narrow task (national security) can effectively perform functions (executive, legislative, and judicial tasks, control over the media, redirection of educational priorities, and even formulation of religious and cultural policies) normally associated with other major state institutions. And how does it affect the triangle of state, Islam, and ethnicity? To answer these questions, we must first examine the adjustments in power and influence *between* the major institutions of Pakistan, especially the political parties, the judiciary, and bureaucracy, on the one hand, and the ever-powerful military, on the other.

CIVILIAN INSTITUTIONS: BROKEN or MERELY BENT?

The historical trajectory of Pakistan's major civilian political institutions would seem to describe a downward curve. Pakistan was a country which began with a full complement of parties, effective bureaucracies, a comprehensive system of laws and courts, a vigorous press, and a small but burgeoning system of higher education. Until recently all of these institutions were in disrepair: the parties were banned, the bureaucracy was held up to ridicule, the press was subject to censorship, the civilian courts were supplanted by a martial law system and a new Islamic legal system, and Pakistan's universities were the literal battleground for opposing political forces, few of which have great regard for higher education itself. Except for the still affluent military, Pakistan was to be undergoing de-institution-alization.

This image is only partly true. The several excellent surveys of Pakistan's political institutions emphasize this political decay, but it is vital to add that from a comparative perspective Pakistan remains an institutionally developed country.[12] Politics is still thought to be a legitimate vocation—although the politicians have difficulty plying their trade—the bureaucracy has shown considerable capacity for re-generation, the press manages to work around a sometimes obtuse censorship, and the universities continue to produce students and scholars that compete effectively in the West. Even the judiciary is capable of making its voice heard although it is much weaker than even under Bhutto. Let us look more closely at three major civilian institutions—the political parties, the judiciary, and the bureaucracy—and see how they have adjusted to the successive crises that have punctuated Pakistan's political history.

The Political Party System

Political parties are everywhere multifunctional institutions. They serve not only as "transmission belts" for public opinion and group interests, but also (especially in Communist countries) as mobilizing agents for the state and instruments of change. Pakistan's parties have never been able to fulfill either of these functions. The party movement which created the state—the Muslim League—was most influential in those areas of British India which did not become Pakistan. While many of the Muslim League's leaders emigrated to Pakistan, their mass base remained in India and this, coupled with the incipient personalistic quality of the party, led to the League's rapid decline as a political force. Yet no other mass party took its place and the political system of Pakistan was dominated by groups that were parties in name only. Some were vehicles for local leaders and others were never far from their feudal roots. The notions of a legitimate opposition, of parties as permanent institutions rather than as instruments of individual power, and of consensus on vital issues were all absent. Nor was the ideology of Islam widely attractive except as a common ground on which to declare a non-Indian identity.

The prospective fragility of Pakistan's party system was recognized by Jinnah before the state became independent. Unlike Jawaharlal Nehru (who served as India's prime minister under a

Governor-General), Muhammad Ali Jinnah chose to become Pakistan's Governor-General. "In this way," according to von Vorys, "he proposed to rise above parliamentary responsibility and direct from his own heights the evolution of Pakistan's political institutions."[13] But Jinnah died shortly after Independence, and the parliamentary path was pursued by his successor, Liaquat Ali Khan, and other politicians for nearly ten years, until Ayub Khan's coup ended Pakistan's unsteady democracy in 1958.

Ayub moved because the system was not working. There were no restraints of individual or institutional loyalty, party organization, or public responsibility upon individual ambition. "The only guide to action, which remained by default, was individual self interest," according to von Vorys. "Holding office became the highest goal."[14]

From the perspective of the civil service, the military, and most other professionals and institution builders in Pakistan, the army's first coup came both as a relief and as an opportunity to reshape Pakistan's political institutions. Ayub Khan eventually turned himself into a political leader (with some initial success) and ruled until 1969, only to be displaced by his army commander-in-chief, Yahya Khan.

Ayub's reign was important in the prominence of *civilian* advisers, and it was in fact more a bureaucratic-military alliance than simple military rule. In a very real sense Ayub's regime more closely resembled the British Raj in its strong central direction and an assumption of bureaucratic omnipotence. His government did provide several years of stability and economic growth and continued the work of building such institutions as the educational system, but Ayub was ultimately brought down by mass protest. The fact that the generals (especially Yahya) were unwilling to trust the politicians only contributed to the irresponsibility of the latter. Pakistan was simply unable to evolve strong political institutions which made military intervention unnecessary—or military institutions which were capable of governing without reliance upon these very fragile political institutions.

The ultimate failure of military nerve took place in 1971 when Yahya refused to allow Shaykh Mujib to form a government after his Awami League had won a majority in the 1970 elections. Had Yahya done so Pakistan would have survived intact, albeit in a different form. But again personal ambition and regional affiliations were too great to resist, and Zulfiqar Ali Bhutto shares responsibility for the breakup of Pakistan and for the decline of party institutions by his unwillingness to see Mujib as Prime Minister.

With a few exceptions, Pakistan's political parties have not had strong organizational roots. Of the parties in the "old" Pakistan the largest ethnic/linguistic party was the Awami League, whose support was entirely in the East Wing; it was nearly equaled in size by the Pakistan People's Party (PPP), which was unashamedly a West Wing party, with strongest roots in the Punjab. After the deaths of their leaders (Shaykh Mujibur Rahman in the case of the Awami League, Bhutto in the case of the PPP) these parties tended toward factionalism: in both cases the cult of the leader has been less effective in death than in life. Despite a strong ideological thrust in both cases party organizational politics tended to be overwhelmed by personalities.

Bhutto and Mujib introduced mass politics in a country which had never experienced this phenomenon, and together they opened up new (for Pakistan) political choices. But even if they had been able to contain their own ambition and maintain organizational coherence, these new choices frightened many in Pakistan (and in Mujib's case, in Bangladesh). Could Bhutto continue to control the mobs? Could he be displaced by a worse rabble-rouser? What if he turned upon those institutions (such as the business community, the military, the bureaucracy, and other parties) which had not been the PPP's enthusiastic supporters? No one was more aware of this discontent than Bhutto himself, and after 1972 he tried to gain leverage over such groups through an adroit mixture of bribery, demagoguery, and—where these did not work—coercion. He ultimately lost control, although in 1977 it was not so much a failure of institutions as the failure of an individual who sought to rise above the very structures he created.[15]

The PPP's policies toward Pakistan's ethnic/linguistic groups and Islamization were both crucial in its rise and ultimate fall. While professing a popular socialism, epitomized by the slogan "bread, clothing, and shelter," the PPP was from the first a predominantly Punjabi party (although Bhutto was himself a Sindhi and the party had deep roots in Sind). But Bhutto was obsessed with regionalism, and he brutally suppressed Baluch armed rebels after they protested his attempt to impose PPP control over the provincial legislature. He also reacted to the post-1971 revival of Islam by introducing his own program of popular Islamization. Bhutto's notoriety as a Westernized secular Muslim undercut this effort, although it did anticipate many of the Islamic programs pursued by Zia.

Between 1977 and 1985 political parties ceased functioning in Pakistan. While they regularly announce "campaigns" or movements to displace the military from power, none posed a serious threat to the regime. Some political activity has been channeled into an appointed Federal Advisory Council, the Majlis-i Shura, a large number of whose members were active politicians.[16] One of the few groups allowed to function freely was the Jama'at-i Islami whose conservative Islamic ideology overlapped with that of Zia ul-Haq. Lending its support to the military regime at first, the Jama'at now distanced itself from Zia, but it still exercises considerable influence on university campuses against both moderate and radical student groups.

Rumors abound that the Majlis will become a partially elected body in its next sitting, or that the provincial elections for local bodies will be expanded, or that general elections will be held.[17] Such rumors, however, have been circulating since 1977, when Zia first promised elections "within three months." National elections will be held only when the military is sure that the results will not threaten its own position, the changes introduced in Pakistani society, or Pakistan's foreign policy. If PPP support withers, the chances for an election increase, although the regime will certainly remember the miscalculation of Yahya, who had not expected the Awami League to win in 1970.

The Judiciary

Up to 1985 three different legal-judicial systems functioned in Pakistan: the British-erived civil courts which trace their structure from the Government of India Act of 1935 and have roots deep in Anglo-Saxon Law; the martial law courts, also derived in part from the British experience but greatly elaborated and refined under successive Pakistani governments; and the Shari'ah (the sacred Law of Islam). One might also add such codes of behavior as Pashtunwali (the traditional tribal code of the Pashtuns) which function in some areas of Pakistan (especially NWFP and Baluchistan) and which in certain matters take precedence over civil codes.

The civilian court system is analogous to that found in India and features a Supreme Court, four High Courts (one for each province), District Courts, and lower courts. From the first years of Pakistan the courts served as a protective agency for those who were in difficulty with the government, and held Pakistan to a reasonably high standard of Indo-British law. Even the military regimes have been concerned that martial law be retroactively sanctified by the Supreme Court.

The judiciary has become the battleground between those who seek to expand the role of Islam in Pakistan and those who wish to maintain the codes, court systems, and legal profession inherited from the British. It has not, unlike other institutions (such as the military), been regarded as an arena of ethnic conflict. Most judges in the respective high courts come from provinces they serve in: the exception is Baluchistan which has not produced many ethnic Baluchi lawyers (Baluchistan did not even have its own High Court until 1971).

Until recently, the lawyers and judges who compromise this civilian court system were under siege from two directions: the military and the Islamizers. The military introduced its own parallel system of martial law courts throughout Pakistan and simultaneously encouraged the development of the Islamic Shari'ah Courts.

The martial law courts were of two types: summary and regular. The summary courts are created to handle specific disturbances (riots, crime waves) and are disbanded when the emergency ends. The "regular" martial law courts were located in most cities and districts and handled violations of the various martial law regulations. Under Zia's regime various activities (gatherings of politicians, defamation of the martial law system, and so forth) were prohibited; these went immediately to the martial law court system, where they were ultimately passed upon by Zia, who presided over the system as Chief Martial Law Administrator (CMLA). However, some activities (violent crimes that may have a political origin) were also justiciable in the regular civilian courts. Local police officers were regularly bribed so that their first information report steers the case into the "proper" court. In some cases, individuals preferred to be tried before the summary and often secret martial law courts, where opportunities for bribery were greater than the open civilian courts. However, all political cases went to the martial law courts, and all arrests of politicians were under the martial law regulations. They were not bailable, nor could the civilian judges issue writs of habeas corpus in such cases; this important restriction on civilian judges was introduced in 1975 by Zulfiqar Ali Bhutto.

In March 1981 a Provisional Constitutional Order further modified the 1973 Constitution and completed the subordination of the superior civil judiciary to the martial law authorities, giving the latter the power to determine whether or not a case would be held before the martial law courts or the civil courts. Theoretically, an army major on martial law duty had more power than the Chief Justice of the Supreme Court of Pakistan. Recognizing the implications of the 1981 Order, the Chief Justice and three colleagues from the Supreme Court and eleven justices from the Sind, Punjab, and Baluchistan High Courts either refused or were not allowed to take the oath under this Provisional Order and lost their jobs.

The Shari'ah Courts have raised more controversy in Pakistan, partly because it was a crime under martial law regulations to criticize the martial law courts. If a case is registered under Islamic law, it will go to an Islamic court at the magistrate or district level. A case can also go to the regular civilian court and will then also be tried under Islamic law (by regular judges). Appeals in such cases go to the Shari'ah Court, located above the High Courts but below the Supreme Court.

Zia first established Shari'ah Benches in 1978, promising to set them up at each High Court and a Shari'ah Appellate Bench in the Supreme Court. Their function was to declare a law invalid if it was repugnant to the Qur'an and Sunna. However, these courts cannot deal with matters concerning Muslim personal law (which differs among Shi'as and Sunnis), the procedures of the martial law courts, the Constitution itself, or fiscal matters. Critics of the Shari'ah system argue that it is a mere sop to the Islamic parties and makes no real impact on civil or military court systems. Nevertheless, the Shari'ah system is being expanded. In 1983 additional legislation was passed in the Majlis-i Shura to establish 150 qazi (religious judge) courts in the districts.[18]

While some have criticized the martial law courts for being lawless, the Shari'ah system may be vulnerable to the charge that there is too much Islamic law. The Shari'ah courts (and civilian courts that handle cases based on Islamic law) have the difficult task of not only administering justice based on a legal code developed in the broader Islamic world, but administering it in the face of hostility from many Westernized Pakistanis, especially the lawyers and judges trained in the Western legal tradition. In 1983, when the Islamic legal codes were being prepared, protest marches were held in major Pakistani cities by women who protested that the Evidence Act did not treat women equally. A cable of protest signed by a number of prominent Pakistani women, including the wife of one cabinet member, reflected wider unease that under the new Islamic codes women would be systematically treated as inferiors in the courts, and ultimately outside of them as well.

Their fears are well-grounded. While it is not surprising to find the Islamic clergy supporting a reduced status for women in Pakistan in accordance with their reading of the Qur'an, this position is also held by some in the military, including President Zia. His government dismisses the protests to the laws of evidence as Hindu-inspired, or un-Islamic, although this event did lead to a slowing of the pace of Islamic reformation.[19]

One consequence of Pakistan's new emphasis on Islam and Islamic courts has been that some opponents of the 1977-1985 martial law regime have resorted to "Islamic" arguments and used these courts when other avenues of protests were shut. In appearing before a military court in early 1983 Benazir Bhutto, daughter of the executed former Prime Minister, argued that the martial law court itself was both un-Islamic and impermissable according to the 1973 civilian constitution of Pakistan.[20] More recently, the All-Pakistan Newspaper Society (APNS) pleaded before the Federal Shari'ah Court in Islamabad that continuation of the Press and Publications Ordinance of 1963 was "repugnant to the Holy Qur'an and the Sunna" because under Islam a person has an absolute right to independent adjudication in a dispute with authorities. Citing chapter and verse of the Qur'an, various newspaper editors and lawyers have argued that the same person cannot be party and judge in the same dispute, precisely the situation held by government newspaper censors.[21]

In both cases there was a mixture of cleverness and desperation in the appeal to Islam by individuals and groups not noted for their past orthodoxy. In a sense, such appeals were a victory for the government's Islamization drive since Islamic symbols and criteria are invoked, but few would believe that in these instances interest in Islam is anything more than tactical and expedient. Those in high places in Pakistan, including Zia, joke about straightening the *qibla*—direction of prayer toward Mecca—of the secular, Westernized opponents of Islamization, but express confidence that these "secular" Muslims will eventually bring themselves into conformity. The latter have done this superficially, but one suspects that if the regime should falter, there will be a strong middle-class reaction against the Islamic courts, Islamic codes of dress and conduct, and restrictions on women in the name of Islam. But the advocates of Islamization are counting on time and the growth of a middle class rooted in more traditional Islamic values and beliefs. The divisions are already apparent within the political party system, the judicial system, and even the military.

The Bureaucracy

Pakistan inherited its bureaucratic structure from British India, and this structure has been virtually preserved intact over the years. Each province has its own locally recruited cadre, but these are inferior to the various central services. In the "old" Pakistan recruiting for these central services initially met no great difficulty, as recruitment, training, and most operations were carried out in English. Problems arose only at the district level when some knowledge of local languages was important, but such difficulties were in themselves not a barrier to the normal functioning of the state bureaucracy. Difficulties did arise in the "old" Pakistan when a disproportionate number of senior civil posts fell to Muhajirs (mainly Urdu-speaking refugees originating from India) or Punjabis, and the situation persists today in Baluchistan where most administrators, even if born in Baluchistan, are non-Baluch. To overcome the continued predominance of Punjabis, Bhutto introduced a quota system for regional representation and tried in particular to encourage Sindhi recruitment, apparently with little success.

However, the imbalance in recruitment to the civil service has apparently never been as great nor as politically consequential as the imbalance in recruitment to the army (discussed below). The members of the Civil Service of Pakistan (CSP) were strong advocates of highly centralized regimes in Pakistan and, beginning with Ayub Khan, they served the various military regimes with enthusiasm and skill. This was not always reciprocated by Ayub, who introduced the first of a series of measures designed to dilute the power of the CSP. Ayub made lateral entry possible, and a number of army officers resigned their commissions to enter civilian service. The attack on the CSP was intensified under Bhutto, who formally abolished it, creating a Central Superior Services (with heavy lateral entry) and a District Management Group which had greatly reduced privileges. Some of these changes were reversed by Zia, who relied heavily upon senior civil servants (as well as a large number of retired generals) for a variety of sensitive administrative tasks. Zia, for example, appointed Ghulam Ishaq, a retired Indian Civil Service (ICS) officer, as Finance Adviser to reorient Pakistan's economic policies, in shambles after Bhutto's attempt to create an instant popular socialist economy.

While restoring some of the prestige and perquisites of the senior civil services in Pakistan, Zia insisted that the civilian bureaucracies conform in externals to his Islamization program. After 1982 all officials working in the secretariats were required to wear "national" dress, time and space had to be set aside for daily prayers (although performing namaz is not compulsory), and Islamic history has been introduced as part of the general training and indoctrination program for all services.

None of these steps can be considered radical, although they have changed the physical appearance of the typical Pakistani government office. Bureaucrats who had to invest in a new wardrobe have now come to accept such attire. The major complaint comes from a few military officers on deputation in civilian positions who lament the unmilitary garb they must wear and the loose fit that makes it easier to inadvertently gain weight. The average bureaucrat sees such practices as a small price to pay for national solidarity or— more importantly—furthering his own career.

The three civilian institutions that we have briefly examined—the party system, the courts, and the civilian bureaucracy— each exhibit a different relationship to Islamic ideas and to Pakistan's diverse ethnic/linguistic composition. The party system reflects the diversity of attitudes toward Islam *and* Pakistan's heterogeneous social structure, but its historical failings are also due to the absence of experience in democratic politics, the inordinate dependence on strong political leaders (three of whom, Jinnah, Liaquat, and Bhutto, met early or untimely deaths), and the inability of party elites to forestall party fissuring. The bureaucracy has its own failings and successes, but these are not closely related to Islam or ethnicity; the senior bureaucrats of Pakistan remain willing to serve whatever civilian or military government holds sway and have thus retained their organizational identity, if not their power. The courts, however, have become a central battleground between "secular" Muslims who resist Islamization and the Islamizers, who have succeeded in establishing a parallel set of religious courts in addition to supplanting civil codes with Islamic ones.

We have frequently alluded to the power of the armed forces. Pakistan has been under military rule for most of its history from Ayub's coup in 1958 to the resignation of Yahya Khan in 1972, and again under Zia ul-Haq from 1977 to the present. Military rule, however, has always had a strong civilian component, as senior politicians and bureaucrats have played an important role in all periods of martial law. Nor has "the military" been a monolith: there have been important dissenters to martial law and particular policies within the military among retired generals. But the military has in fact been the most important political institution in Pakistan for much of its history and has repeatedly attempted to practice corrective surgery on other important governmental and political institutions. It is important, therefore, to examine closely the armed forces' relationship to Pakistan's ethnic diversity and Islamic ideology. What we will see in this regard is that ethnic imbalance has always been a critical political factor in state politics, and that the army's new interest in Islam may yet prove to be its most important achievement.

MILITARY INSTITUTIONS: POWER and POLICY[22]

Of Pakistan's institutions, one, the military, has remained untouched. It was too powerful for civilians to tamper with and virtually ran itself without outside interference. Only when it was defeated by the Indian Army in 1971 were there attempts by Bhutto to restructure it, and some of these attempts may have only hastened his own downfall.

Our primary interest in the armed forces lies with the Pakistan Army (the politically most powerful service), and, within the army, the officer corps. The attitudes, professionalism, regiment or branch origins, and shared formative experiences of its young officers are likely to shape Pakistani politics beyond the year 2000, just as the experiences undergone by Zia ul-Haq in the 1940s shape his behavior today. Our focus will be on four linkages: between the army and Pakistan's ethnic groups, the army and Islam, the army and other important state and political institutions, and the army and foreign policy.

Ethnicity and Representativeness

The maintenance of proportionate representation of important ethnic groups in the military has important symbolic and practical dimensions. The symbolic dimension of military service is self-evident: if a Pakistani cannot fully share the obligations and rewards associated with such a central state institution as the military, he is not a citizen in the full meaning of the word. Conversely, the dominance of a particular region within the military is often seen by others as a potential threat.

The practical dimensions of ethnic representativeness are no less important. In dealing with conflict within a region (such as Baluchistan) it is essential to have within the military and security forces individuals from that region who understand the local languages, terrain, culture, and aspirations. Yet there are dangers associated with such a practice. First, the military trains its members in the art and science of violence, and a continual flow of veterans from the army back to a rebellious area may strengthen the capacity of the rebels. Second (and apparently of great importance in the Lahore riots of 1977), disturbances in a particular region are quickly felt in military units drawn from that region. Such forces cannot be trusted to control a crowd possibly made up of their own kin.

The British who ran the old Indian Army strongly believed that India was a series of disparate, segmented societies, an agglomeration of "nations" with different characteristics and attributes. They concluded that not only were some ethnic groups inherently more martial or warlike than others but that such groups had to be counterbalanced to ensure that they would not unite against the British or exploit regions and castes and religious communities that were "weaker." The idea of the "martial races" had complex origins, some based on myth, some rooted in South Asian tradition—which antedates the British—of ranking different ethnic groups according to their military-like qualities, including not only ferocity (in which the Baluchi excel) but also adaptability to discipline and organization. But this view of "martial races" did partially reflect actual regional, religious, cultural, and ethnic differences among Indians. It also led to a serious imbalance of recruitment in the old Indian Army and to the dominance of Punjabis in the sepoy ranks and later in the officer corps. The British found that Punjabi Muslims made very good soldiers, and often good officers. Punjabis took to discipline better, recruitment among Punjabis was easier, and the nomadic Baluchi had the disconcerting habit of decamping without notice. By the beginning of World War II the largest single class in the Indian Army was Punjabi Muslims.

Upon achieving independence Pakistan found that it had something like 60 percent Punjabi Muslims as sepoys and in the officer corps. The second largest group was drawn from the Pashtun Muslims of the North-West Frontier Province (one of the few ethnic groups Punjabis respect). Pashtuns although a minority, play a major role in the officer corps. (Zia, in fact, is the first Punjabi to serve as head of the army, all of his predecessors being Pashtuns.)

From the beginning these Punjabi and Pashtun officers claimed a special position in the new state of Pakistan: they stressed that the virtues of Pakistan were their virtues and that the Islamic character of Pakistan was reflected in the Islamic character of the military. In popular publications as well as in the military schools the history of Pakistan was traced to Muslim dominance in South Asia, and Pakistanis were portrayed as the natural conquerors of the region by virtue of their purer religion and their martial characteristics. These assumptions led to the grotesquely inflated belief of the martial superiority of Pakistan's Army over "Hindu India." The Indians had within their ranks some near-martial races—Sikhs, Gurkhas, and Rajputs were shown particular respect—but the Indian Army was "contaminated" by such nonmartial groups as Tamils, Telugus, Gujaratis, and—fatally—Bengalis.

No regular Bengali Muslim army units had been raised during World War II. The Pakistan Army immediately raised two battalions of the new East Bengal Regiment (EBR) in 1948. These and subsequent Bengali units were organizationally significant because they were the only single-ethnic units in the new Pakistan Army and were officered entirely by Bengalis. After Independence the Pakistanis had systematically mixed different army units—but not Bengalis. While Bengali units were slowly expanded, there was strong resistance within the Pakistan Army to greatly expanding East Bengali representation in the military, and considerable distaste for the quality of Bengali officers and other ranks.

We now know the consequences of discriminatory treatment against Bengali officers and soldiers. They became the backbone of armed resistance to the Pakistan Army during the civil war in the East wing; despite warnings, the Pakistan Army leadership never could make up its mind as to whether the Bengali units should be expanded into full partnership or completely eliminated. Since the army was running the country, the exclusion of East Pakistanis also had very broad political implications.

This discussion of the military origin of the old Pakistan's destruction is offered as a reminder of the central symbolic and practical importance of ethnic representativeness within the military when it dominates the politics of a country. It raises the question: Could it happen again? The question is relevant and worth examining since the present Pakistan Army's units and officer corps are hardly more representative than the old one, with a few districts of the Punjab and NWFP still as dominant.

Before Independence, more than 77 percent of the wartime recruitment from what became Pakistan had been from the Punjab, 19.5 percent from NWFP, 2.2 percent from Sind, and just over 0.06 percent from Baluchistan (and of this number, 90.7 percent had served in the army). Today, the percentages have not changed dramatically. Seventy-five percent of all ex-servicemen come from only three districts in the Punjab (Rawalpindi, Jhelum, and Cambellpur) and two adjacent districts in NWFP (Kohat and Mardan), so the army as a whole is still ethnically unrepresentative. These five districts are part of or adjacent to the Potwar region of Pakistan—very poor, overpopulated, underirrigated, and on the path of countless invasions of South Asia—and between them, they contain only 9 percent of the male population of Pakistan.

Since the departure of the Bengalis, all regular units of the "new" Pakistan army are now integrated in that they are supposed to contain a fixed ratio of Pakistanis from several regions.[23] Each of the four major infantry regiments (Punjab, Baluch, Frontier Force, Sind) recruits on a national basis through a central system of recruiting officers. However, because of the large numbers of Punjabis, some units (even in the Baluch Regiment) have no Baluchis and very few Pashtuns or Sindhis. The problem is further complicated in that quotas are by region, not by ethnic group. Thus a Pashtun living in the Punjab is counted as a Punjabi, and a Punjabi living in Baluchistan is counted as a Baluch.

The disproportionate representation of ethnic Punjabis in both the officer corps and the other ranks has changed greatly since 1971, in that very few Bengalis served in the military although they were half the population. Still, while exact figures are unavailable, it is likely that Punjabis remain slightly overrepresented at both levels, Pashtuns receive about proportionate representation, and Baluchis and especially Sindhis are underrepresented. Since there is no conscription, little can be done to draw in reluctant or uninterested ethnic groups.

There is now more awareness of the dangers of an ethnically unrepresentative army. A predominantly Punjabi army is particularly sensitive to political unrest in the Punjab itself. Large numbers of Baluch or Sindhis in the military would mean a better-trained and disciplined population in two provinces with separatist sentiment. Moreover, if ordinary citizens from Sind or Baluchistan do not make good soldiers—or if they were not interested in participating in the defense of the country *as* soldiers—what does this imply about their loyalty to the state of Pakistan, and the loyalty and officer-like qualities of Baluch or Sindhis who join the officer corps? What lesson is to be drawn by such groups in the face of Punjabi dominance? The former Chief Justice of the Supreme Court raised this issue in the army's professional journal. Justice Hamoodur Rahman reminded his readers that the main culprits in the disintegration of the old Pakistan were Punjabis and that this gave rise to a feeling of Punjabi domination which in its turn propelled into prominence "regionalistic and parochial aspirations."[24] The dilemma was recently summed up from a military perspective by a senior retired lieutenant-general who had been a close associate of Ayub Khan: "The idea is to get more Sindhis in and the response is not there! It is like the Bengalis—the attempt to do it was there, the response was weak, but as I saw it, the attempt [to bring in Bengalis] was late—but there were those who could say, "See, if you had done it earlier, see what happened later?" Had we rushed it, would things have been worse?"[25]

The Army and Islam

After independence there was little detectable concern about the relationship between the military, Islam, and the state of Pakistan. Other than trivial steps such as replacing British slogans and symbols with Islamic ones, no outward change in the appearance of the officer corps and various military establishments took place. Primary attention had been given to building an organization and the development of strategic doctrine. The close relationship first with the British and then the United States military encouraged deferral of the issue of Islam: it was enough that the army served an Islamic state.

In time, however, the failures of the Pakistani political system coupled with the recruitment of officers from more traditional sectors of Pakistani society increased the salience of the question of the relationship between army and state in an Islamic country. Officers began to ask what other national models might be more relevant to their army than the secular British or American patterns, and the military has started to take seriously Islamic history and Qur'anic doctrine, although the basic institutions of the army still follow Western lines. The present army is an uneasy blend, especially in matters of doctrine. The Shi'a-Sunni schism does not play a major role within army politics, although it certainly has been a factor from time to time. It was rumored, for example, that Yahya Khan was particularly vulnerable as Commander-in-Chief because he was a Shi'a, and

Shia's are somewhat resentful that certain foreign training posts are closed to them (most importantly, Saudi Arabia). The army is, however, increasingly "Islamic" in that regulations against drinking are now seriously enforced, although prayer is left up to the individual and technical military subjects remain untouched.

Comparatively, the most relevant model is the Israeli defense force. Pakistanis respect the mix of democracy, religion, and fighting qualities that they see in Israel (although they certainly oppose Israeli *policy*) and would like Pakistan to emerge as a kind of Islamic Israel. There are other analogies. One distinguished retired general argues that Pakistan "cannot have an army and a political system which is derived from secular, Western models. The comparison should be with the Catholic states of Europe: how long did they take to work out a relationship between the army and the state?"[26] This view more closely resembles Muhammad Iqbal's philosophy of autonomous Muslim states than Jinnah's semisecular Pakistan, and it seems to be accepted by the present military leadership.

Under President Zia, there is a systematic attempt to construct a state and an army along Islamic lines, yet still to be "modern" and efficient. In the years since he has come to power Zia has extended and reinforced the Islamization of Pakistan, introducing a number of banking and commercial practices based on Islam, punishments drawn from the Qur'an, and the "Islamic" reform of many parts of Pakistani society.

The central question is: Why has the military pursued this policy of Islamization of the state when many of its *own* institutions are quite un-Islamic in origin? Is Islamization merely a diversionary tactic used by the generals to keep the most Westernized segments of Pakistan off balance? Or, is the policy due to the religiosity of Zia and his advisers?

Neither answer seems to be exactly correct. Zia is a devout Muslim but no fanatic, yet he and others take Islamization quite seriously. The view of the senior leadership was best expressed by one senior retired general, who provided this analysis of the weaknesses of Pakistani society and how Islam serves as both a goal and a corrective:

> We [the leadership] are progressive and enlightened individuals. But Islamic laws have been brought in [chopping off hands, lashes]. Are we hypocrites? Well, there *are* good laws, but they require a good society, the two things have to go side by side. The development of the world has not been uniform: within certain countries

also the development has not been uniform. In the West, for example, law can be enforced uniformly, it will be acceptable practically to everybody as being the law at the time, because the whole society has grown upward simultaneously. In the East it is not so. In Pakistan, for example, you find people who live in caves! You can find people living by centuries, till the 21st, leave alone the 20th. So, a law which a man of the 20th Century considers to be modern and civilized is considered to be uncivilized for a man living in the 14th Century. And there are people here living in caves, in a pre-historic period!

I think we are trying to civilize people here, whereas in the West the people are becoming animals, going towards the other direction; for me, homosexuality is such a big crime against humanity. Chopping off hands for stealing in Pakistan, I do not consider to be against humanity. You consider such things [liberation of laws concerning homosexuality] to be a step forward, we consider it to be against human nature.

And, he concluded, expressing the view of virtually the entire leadership of Pakistan in the Zia years:

We do not accept that the West goes out to impose its views on us. We do not cry or shout about what Sweden has done—they have authorized their children to go to court against their parents—now this is destroying human civilization which has been developed by this race of human beings over centuries. It is wrong, totally wrong, but if we had done it, the whole of the West would have started shouting "look how uncivilized and backward those Pakistanis are." You people have a friend in Pakistan. You can always find fault, but you will destroy us, with what result? The West is looking for an ideal society, but is an imitation of that ideal for us? I think it would depend on the situation: you cannot impose a proper type of culture, civilization, without considering the basic structures of that society.[27]

The inner tensions and contradictions in this view are clear. The typical officer is highly Westernized in appearance and in his values, yet he is Muslim and Pakistani and rejects much of what he believes to be the degradation of the West. More officers come from devout families than in the past, and more believe that religion and public life *should* mix. Fewer and fewer come from secularized Muslim families who believe that religion and public life should *not* mix, and young Pakistanis who hold this view tend to go into professions other than the military. Further, those officers who do not feel strongly about the mixing of religion and reform have been swept up in the wave of Islamization as part of a general search for ideology within the military after the disaster of 1971. This defeat persuaded some officers that Pakistan was being punished for not being true to its original (Islamic) purpose; other officers do not feel quite this strongly but recognize Islam as an important unifying factor in maintaining the integrity of the army and the state and as a link between these institutions.

Islam does not provide a complete model or pattern, certainly to the more well-informed and highly trained officers. The Pakistani military is trying to work for an amalgamation of two cultures. their approach is to draw upon their own professional experience and careers: if good government works within the military, if it can be imposed by adherence to regulations, law, and tradition, then the broader society should be amenable to the same kind of orthosocial control. Zia and some around him who hold these views know that they have not been able to persuade many Western-educated Pakistanis of their correctness, but this only confirms their view of un-Islamic rot in Pakistan and the need to persevere.

The Army and the State

When Zia ul-Haq assumed power in 1977, he promised that he would hold elections within ninety days. The promise was repeated and only recently fulfilled. Zia has rejected the suggestion that *he* enter politics, aware that Ayub's experiment along these lines ended in disaster and a second coup. Zia's power rests upon his command of the army, and it would not permit him to play a partisan role while remaining Chief of the Army Staff.

Two contesting theories have been offered to explain not only Zia's coup, but earlier intervention by the military in Pakistan. On the one side, many academic and civilian critics regard the Zia martial law regime as the latest in a series of military governments, which themselves are a cover for Punjabi/West Pakistani dominance, or antidemocratic values held by the generals, or both. On the other side, the military defends its actions by pointing to civilian incompetence and misrule and believes that the military—the soldiers—may be the only truly national, patriotic, and efficient institution left in Pakistan.

There is evidence to support either view. We need not rehearse these arguments again, as ample literature already exists on the subject.[28] However, two further arguments are important in understanding how the military came to power, how it continued to rule, and how it might yet fully withdraw. The first relates to the notion widely held in Pakistan of "democracy," the second to the military's ambivalence about governing the state.

In Pakistan the confrontational dimensions of democratic government are emphasized: Democracy thus seems synonymous with hostile and uncompromising opposition to established governments, even legitimizing outrageous and destructive behavior. This kind of "democracy"—unscrupulous campaigning, public libel and slander, betrayal of party loyalties, misconduct in government, and so forth—is seen as a threat to the state itself. Accordingly, security and bureaucratic elites regularly support repressive measures in the face of such behavior, and they also tend to exaggerate the dangers of such behavior.

The image of democracy gone berserk is widely held within the military and civilian bureaucracies of Pakistan. As in the case of the general quoted above, it is often argued that Pakistan is not yet ready for democracy—that Pakistanis lack the necessary level of education, culture, or maturity to make democracy work, and that the military must therefore stand by as guardians ready to intervene. This narrow conception of "democracy" has its origins in the colonial experience when British officials made the same argument. This theory of democracy and cultural/political backwardness has dominated Pakistani elite military and bureaucratic thought since Independence.

A second vital point in understanding military rule concerns the moral and legal ambiguity felt by the armed forces toward governing the state. The military ruled in the name of the 1973 Constitution (albeit virtually transformed by various martial law decrees) and continued to promise elections. The martial law regime offered this symbolic compliance with democratic politics not only to humor its American allies or to hoodwink gullible Pakistanis but because it was concerned about the legitimacy of its *own* rule, just as previous martial law regimes saw to it that successor civilian governments legitimated their actions. The military did not want to be accused of treason by a successor civilian government bent on revenge.

The military was and is nervous about its own power. While there has been some public discussion of a system that would give the military a formal constitutional role (as in Turkey), there is still no consensus within the senior ranks about the propriety of such a role and its compatibility with "democracy," i.e., civilian rule. Further, some openly oppose such a role as incompatible with their notion of military professionalism and likely to damage the military itself by association with corrupt or incompetent civilian regimes.

The ambiguity of the military toward state power and its extreme sensitivity toward internal security problems in turn are clearly demonstrated in the ill-fated attempt to create a paramilitary force in Pakistan. Such paramilitary forces have been created in a number of new states.[29] They generally serve two vital purposes: they act as a buffer between the regular armed forces and society, allowing the military to concentrate upon professional matters, and they can be used to balance the armed forces politically and make a coup harder to plan.

Unlike India, where civilian governments raised a number of parliamentary forces after 1968, Pakistani leaders did not consider the issue until 1972. Ayub and Yahya were army men, their power rested on the support of the army, and they felt confident that the army could and should be ready to handle domestic law and order problems. More than its sister army in India, the Pakistan Army inherited something of the paternalist autocracy that characterized the Punjab school of administration of British India. Although some of the perquisites of such a system included opportunities for corruption and bribery by the officers, the army stood by to help civilian authority when necessary, and even supplant it.

This pattern was broken when Zulfiqar Ali Bhutto created the Federal Security Force in 1972 as both a buffer and a counterweight. The army, shattered by its defeat in East Pakistan, accepted the FSF, although some senior retired officers refused to accept Bhutto's offer of appointments in the force. Tolerance turned to fear, however, and then to hatred. Bhutto used the FSF as a private police force and began equipping it with arms that rivaled those of the military—some retired officers now characterize the FSF as an incipient Nazi SS. When Bhutto was overthrown in 1977, one of Zia's first acts was to abolish the FSF. The army is again the second line of defense against internal disorder and remains highly sensitive to domestic law and order problems. It has a domestic intelligence service of its own and interacts closely with local police and intelligence services. Virtually all army units have some secondary law and order assignment since they are generally stationed within marching distance of some important civilian population centers (most of the army is in the Punjab, as are most of the cities of Pakistan).

The recent spell of military rule was certainly not "democratic" politics, but Zia and other generals (and not a few civilians) would defend it as "good government." Economic stability and law and order have returned to Pakistan and foreign policy is well managed. The system allowed consideration of slightly divergent points of view, and public discussion of important issues in the press and in the Majlis-i Shura. Unlike previous martial law regimes, however, the military has tried to share the implementation of martial law with civilians and has kept the various civilian ministries functioning. Zia, in his capacity as Chief Martial Law Administrator, was known to issue an order to a particular ministry, which in turn has either appealed this through the martial law hierarchy or taken it back to him via the Cabinet (in his capacity as President). Then, as President, Zia has at times reversed the martial law directive he originally approved. The same process occurred in the four provinces where the governors were also martial law administrators. In the eyes of many Pakistanis this was a poor substitute for popular democratic government, but it was not quite the draconian rule often associated with military governments elsewhere.

The Army, External Relations, and Power

The foreign policy dimensions of domestic politics cannot be ignored in the case of a state recently dominated by the military and facing substantial external threats, especially when that state has many dissident ethnic groups with ties abroad and when the armed forces are dependent upon foreign powers for their military hardware. Politics in Pakistan is linked to foreign policy in at least five ways.

The first is the connection between dissident ethnic and linguistic minorities and foreign governments. Pashtuns, Kashmiris, Baluch, and Sindhis must be placated, for they do have a limited option elsewhere. The Pakistan government may find itself pressed at home if one or more of its neighbors decides to meddle.

Second, Pakistan's heavy defense expenditures may affect not only the growth of the entire economy but also the distribution of resources among the provinces. Sindhis and Baluch in particular see little economic benefit from Pakistan's heavy defense burden, and they and other minority provinces often encounter the military only as a hostile force.

Third, the army has continued Bhutto's efforts to place Pakistan in the Islamic world. Bhutto was seeking a way back into the international community and saw an opportunity to gain access to the rich resources of the oil states. But the military added its own perspective to Bhutto's Islamic foreign policy. The military sees itself as the strategic *center* of the Muslim world, having the best training facilities of any Muslim state and maintaining military missions in over twenty countries. These operations have brought it great prestige and considerable financial rewards, a neat conjunction of personal, bureaucratic, and Islamic interests.

Fourth, if Pakistan does go nuclear, the stakes in domestic politics in any future coup or transfer of power are raised. Not only will there be a struggle for control over such weapons, but foreign governments will feel that they have a direct and vital interest in such a struggle. Indeed, the emergence of an unstable and disorderly Pakistan as a nuclear power may be too great a provocation for some neighbors. Although some believe that once states acquire nuclear weapons they become reasonably trustworthy, no one familiar with Pakistan's violent tradition of political succession would share this optimism.

Finally, despite a major attempt by Bhutto to build a domestic arms industry, Pakistan remains dependent on foreign nations for its hardware and financing. Virtually all air force equipment is Chinese, American, or French in origin, most armor is Chinese or American, and other weapons, ships, and equipment come from these and a few other sources. If the armed forces fully yield power to civilians, they are likely to want a veto over foreign policy decisions, particularly those affecting weapons suppliers, and they are unlikely to tolerate a civilian leadership which dramatically reduces arms levels.

CONCLUSIONS and PROSPECTS

Pakistan came into existence as the expression of an idea with a very brief history. Yet Pakistan was born with a developed set of state institutions that had been forged in an imperial context to assist the British in governing a multiethnic and multireligious territory of continental dimensions. Other large states shaped their bureaucracies and institutions over the years but, in Pakistan, the institutions came first and have tried to shape the state.

The ethnic imbalance of these institutions was deliberate. Especially in the case of the military, Pashtuns and Punjabi Muslims were overrepresented both because of their desire for military service and because of the impunity with which they could be used in non-

Muslim regions. In the case of the civil services, where selection was more by aptitude than traditional interest, some regions were under-represented because of the disparity in educational levels among Pakistan's provinces.

It was not surprising then when the state ran into difficulty, the military would emerge as a political force, backed by the senior civilian bureaucracy. Nor was it surprising that the ethnic imbalance within these and other institutions turned out to be fatal to Pakistan in 1971 when a major ethnic group, the Bengalis, broke away.

What *was* surprising was that Islam failed to provide the glue to hold Pakistan together. But "Islam" often meant little more than anti-Hinduism or a longing for freedom from oppression. Bengalis weighed the balance and came to the conclusion that they could be free of both Indian and West Pakistani dominance if they had their own state. These calculations are made today in the North-West Frontier Province, Baluchistan, Sind, and even Kashmir, and though some have opted for separatism, another breakup is less likely to recur than some observers have argued.

First, the ethnic imbalances in the services, the bureaucracies, the professions, and even in politics are not as severe now as in the "old" Pakistan. Nor are the cultural differences as great between Sindhi, Punjabi, Baluch, and Pashtun as between each of these and Bengalis. Pakistani elites have yet to find an institutional formula short of British-style parliamentary democracy and more than dictatorship-by-consensus. But effective institutions are possible only if the dominant ethnic group, the Punjabis, recognize the necessity for power sharing.

Second, external events have changed the context of Pakistani politics. The ethnic groups that are most discontented with Punjabi dominance do not constitute viable and distinct entities and would need considerable outside support to survive, especially from India or the Soviet Union. Although some non-Punjabi leaders have announced their break with Pakistan, many others are concerned over foreign influence to see common interest with Punjabis in reforming or reconstructing the present Pakistan.

Third, Islam, which failed to provide the path for Pakistan in the past, offers a peculiar kind of attraction today. It provides a domestic rallying point and frame of reference and defuses the orthodox right-wing parties who are still capable of generating mass protests. Externally, it is useful as part of a revivified foreign policy. Though Zia and the Islamizers run the risk of creating a Khomeini-type revolution, they regard this risk as quite low. The clergy of Pakistan are neither as powerful nor as central to the political life as those in Iran, for they are divided between Sunni and Shi'a and are balanced by a more developed professional and political community (including the army) than in Iran. Islam is available for state-building purposes. The military and their civilian supporters need not follow the Shah's or Turkey's model of a secular Muslim state.

What remains troubling, however, is the military's ambivalent relationship to the political parties and constitutional government. Military rule is regarded as illegitimate in Pakistan not because it has meant the domination of a Punjabi officer corps—although that is a factor in non-Punjabi grievances—nor because the military has Islamized the country—that was initiated by Bhutto—but because there is no theoretical or practical justification for military rule beyond expediency. The illegitimacy of military rule remains even as it is thought to be occasionally necessary.

Ayub tried to deal with this tension by turning himself into a politician, only to lose the respect of the military. Yahya, a man more limited in ambition, did hold Pakistan's first free election but lacked the nerve to act upon the results. Until recently Zia resisted the political path and distrusted the electoral process. He is more willing than his predecessors to undertake what he regards as the necessary Islamic and political reforms to make Pakistan unified. Zia feels that one can be a good Muslim and a good (Westernized) professional—he sees himself as a model—and asks only that Pakistan's lawyers, students, professors, journalists, doctors, bureaucrats, and politicians conform to the pattern—that they straighten out their "qibla." But the armed forces are perhaps the least qualified institution to lead a cultural revolution.

Yet there were a few important qualities of the martial law regime of 1977–85 that offered some hope. Because of the terrible ordeal undergone by the army, its senior officers, especially Zia, were more realistic than their predecessors about their external strategic and internal political situation. The present military hierarchy have no illusions about Pakistan's military might, about their capacity to rule by threat, or about the ability of Pakistani politicians to govern. they also have strong foreign support from a number of countries, which has meant a new influx of economic assistance, weapons, and political support. If a balance of Pakistan's prospects for state building were to be drawn, it would not be unfavorable for the short run— the next few months or even years. But one hesitates to speculate beyond that.

Postscript, May 1986

Events in Pakistan moved with dramatic speed after this chapter was completed in August 1984. I have changed the text to the past tense, but my cautiously optimistic conclusions remain unaltered.

President Zia held a national referendum in December 1984 on two questions: the propriety of Islam as Pakistan's guiding philosophy, and his right to continue as President through 1990. The answer in both cases was "yes," although the turnout for the referendum was low. Zia then held successful nonparty general elections at the national and provincial level in February 1985, and Mohammed Khan Junejo became Prime Minister in March. Junejo was a relatively unknown Sindhi politician with a reputation for honesty.

After keeping his promise to restore civilian government Zia continued the process of demilitarization. By the end of 1985 the National Assembly had passed a bill amending the 1973 Constitution. The amendments incorporated many martial law regulations that Zia had promulgated since 1977 and also indemnified from prosecution those associated with the martial law system. Martial law was completely ended in Pakistan by the end of 1985, and the country was (for the first time since the 1950s) free from any martial law or "emergency" proclamations. A fully civilian government headed by Prime Minister Junejo was sworn in on January 28, 1986. Nearly full press and political freedoms have been restored to Pakistan, as have political parties. However, Zia continued in his position as head of Pakistan Army as well as President through mid-1986.

During this transition period there was a marked decline in the political role of Islam. The Jamaat did badly at the polls, although its strength had always been in organizational not electoral politics. Women politicians have been prominent, most notably Bhutto's daughter, Benazir. She made a triumphal return to Pakistan in April 1986 (having boycotted the elections) and expects to challenge both Junejo and Zia. However, Benazir was cautious in her early statements about the military: it is now a constitutional violation instead of a martial law violation to criticize the armed forces. (This was also the pretext for banning at least one scholarly book on the Pakistan army.)

While post-martial-law politics are fluid and unpredictable, it was evident that all concerned—Zia, the military, Benazir Bhutto and the PPP, and Junejo and his ruling Pakistan Muslim League—

remember Pakistan's calamitous political history and were eager to avoid provocation. To repeat my conclusion of 1984: Pakistan's short-term prospects are encouraging: democracy has been gradually but almost fully restored to Pakistan. The long-term prospects are still uncertain. Pakistan has the requisite formal institutions, considerable material and human resources, and a deeply rooted democratic tradition. Has it, however, learned from its own past?

NOTES

1. "The state" is not a mythical entity, but achieves concrete expression in the various institutions which purport to act on behalf of the state and its interests. See Ernst Cassirer, *The Myth of the State* (New York: Anchor, 1955).

2. Samuel P. Huntington, *Political Order in Changing Societies* (New Haven, Conn.: Yale University Press, 1968).

3. Katherine Chorley, *Armies and the Art of Revolution* (reprint ed.; Boston: Beacon Press, 1973), p. 243. For a similar view see Stanislav Andreski, *Military Organization and Society* (Berkeley: University of California Press, 1968).

4. See Arend Lijphart, *Democracy in Plural Societies: A Comparative Exploration* (New Haven, Conn.: Yale University Press, 1977).

5. A recent rediscovery of this integrated into a broader theoretical and historical framework is presented by Theda Skocpol, *States and Social Revolutions: A Comparative Analysis of France, Russia, and China* (Cambridge: Cambridge University Press, 1979), p. 30. See also Eric A. Nordlinger, *On the Autonomy of the Democratic State* (Cambridge, Mass.: Harvard University Press, 1981).

6. Elias Canetti, *Crowds and Power,* trans. Carol Stewart (New York: Seabury Press, 1978), p. 141.

7. See William L. Richter, "The Political Dynamics of Islamic Resurgence in Pakistan," *Asian Survey,* 19:6 (June 1979), pp. 547–57.

8. There are many studies of this process and of the breakup of Pakistan in 1971. For a Bangladeshi perspective see Rounaq Jahan, *Pakistan: Failure in National Integration* (New York: Columbia University Press, 1972); and for an informed military analysis see Fazal Muqeem Khan, *Pakistan's Crisis in Leadership* (Islamabad: National Book Foundation, 1972).

9. Selig S. Harrison has discussed this at length in *In Afghanistan's Shadow: Baluch Nationalism and Soviet Temptations* (New York: Carnegie Endowment for International Peace, 1981).

10. The states that might be most concerned include two of Pakistan's neighbors, Iran and India. The latter is currently witnessing in the Punjab and Assam two major ethnic/linguistic/religious disputes.

11. There has not, however, been the kind of agreement found in Lebanon and several European democracies and other states which Lijphart would term "consociational."

12. There are a number of excellent recent books about Pakistani political and administrative institutions. See Lawrence Ziring, *Pakistan: The Enigma of Political Development* (Boulder, Colo.: Westview Press, 1980); and, slightly older, Henry F. Goodnow, *The Civil Service of Pakistan* (New Haven, Conn.: Yale University Press, 1969).

13. Karl von Vorys, *Political Development in Pakistan* (Princeton, N. J.: Princeton University Press, 1965), p. 124.

14. Ibid., p. 125.

15. Bhutto's own writings demonstrate some of this ambition; for the best biography and political analysis see Salmaan Taseer, *Bhutto: A Political Biography* (London: Ithaca Press, 1979); and Shahid Javed Burki, *Pakistan Under Bhutto, 1971–1977* (New York: St. Martin's Press, 1980).

16. About 100 of the 288 named members of the Majlis came from legally defunct political parties, including as many as sixty members of Bhutto's People's Party. For a discussion see Marvin G. Weinbaum and Stephen P. Cohen, "Pakistan in 1982: Holding On," *Asian Survey,* 32:2 (February 1983), pp. 123–32.

17. See the 1986 "Postscript" (pp. 329–30) for recent developments.

18. Karachi Domestic Radio, *Foreign Broadcast Information Service,* 22 January 1983.

19. The laws of evidence draft was summarized in *Overseas Dawn,* 10 March 1983, which also carried the text of the telegram and the names of the signatories on 14 april 1983.

20. See Agence France Press reports of 26 and 29 March 1983 in *Foreign Broadcast Information Service,* 28 March and 1 April 1983.

21. *Overseas Dawn,* 19 May 1983.

22. Some of the following is based on Stephen P. Cohen, *The Pakistan Army* (Berkeley: University of California Press, 1984).

23. An exception and an important ethnic halfway house in the security forces are the various scout and ranger units operated by the Pakistan Army. These are commanded by regular commissioned officers on deputation from their "home" regiment, but are manned entirely by soldiers drawn from the local region in which the unit (such as the Khyber Rifles or Pishin Scouts) serves. While the scout units are well trained and adapted to local conditions, they are not required to master complex military technologies or operate as part of a larger standard military formations.

24. Retired Chief Justice Hamoodur Rahman, "Ideology of Pakistan: The Raison d'etre of our Country," *Pakistan Army Journal,* June 1978, p. 9. Also see the writings of former Chief Justice Muhammad Munir, *From Jinnah to Zia* (Lahore: Vanuard Books, 1980).

25. Interview, 1980.

26. Interview, 1980.

27. Interview, 1980.

28. See Gerald Heeger, "Politics in the Post-Military State," *World Politics,* 29:2 (January 1977), pp. 242–62; Hasan Askari Rizvi, *The Military and Politics in Pakistan 1947–1986* (Lahore: Progressive Publishers, 1986); Eqbal Ahmad, "Pakistan: Signposts to What?," *Viewpoint* (Lahore), 18 May 1974; and "Zia is No spokesman," *New York Times,* 1 October 1980, for contrasting views.

29. For the best discussions of the political role of paramilitary forces in developing countries see Morris Janowitz. *Military Institutions and Coercion in the Developing Nations* (Chicago: University of Chicago Press, 1977).

12

ISLAM: IDEOLOGY and POLITICS in PAKISTAN

JOHN L. ESPOSITO

SINCE PAKISTAN'S ESTABLISHMENT AS A SEPARATE STATE in 1947, Pakistanis have struggled with the meaning of their identity.[1] During the latter half of the 1970s Islam reemerged dramatically in Pakistani politics, used first by those who toppled the government of Zulfiqar Ali Bhutto in 1977, then by those who sought to legitimate the martial law regime of his successor, General Zia ul-Haq. Islamic ideology has been put forward as the basis for creating a sense of national unity. Some Pakistanis have called for a more Islamic system of government, *Nizam-i Islam* (the system of Islam). For many, Islamic ideals and Islamic institutions are necessary to realize Pakistan's original raison d'être, to define it more clearly, and to unite otherwise disparate regional/ethnic groups into a nation-state.

This chapter will review and analyze the role of Islam in state formation and mass politics in Pakistan, focusing specifically on the contemporary reassertion of Islam in Pakistan's political development. The Islamization of state and society—its institutions, laws, regulations, programs, and policies—will be described and assessed. The issues and problems that emerge from this process not only contribute to our understanding of contemporary Pakistan but also address underlying issues and problems that face other Muslim countries as they seek to Islamize their societies.

ISLAM in the FORMATION of PAKISTAN

The independence movement in the Indian subcontinent flowered during the period between World War I and World War II. In the early

333

years Hindu and Muslim leaders of the Indian Nationalist Movement sought a united front. However, as religion was an integral part of the two great traditional cultures—a source of strength which inspired and assured as well as preserved their identity and way of life— Hindu and Muslim communal fears ultimately undermined any union. Muslims were concerned about their rights in a predominantly Hindu, albeit secular, state. This concern moved Muslim leaders like Muhammad Iqbal and Muhammad Ali Jinnah to call for a separate Indian Muslim state. Convinced that communalism was both the existent reality and an absolute necessity for survival of Muslims' identity and way of life, Iqbal declared at the All-Parties Muslim Conference of Delhi: "The Indian Muslim is entitled to full and free development on the lines of his own culture and tradition in his own Indian Homelands."[2] However, by 1930, in his now famous "Presidential Address," Iqbal called for the formation of a separate Muslim state:

> I would like to see the Punjab, Northwest Frontier Province, Sind and Baluchistan amalgamated into a single State. Self-government within or without the British Empire, the formation of a consolidated North-West Indian Muslim State appears to me to be the final destiny of the Muslims, at least of North-West India.[3]

Similarly, although Jinnah had sought at first to work with the Congress Party and its leaders (Jawaharlal Nehru and Mahatma Gandhi), by 1940 Jinnah was speaking of the two nations of India—Muslim and Hindu:

> It is extremely difficult to appreciate why our Hindu friends fail to understand the real nature of Islam and Hinduism. They are not religious in the strict sense of the word, but are, in fact, different and distinct social orders, and it is a dream that the Hindus and Muslims can ever evolve a common nationality, and this misconception of one Indian nation has gone far beyond the limits. . . . The Hindus and Muslims belong to two different religious philosophies, social customs, literatures. They neither intermarry nor interdine together and, indeed, they belong to two different civilizations which are based mainly on conflicting ideas and conceptions. Their aspects on life and of life are different. It is quite clear that Hindu and Musalmans derive their inspiration from different sources of history. . . . To yoke together two such nations under a single state, one as a numerical minority and the other as a majority, must lead

to growing discontent and final destruction of any fabric that may be so built up for the government of such a state.[4]

Jinnah and the Muslim League harnessed Islamic symbols and slogans to forge a mass movement whose goal was a separate nation—a Muslim homeland wherein Muslims might be free to pursue their way of life. Their goal was realized in August 1947 when the Indian subcontinent was partitioned into two separate nation-states—India and Pakistan.

At its founding Pakistan was a nation whose Western and Eastern wings (West and East Pakistan) were separated by more than one thousand miles of Indian territory. Islam had given birth to Pakistan, thus providing the ideological basis for a state that lacked any of the usual prerequisites for a nation-state—territorial integrity, sense of national community, or linguistic unity. Tribalism, regionalism (the Punjabi, Baluchi, Sindhi, and Pashtun), and linguistic diversity (five major linguistic families and thirty-two spoken languages) abound. Early problems of nation building were compounded by Muslim-Hindu communal rioting and mass migration. Pakistan has weathered the untimely death of its founder-architect Jinnah in 1948 and the subsequent assassination of the first Prime Minister, Liaquat Ali Khan, three martial law regimes and three constitutions, the loss of East Pakistan (Bangladesh) in 1971, and the overthrow and hanging of its most recent Prime Minister, Zulfiqar Ali Bhutto.

Despite Pakistan's commitment to Islam, the Islamic character and form of the state has never been systematically addressed or adequately resolved.[5] Ideologically, Pakistan has remained suspended between the ambiguity of her founder's call for a Muslim homeland and the varying expectations of the majority of the religious establishment and populace for an Islamic state. When deemed opportune, governments or religious leaders have appealed to Islam for their political purposes. Substantively, while religious traditionalists have advocated an Islamic state based upon the *Shari'ah* (the sacred Law of Islam), Pakistan has, in fact, generally followed Western models of political, legal, social, and economic development. The problems raised in using Islam to forge a national consensus and identity are demonstrated by two examples: the debate surrounding the drafting of Pakistan's first constitution (1956), and the turmoil engendered by Ayub Khan's (1958–69) modernist brand of Islam. The basic ideological questions were: What does it mean to say that Pakistan is a modern Islamic or Muslim state? How is its Islamic character to inform the ideology and institutions of the state?

The process of framing Pakistan's first constitution lasted nine years. The constitutional debate provided an arena for a protracted battle between conservative religious leaders and modernist factions—the former more inclined to a revival of a past ideal, the latter to modernization and reform through the adoption of Western-based models of development. The Constitution of 1956 reflected the long years of debate and the sharp differences between traditional religious and modernist elites.[6] The final document substantially incorporated many facets of a modern parliamentary democracy (popular sovereignty, a political party system, equality of all citizens) to which several Islamic clauses or provisions were added to respond to the expectations and demands of religious leaders. Among the principal Islamic provisions were: the state was to be called the Islamic republic of Pakistan;[7] Pakistan was to be established as a democratic state based upon Islamic principles;[8] the head of state must be a Muslim;[9] an Islamic research center was to be established to assist in the "reconstruction of Muslim society on a truly Islamic basis";[10] and finally, the "repugnancy clause" stipulated that no law contrary to the Qur'an and sunna of the Prophet could be enacted.[11]

The Constitution of 1956 demonstrated the unwillingness to articulate and implement an Islamic ideology. It skirted the question of the Muslim or Islamic character of the state for it lacked any systematic statement and implementation of an Islamic rationale. Modernists had a document whose few Islamic provisions caused a minimum of inconvenience. While religious leaders had called for an Islamic state based upon the full implementation of the Shari'ah, they settled for a legal system in which no law could be repugnant to Islam. The relationship of modern constitutional concepts to Islamic principles was asserted but not delineated. These unresolved constitutional questions and inconsistencies illustrate the ideological quandary that has continued to resurface throughout Pakistan's history.

The rule of Field Marshal Ayub Khan (1958–69) provides a second major example of the failure to achieve a national consensus on the meaning, character, and implementation of Pakistan's Islamic ideology. Ayub Khan's coup d'etat brought a military government committed to a strong centralized national government and rapid socioeconomic development. At the same time, Ayub Khan's modernization program included an attempt to introduce and implement modern reformist Islam. He emphasized the need to "liberate the spirit of religion from the cobwebs of superstition and stagnation which surround it and move forward under the forces of modern science and knowledge."[12] Since he held the religious establishment chiefly responsible for the stagnant state of Islam and viewed the ulama (clergy; literally, the "learned men") as ill prepared to meet the demands of modernity, Ayub tended to ignore or diminish the role of the religious elite. Ayub's modernist outlook was reflected quite clearly in the new Constitution of 1962, the establishment of the Advisory Council of Islamic Ideology, and the Islamic Research Institute, as well as the reforms embodied in the Muslim Family Laws Ordinance (1961). Religious leaders saw such steps as a direct challenge to the traditional role of the ulama as the guardians of Islam and advisers to Muslim governments. An ideological battle was thus joined between a regime which sought to impose its modernist interpretations of Islam and a religious elite that resisted both the displacement of their traditional role and authority as well as their more conservative religious world view. Once again, the struggle between modernist and traditionist factions resulted in minimizing the potential of these mechanisms of reform.

The new Constitution of 1962 generally adopted the Islamic provisions of the 1956 Constitution. There were, however, some significant changes. The new document initially omitted "Islamic" from the official name of the republic and the divine sovereignty phrase, which limited the power of the state, "within the limits prescribed by Him," but, under strong public pressure, these Islamic provisions were again restored by the first Amendment Bill of 1963.

Perhaps the most notable Islamic provisions of the new constitution occurred in "Part X, Islamic Institutions" which, following the lead of the Constitution of 1956, called for the establishment of an Advisory Council of Islamic Ideology and an Islamic Research Institute, the former concerned with legislation and the latter with research, especially on Islam in the modern world. The functions of the Advisory Council of Islamic Ideology were to make recommendations to the government regarding provisions that might better enable Muslims to lead their lives in conformity with the tenets of Islam; and to advise the government as to whether proposed legislation was repugnant to Islam. The role of the Central Institute of Islamic Research, which had been mandated by Article 197 of the Constitution of 1956, was to define Islamic fundamentals in a rational and liberal manner so as to bring out their dynamic character in the context of the modern world. In this regard, the Research Institute could be asked by the Advisory Council to gather materials and submit an opinion on a particular legislative proposal.

The issue of Muslim family law reform became a major point of contention between Ayub Khan and the religious establishment.

The Commission, which had been established in 1955, was dominated by lay modernists (three men and, even more objectionable for traditionists, three women) with only one representative of the ulama. Moreover, the Commission's Majority Report issued in 1956 did not simply restrict its recommendations to regulations obtained by *taqlid* (the following or imitation of tradition) or selection from medieval *fiqh* (Islamic jurisprudence), but rather asserted its right to depart from tradition and exercise *ijtihad* (individual reasoning or interpretation) in drafting reforms in Muslim family laws (marriage, divorce, and inheritance). In his Minority Report the lone representative of the ulama attacked the competence and credentials of the Commission's lay members to interpret Islamic law and accused them of "distorting the religion of God and the worst type of heresy. . . . [Their recommendations] reflect subservience to the West of some of the members and their displeasure with Islam, [constituting] an odious attempt to distort the Holy Qur'an and the Sunna with a view to giving them a western slant and bias."[13]

After five years of heated debate the legislature passed, with strong backing from Ayub Khan, a weakened version—the Muslim Family Laws Ordinance of 1961—over strenuous objections from religious leaders. Moreover, in 1963 an attempt to repeal the new law was defeated in the National Assembly after some twenty hours of debate. As discussed below, the contemporary resurgence of Islam has brought fresh attempts to either amend or repeal the Muslim Family Laws Ordinance.

Thus, during the first decades of Pakistan's existence, modernist elites succeeded in establishing a functioning state and society, but little headway was made in determining the Islamic character of Pakistan's ideology to provide the basis for national unity and political integration. While there had been general agreement regarding the need for a Muslim homeland, what that agreement meant was far from clear.

ISLAMIZATION in CONTEMPORARY PAKISTAN

The Bhutto Period (1971–77)

When Zulfiqar Ali Bhutto decisively won the national elections in 1970 and became the head of state in 1971, few expected that this secularist, representing the socialist platform of his Pakistan People's

Party (PPP), would be the Initiator of Islamization in Pakistan. Most observers believed that while religious sensitivities had to be respected, Pakistan would generally continue in its political and social development along a de facto Western, secular path. However, several factors contributed to a significant revival of Islam in Pakistan's politics: a post-Bangladesh identity crisis, the Arab oil crisis, and internal politics.[14] As a result, Islam became a major theme in Pakistan politics; indeed, by the end of Bhutto's rule, it had become the dominant theme.

The loss of East Pakistan, after a bloody civil war which led to the formation of an independent Bangladesh in 1971, seemed a testimony to the failure of Islam to provide national cohesion and solidarity and led to a renewed concern with questions of national identity and unity.[15] Not only had Pakistan lost more than half of its population and part of its territory to the Bengalis of East Pakistan, but resentment of Punjabi dominance and strong ethnic nationalist and separatist sentiments could be found within West Pakistan among Baluchis, Sindhis, and Pashtuns as well. Jinnah had foreseen and warned against these very threats to Pakistan's basis for existence: "If we begin to think of ourselves as Bengalis, Punjabis, Sindhis, etc., first, and Muslims and Pakistanis only incidentally, then Pakistan is bound to disintegrate."[16] To deal with the situation, Bhutto, domestically, sought to establish a sense of national unity behind a populist, socialist program which promised to redress the acute socioeconomic disparities in Pakistan. Internationally, Bhutto determined to draw closer to the Arab oil-producing countries for aid and, toward this end, progressively emphasized their common Islamic identity and bond. Hosting an Islamic Summit Conference in Lahore in 1974 strikingly symbolized his new initiatives in the Middle East. The summit, attended by heads of state from around the Muslim world, provided a forum for Libya's Colonel Muammar Qaddafi who addressed throngs of Pakistanis at the Badshai Mosque in Lahore. Bhutto permitted Egyptian President Anwar Sadat to mediate between Pakistan and Bangladesh and agreed to restore diplomatic relations with Bangladesh in the name of Islam. The Bhutto government also initiated programs to encourage the study of Arabic and fostered an increasing number of religious conferences to which representatives from other Muslim countries were invited.

Despite all of his efforts in the name of Islam, the Jama'at-i-Islami and other religious parties continued to oppose Bhutto. In reacting to this internal political pressure from religious critics, Bhutto increasingly responded to them on their own ground—

through appeals to Islam to legitimate his programs and policies. Bhutto's PPP had been the only party since the Muslim League to establish itself as a mass political party with its populist, socialist slogan "*roti, kapra, aur makan*" (bread, clothing, and shelter) and "*zamin kashtkaron ko*" (land to the tiller). These and other social policies such as nationalization of basic industries (cotton, iron and steel) and of financial institutions—alienating many industrialists and other private entrepreneurs—and land reform (1972) were progressively equated with Islamic social justice. Phrases like *Musawat-i-Muhammadi* (the equality of Muhammad or Muhammad's egalitarianism) and *Islami Musawat* (Islamic equality) became part of the PPP's rhetoric. A new newspaper, *Musawat*, was founded which, somewhat like the journal *Minbar al-Islam* in Gamal Abdul Nasser's Egypt, provided an organ for the Islamic justification of the PPP's policies by appealing to the Qur'an, the Sunna of the Prophet, and the practice of the *Khulafah-i-Rashidun* (rightly guided caliphs).

In addition, in 1974 Bhutto yielded to the decades-long campaign of religious leaders to have the Ahmadiyah declared a non-Muslim minority. Muslim religious leaders had long maintained that the Ahmadiyah recognized their founder, Ghulam Ahmad, as a prophet and thus rejected a pillar of Islam—that Muhammad was the final prophet of God. Since they viewed the Ahmadiyah as non-Muslims, they especially objected to their holding important positions in government and the military. In addition to provisions in the 1973 Constitution which required that both the President and Prime Minister be Muslims, the oath of office was amended to include an affirmation of the finality of Muhammad's Prophethood.

Appeals to Islam reached their zenith in the March 1977 general elections. Shortly after elections were announced in January, nine political parties joined under the umbrella of Islam to form an opposition block, the Pakistan National Alliance (PNA). The Alliance drew its support from the Islamic religious parties and from the middle class and included the Pakistan Muslim League, National Democratic Party, Tehrik-i-Istiqlal, and others. However, its direction, leadership, and organization came from the Islamic religious parties: the Jama'at-i-Islami (JI), the Jami'at-i-Ulama-i-Pakistan (JUP), and the Jami'at-i-Ulama-i-Islam (JUI). Mawlana Mufti Mahmud (JUI), assisted by a council composed of leaders of the member parties, including Mian Tufail Muhammad (JI) and Mawlana Ahmad Shah Noorani (JUP) assumed leadership of the PNA. Although member parties spanned the political spectrum, the PNA's symbols and slogans were stated in an Islamic framework, e.g., "Islam in Danger" and "*Nizam-*

i-Mustafa" (the system of the Prophet). The vast network of ulama and mosques and their associated *madrasahs* (advanced schools for Islamic learning) were employed as centers for PNA political organization and communications.

Much PNA support came primarily from the middle class (traditional and modern): urban intellectuals who had supported Bhutto's early socialist platform and were now alienated by his purge of the more leftist elements in his cabinet in 1974; and bazaaris (small traditional businessmen, merchants, and artisans) and members of the "new" middle-class professions (teachers, doctors, clerical workers, university students, and other professionals) for whom Bhutto's political and economic reforms resulted in an increased sense of powerlessness and alienation.

While many in the middle class had been attracted by the PPP's 1970 election manifesto which promised modernization and the destruction of feudalism, the impact of many economic as well as political reforms hit the middle class hardest. Many believed that Bhutto's populist promise of "bread, clothing, and shelter" for all was being accomplished not through the breakup and redistribution of feudal interests but at the expense of the middle class. This seemed further confirmed after 1974 by Bhutto's policy shift away from his socialist platform and the inclusion within the PPP and Bhutto's administration of the very feudal landlords whose power he had earlier pledged to eliminate. Bhutto's political reforms had also meant tighter control by the PPP of government (administrative-bureaucratic) and district-level officials as primary emphasis was placed on party loyalty and connections rather than merit. Moreover, Bhutto's autocratic rule was reflected in a government that increasingly resorted to media censorship, the "policing" of its own Federal Security Force, political harassment, arrests, and imprisonment.

The middle-class nature of the PNA movement was reinforced by the presence and leadership of the religious parties whose traditional base of support has always come primarily from among the urban and town-based middle class. Mawlana Mawdudi's Jama'at-i-Islami was particularly important to the PNA both organizationally and ideologically. In his extensive writings on Islamic state, society, and law, Mawdudi offered an alternative vision, a coherent Islamic ideology, which rejected Westernization and maintained that Islam provided a political, economic, and social system for modern man. Not only a Mawdudi the most widely read religious writer among the educated classes in Pakistan but, through the translation and distribution of his works, his interpretation of Islam has become an integral part of the rhetoric and ideological statements of Islamic revivalism throughout the Muslim world.

The religious leadership (both in the political parties and ulama) had, from the start, rejected Bhutto's socialism as un-Islamic. Bhutto's personal lifestyle and his government were denounced as anti-Islamic. Bhutto's regime, they argued, had led to political and social corruption and the breakdown of law and order. In its place they called for national unity rooted in Pakistan's Islamic raison d'ê-tre in which Islamic brotherhood and solidarity would transcend regional, linguistic divisions. They emphasized that the only means to achieve this was a return to Islamic law, the Shari'ah, which provided the blueprint for a truly democratic, egalitarian society based upon Islamic social justice. The introduction of an Islamic system of government would avoid the extremes of corporate capitalism and state socialism, substitute Islamic values for their excessive materialism and secularism, support small industry and business interests, counter the corruption and spiritual malaise of the Bhutto years, and thus realize for the first time Pakistan's destiny as an Islamic state and society. The PNA election manifesto accordingly reflected the concerns of this religious and middle-class alliance.

In order to counter his Islamic opposition with its popular appeals to Islam, Bhutto and his PPP increasingly placed themselves under the banner of Islam. As their emphasis shifted toward Musawat-i-Muhammadi, their use of the term "socialism" had now receded into the background. The new PPP election manifesto included provisions which promised greater Islamization of society such as a commitment to center community life more firmly upon the Qur'an and to have Friday replace Sunday as the weekly holiday.

Thus, in the 1977 elections campaign, the lines of battle were drawn between a broad coalition of the religious parties and the middle class which supported the PNA and the new alliance of the upper and lower classes which supported Bhutto's PPP. Despite their appeals to Islam, however, the PNA clearly did not have the votes, and Bhutto and the PPP scored what appeared to be an impressive victory in the general elections of 7 March 1977. However, amidst charges of widespread poll irregularities, the PNA boycotted the provincial elections of 10 March and renewed their political action. The mosques of the country became the centers not only for Friday *jum'ah* (communal prayer) but also for political agitation. The *khutbah* (Friday sermons) concerned "Islamic politics," and a community gathered for prayer was easily transformed into a political rally and march. Responding to widespread disturbances, the Bhutto government imposed martial law and curfews. As PNA activities increased, Bhutto sought to diffuse their appeal by announcing further Islamization measures such as the prohibition of alcohol, gambling, and nightclubs. Implementation of these Islamic provisions and promises to introduce other Shari'ah laws served to reinforce the Islamic character of the conflict. Most importantly, a turning point had been reached. Islam and Pakistan's Islamic identity had reemerged as the dominant theme in Pakistani politics in a manner and to a degree that had not been seen since its establishment.

The Regime of Zia ul-Haq (1977–)

The anti-Bhutto movement came to an abrupt halt with the bloodless military coup d'etat which brought General Zia ul-Haq to power on 5 July 1977. As Chief Martial Law Administrator (CMLA) and President, Zia ul-Haq, from the inception of his regime, legitimated his coup and subsequent rule through demands for Nizam-i-Mustafa—the system of the Prophet—or, as it is more commonly called, Nizam-i-Islam—the system of Islam. Bhutto's downfall was progressively attributed to his unIslamic behavior and Zia declared his commitment to "transform the country's socio-economic and political structure in accordance with the principles of Islam."[18] Toward that end he took a number of steps. He reconstituted the Council of Islamic Ideology in 1977. Its membership of seventeen included two judges from the High Court or Supreme Court (sitting or retired), one of whom serves as Chairman, six ulama (four Sunni and two Shi'a), and one woman. Other members come from specialized fields such as law, economics, and banking. The scope of the Council was broadened so that it might serve as the President's chief advisory council recommending the best means for introducing a more Islamic system of government. In particular, three areas of immediate concern were targeted: the Islamic taxes *zakat* (almsgiving, the third pillar of Islam) and *ushr* (agricultural tax on productive land), a economy free of *riba* (interest), and an Islamic penal code.[19] Zia's military regime subsequently forged an alliance with the PNA. Some parties like the JUP refused to participate, while others, especially the JI and JUI, accepted the opportunity to advise and assist a government that had taken up the banner of Nizam-i-Islam. Individuals noted for their strong commitment to Islam and Nizam-i-Mustafa were appointed to such cabinet positions as the Ministries of Law, Religious Affairs, Information, and Production and Planning.

In December 1978, at the time of the Islamic New Year, the President proclaimed Pakistan's new beginning in an address entitled "Measures to Enforce Nizam-i-Islam." In addition to declaring the intention of his government to introduce reforms in the areas which were under study by the Council of Islamic Ideology, Zia announced the creation of Shari'ah Benches Courts to determine whether or not specific existing laws were repugnant to Islam. Finally, several months later, in February 1979, as Chief Martial Law Administrator, Zia formalized the commitment of his government to Nizam-i-Islam in a speech, and subsequently in his *Introduction to Islamic Laws*. Appealing to the traditional Islamic belief that Islam is a total way of life, he announced a series of reforms in worship and in the legal, economic, and educational system. Since that time Islamization has continued to be a prominent part of Pakistan's politics and life, and other Islamic measures and proposals affecting politics, law, the courts, economics, education and culture, and women have been introduced. We will examine the impact of Islamization in each of these areas.

The Political System

Politically, Islam has been used throughout Zia's rule as the source of legitimation. Although Zia promised elections within ninety days of his July 1977 coup, elections in Pakistan were postponed twice—in October 1977 and again in November 1979. The primary reason cited for the postponement and then cancellation of elections in 1979 and the outlawing of political parties was that Pakistan's political system was not Islamic. The Council of Islamic Ideology, a government-appointed body which includes religious leaders as well as experts in secular fields such as banking, economics, and law, ruled that, pending further recommendations of the Council, Pakistan was to continue under martial law without an elected president, national and provincial assemblies, and political parties. Pakistan, under Zia, sought a "new political system according to Islam."

These actions produced broad-based opposition including not only Bhutto supporters but also the PNA members who found themselves disenfranchised and their parties declared "defunct." All publicly denounced the continuation of what was originally to be a brief interim government and called for a restoration of the democratic process in Pakistan. Both secular and religiously oriented parties joined together in demanding elections. Even religious leaders like Mian Tufail Muhammad, successor to Mawlana Mawdudi as Amir of the Jama'at-i-Islami, emphasized that a military government is not Islamic. They argued that the Zia government could not claim to be an expression of Nizam-i-Islam since the head of an Islamic state should be chosen or elected by the people and is, himself, subject to the Shari'ah or sovereignty of God's rule. Zia ul-Haq was criticized for placing his rules and laws above the Shari'ah. Whereas the only norm guiding the Shari'ah Courts should be the Qur'an and Sunna, in fact, General Zia exempted his martial law regulations, taxation, and banking from the Court's purview. Moreover, he had declared that Shari'ah Court decisions in themselves could not delete or change an existing law; only the action of the CMLA, i.e., an ordinance issued by General Zia as Chief Martial Law Administrator, could do so.[20]

In June 1981 Zia reconstituted the Council of Islamic Ideology. The Council's first order of business was consideration of Pakistan's Islamic system of government, including the question of national elections. Council members agreed upon guidelines, among them:

1. According to Islam, *shura* (consultation) is essential in the affairs of state and is synonymous with people's participation.
2. Consultation in Islam has the following three aspects;
   a. Consultation in the affairs of state
   b. Consultation in the election of the head of state
   c. Consultation in the election of the *Majlis-i Shura* (Federal Advisory Council)
3. A presidential form of government is "nearer to Islam"
4. Elections are "not non-permissible" in Islam.

On 12 November 1981, as the Ideology Council was about to issue its recommendation regarding Pakistan's political system, General Zia requested that, in order to assure a broader base of consultation and input, the Council survey leading elements of society through a questionnaire. The Council formulated a series of questions concerned with the nature of an Islamic state: the qualifications, election, and term of office for the head of state; the role and powers of the Majlis-i-Shura; the role of political parties in Islam; and the voting franchise for women and minorities. This questionnaire was circulated to some 285 individuals and institutions, representing such constituencies as bar associations, women's groups, religious leaders, legal experts, government leaders and officers of the registered defunct political parties with a deadline of 31 January 1982. The questionnaire required written responses which the Islamic Ideology Council was to summarize and incorporate in their final report and recommendations. The net result of this process was to further delay elections and the implementation of an elected system of government.

In 1982, President Zia, without consulting the Ideology Council, appointed a Majlis-i-Shura, Federal Advisory Council, of 350 members to serve during this "transitional stage" until an elected national assembly was constituted. The stated purpose of the Majlis was to "create conditions in which the country could attain a democratic, Islamic polity,"[21] and its role was strictly advisory since only General Zia, as Chief Martial Law Administrator, can legislate. The four major concerns of the Council were: "(a) to help the government accelerate the process of Islamization; (b) to create conditions congenial for the establishment of Islamic democracy; (c) to apprise the government with its views on important international issues; (d) to assist the government in overcoming social and economic difficulties faced by the people."[22]

The Majlis began meeting in January 1982. Members came from a cross-section of Pakistani society, including members of the now defunct political parties as well as women and minorities. Most of those selected were not among Pakistan's more prominent political figures. Although others refused to cooperate with the government by accepting a seat, some used their new position to question both domestic and foreign policy.

However, the majority of the "defunct" political parties continued in opposition, organized in an alliance called the Movement for the Restoration of Democracy (MRD). Notable exceptions were the Jamaat-i-Islami and the Muslim League, who chose not to join. On August 12, 1983, Zia ul-Haq promised national and provincial legislative elections before March 1985; however, they were to be on a nonparty basis. The MRD mounted a protest movement but failed in a challenge which left many of its leaders in prison.

Law

Pakistan's law, which is called Anglo-Muhammadan Law and which evolved as a result of colonial rule, combines British and Islamic law. If Islamic law is to provide the blueprint for Muslim society, it is not surprising that a strong emphasis has been given to the introduction of Shari'ah law. Prior to Zia, the only major attempt at Islamic legal reform occurred in 1961 with the passage of the Muslim Family Laws Ordinance which introduced changes in marriage, divorce, and inheritance. Under martial law, further Islamic measures (affecting substantive law and the judiciary) were introduced. The 1973 Constitution was "augmented" by a series of martial law regulations, such as those which banned political parties and prohibited newspapers from political commentary and criticism. In effect, with the dissolution of the National Assembly, these martial law ordinances constituted the only legislation possible and thus Zia ul-Haq as CMLS was the sole lawmaker. Accordingly, Islamic laws were introduced through a series of proclamations in such areas as fasting, prayer, penal law, and economics.

Another area of legal reform affected the observance of Ramadan. Since the fast of Ramadan is one of the five pillars of Islam, public observance of Ramadan has always been expected in Pakistan. However, actual observance has varied significantly, subject to personal conscience and to peer pressure. Under the Zia government, the state assumed the power of public enforcement, and prosecutions have occurred. Public consumption of food or drink and smoking during Ramadan are punishable by a sentence of up to six months. In addition, dance and musical productions have also been curtailed during Ramadan.

Observance of Friday as the weekly holiday, instituted under Bhutto's government, continued in the Nizam of Zia, and ordinances were issued requiring that government workers be provided with the time and a suitable place to perform namaz (Islamic worship or prayer), salat (the five daily prayers required of Muslims, the second pillar of Islam). Companies which conduct business on Friday are required to close during the noon hour to permit workers to attend jum'ah prayers.

The most prominent and, at times, controversial area of legal reform has occurred in Pakistan's Penal Code, in particular, the imposition of *hudud* punishments (Qur'anically or prophetically prescribed punishments for certain crimes), for drinking, theft, *zina* (adultery), and *qazf* (false accusation), i.e., bearing false witness regarding sexual crimes. Instead of imprisonment and/or fines (as punishment) for *hudud* crimes, the amended penal code stipulates amputation of the hand for theft, *rajam* (stoning) for adultery, and flogging for fornication and drinking. However, the imposition of *hu-*

dud punishments by any court must be reviewed and confirmed by the Shari'ah Court and then given final approval by General Zia before being enforced.

Prior to 1977, sale and consumption of alcohol were permitted in private homes and in international hotels. In April 1977 Ali Bhutto, to counter his Islamic critics, prohibited the sale and consumption of alcohol by Pakistani Muslims and specified a sentence of six months and/or the fine of Rs. 5,000 ($500). The Zia government extended the prohibition of alcohol to include all Muslims, whether foreign-born or Pakistani. Non-Muslim Pakistanis are restricted in the amounts they may purchase. The consumption of alcohol by other non-Muslims in international hotels is limited to private areas and to hotels with a license. Moreover, under the Prohibition Order of 10 February 1979, drinking is liable to hudud or *tazir* (imprisonment for up to three years and/or flogging not to exceed thirty stripes) punishment. A Muslim found guilty of drinking intoxicants based upon his/her confession or the testimony of at least two adult male Muslim witnesses, who themselves have satisfied the court as to their *tazkiyah al-shuhood* (truthfulness) and their abstention from *kabir* (major sins), is subject to the *hudud* punishment of eighty stripes. If the above criteria are not met, but the court is satisfied that sufficient evidence exists for a guilty verdict, then the individual is liable to tazir punishment.

While public floggings for drinking violations and other hudud crimes have taken place, they have been curtailed due both to internal criticism as well as to adverse publicity in the international media. Amputations have been imposed by the court, but none has occurred since physicians have refused to perform them. A sharp controversy has surrounded the imposition of stoning for adultery. Although ordered by the courts, such verdicts were appealed to the Shari'ah Court, and, in a surprising decision, the Court, by a vote of four to one, ruled that *rajam* is repugnant to Islam. The majority based their decision on the fact that the punishment of stoning is not to be found in the Qur'an. The government appealed the decision to the Supreme Court, and, in addition, reorganized the Shari'ah Court to include three ulama among its members and expanded its jurisdiction so that the Court can review its previous decisions. Subsequently, the Federal Shari'ah Court did reverse itself with conservative members arguing that *rajam*, although not based on a Qur'anic text, is rooted in Prophetic tradition. Defenders of this provision argue that such a severe punishment will serve to deter the most blatant violations of public morality and that normally conviction will be rare since Islamic law requires four eye witnesses to the act itself.

What has proven to be especially significant with regard to enforcement to *hudud* penalties is the tendency of the government to emphasize that certain Islamic provisions presume the existence of a socially just society before they can be implemented. President Zia has increasingly used this argument as a rationale for his resistance to specific demands from more conservative religious leaders. A similar line of thinking has been advocated by heads of the Federal Shari'ah Court and the Islamic Ideology Council.[23]

Shari'ah Courts

In 1978 the government announced the creation of Shari'ah Benches or Courts. Pakistan's Shari'ah Courts are essentially courts which determine whether or not a specific law is contrary to the Shari'ah. This was heralded by the government as a major step in the Islamization of Pakistan's legal system. Five Shari'ah Benches were constituted[24]: one at the High Court in each of Pakistan's four provinces (Lahore, Peshawar, Karachi, and Quetta) and an Appellate Shari'ah Bench at the Supreme Court in Islamabad. Each Shari'ah Bench consisted of three justices from the court. The court's jurisdiction included the review of petitions from individuals or the federal or provincial governments which challenged any law as repugnant to Islam, i.e., the injunctions of Islam as found in the Qur'an and Sunna. However, the court was barred from reviewing laws in three areas (the constitution and martial law ordinances, family law, and fiscal law) for a period of three years. Shari'ah Bench decisions could be appealed to the Appellate Shari'ah Bench of the Supreme Court. Laws or provisions found to be un-Islamic are to be amended through legislative action taken by General Zia ul-Haq.

In late May 1980 the four Shari'ah Benches of the High Court were reorganized and centralized into the Federal Shari'ah Court.[25] From its seat in the capital, Islamabad, the Court travels as a circuit court to each of the provinces to hear petitions.

Significantly, the membership of the Shari'ah Court has been changed from an ad hoc panel consisting of three provincial High Court Justices constituted for each Shari'ah-related case to a single fixed federal panel of eight judges—five of whom must be Justices (sitting or retired) and three of whom must be ulama whose primary qualification is as an alim (religious scholar) and not as a lawyer or judge. Prior to this, the ulama served only as advisers to the court. On the positive side, the reconstitution of the Shari'ah Court assures that Shari'ah judges are men who are more qualified in Islamic law and also that their interpretations are more centralized and thus consistent. On the negative side, the court now consisted of a fixed panel of judges, all of whom have been appointed by Zia ul-Haq. Although their decisions remain subject to appeal to the Appellate Shari'ah Bench of the supreme Court, final authority continued to rest with General Zia.

Since their inception the Shari'ah Courts have reviewed a broad spectrum of suits ranging from challenges to the legitimacy of Pakistan's Constitution and law to the acceptability of cinema, from the stoning of adulterers to government-enforced land reform. The Court has also continued the work of the Islamic Ideology Council in reviewing all of Pakistan's legal codes to identify and rectify those aspects or provisions that are un-Islamic. It is important to note that Islamization of law is not seen as totally replacing Pakistan's Anglo-Muhammadan legal system with classical Islamic law or developing a new system but rather surging its current system of un-Islamic provisions.

The introduction of Shari'ah Courts and Shari'ah laws has had an impact on the legal profession. Many are resistant to what they see as a retrogressive step. Moreover, because Shari'ah law had not been part of their legal education, many judges and lawyers are at a disadvantage. This was especially true under the earlier Shari'ah Court system in which a court was constituted from High Court judges regardless of their familiarity with Shari'ah law. Thus, there is a necessity to rely upon outside experts, in particular, the ulama whose interpretation of Islamic law tends to be less flexible. The current Federal Shari'ah Court system does include ulama as judges. In addition, law schools have added an extra year of Shari'ah law to their curriculum and the government has established a Shari'ah College. The latter began in October 1979 as a separate faculty of the Quaid-i Azam University (formerly Islamabad University) and in November 1980 became part of a new institution—the Islamic University.

Other changes have subsequently been made in the judiciary: the introduction of *qazi* (religious judges) courts and the creation of the office of *Muhtasib-i A'la* (Office of Ombudsman). A bill (Qazi Courts Ordinance, 1983) establishing qazi courts was passed on 20 February 1983 by the Majlis-i Shura. Qazi courts hear cases concerned with Islamic law at the local level, a further step toward an

Islamic system of justice. Since qazis apply Islamic law, many of these judges are recruited from the madrasahs, from the ulama, and from the graduates of the Islamic University. As with the Shari'ah Courts, critics of the qazi system include the legal profession (the Bar Council, for example, at its convention in September 1982 rejected the Qazi Courts Ordinance[26]) as well as certain women's organizations. Unlike the traditional Islamic institution or office of *muhtasib* (supervisor of public behavior and morality), the Muhtasib-i A'la serves in a more restricted capacity as an ombudsman who investigates charges of maladministration against government ministers, agencies, and corporations.[27]

Economics

Under an Islamic system of government, religion is integral to economics as well as politics and law. Islamic thought provided guidelines in the past for taxation, banking, land ownership, rent, and income distribution.[28] Therefore, Muslim revivalists in Pakistan as well as other Muslim countries assert the need to Islamize the state's economic system in order to counter major social problems such as corruption and the concentration of wealth and to create a socially just society.[29] To achieve such goals, the ulama in Pakistan have supported measures to abolish interest and to introduce zakat.[30]

Islamic economic measures have formed an integral part of Zia's Islamization program and affect questions of private property, taxation (zakat and ushr), and interest (riba). In response to the financial concerns of industrialists and landowners and the objections of religious leaders to the Bhutto government's socialism whether Western or Islamic, both Zia and the Shari'ah Courts have reaffirmed the right to private property as the Islamic norm. However, the Shari'ah courts have upheld previous land reform and nationalization measures under the governments of Ayub Khan and Ali Bhutto, citing in their decisions Islamic teaching that all land belongs to God and that the right of private property is limited by the demands of social justice.

The introduction of zakat and ushr as well as the establishment of interest-free banking have been the more substantive and controversial measures. Zakat was announced in February 1979, and a Zakat Fund was created with substantial financial assistance from Saudi Arabia and the United Arab Emirates. A multitiered elected administrative system extending from the Central Zakat Administration to councils at the district (65), subdistrict (285, tesil), and rural (32,000) levels was set up to collect and distribute zakat. A wealth tax of 2-1/2 percent was to be levied on income and assets in excess of Rs. 2,000 ($200) and deducted at the end of Ramadan. Zakat was to be deducted directly at the source, i.e., directly from bank savings accounts and other financial assets such as investment shares, annuities and insurance. In its first year Rs. 860 million ($86 million) was collected.

Ushr, the agricultural tax on productive land, announced by the government but delayed, was finally instituted in May 1983. Although traditional law distinguished between the produce from unirrigated (barani) lands, taxed at 10 percent, and canal-irrigated lands, taxed at 5 percent, the ushr has been uniformly set at 5 percent.[31] The tax, while compulsory, is paid voluntarily. Zakat Committees, which have been renamed Zakat and Ushr Committees, monitor compliance by randomly sampling the landowners in their districts.

Implementation of zakat and ushr, however, has encountered a number of difficulties. One problem arose when the first deductions took place without warning and was announced after the fact. On 20 June 1980 President Zia at the Friday prayer in Islamabad promulgated the zakat and ushr ordinance, and that evening on television the Administrator General of the Zakat Fund notified the nation that banks would be closed the following day in order to deduct the zakat from accounts. This action exacerbated a climate of apprehension and distrust that already existed. It also created injustices. For example, those who borrowed money and placed it briefly in their savings account one day discovered on the next that they had lost 2-1/2 percent of their loan.

A second major problem occurred when the Shi'a community objected vociferously to the zakat order. According to the Shi'a school of legal thought (Ja'fari fiqh), zakat is not compulsory on capital and trading money, thus differing with Hanafi-based sunni prescriptions. In July 1980 some 15,000 Shi'a marched in a demonstration in Rawalpindi against compulsory zakat. Violence and bloodshed ensued. After a prominent Shi'a alim resigned from the Council of Islamic Ideology, a special subcommittee of ulama (three Sunni and three Shi'a) was established to iron out the differences. The government finally responded, and current legislation permits a Muslim to file for an exemption by stating that zakat is not enjoined by his "faith and fiqh."

A third criticism of zakat and ushr measures has come from various quarters. Some Muslims resent the government's taking over what is regarded as one's private obligation before God to look after needy family and friends. The current system is perceived as the government's bureaucratization of a personal, charitable duty and as now subject to mismanagement and misappropriation. Religious leaders also find fault with the government for not implementing zakat and ushr immediately and in their entirety. They and others point out that this partial approach has favored the wealthy— businessmen who do not pay zakat on hidden assets (business inventory) and landowners who have thus far avoided the ushr—and resulted in collection of only one quarter of the estimated revenue.[32] Thus, the needy are often denied adequate assistance, sometimes receiving no more than Rs. 40 rupees ($4.00).

Of the Islamic economic changes the most potentially far-reaching was the abolition of interest. Early in his administration Zia ul-Haq committed himself to the abolition of the "curse of interest."[33] The Council of Islamic Ideology established a Panel of Experts in Economics and Banking with whom it worked closely, and in June 1980 the Council issued its 127-page report advocating a gradual approach to the Islamization of Pakistan's economy with implementation of three stages over a three-year period,[34] culminating in the elimination of interest from all domestic financial transactions. By 1 January 1982 "banks would cease to accept fresh deposits on the basis of interest and would instead accept deposits on a profit/loss sharing basis. Interbank transactions would also be brought under a profit/loss sharing system. The State Bank would abandon the system of providing finance to banks and other financial institutions on the basis of interest."[35]

This timetable was not met. However, a number of economic reforms were implemented. In January 1981 interest-free banking accounts were introduced on a voluntary basis in all (7,000) branches of Pakistan's commercial banks, all of which are nationalized. The system, called profit/loss sharing (PLS), is based upon traditional Islamic banking institutions. Under PLS the depositor and the bank enter into a partnership in which both share in the profit or losses. Money is invested in a selective portfolio, some of which consists of government-owned companies which are secure and known to be profitable. The PLS system is optional and applicable to savings and fixed deposit (time deposit) accounts. By the end of the first year approximately 25 percent of the total number of accounts operated on a PLS basis and they have continued to return a profit which has exceeded interest-bearing accounts.

Three additional government institutions have also been

placed on an interest-free basis: the House Building Finance Corporation (HBFC), the National Investment Trust (NIT), and the Investment Corporation of Pakistan (ICP). The House Building Finance Corporation provides mortgages for lower-and middle-class people to build and/or purchase houses or apartments. Under the current system the HBFC and the individual enter into a "joint investment," not an interest-bearing mortgage or loan. The National Investment Trust and the Investment Corporation of Pakistan both issue government-backed mutual funds. Money from the purchased units or certificates is used by the investment corporation to purchase shares in companies. Profits (dividends from purchased stocks or moneys from the appreciation of purchased stocks) are shared by the holding company and the investors. Likewise both the corporations (NIT and ICP) and the investors share in any losses. The ICP also functions as a brokerage house providing a network of branch offices for the purchase of other stocks. In addition, clients can borrow funds from ICP for investments. This service is provided on a noninterest, "participation" basis. If, for example, an individual has 40 percent of the needed capital and ICP provides the additional 60 percent, the distribution of profits is in reverse proportion. While this percentage favors the individuals, the same allocations also pertain to losses.

However, total change in the economy has proven more difficult than the implementation of individual economic measures. Indeed, the Council of Islamic Ideology has again reiterated its call for the complete and immediate elimination of interest from the economy. And as early as May 1980 a special Committee on Islamization appointed by the Finance Minister had cautioned in its report "An Agenda for Islamic Economic Reform" that "the Islamic rejection of interest is in effect a rejection of the entire capitalistic system: an interest-free economy is in fact an exploitation-free economy."[36] The Committee stressed that the abolition of interest must be part of a far more comprehensive and complex process, the development of a complete economic system without which an interest-free economy would neither be possible nor effective:

> The abolition of interest is part of a fundamental restructuring of the whole spectrum of production, consumption and distribution relationships on the Islamic lines. However, the search for such a system must be gradual to let the interaction between theory and practice . . . produce an economic system which corresponds to the overall vision of an Islamic economic system.[37]

Zia ul-Haq's government has not adopted this more comprehensive outlook. Instead, it continues to advocate and pursue a more fragmented, ad hoc, gradualist policy of Islamic economic reform which tends to satisfy no one. Perhaps to blunt some of its critics, in March 1983 the government hosted its Second International Conference on Islamic Economics. In his inaugural address President Zia ul-Haq announced the establishment of an International Center for Islamic Economics to be located at the Islamic University and headed by Professor Khurshid Ahmad, former Minister of Planning and Development in Zia's early coalition with the PNA, a long-time leader in the Jama'at-i Islami, and an authority on Islamic economics. In July 1985 the Pakistan government announced the abolition of interest on all banking accounts.

Education

Education and cultural reforms constitute a crucial part of Zia ul-Haq's Islamization program. Throughout government literature on Islamization, in the statements and ordinances promulgated by Zia ul-Haq, the Ideology Council, and the Shari'ah Courts, or in reports by special committees such as the Panel on Islamic Economics and Banking, the importance of Islamizing society and of an Islamic outlook and attitude is stressed so as to promote awareness, appreciation, and compliance with Islamic measures. A series of changes, real and symbolic, have been introduced to underscore the government's commitment to strengthen Pakistan's national identity through a reaffirmation of its Islamic-Pakistani identity—to produce what Zia has called "a new generation wedded to the ideology of Pakistan and Islam." This ever-burgeoning number of regulations and programs involves areas ranging from language and dress to mass media and education.

Urdu replaced English as the medium of instruction in schools and assumed a more prominent place in public life (government and media) as Pakistan's national language. Virtually all television and radio programs broadcast in Urdu. General Zia called upon all Pakistanis to wear national attire during working hours. Civil servants, university professors, and businessmen were asked to trade their suits for traditional, national attire. While there was initial compliance, especially in government offices and schools, there was also widespread resistance. To counter some objections, it was even suggested that the wearing of regional dress alternate with national dress. Increased emphasis on Pakistani-Islamic identity and fraternal ties with Arab-Muslim countries has resulted in an increased emphasis on the use of Arabic in education and the renaming of cities, streets, and public facilities. For example, the city of Lyallpur is now Faisalbad, Islamabad University became Quaid-i Azam University.

In the mass media—radio, television, and print—programs on national and/or Islamic history and culture were prominent. At the same time, censorship of movies and television commercials and restrictions on coverage of "un-Islamic" activities increased sharply. Ironically, the emphasis on both Islamic and Pakistani identity has sometimes led to contradictions. For example, more traditional religious leaders have attacked public performances and media coverage of national dance and music programs as un-Islamic.

Islamization of the informal means of education has been accompanied by reforms in Pakistan's formal educational system as well. *Islamiyyat* (Islamic studies) courses are required at the university level as well as preuniversity education. The Department of Education has for several years been engaged in reviewing curricula and textbooks both to eliminate un-Islamic materials as well as to revise and develop curricula and books that foster Islamic-Pakistani values. A 1982 government-sponsored conference on "Islamization of Knowledge" attended by government ministers, Pakistani intellectuals, educators, and religious leaders, as well as Muslim leaders from abroad sought to lay the groundwork for a program to Islamize Pakistan's system of education—its methods and content. However, substantive change has not yet occurred. Moreover, in addition to alienating those Muslims who resent such regulations as required Islamic studies courses, religious minorities have pressed for their own required courses.

No single institution better symbolizes the Islamization of education than the Islamic University in Islamabad, established in 1980. The university combined the Shari'ah College, which was founded in 1978 at the Quaid-i-Azam University in Islamabad, the Islamic Research Institute, which has existed since 1962, and several new institutes on education and Islamic history. These institutes and their curricula reflect the religious and cultural concerns of the Zia administration. "Islam enjoins upon the *Ummah* [Islamic community] to establish a just and humane world order," Zia's Ordinance establishing the university states. "The purpose of education is to produce people who are imbued with Islamic learning and character and capable of meeting economic, social, political, technological, physical, intellectual and aesthetic needs of the society."[38] The university should thus seek to fuse Pakistan's dual or parallel systems of secular and religious learning "so as to provide an Islamic vision for those engaged in education and to enable them to reconstruct human thought in all its forms on the foundations of Islam."[39]

The Islamic University began to function in 1981, and approximately 250 students are enrolled. The teaching staff includes scholars from other Muslim countries (especially Egypt, Jordan, and Saudi Arabia), many trained at Islamic institutions such as al-Azhar and Medina Universities. The university consists of three faculties and related institutes: Faculties of Usul al-Din (Religion), of Shari'ah (Islamic Law), and of Social Sciences (Economics), plus the Islamic Research Institute, Institute for Training in Shari'ah, and the Institutes of Islamic History, Culture, and Civilization, and of Education.

The faculties of the Islamic University train teachers and *imams* (prayer leaders) for the mosques and judges for the new qazi courts. The curriculum is designed to combine Western education with the traditional Indo-Muslim system of madrasahs. To accomplish this, the usual two-year course of study for a degree has been extended to four years. The first year is devoted to an intensive study of Arabic and English to enable students to work with Islamic as well as Western sources. Interestingly, this approach sharply contrasts with other universities whose medium of instruction has been changed from English to Urdu. After the basic first year, students at Islamic University devote three years to the study of traditional subjects such as *Qur'an qirat* (Qur'an recitation), hadith (sacred traditions of Islam), and fiqh (Islamic jurisprudence), and modern disciplines such as economics and sociology.

The Institute for Shari'ah Training has a twofold purpose. As the major training center in Shari'ah law, it offers a post-graduate degree (LLM) in Islamic law, and it conducts three-month training seminars in Islamic law for judges, lawyers, and police officials. The Islamic Research Institute mentioned earlier in this study has been incorporated within the university with no change in its functions. The Institutes of Education and Islamic History have only recently been initiated.

Women

Islamization has focused attention on the status and role of women in Pakistan. It has caused increased apprehension among professional women who fear that government policies and the increasingly vocal protestations of the mullahs (religious leaders) will mean increased restrictions and loss of any gains made thus far. To express their various concerns about the impact of Islamization on the status of women in a Muslim society, they have formed such groups as the Women's Action Forum in Karachi. Viewed by conservatives as simply a small Westernized elite, these women continue to organize conferences and speak and write about women's issues. They see increased emphasis on national dress and covering the head (with a veil or scarf) as symbolizing a reinforcement of traditional regressive attitudes and customs toward women which rendered them second-class citizens. Many are quick to argue that while veiling and seclusion are not truly Islamic, they have been the practiced norm in Pakistani society where *purdah* (seclusion or separation of the sexes) as well as the wearing of the *burqa* or *chador* (veil) have been very much in practice, and where sexes used to be separated in buses, banks, educational institutions, and many offices. The strength of the "purdah mentality" (regarding women's modesty) among lower and middle classes is witnessed by the wide debate in the newspapers as to whether a sari is Islamic, by incidents in which women with uncovered heads have been reprimanded, even accosted in public, and by a popular television teacher/preacher's refusal to permit women in his television audience.[40] This latter event was especially troublesome since women activists had considered this lecturer to be moderate in his Islamic teachings, and his audiences had heretofore been mixed. His new posture increased fears that the Zia regime was allowing a far more pervasive phenomenon to surface. In this regard women have pointed to the *fatwa* (formal legal opinion) by Mawlana Noorani, leader of the JUP, declaring that women may not hold political office, and to the government's decision to restrict Pakistan's women's hockey team from playing before mixed audiences. Moreover, the example of the postrevolutionary Iranian Islamic government's actions regarding women's status—from dress to employment to the repeal of the Family Protection Act with its reforms in marriage, divorce, and inheritance—have reinforced women's fears that Pakistan's mullahs will push the government along a similar path. Conservative mullahs have become increasingly vociferous in matters relating to women and, among other things, have in their public mosque and media statements called for the repeal of Pakistan's Muslim Family Laws Ordinance of 1961, separation of the sexes in society and wearing of the chador. The government-appointed and -supported Council of Islamic Ideology itself found that three provisions in the Family Laws Ordinance were un-Islamic and had recommended their repeal;[41] the three provisions required a male to obtain permission to contract a polygamous marriage or to divorce his wife and granted inheritance rights to orphaned grandchildren. General Zia, seeking to reassure women activists, indicated that he would approve only the repeal of the inheritance provisions. Women objected to this compromise, and the mullahs viewed it as a total capitulation.[42]

Women find three other causes for continued concern—the creation of separate women's universities, the introduction of qazi courts, and the revision of the Laws of Evidence Act. Women's universities are viewed as acquiescing to religious pressures for separation of the sexes. Women fear that this will lend credibility to the belief that Islam requires such separation of the sexes and will, in the long run, spread to other educational institutions. Indeed, women were originally excluded from the Islamic University. Although finally admitted to the university, they are educated in separate facilities. Thus, many women find reason for their concern that Islamic education will be equated with separation of the sexes. In addition, degrees from new women's universities could make their credentials less competitive with those of males from established universities.

The establishment of qazi courts involves reconstituting religious courts manned by judges drawn from the ulama. Given the conservative character of the majority of the ulama and their tendency to simply turn to the world view of classical Islamic jurisprudence, with a minimal recognition of the need for reinterpretation, women anticipate serious difficulties. For many women the revision of Pakistan's Evidence Act in 1983 confirmed their worst fears. The draft submitted by the Islamic Ideology Council and supported by the vast majority of religious leaders advocated the implementation of the traditional legal viewpoint that the evidence of two women equals that of one Muslim male. The law enacted in 1984 was a modified version which equates the evidence to two women to one Muslim man in specified cases in particular those relating to financial matters. This legal position is based upon Qur'anic teaching and traditional patriarchal practice whereby men bear the ultimate duty and responsibility for the support and finances of the family. This same outlook informed the 1984 version of the law governing compensation or *dija* (blood money) in which compensation for the death or injury of a Muslim man exceeds that for women.

CONCLUSION

On December 29, 1984 Zia called for a surprise referendum on his Islamization program. Despite an opposition boycott and amidst charges of election irregularities, an overwhelming majority voted approval of the referendum: "To approve policies to conform the nation's laws with Islam and the peaceful transition of power to elected representatives." Zia interpreted the result as a mandate to continue as president for a five-year term. In December 1985, Zia officially lifted martial law as a first step towards the restoration of civilian rule. National elections were held on February 25, 1985, followed by provincial assembly elections (February 28) on a nonparty basis. Although the MRD again boycotted the election, more than fifty percent of the voters turned out to vote for independent candidates and members of the Jamaat-i-Islami and the Muslim League who ran as individual (nonparty) candidates.

The return to civilian government has not brought stability. The MRD has continued in its opposition and more recently (April 1986) Benazir Bhutto, the daughter of Zulfiqar Ali Bhutto, has returned to Pakistan also calling for new elections. Zia and the military have not missed the message inherent in the unusually large crowds that have greeted Benazir Bhutto, many of whom are there to voice opposition to Zia's rule rather than support for Bhutto. This pressure has increased the government's tendency, since late 1984, to emphasize its commitment to civilian rule and to moderate its Islamic rhetoric and Islamization programs.

Islamization in Pakistan has traveled a rocky road. When Zia ul-Haq assumed power in July 1977, both because of his own religious belief and because of the climate of Pakistani politics, he committed his regime to the implementation and enforcement of an Islamic system of government to legitimate his rule and to provide a basis for national identity and unity. Greeted with skepticism by some and with enthusiasm by many, the process thus far has progressively led to frustration, disillusionment, and opposition.

The political expectations and aspirations of both secularists and religious factions have been thwarted. Not only was Bhutto's PPP dethroned and cast into the role of opposition party, but the PNA parties quickly discovered that they had won a Pyrrhic victory. National and provincial elections were postponed in 1977 as rule by martial law was extended, and within two years the PNA, like all political parties, was banned. All this had been done in the name of the very Islamic order that the PNA had advocated and fought for.

Perhaps the most fundamental questions which have arisen from Pakistan's recent experiment in Islamization are: "Whose Islam?" and "Why a negative Islam?"

Religious leaders, who initially applauded and supported the government's commitment to the establishment of an Islamic system of government, have, in particular, become increasingly disillusioned. Participation in the government has given way to opposition. Many are critical of the slow pace of Islamization. They had expected and demanded full and immediate implementation of Islamic measures such as zakat, ushr, and interest-free banking.[43] What they deemed a one-year process in 1977 when Zia came to power is still incomplete. Of equal importance, Zia ul-Haq, and not the ulama nor the religious parties JI, JUI, and JUP, has ultimately been the final interpreter of Islam. Islamic regulations have but one source—Zia ul-Haq—and even the Shari'ah Court's authority is circumscribed by the executive. Zia's martial law regulations are not subject to its jurisdiction, and Zia must endorse the Court's decisions before they can take effect.

Broader criticism from many quarters focuses on what is often described as the government's manipulation of Islam to postpone elections and outlaw political parties. The creation of the Federal Advisory Council and its Islamic designation as a Majlis-i Shura have not allayed critics who charge that such steps are not Islamic but another tactic to delay elections. Many religious leaders point out that military rule cannot be defined as Islamic government and that even the elected head of an Islamic state does not have the right to appoint a majlis whose members should be elected. Although they welcomed the overthrow of Bhutto by Zia ul-Haq, religious leaders joined with other segments of the population in demanding free elections. Whatever the meaning of Islamic democracy, elections and representative government were called for by all.

"Whose Islam?" is for many tied to a related question: "Why a negative Islam?" The Islam which Zia ul-Haq's regime has implemented is criticized as simply one of restrictions, *hudud* punishments, taxation, and political control. This quandary underscores a dual problem that has confronted Pakistan (and many other Muslim countries) throughout its existence: inability to agree on the content of Islamic belief and the need for reinterpretation and/or reform. Pakistanis have found it easier to rally under the umbrella of Islam in opposition movements, e.g., against British and Hindu rule or, more recently, against the Bhutto regime, than to agree upon what Islam and an Islamic state are.

An early and still important example of this difficulty is reflected in the Munir Report of 1954. In 1953 anti-Ahmadiyah riots
swept the Punjab Province. In their wake the government appointed
a Commission of Inquiry headed by Justice Muhammad Munir. After
extensive hearings and testimony, the Commission Report, commonly referred to as the Munir Report, drew several conclusions
which continue to be true today. While the ulama could agree that
the Ahmadiyah were not Muslims, they were unable to reach any
agreement among themselves on such basic questions as who is a
Muslim, or what is the nature of an Islamic state. Ominously, the
Report concluded:

> Nothing but a bold orientation of Islam to separate the vital from the
> lifeless can preserve it as a World Idea and convert the *Musalman*
> into a citizen of the present and the future world from the archaic
> incongruity that he is today. It is this lack of bold and clear thinking,
> the inability to understand and make decisions, which has brought
> about in Pakistan a confusion which will persist and repeatedly cre-
> ate situations of the kind we have been inquiring into until our lead-
> ers have a clear conceptions of the goal and of the means to reach
> it.[44]

Zia ul-Haq's interpretation and application of Nizam-i-Islam
have neither won popular support nor inspired national unity. Yet he
remains in power and Islamization of state and society has for many
years served as the regime's ideological commitment and goal. This
may be attributed not only to his political skills and the strength of
the military but also to a lack of an acceptable alternative.[45] This has
been especially true for the religious establishment and the majority
of middle-class interests for whom a return of the PPP represents a
real danger. More broadly, some believed that ending military rule
and holding elections would almost certainly lead to political chaos.
Fear of political instability was heightened by the Soviet presence in
Afghanistan. Against this backdrop Zia ul-Haq has thus far skillfully
managed the diverse political and social forces in Pakistan.

For the military elite Islamization provided the rationale for
their continued rule at the national and provincial levels, holding key
positions in the government and related institutions and agencies.
For the middle levels of the military, appeals to Islam were effective
because of their less Westernized, more traditional social backgrounds.

The civilian bureaucracy has learned to survive many governments and retain its control of the state's management. While some Islamic measures have proved annoying for some, civilian bureaucrats remain the backbone of day-to-day government, secure in their positions under a government whose Islamization policy has not substantially altered the sociopolitical realities of Pakistani life. Similarly, for most businessmen and landowners, Islamization has not posed a direct threat to their interests. The government has repeatedly endorsed Islam's recognition of private property and eschewed socialist measures or further nationalization.

While some religious leaders criticize Zia for moving too slowly or for his political controls in the name of Islam, Zia's regime continues to enjoy the ambivalent, if not reluctant, support of the ulama. The current government still provides an Islamic as opposed to a socialist (PPP) or secularist alternative. Zia is personally devout, he espouses their ideological commitment, he continues to consult with religious leaders in implementing Islamic measures and institutions such as the qazi courts, and he often supports their Islamic programs and conferences. Most ulama thus do not see a better Islamic alternative to the Zia regime.

The current Islamization program has also exacerbated problems of religious sectarianism—both between Sunni and Shi'a as well as among Sunni Muslims themselves—and their ability to split society. Although no statistics are kept, the Shi'a constitute perhaps 25 percent of the population,[46] in a largely Sunni nation. Historically, religious differences have resulted in clashes between the two communities. Zia's introduction of Islamic measures like zakat, ushr, and *hudud* punishments aroused the Shi'ite community who complained that their *madhhab* (school of traditional legal thought), namely, Ja'fari fiqh, differed in its prescriptions from the Hanafi-based Sunni fiqh. Thus, for the Shi'a, Islamization did not simply mean the implementation of Islamic law in their lives but of Sunni Hanafi law in particular. As noted earlier, Shi'a demonstrations in 1980 against zakat led to violence and bloodshed. Although the government amended the zakat ordinance to exempt anyone who believes compulsory deduction of zakat is against his madhhab, tensions continue between Sunni and Shi'a over a variety of issues. In early March 1983 there were several clashes in Karachi over the construction of a Shi'a center in a Sunni neighborhood. A mob set fire to the center and allegedly desecrated a Qur'an, a number of people were killed, and Sunni organizations called for the expulsion of the Iranian Consul General for his involvement.

Of equal significance are the often overlooked religious differences among Sunni Muslims. Pakistani Sunni Muslims distinguish themselves into sects according to their school: Deobandi, Brelevi, Wahhabi, Ahl al-Hadith, and so forth. Accompanying the resurgence of Islam in Pakistan and the greater emphasis on its Islamic character has been a proliferation of religious literature, much of which emphasizes these various Sunni sectarian differences in belief and practice. In February 1983 provincial governments were directed to prohibit mosque sermons "against the faith of one sect or the other."[47] These differences, coupled with the lack of hierarchical structure in Sunni Islam and the long-standing personal rivalry among Sunni ulama, have been a major factor in the failure of religious groups to unite.

Perhaps the most important desideratum for Islamic reform continues to be education. Islamization "from above" is a risky proposition unless accompanied by Islamization "from below." Effective change cannot simply be mandated or legislated. Societal acceptance is based both upon involvement through representation in the process of change and upon understanding, attitudes, and values. Islamic revivalists have thus emphasized (1) dawah ("call" to Islam, missionary activity) of the Muslim populace as much as conversion of non-Muslims, and (2) Islamization of education.

Muslims not only in Pakistan but in other areas of the Muslim world stress that the primary, immediate task is the creation of an Islamic society. Only then can an Islamic government or political order be successful. However, whether the growing emphasis on educational reform and the Islamization of education will reinforce a conservative fundamentalism or foster a mere reformist outlook and approach is a critical question.

Discussions of tradition and modernization in Muslim societies often distort reality by positing an absolute dichotomy between "worldly wise" modern educated elites and "tradition-bound" ulama. In fact, both share a common political and socioeconomic milieu and thus will often agree upon major political and social issues. However, because of their differences in training and outlook, common views regarding the problems of society and the means of bringing about a change in government give way to sharp differences of opinion as to what should be the actual content of reforms. Therefore, in fulfilling the first objective of dawah in educational reform either modern secular and traditional religious education must be fused or each must broaden its curriculum—the modern secular to include more Islamiyyat courses, and the madrasahs more education in modern disciplines.[48] The second, and perhaps most important, objective—the Islamization of education—requires a fuller awareness and deeper appreciation of the dynamic, synthetic, creative character of early Islamic history and the process of Islamization. Only then will the duality of education with its "separate" mentalities or communities—traditional religious versus modern secular—be overcome through the formation of a generation of citizens who, despite differences, share a common sense of and pride in their history and identity. For a Muslim community for whom Islamic history and tradition are so normative, such an appreciation would provide a rationale for an openness to substantive change.[49] Islamization would be understood as an outlook on life as much as specific prescriptions.

However, what will the nature of that Islamization be? Will it tend to return to the past in order to impose its regulations and practices uncritically upon the present, or will it be a return to the sources of Islam in order to distinguish between original revealed sources and historically developed forms and, thus, to reapply the Shari'ah to the changing needs of Muslim society? Will Islamization seek to repeat a past process characterized by adaptation and change, or will it repeat not the process itself but the particular historical forms or products of that process?

The dimensions of the problem of Islamization may be understood in terms of classical Islamic categories: taqlid-ijtihad, Shari'ah-fiqh. For the vast majority of Muslims in Pakistan, taqlid (following or imitation of tradition) continues to be the norm. However, this problem is more subtle than simply the pursuit of taqlid and rejection of ijtihad (individual reasoning or interpretation). In addition to the predominance of strong conservative elements, there are those who, despite their theoretical acceptance of ijtihad, continue to labor with a "taqlid mentality" or outlook. When faced with most specific, practical questions, they instinctively rely upon the medieval fiqh (law) manuals rather than undertaking a fresh interpretation in light of revealed sources. This attitude can be seen in a host of disputes regarding which items are subject to zakat and ushr, at which specific bodily point should the hand be amputated, what the status and role of women should be in Muslim society, or how an Islamic economic system can be implemented. For many, fiqh continues to be equated with Shari'ah, in practice if not in theory. More often than not, there is little practical acceptance of the relativity of many man-made regulations in the legal manuals. The insistence of Muslim reformers on the need to distinguish between eternal, immutable Shari'ah principles and values which are rooted in the Qur'an and Sunna of the Prophet, on the one hand, and their understanding, interpretation, and application in time and space which were embodied in fiqh during the formative period of Islam, on the other hand, has too often had little impact. Laws and regulations which were conditioned by their sociohistorical milieu are not seen as changeable forms but rather as immutable prescriptions. Islamic law is not seen as a blueprint based upon and inspired by revelation and then developed and designed to meet the needs of a specific time and place. Rather, the corpus of law, as preserved in legal manuals, is often treated as if it were itself revealed.

In light of the above attitudes, education becomes critical. Real change cannot simply be decreed or legislated. Effective implementation of change depends upon acceptance and internalization by the community—the majority of the population and its religious leadership, the ulama and mullahs who remain crucial actors in the process of change. In order to overcome the current bifurcation in Muslim society, caused by Pakistan's dual (madrasah and modern) educational program, and to restore a greater awareness of the dynamic, creative nature of Islamic history and the process of Islamization as practiced in the past, educational reforms are of primary importance. Only then will needed changes come to be appreciated and seen as Islamically acceptable and not simply dismissed as an aping of the West.

During the last decade Islam became a dominant theme in Pakistan's politics, ranging from agitational politics to the establishment of new political, legal, and economic institutions. If Islamization of politics and society is a desired goal for many Muslims, the Pakistani experience provides some measure of both the possibilities and pitfalls of this process. Whether defining Pakistan's Islamic identity can move beyond slogans, opportunistic manipulations, and a conservative fundamentalism constitutes Pakistan's present challenge.

NOTES

This chapter is adapted in part from John L. Esposito, "Islamization: Religion and Politics in Pakistan," *Muslim World*, 72:3-4 (July–October 1982), pp. 197–223, and *Islam and Politics* (Syracuse, N.Y.: Syracuse University Press, 1984).

1. Wilfred Cantwell Smith, "Pakistan: Islamic State," chap. 5 in *Islam in Modern History* (Princeton, N.J.: Princeton University Press, 1957), pp. 206–55; John L.

Esposito, "Pakistan: Quest for Islamic Identity," in *Islam and Development: Religion and Sociopolitical Change*, ed. John L. Esposito (Syracuse, N.Y.: Syracuse University Press, 1980), pp. 139–62; Asaf Hussain, *Elite Politics in an Ideological State* (Kent, England: Lawsons Publishers, 1979).

2. Muhammad Iqbal, "Presidential Address," in *Thoughts and Reflections of Iqbal*, ed. S. A. Vahid (Lahore: Muhammad Ashraf, 1964), p. 169.

3. Ibid., pp. 170–71.

4. Jamil-ud-din Ahmad, ed., *Speeches and Writings of Mr. Jinnah* (Lahore: Muhammad Ashraf, 1952), vol. 1, pp. 177–78.

5. Fazlur Rahman, "Islam and the Constitutional Problems of Pakistan," *Studia Islamica* 32:4, (December 1970), pp. 275–87; and Fazlur Rahman, "The Ideological Experience of Pakistan," *Islam and the Modern Age*, 2 (1971), pp. 1–20.

6. See Leonard Binder, *Religion and Politics in Pakistan* (Berkeley: University of California Press, 1961); E. I. J. Rosenthal, *Islam in the Modern National State* (Cambridge: Cambridge University Press, 1965), pp. 181–281; Rahman, "Islam and the Constitutional Problems of Pakistan," pp. 275–87; Smith, *Islam in Modern History*, pp. 206–55.

7. *Constitution of the Islamic Republic of Pakistan* (Lahore: Government of Pakistan, March 1956), pt. 1, art. 1.

8. Ibid., Preamble.

9. Ibid., pt. 4, art. 32.

10. Ibid., pt. 12, art. 197.

11. Ibid., art. 198.

12. As quoted in M. Ahmed, "Islamic Aspects of the New Constitution of Pakistan," *Islamic Studies*, 2:2 (June 1963), p. 262.

13. John J. Donohue and John L. Esposito, eds., *Islam in Transition: Muslim Perspectives* (New York: Oxford University Press, 1982), p. 205.

14. William L. Richter, "The Political Dynamics of Islamic Resurgence in Pakistan," *Asian Survey*, 19:6 (June 1979), pp. 547–57.

15. See, for example, Waheed-uz-Zaman, ed., *The Quest for Identity* (Islamabad: Islamabad University Press, 1973).

16. *Jinnah's Speeches as Governor General of Pakistan 1947–1948* (Karachi: Pakistan Publications, n.d.), p. 104.

17. Philip E. Jones, "Islam and Politics Under Ayub and Bhutto: A Comparative Analysis" (Paper presented at the Seventh Conference on South Asia, Madison, Wisc., November 1978).

18. *Dawn*, 30 September 1977.

19. Ibid.

20. Interview with Mian Tufail Muhammad, Mansoora, 7 January 1982.

21. *Pakistan Affairs*, 35:1 (1 January 1982), p. 1.

22. *Al-Mushir*, 24:1 (Spring 1982), p. 21.

23. Confirmed in interviews in Islamabad with General Zia ul-Haq, 9 January 1982; and Justice Tanzil ur-Rahman, Chairman, Islamic Ideology Council, 5 January 1982; and with Justice Aftab Hussein, Chairman, Federal Shari'ah Courts, in Lahore, 6 January 1982.

24. *Superior Court's Shariat Benches Order* (Islamabad: *The Gazette of Pakistan,* 10 February 1978).

25. *Federal Shariat Court (Procedure) Rules, The All Pakistan Legal Decisions* (PLD), vol. 33 (Islamabad: Government of Pakistan, 1981).

26. *Dawn Overseas,* 17–23 September 1982, p. 4.

27. "News from the Country," *al-Mushir,* 23:3 (Rawalpindi, 1981), p. 115.

28. John Thomas Cummings, Hossein Askari, and Ahmad Mustafa, "Islam and Modern Economic Change," in Esposito, ed., *Islam and Development,* pp. 25–47.

29. See, for example, Ayatullah Mahmud Taliqani, "The Characteristics of Islamic Economics"; Khurshid Ahmad, "Islam and the Challenge of Economic Development"; M. Umar Chapra, "The Islamic Welfare State"; and Abul Hasan Bani-Sadr, "Islamic Economics: Ownership and Tawhid," in Donahue and Esposito, eds., *Islam in Transition: Muslim Perspectives,* pp. 210–16, 217–22, 223–29, 230–35.

30. Mumtaz Ahmad, "Perceptions and Attitudes of the Ulama to Problems and Policies of Economic Development in Pakistan," iin Marc Gabrieu, ed., *Asie Du Sud: Transitions Et Changements,* (Paris: CNRC, 1979), p. 264.

31. *Zakat and Ushr Ordinances, 1980* (Islamabad: Government of Pakistan, 1980), p. 33.

32. Interview with professor Khurshid Ahmad, Director, Institute of Policy Studies, member of the Jama'at-i-Islami, and former Deputy Minister of Planning responsible for the original government proposal, in Islamabad, 5 January 1982.

33. *Introduction of Islamic Laws* (Islamabad: Government of Pakistan, 1979), p. 16.

34. *Report of the Council of Islamic Ideology on the Elimination of Interest from the Economy* (Islamabad: Government of Pakistan, 1970).

35. Ibid., p. 30.

36. *An Agenda for Islamic Economic Reform* (Islamabad: Pakistan Institute of Development Economics, 1980), p. v.

37. Ibid., p. vi.

38. *Islamic University Ordinance* (Islamabad: Government of Pakistan, 1980), p. 5.

39. Ibid., p. 6.

40. *The Times* (London), 22 February 1982, p. 6.

41. For an extended treatment of Muslim family law reform in Pakistan and its methodological problems see John L. Esposito, *Women in Muslim Family Law* (Syracuse, N.Y.: Syracuse University Press, 1982), especially chap. 3.

42. Interview with General Muhammad Zia ul-Haq, in Islamabad, 8 January 1982.

43. See, for example, the comments of Mawlana Ahmad Noorani, President of the JUP, in *Dawn,* 1 October 1979, p. 3.

44. *Report of the Court of Inquiry constituted under Pubjab Act II of 1954, to inquire into the Punjab disturbances of 1953* (Lahore: Government of Pakistan, 1954), pp. 231–32. See also Muhammad Munir, *From Jinnah to Zia* (Lahore: Vanguard Books, n.d.), pp. 38–73.

45. Pakistan's continued inability to achieve any consensus in theory or practice regarding the Islamic nature and character of the state was demonstrated by a debate in the media in which more than one hundred leaders (ulama, politicians, military officials, intellectuals) discussed the nature of an Islamic state. Their positions ranged from advocating dictatorship to popular democracy, from a one-party to a multiparty political system (the author wishes to acknowledge his debt to Mumtaz Ahmad for this information).

46. This is an approximate figure since there are no reliable statistics. Estimates often range from 5 percent to 25 percent.

47. *Dawn Overseas*, 3 February 1983, p. 4.

48. Esposito, "Pakistan: Quest for an Islamic Identity," in Esposito, ed., *Islam and Development*, pp. 161–62.

49. Esposito, *Women in Muslim Family Law*, chap. 5.

INDEX

Abdali, Ahmad Shah. *See* Durrani, Ahmad Shah
Abdali Tribes, 28–29, 66n, 67n
Abdul Ghaffar Khan, 287–88, 290–91
Abdul Hay (of Panjsher Valley), 70n
Abdul Quddus Khan, Sardar, 47
Abdur Rahman, Amir, 52, 117, 129; centralization policies of, 39–40, 92; consolidation of, 37–39, 111; control of religious establishment, 38–39, 93–94; and the Hazaras, 90, 110, 128
Adams, Richard N., 77
Advisory Council of Islamic Ideology, 337. *See also* Council of Islamic Ideology
Afghan army. *See* Afghan military
Afghan bureaucracy, 15, 65; historical development of, 53, 59–60, 92; incorporation of the clergy in, 9, 135, 149; inefficiency of, 8, 60; language issue and, 113; minorities in, 96; in rural areas, 115
Afghan Constitution (1923), 47, 131–32
Afghan Constitution (1964), 56, 60, 63, 116, 153n
Afghan economy, 121; features of, 31, 40, 107, 109; historical development of, 36, 40, 55, 59, 63, 96, 117
Afghan elite: educated, 131; educated rural, 125; Kabul, 135–36; landed, 15, 40; ruling, 36, 44, 120, 137; rural aristocratic, 10, 63; traditional aristocratic, 61; traditional religious, 53; urban, 75
Afghan government: and Afghan resist-

ance, 119, 138–39; and the clergy, 93, 129; and ethnic groups, 23, 64–65, 75–76, 94–96, 113, 118, 128; historical expansion of, 24, 30–31, 36–37, 39, 44, 47–49, 52–55, 58–65, 91–94, 96–98, 104, 113–14; Marxist seizure of, 9, 13, 20, 77, 117–19; and outside powers, 91; and Pakistan, 112, 284; and religious establishment, 34, 129–31, 134–35; and rural population, 54, 61, 82, 96–99, 115–16. *See also* Afghanistan, Afghan state
Afghan military: historical evolution of, 15, 30, 36, 38, 39, 45–46, 48, 51, 53, 55, 59, 61–62, 97, 111, 113, 117; and Jami'at, 145; and Jews and Hindus, 131; and Soviet domination, 15, 114
Afghan Millat, 143
Afghan minorities: access to Monarchs, 133; and Marxist government, 117–18; and the State, 8, 13
Afghan monarchy: evolution of, 9, 36–37, 54, 111–12, 133; and the Great Game, 36; and the Marxist camp, 117, 119–20; and Pashtunistan, 284
Afghan nationalism: and Baluchistan, 273; emergence of, 43, 70n; and Islamic Alliance, 136; as Pashtun nationalism, 9, 30, 56, 59; and Soviet presence, 19, 138–39
Afghan refugees, 4, 6, 121, 137, 143, 291. *See also* Afghan resistance; Pashtun refugees
Afghan resistance: fragmentation of,

371

THE STATE, RELIGION, AND ETHNIC POLITICS

was composed in 10-point Palatino and leaded 2 points on a Compugraphic Quadex 5000
by BookMasters;
printed by sheet-fed offset on 50-pound, acid-free Glatfelter Eggshell Cream,
Smyth sewn and bound over binder's boards in Joanna Arrestox B
by Maple-Vail Book Manufacturing Group, Inc.;
with dust jackets printed in two colors
by Philips Offset Company, Inc.;
and published by

SYRACUSE UNIVERSITY PRESS
SYRACUSE, NEW YORK 13244-5160

A central theme of the book is the importance of ethnolinguistic and religious identities, and the corresponding weakness of nationalism as the basis of civil society in all three countries. To what extent the present ruling elites—the military in Pakistan, the People's Democratic Party in Afghanistan, and the clerical establishment in Iran—will succeed in their efforts to create strong states in societies where political institutions do not cut across diverse religious, ethnic, and class divisions is a major question raised by this volume.

This collection of essays by an outstanding group of anthropologists, historians, political scientists, and Islamicists is one of the first attempts to look at the issues of the state, religion, and ethnic politics from a comparative and historical perspective.

This volume is sponsored by the Joint Committee on the Near and Middle East and the Committee on South Asia of the American Council of Learned Societies and the Social Science Research Council.

ALI BANUAZIZI is Associate Professor of Social Psychology and Modern Iranian History at Boston College, a past editor of *Iranian Studies*, and the author of a number of articles on Iran and the Middle East.

MYRON WEINER is Ford International Professor of Political Science at the Massachusetts Institute of Technology and author of *India's Preferential Policies* and *Sons of the Soil: Migration and Ethnic Conflict in India*.